# THE BOO

# An Encyclopedia of Proof That The Black Man is God

## New Revised Edition

True Islam

A-Team Publishing

Atlanta

# THE BOOK OF GOD: New Revised Edition

First Printing: Second Edition
September 2007

# CONTENTS

# Introduction

The Honorable Elijah Muhammad says in *Message to the Black Man of America*:

> For thousands of years, the people who did not have the knowledge of the person, or reality, of God worshiped their own ideas of God. He has been made like many things other than what He really is.

Compare this with the observation by James L. Kugel, former Starr Professor of Hebrew Literature at Harvard University and currently Director of the Institute for the History of the Jewish Bible and Professor of Bible at Bar-Ilan University in Israel:

> The God of the world's great religions – all-powerful, all-knowing, invisible, and omnipresent – has been a staple of Western thought for some time. *Yet...this God is not the same as the God of most of the Bible*, the God who appeared to Abraham, Moses, and other biblical heroes. That God, the 'God of Old,' was actually perceived in a very different way.[1]

Here is a world-renowned biblical scholar affirming something the Hon. Elijah Muhammad said forty years ago: the world today is worshipping a god that is different from the true God of the Bible, what Kugel calls the 'God of Old.' Who is this 'God of Old,' the God of the Prophets? How was he perceived by ancient Israel and the biblical authors? How is it, why is it, that that this God is no longer acknowledged or worshipped by the Jewish and Christian worlds who claim the Bible as the foundation of their faith?

The most important of all questions is the question of the reality or person of God. The Hon. Elijah Muhammad's proclamation in 1934 that God came to him in the person of a

---

[1] James L. Kugel, *The God of Old: Inside the Lost World of the Bible* (New York: The Free Press, 2003) front jacket.

man, one W.F. Muhammad, offended, and offends Jews, Christians and Muslims alike. Contrary to popular theological wisdom the Hon. Elijah Muhammad taught that God is not a formless, immaterial spirit. God is a man. But more than that: God, he declared, is a Black man, indeed, *the Black Man*. Not man as we currently understand man; but Man as he was before the great "Fall of Man." This Man is divine, Supreme in knowledge, wisdom, understanding, holiness and power. He has power over all that is, and has come into the world, out of "hiding," to redeem his Chosen People who have been trampled upon by the nations of the earth. Muhammad said:

> The Black Man is the God of the Earth. He is the Creator. I don't care how you have been mistreated, still your Father was a Black Man and He is the One who created this Earth and is now taking it over. This is our Earth.[2]

Master Fard Muhammad (T.W.P.I.D.F.) told the Hon. Elijah Muhammad:

> They just waited. They're so glad that the day has come now that they can show you now that THE BLACK MAN IS GOD.[3]

The Hon. Elijah Muhammad proceeded to describe for us, in broad outline, the process by which God became a Black man. It began, Muhammad said, with an atom hidden in a primordial triple-darkness. From that atom and that darkness God built up, over trillions of years, his black body. Jewish, Christian, and Muslim theologians were aghast and wasted no time, spared no epithet in condemning Muhammad and his teaching as unbiblical and un-Islamic. Many who have heard this teaching dismissed it as a dangerously extreme display of racial pride - an

---

[2] Elijah Muhammad, *Theology of Time*, Lecture Series printed transcript by Abass Rassoul (Hampton: U.B.U.S., 1992), 125.

[3] Elijah Muhammad, *Our Savior Has Arrived*, 1974, 56.

understandable, though unacceptable reaction to centuries of racial degradation at the hands of white America.

Answering the question Who is God is of paramount importance to the whole world. It is of particular importance, however, to Black people because, in so doing, we solve the mystery of our own beginning. Current evolutionary theory, while acknowledging that the first humans were "probably" Black, place the origin of these aboriginal Black folk in the tree hopping primates of Africa. Accordingly, they say, when the Black Man of today looks at his reflection in a mirror, what he is seeing is nothing more than an advanced ape. The Hon. Elijah Muhammad, on the other hand, took a different position. According to him, when the Black Man looks at his reflection he is witnessing, not an advanced ape, but a descended God.

It is time to revisit the teachings of the Hon. Elijah Muhammad academically. The question his doctrine raised in regards to the nature of God absolutely must be answered if Black People are going to have a true knowledge of themselves. We now come on the heels of the Era of Afrocentricity, during which invaluable information has been uncovered and dispensed showing the greatness of our African past. But through it all, we are no closer to a true Knowledge of Self because the Afrocentric movement did not address the question Who is God. Consequently, our self knowledge, at best, could only be asymptotic. We recall in our high school algebra class that an asymptote is a downward sloping line on a graph which endlessly gets ever so close to the x-axis but never crosses. It is never tangent. Regardless of how learned we are in African history, regardless of how many kings we can name or contributions to civilization we can cite, until we can correctly answer the question of 'Who is God' we will never cross the threshold of true Knowledge of Self.

The average God-fearing individual reacts vehemently against such teaching of God being a human being. It is believed by most Jews, Christians, Muslims, and others that God is a spirit independent of a material body. But the Bible teaches that during this time God's true reality would not be known until the End of Time. Rev. 10:7 says:

3

But in the days of the voice of the seventh angel, when he begins to sound, THE MYSTERY OF GOD SHOULD BE FINISHED, as He hath declared to his servants the prophets.

A mystery is that which is unknown. God's reality was unknown for thousands of years and was to remain so until the Seventh Angel sounded in the Last Days. Thus, the masses who worshipped God prior to the sounding of the Seventh Angel would be worshipping other than his true reality; that would be unknown to them. When 'The Mystery' is finally finished and the Secret revealed, the masses who have been worshipping other than God would stand in shock and consternation upon learning his true nature. The Voice of the Seventh Angel has sounded and the Secret of God has been revealed. In this work, *The Book of God*, I hope to provide some of the evidence demonstrating that it was indeed the Hon. Elijah Muhammad who revealed the Secret.

# CHAPTER I

# *Is God A Spirit?*

"God is a spirit, and they that worship him must worship him in spirit and in truth." John 4:24, KJV

## 1.1. *Spirit as Energy*

The hallmark of the major western religions (Judaism, Christianity, and Islam) is their belief in God as an immaterial spirit, detached from and having no connection with any physical body. The above referenced verse from the Book of John has been the Christian world's scriptural "proof" that God is in fact a formless spirit, not a man. And though we concur 100% with John 4:24, for *God is spirit*, we believe the Christian world has greatly misunderstood and misinterpreted this most revealing scripture.

The proper interpretation of this verse depends on our understanding it in its original context. The literal translation of both the Greek (*pneuma*) and Hebrew (*ruah*) words here rendered "spirit" is "breath" or "air."[4] This breath or "air in motion" is, according to the ancients, the intrinsic life-force which animates all things. It is the *prana* of the Hindus and the *ba* of the ancient Egyptians. Wade Nobles, in his *African Psychology*, describes the *ba*:

> The BA was the second (of seven divisions) of the psychic nature. It represented the transmission of the breath of life. The ancients believed that there was only one power, which was symbolically represented as 'THE BREATH,'

---

[4]*Theological Dictionary of the New Testament*, translated and edited by Geoffrey W. Bromiley (Grand Rapids, Mich.: Erdmans, 1964-) 6:365 s.v. *pneuma*; *Theological Dictionary of the Old Testament*, edited by G. Johannes Botterweck and Helmer Ringgren and translated by John T. Willis (Grand Rapids, Mich.: W. B. Eerdmans Pub. Co., 1974-) 13:365- s.v. *ruah*. See also True Islam, **The Truth of God: The Bible, the Qur'an and the Secret of Black God** (Atlanta: All in All Publishing, 2007) 28-35.

and that this power or breath was transmitted from the ancestors to the descendants. The ancients believed that this power or energy has always existed and will always exist. The *Ba* was the invisible source, like electricity, of all visible functions. The *Ba* was in effect the vital principle which represented the essence of all things.[5]

This "Breath" of John 4:24 is therefore the intrinsic essence of all material reality.[6]

Webster's *Ninth Edition* defines air as "breath" or "the gaseous mixture surrounding the earth." A gas is a loose assortment of various types of atoms. An atom, in turn, is an extremely tiny "ball of energy." Fritjof Capra, in his *TAO of Physics*, observes:

Atoms consist of particles and these particles are not made of any material stuff...The discovery that mass is nothing but a form of energy has forced us to modify our concept of a particle in an essential way. In modern physics...particles are not seen as consisting of any basic 'stuff,' but as bundles of energy.[7]

Energy, then, is the root of air and thus the root of spirit. Both "spirit" and "matter," the incorporeal and the corporeal, are two manifestations of the same One Reality. Theologians call this One Reality God. Philosophers call it "THAT." Scientists call it Energy. Energy is eternal, according to the Law of Conservation of Energy, which states that energy is neither created nor destroyed, but constantly transforms. But whether we call It God, That, or Energy, this one essence is the same and from It sprung both matter and spirit. Madame Blavatsky, matriarch of Theosophy, notes: *"Spirit and Matter, or Purusha and Prakriti, are but two primeval aspects of the One and Secondless."*[8] The two are *"different*

---

[5]Wade Nobles, *African Psychology* (Oakland: Black Family Institutions, 1986) 36.

[6] See further True Islam, *The Truth of God*, 28-35.

[7]Fritjof Capra, *TAO of Physics* (Boston: Shamballah, 1991) 202-3.

[8]H.P. Blavatsky, *The Secret Doctrine* (New York: Theosophical Publishing Company, 1888) I: 51.

*forms of the same basic 'stuff'-in much the same way that ice and steam are different forms of water."9*

This One Reality has been found in every major world religion to be "the beginning" from which all else springs. The Hindus called it *Parabrahm*. The Zoroastrians called it *Zeruana Akerne*. To the Egyptians it was *Kneph* and to the Jews *Ain Soph*. Whatever it was called, it represented to all the "unmanifested deity," "the latent, causeless cause."10 This One Reality (Energy) manifests itself through spirit, and spirit manifests itself through matter.

This is indeed how John 4:24 was intended. The word *pneuma* was used because it conveyed this meaning of materiality. Grace Jantzen, in **God's World, God's Body**, observes:

> Scripture does say, of course, that God is Spirit (*pneuma*). But *pneuma*, in the Greek text of that time, did not necessarily indicate incorporeality as we would expect; in fact, it was sometimes taken to imply the reverse. We can observe this in the Stoic philosophy of the time, where *pneuma required* corporeality. According to Stoicism, God and the world are composed of the same stuff. The creative fire which rules the universe is *pneuma*...11

According to the Stoics "*God is a spirit that permeates all things and contains all things within Himself.*"12 The Church Father Origen (A.D. 185-253) acknowledged that it was this same verse, John 4:24, which early Christians used to prove that God did in fact possess a material body. He says:

> I know that some will attempt to say that, even according to our own Scriptures, God is a body, BECAUSE...they find it said...in the gospel according to John, that 'God is a

---

9Dr. Robert Gange, **Origins and Destiny: A Scientist Examines God's Handiwork** (Dallas: Word Publishing, 1986) 13.

10Blavatsky, **Secret Doctrine**, I:6-7.

11 Grace Jantzen, **God's World, God's Body**, (Philadelphia: Westminster Press, 1984) 22.

12 G. Stroumsa, "The Incorporeality of God," **Religious Studies** 13 (1983): .346.

Spirit'...Spirit according to them [is] to be regarded as nothing else than a body.[13]

The early Christians, like the peoples of antiquity, understood that the Spirit, as a rule, manifests itself through a material body.

This is exactly as taught by the Honorable Elijah Muhammad. He says:

> Materials from the Earth give us a body for breath to enter. When breath entered the body it made a sound and from the sound I could walk and I could guide myself. The Breath of Life. Every human being that is born of parents, if it does not breathe the breath that is carrying the Earth and that we are all breathing, it won't live. We say it is stillborn. But he (devil) made you look at it differently. He made you to look at breath as something of a spirit or a body we can't see. That's right too. We can't see the air that we are breathing unless we get a microscope. Then we can see the very Atom of Life in the air. Those Atoms of Life in the air are the things that give us life[14]...The biggest 'soul' we have is air...The real soul that they preach to you about is your breath...The human soul is nothing but a person's life. It is not something which is separate from body in which we are in. If you study the theological side of it, it only means our breath. That is the soul, our breath. The Bible teaches you that when God made Man He breathed into the Man the Breath of Life, then He became a Living Soul.[15]

## 1.2. *God as Spirit and Matter*

The Western world has juxtaposed spirit and matter in such a way that the two are seen as mutually exclusive. This is not, however, how

---

[13] Quoted from D.L. Paulsen, "Early Christian Belief in a Corporeal Deity," *Harvard Theological Review*, 83 (1990): 109.

[14] In V. Valerian's *Matrix IV*, 405 we read, "Just the act of breathing, with each breath you inhale $10^{22}$ atoms from the universe. It is an astronomical amount of raw material that comes from everywhere and ends up as renewed cellular structure in the body."

[15] Muhammad, *Theology of Time*, 241-2.

the original peoples of antiquity understood the spirit-matter dichotomy. To them, spirit and matter were two aspects of the whole, and the whole depended on the harmonious union of the two. Wade Nobles notes:

> Reality for the ancients was always conceived of as the synthesis of the visible and the invisible, the material and the immaterial, the cognitive and the emotive, the inner and the outer.[16]

He says the Supreme Being according to the ancients was *"simultaneously 'spiritual' and 'material'."* Egyptologist Theophile Obenga observes:

> The opposition between 'matter' and 'spirit' does not exist in ancient Egypt where nature forms a whole, matter and consciousness intermingled...Spirit and matter are both modes of the same reality.[17]

Fritjof Capra concurs:

> Since motion and change are essential properties of things, the forces causing the motion are not objects from the outside, as in classical Greek view, but are an intrinsic property of matter. Correspondingly, the Eastern image of the Divine is not that of a ruler who directs the world from above, but a principle that controls everything from within.[18]

The change of view can be traced back to Rene' Descartes' seventeenth-century philosophy, now known as the "Cartesian Split," which at least popularized the spirit-matter dualism. Marcel Mauss, writing in *What is Matter: History of the Concept and Present Conception*, says:

---

[16] Nobles, *African Psychology*, 36.

[17] Theophile Obenga, "African Philosophy of the Pharonic Period" reprinted in Ivan Van Sertima's *Egypt Revisited* (New Brunswick: Transaction Books, 1989) 302.

[18] Capra, *Tao of Physics*, 24.

The 'matter-spirit' opposition is much more recent. It came along with the notion of matter as purely mechanical and geometric which dates back perhaps to Galileo, certainly to Descartes...This notion of matter purified of all spiritual element developed for the most part in France and Great Britain.[19]

According to the Wisdom of the ancient Black man and woman, matter and spirit are mutually co-dependent and the "whole" is the product of their synthesis. We all experience this profound truth in our lives. All of us who have electricity running through our homes know that copper wiring is absolutely necessary for our use of the electric current. The copper wire serves as a transmitter of that current. If the wire is damaged, the electricity is left suspended - unable to be made manifest - until more wire is put down. The current represents the Spirit of God. The wire represents the transmitters of God's Spirit, the human body.[20]

To the ancients, Spirit was masculine and Matter was feminine.[21] They were represented as Twin Gods, male and female, called the Mother and Father of Man.[22] Sometimes they were shown in a sensual embrace, as in *Shiva* and *Shakti* of India (Figure 1). This represents the sensual embrace between Spirit and Matter.

At other times, the two gods are welded into one androgynous deity. All over the earth, God was often depicted as a Great Hermaphrodite, a man with male and female organs.[23] The profane and unlearned took this representation on face value and thus imagined God as a being who actually possessed both sets of organs – a true hermaphrodite. The initiated, on the other hand, understood this to signify the spiritual-material nature of

[19]Marcel Mauss, "Concepts which Preceded Matter," in his *What is Matter* (1945), 778.

[20] See especially the Hon. Louis Farrakhan, "Who Is God" Saviors Day Lecture at Christ Universal Temple, Chicago, Illinois. February 24, 1991.

[21]Manley P. Hall, *Man: Grand Symbol of the Mysteries* (Los Angeles: Philosophical Research Society, 1972) 44.

[22] Albert Churchward, *Signs and Symbols of Primordial Man*, (London: George Allen & Company, LTD., 1913) 60.

[23] Godfrey Higgins, *Anacalypsis* (1836; Brooklyn: A&B Book Publishers, 1992) I:37.

Figure 1
Stone sculpture of Shiva and Shakti in sensual embrace. Khajuraho, India.

God/Man. This is true as well with the image of God with two faces, a man's and a woman's, turned in opposite directions. This is God as Spirit (Man) and Matter (Woman).

The sages of alchemy revealed the secret of their 'Great Work' in these words:

> Make the fire to burn in water, and make the water to feed the fire. In this lies the greatest wisdom.

This alchemical adage sums up the true nature of the alchemist's work - the ultimate unification of opposites.[24] This adage was symbolized by the great Hermaphrodite. According to Manly P.

---

[24] True & Living Allah, *Who is The Founder of Unlike Attract and Like Repel*, 17.

Hall, the term *hermaphrodite* derives from the Egyptian Gnostic god Hermaphroditus. This name in turn is a compound of *Hermes* and *Aphrodite*. Hermes is the god of Fire and Aphrodite is the goddess of water.[25] Thus, Hermaphroditus or a Hermaphrodite is a symbolic restatement of the Hermetic adage, "Make Fire to burn in Water..."[26] Hall thus notes:

> the two great opposites of Nature - father and mother principles - have been united in him (the Great Hermaphrodite). Therefore, he is said to be a son of the Hermetic Marriage. He is his own father and his own mother...[27]

The "Hermetic Marriage" is the marriage of the male and female principles in Man/God, the marriage of spirit and matter.

### 1.3. *The Temple of God and the Black Man's Body*

MAN is called by the ancients "the Son of the Two," the "Two" being Spirit (Father) and Matter (Mother).[28] And according to all scripture, the Spirit of God uses the human body to convey or manifest Itself. Thus, MAN's body is called "the Temple of God." Paul says in I Cor. 3:16-17:

> Know ye not that ye are the temple of God, and that the Spirit of God dwelleth in you? If any man defile the temple, him shall God destroy; for the temple of God is holy, WHICH TEMPLE YOU ARE.

---

[25] Manley P. Hall, *Melchizedek and the Mystery of Fire* (Los Angeles: Philosophical Research Society, 1996) 49.

[26] True & Living, *Who is The Founder*, 18

[27] Manley P. Hall, *The Hermetic Marriage* (Los Angeles: Philosophical Research Society, 1996) 42.

[28] Blavatsky, *Secret Doctrine*, I: 41.

The sacred temples of the ancients were constructed to reflect the human body (Figure 2).[29] R.A. Schwaller de Lubicz, in his famous *The Temple In Man*, says of the great House of God called the Temple of Luxor from pharonic Egypt:

> The outline of a human skeleton - traced according to anthropometrical methods and very carefully constructed, bone by bone - was superimposed on the general plan of the temple. The head...is located exactly in the sanctuaries of the covered temple; the sanctuary of the barque of Amun is the oral cavity; the chest is located in the first hypostyle of the covered temple and ends with the temple's platform. The abdomen is represented by the peristyle court, and the pubis is located exactly at the door separating this peristyle from the colonnade of Amun. This marvelous colonnade is, in fact, dedicated to the femurs, the thighs; the knees are at the site of the gate in front of which sit the two colossi, marking the entrance to this colonnade...One might be tempted to think this skeleton had been constructed to be superimposed on the temple. But any skeleton...can be projected thus on the plan of the temple and will coincide with it. Moreover, all the proportions of the skeleton may be checked against the actual measurements of the temple.[30]

He concludes:

> The Temple of Luxor is indisputably devoted to the Human Microcosm. This consecration is not merely a simple attribution: the entire temple becomes a book explaining the secret functions of the organs and nerve centers.

---

[29]Manley P. Hall, *The Secret Teachings of All Ages* (Los Angeles: Philosophical Research Society, 1988) LXXIV.

[30]R.A. Schwaller de Lubicz, *The Temple In Man* (Rochester: Inner Traditions International, 1977) 21-24.

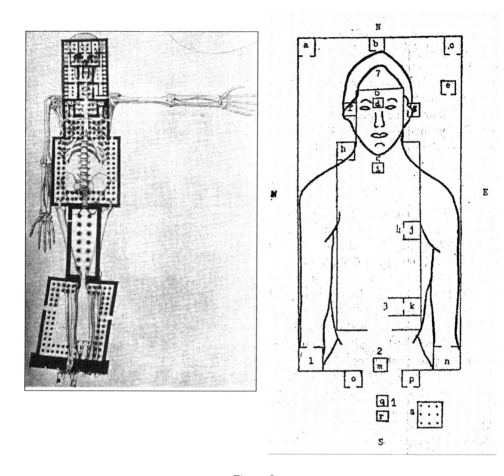

Figure 2

Whether it is the Temple of Luxor in ancient Egypt or the Prasada Temples of
Hindu India, sacred architecture reflected the Divine Anatomy.

Likewise, the Great Pyramid of Gizah was constructed to reflect the Human Microcosm. Hall observes,

> The base of the Pyramid...represents the four material elements or substances from the combination of which the quaternary* body of man is formed. From each side of the square there rises a triangle, typifying the threefold divine being (Spirit of God) enthroned within every quaternary material nature...The three main chambers of the Pyramid are related to the heart, the brain, and the generative system - the spiritual centers of the human constitution. The triangular form is also similar to the posture assumed by the body during the ancient meditative exercises.[31]

In the depths of the recesses of the Great Pyramid there dwells the "Holy of Holies," a most august soul who never left the Temple and whose audience only the "initiated" could seek. He resided in the Temple "as God dwells in the hearts of men."[32] This "Illustrious One" represents the Spirit of God dwelling in the real House of God, the Human Body. This is the Ka'aba in Mecca or Cathedral in Rome.

This is true and consistent in a number of traditions. In the Qaballah of the Jews, *Ain Soph* (which is the Jewish "Supreme All" or Spirit) uses the body of the first MAN, Adam Qadmon ("ancient man"), as the *mercabah* or throne-chariot through which It manifests Itself.[33] The *Zohar*, the central text of Qaballah, says:

> The Infinite Unity (*Ain Soph*), formless and without similitude, after the form of the Heavenly Man was created, used it. The Unknown Light used the (heavenly form) as a chariot through which to descend, and wished to be called by this form, which is the sacred name Jehovah.[34]

---

[31]Hall, *Secret Teachings of All Ages*, XLIV.

[32]Ibid., XXIV.

[33]Blavatsky, *Secret Doctrine*, I: 214.

[34]Ibid., I: 356. On the association of Adam Qadmon and the sacred name Jehovah see below.

In the *Laws of Manu*, which is an ancient Hindu writing, the Eternal All of the ancient Indians is called *Parabrahm*. He (IT) manifests Itself through the male God *Brahma*, the Creator.[35] *Brahma* is called *Kali Hamsa* which means "Black Swan." *Parabrahm* is then called *Hansa-vahan*, which means "he who uses the swan (*hansa*) as His vehicle (*vahan*)."[36]In other words, the black body of Brahma is the vehicle (swan) in which the Absolute All manifests Itself. A Black aquatic fowl - whether swan, goose, pelican, or dove - is often used to symbolize the vehicle through which the Spirit of God conveys Itself.[37] *Ain Soph* is called "The Fiery Soul of the Pelican."[38] According to the Greeks, the city of Delphi was founded by the Spirit of God in the form of a Black Dove.[39]

What is the significance of all these Black birds being associated with the transmission of the Spirit of God? Madame Blavatsky, in **The Secret Doctrine**, says:

> Darkness is always associated with the first symbol and surrounds it - as shown in the Hindu, the Egyptian, the Chaldeo-Hebrew and even the Scandinavian - hence black ravens, black doves, black waters and even black flames; the seventh tongue of Agni, the fire god being called 'Kali,' 'the black'...Two 'black' doves flew from Egypt and settling on the oaks of Dodona, gave their names to Grecian gods. Noah lets out a Black raven after the deluge, which is a symbol for the Cosmic *pralaya* (absolute rest or sleep), after which began the real creation...Odin's black ravens fluttered around the Goddess Saga and 'whispered to her of the past and future.' What is the real meaning of all these black birds? They are all connected with the primeval wisdom, which flows out of the pre-cosmic Source of all...and they all have an identical meaning and relate to the PRIMORDIAL ARCHETYPAL

[35]Ibid., I:333, 345.

[36]Ibid., I: 77-80.

[37] Higgins, *Anacalypsis*, I:112. This is because the aquatic fowl is known to "move on the face of the waters" like the Spirit does.

[38]Blavatsky, *Secret Doctrine*, I: 80.

[39]Higgins, *Anacalypsis*, I:112.

# MAN (ADAM QADMON) THE CREATIVE ORIGIN OF ALL THINGS.[40]

Adam Qadmon, THE ORIGINAL BLACK MAN, is the *Kali Hamsa* through which the Spirit of God is conveyed to the world. He was the first emanation from the darkness of Mother Space. The Honorable Elijah Muhammad says in *Theology of Time*:

> You are being taught that the Black Man is the first creature in the Sun. You must realize that the Black Man was the first to see the light after coming out of darkness. He came out of total darkness and he was dark...His own color corresponds with the conditions of what is now the Heavens and Earth, that was nothing then but total darkness.[41]

---

[40]Blavatsky, *Secret Doctrine*, I: 443.

[41] Muhammad, *Theology of Time*, 107.

## CHAPTER II

# *The Black God in History*

## 2.1. *The Universal Worship of the Black God in Antiquity*

The whole world at one time knew that the Black man was He through whom the Supreme All manifested Himself. J.A. Rodgers, in his **100 Amazing Facts About The Negro**, says,

> Nearly ALL THE ANCIENT GODS OF THE OLD AND NEW WORLD WERE BLACK AND HAD WOOLY HAIR...'From the texture of the hair, I am inclined to assign to the Buddha of India, the Fuhi of China, Xaha of the Japanese, the Quetzacoatel of the Mexicans, the same and indeed an African or rather Nubian origin.

Figure 3
Black Buddha in ancient Temple at Nara, Japan (From Rashidi and Sertima, *African Presence*, 322)

Godfrey Higgins, in his prodigious work, *Anacalypsis: An Inquiry into the Origins of Languages, Nations, and Religions*, notes also,

> We have found the black complexion or something relating to it whenever we have approached the origin of nations. The Alma Mater, the Goddess Multimammia, the founders of the Oracles, the Memnon of first idols, were always black. Venus, Jupiter, Apollo, Bacchus, Hercules, Asteroth, Adonis, Horus, Apis, Osiris, and Amen: in short ALL THE...DEITIES WERE BLACK. They remained as they were first...in very ancient times. [42]

The civilizations of antiquity understood that the Most High, who is spiritual, manifested or conveyed Himself through the body of the Black man. This understanding of God's self-manifestation is referred to as *anthropomorphism*. Anthropomorphism is a Greek word coming from *anthropos* meaning 'man' and *morphe* meaning 'form.' It represents belief in God manifesting Himself in human form. For reasons we shall discuss later, the Black man's physical make was chosen by the Most High as the best conductor of His Spirit. Thus, in all of the great civilizations of the Original People, God was understood to be a man - a Black man. The *Jewish Encyclopedia* notes: *"Anthropomorphism is, of course, met with among ALL THE PEOPLES of antiquity, NOT EXCLUDING THE MOST ADVANCED."* [43]

### 2.1.1. *The Black God of Ancient Egypt*

In the great civilization of Ancient Kemet, God was understood in anthropomorphic terms. Egyptologists E. Wallace Budge, in *The Gods of the Egyptians*, observes that *"the Egyptian's...gods (were) in their own image, only they attributed to them super-human powers."* [44] Cheik Anta Diop, in *African Origin of Civilization* says also,

---

[42] Higgins, *Anacalypsis*, I:286.

[43] "Anthropomorphism," *The Jewish Encyclopedia* (1925) I:622.

[44] E.W. Budge, *The Gods Of The Egyptians* (New York: Dover Publications, 1969) 40.

Thus we can understand why the Egyptians always painted their gods black as coal, *in the image of their race, from the beginning to the end of their history.*[45]

In spite of references to the Egyptian's "gods," these ancient Blacks worshipped one Supreme God. His name changed with time, but whether He was called *Ptah, Ra, Amun,* or *Atum,* there was acknowledged One God from whom all others sprung and who is above all. Manley P. Hall, in *Man: Grand Symbol of the Mysteries,* says:

Eusebius, on the authority of Porphyry, wrote that the Egyptians acknowledged one intellectual author or creator of the world; that they worshipped him in a...human form AND DARK BLUE COMPLEXION (Blue-Black).[46]

Figure 4
Amun, Black God of ancient Kemet

[45] C.A. Diop, *The African Origin of Civilization: Myth or Reality* (Westport: Lawrence Hill & Company, 1967) 75.

[46] Hall, *Man: Grand Symbol of the Mysteries,* 71. On the meaning of the Blue-Black color of the gods see True Islam, *Truth of God,* 134-54 (§ 5.3 "The Blue-Black Creator-God" and § 5.4. "The Self-Created Blue-Black Creator").

It is said that the early Egyptians worshipped animals or God in animal form. But this is not the case. The adoration of God in theriomorphic ("animal form") terms was a late development in the religious history of Egypt. James Breasted, in *A History of Egypt*, says:

> But the animal-worship, which we usually associate with ancient Egypt, IS A LATE PRODUCT, BROUGHT FORWARD IN THE DECLINE OF A NATION AT THE CLOSE OF ITS HISTORY. In the (early) periods, IT WAS UNKNOWN; the hawk, for example, was the sacred animal of the sun-god, and as such a living hawk might have a place in the temple, where he was fed and kindly treated, as any such pet might be; BUT HE WAS NOT WORSHIPPED, NOR WAS HE THE OBJECT OF AN ELABORATE RITUAL AS LATER.[47]

The animals only represented and symbolized particular attributes or characteristics of the God. The hawk, because of the heights that it soars up in the sky, merely represented that quality of the Sun God. It was not, however, identified as the Sun-God. In *Religions of the World*, edited by D. Reisman, we learn:

> This does not mean the Egyptians worshipped animals, however. In the ancient world, animal forms were commonly used to characterize and symbolize the sacred.[48]

### 2.1.2. *The Black One of the Indus Valley*

Another great civilization and religious center established by the Black man and woman is found on the sub-continent of India, called the Indus Valley Civilization. This civilization goes back to 6-7,000 B.C. and reached its apex in Mohenjo-Daro around 3,000 to 2,500 B.C. These ancient Blacks likewise acknowledged that the Most High manifested Himself in the form of a man - a Black man.

---

[47] J. Breasted, *A History Of Egypt* (New York: Charles Scribner's Sons, 1942) 60.

[48] D. Reisman, *Religions of The World* (New York: St. Martin's Press, 1993) 50.

Figure 5
'The Black One' of ancient India.


The religion of the ancient Indians is known primarily from figurines and seals, for the language has not been fully deciphered. Anthropomorphic figurines were found representing male gods and female goddesses.[49] On the seals, the goddess is represented as a slender woman with a headdress, sometimes a crescent-shaped headdress, and sometimes bovine horns protruding out. She is also usually shown with a long pony-tail and a skirt.

The most famous seal, however, is that of the male god, called the *Proto-Sivaic Seal* (Figure 5). A male god is depicted sitting in yoga-fashion on a throne. Large bovine horns protrude from his very stylized headdress. Around the God are a tiger, buffalo, elephant and rhinoceros. He has since been called "the Lord of the Beasts." Inscribed on the seal is the appellation, "the Black One, the Black Buffalo."[50] The bovine, either Bull or Buffalo, was the

[49] "Indus Valley Religion," *The Encyclopedia of Religion*, 7: 220.

[50] Ivan van Sertima, *African Presence in Early Asia* (New Brunswick: Transaction Books, 1988) 96.

universal icon of the Black God because it represents power and dominion.[51] This Black god is identified by the Buffalo signifying his power and dominion and status in the Indus Valley religion. The fact that this Black deity is the supreme power of Mohenjo-Daro is shown in another seal where the Mother-goddess which we have just looked at is shown kneeling down and worshipping the Black One.[52]

The name of the Supreme God in India, like in Egypt, changed with time and area. But whether He was called Brahma, Indra, or "The Black One," He was always said to manifest Himself in human form. Stewart Elliot Guthrie, in *Faces in The Clouds*, says:

> Gods and humans are both similar and continuous in India, where the 'man-god continuum is central and crucial.'....Hindu myths include a time when gods and humans lived together and humans who aspire through austerities to the position of Indra, chief of the gods.

### 2.1.3. *The Black God of Ancient Sumer*

Ivan Van Sertima, in his *African Presence in Early Asia*, has shown that the indigenous people of the Sumerian Civilization were Black. Between 1889 and 1900, 30,000 texts were unearthed at Nippur, Lagash, the religious center of ancient Sumer. The texts, which are from the 2nd and 3rd millennium B.C., have helped us to have a clearer understanding of the religion of these ancient Blacks. Samual N. Kramer, in his book *History Begins at Sumer*, observes,

> (The stories) illustrates vividly the anthropomorphic character of the Sumerian Gods. Even the most powerful and most knowing among them were regarded as human in form, thought, and deed.[53]

---

[51] See True Islam, *Truth of God*, 129-34 (§ 5.2. "The Black God and His Black Bull").

[52] Sertima, *African Presence*, 68.

[53] S.N. Kramer, *History Begins at Sumer* (London: Thomas & Hudson, 1959) 138.

T. Jacobsen, in "Primitive Democracy in Ancient Mesopotamia," asserts

> The Sumerians and Akkadians pictured their gods as human in form, governed by human emotions, and living in the same type of world as did men.[54]

The Sumerians believed in One Supreme God who was called *Anu*, who was Black.[55] Anu was the Father and King of all the gods. His realm was the expanse of the heavens. Cheik Anta Diop suggest that the name comes from *An*, which means "man."[56] Anu was accompanied by his wife, the Mother-Goddess called *Antu*. All the other gods, which were "his children" - Enki, Marduk, Ishtar, and the rest - were human in form.

### 2.1.4. *Black God, White Worshipers*

*Ahura Mazda*, the God of Zarathustra (Zoraster) and the Persians, was likewise a Man (Figure 6) with a blue-black body.[57] William Bramley, in *The Gods of Eden*, observes,

> Ahura Mazda is depicted in some places as a bearded human figure who stands in a stylized circular object...Ahura Mazda was a humanlike 'God'.[58]

---

[54] T. Jacobsen, "Primitive Democracy In Ancient Mesopotamia," *Journal Of Near Eastern Studies* 2 (1943): 167.

[55] See True Islam, *Truth of God*, 131.

[56] Diop, *African Origin of Civilization*, 77.

[57] On the blue-black body of the gods see True Islam, *Truth of God*, 134-54 (§ 5.3 "The Blue-Black Creator-God" and § 5.4. "The Self-Created Blue-Black Creator").

[58] William Bramley, *The Gods of Eden*, (New York: Avon Books, 1989)114-5

Figure 6
Ahura Mazda, Persepolis, Persia

The Greeks worshipped the Black God as well. Zecharia Sitchin says,

> The Greeks described their gods as anthropomorphic, as physically similar to mortal men and women, and human in character: They could be happy and angry and jealous; they made love, quarreled, fought; and they procreated like humans, bringing forth offspring through sexual intercourse-with each other and humans.[59]

According to Godfrey Higgins, "*The Greek gods were adaptations of the Egyptian ones. Hence, the earliest ones of Greece WERE BLACK.*"[60] Zeus, the Supreme God of the Greeks, was Black (Figure 7).

---

[59] Z. Sitchin, *The 12TH Planet* (New York: Avon Books, 1978) 52.

[60] Ishakamusa Barashango, *God, The Bible, and the Black Man's Destiny* (Silver Spring: IVth Dynasty Publishing, 1982) , 2.

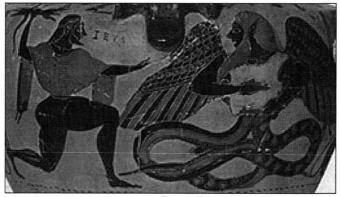

Figure 7
Zeus and Typhon. Chalcidian black-figure hydria c. 540-530 BC

In a number of areas Whites worshiped the Black God under the name 'Ham.' Charles Finch, in his *Echoes of the Old Darkland*, observes that the Hebrew word "Ham" derives from the Egyptian "Cham" and means "Black." Higgins says:

> By the Syrians the Sun and Heat were called...'*hme*,' Chamha; and by the Persians Hama...Mr. Bryant shews (sic) that Ham was esteemed Zeus of Greece, and the Jupiter of Latium...Mr. Bryant says, 'The worship of Ham...as it was the most ancient, so it was the most universal of any in the world. It was at first the prevailing religion of Greece; and was propagated over all the sea-coast of Europe, from whence it extended itself into the inland provinces. It was established in Gaul and Britain; and was the original religion of this island, which the Druids in after times adopted.[61]

Rev. Ishakamusa Barashango thus concludes,

> Thus we see, that in ancient times, ALL THE IMAGES OF GOD OR WHAT THE ANCIENTS THOUGHT GOD LOOKED LIKE, or as he was revealed and manifested to

---

[61] Higgins, *Anacalypsis*, I: 45.

them, had FEATURES OF THE INDIGENOUS
AFRICANS...[62]

## 2.2. *Of Gods and Men*

All over the earth it was understood that God manifested
himself in human form. Stewart Guthrie concludes,

> Indeed, gods and humans are both similar and continuous
> to most parts of the world. Gods may be jealous of
> humans or infatuated with them, may make love or war
> with them...In many cultures gods are not eternal but are
> born...They may die of old age or be killed...They may be
> the ancestors of humans...They eat and drink, sometimes
> ambrosia or other unearthly delicacies, but also milk (from
> the dairy herds) and other human foods...
> A.F.C. Wallace notes that the Great Gods of Dahomey are
> 'humanlike beings' with an 'active social life' including sex,
> war, and economic enterprises. Erland Ehnmark says a
> 'richly developed anthropomorphism is by no means
> peculiar to Homer'... In Siberia, 'countless tales relate how
> God has a magnificent home in the (heaven)...a wife and
> children, servants, cattle, and other property.' The Koryak
> Supreme Being is an 'old man living in a settlement in
> heaven and having a wife and children...In Polynesia,
> Ehnmark finds little difference between gods and powerful
> chiefs. Similar examples of humanlike gods are legion.
> Although we know the Greek gods for their
> anthropomorphism, they are by no means exceptional.[63]

The ancients understood that God and Man were of the same
nature, the only difference being that God was Supreme in all of
His activities whereas Man has fallen (see below).

The sacred world of the gods - as recounted in myth - was
not just the ideal toward which men and women should

---

[62] Barashango, *God, the Bible, and the Black Man's Destiny*, 3.

[63] S. E. Guthrie, *Faces in The Clouds* (New York: Oxford University Press, 1993) 190-1

aspire, but was the prototype of human existence; it was the original pattern or the archetype on which our life here below had been modeled. Everything on earth was thus believed to be a replica of something in the divine world...There was no gulf between human beings and the gods. The natural world, men and women and the gods themselves all shared the same nature and derived from the same divine substance. The pagan vision was holistic. The gods were not shut off from the human race in a separate, ontological sphere: divinity was not essentially different from humanity...The gods and human beings shared the same predicament, the only difference being that the gods were more powerful and were immortal.[64]

## 2.3. *One God*

We have talked about "gods" in the plural, but these other "gods" were the "children of God." Just as it is written in Psalms 82:6, *"I have said, 'ye are gods, and all of you are children of the Most High."* Such gods as Enlil, Ba'al, Ishtar, and Horus, were all children of the God. But in all these civilizations there was the acknowledgment of the supremacy of the One Creator God.

All over the earth, the Black man and woman knew God. We knew Him under different names because we spoke different languages. But as you continue through this work you will see that they all spoke about the same God. God has 10,000 beautiful Names. 9,999 of them represent His attributes or an aspect of His nature. *Ptah* means "the Opener," but God is also the Closer. *Amun* means "the Hidden," but the *Holy Qur'an* says God is *"The Hidden and the Manifest* (57:3)." *Ahura Mazda* means "Lord of Wisdom" but He is also Lord of Understanding. All of these names represent various aspects of the nature of the one God. Albert Churchward, in his ***The Signs and Symbols of Primordial Man***, notes,

At the same time we must not forget that all of these different names of gods were simply the attributes of the

[64] Karen Armstrong, *A History of God* (New York: Ballantine Books, 1993) 5, 7.

One God.  In the 17th chapter of the (Egyptian) Ritual it says: 'His names together compose the cycle of the gods'...The aboriginal Australians have a legend about Bymee, 'The Great Father...,' as having a totem name for every part of his body, even to a different one for each finger and toe, which is simply the various attributes of the 'Great Spirit Father.'....In the 17th chapter of 'The Book of the Dead' it is said: 'I am the Great God-self created, that is to say, who made his names' - 'the company of the gods of God.'[65]

The tenth-thousandth name is *Allah*, for it represents the synthesis of All of God's great Attributes.  "Allah" means "All In All." According to Godfrey Higgins, Allah is the etymological root of the English word "all."[66]  Thus, when one says Allah, he/she simultaneously says Ptah, Amun, Brahma, Yahweh, Ahura Mazda, Ain Soph, Vishnu, ect.  All of God's beautiful Names are spoken when His name Allah is spoken.

## 2.4. *Allah, Black God among Ancient Black Arabians*

In Dr. Yosef Ben Jochannan's **African Origin of the Major Western Religions,** he states that Prophet Muhammad of Arabia (P.B.U.H.) took the pagan goddess *Allat* and transformed her into the male god Allah. [67]  I have great respect for Dr. Ben, but history reveals this not to be the case. The name Allah was the name of the Supreme God in Arabia and throughout the so-called Middle East (which was originally populated by Black People[68]) long before Muhammad was ever born. W. C. Tisdall, in his *The Original Sources of the Qur'an,* points out:

---

65 Churchward, *Signs and Symbols*, 62.

66 Higgins, *Anacalypsis*, 2:284, 408.

67 Y.B. Jochannan, *African Origin of the Major Western Religions* (Baltimore: Black Classic Press, 1970, 1991) 212, 215.

68 Ivan Van Sertima, in his *African Presence in Early Asia* (page 8) notes: "Arabia...like much of Asia was initially populated by Blacks. Some surviving black populations, known as the Veddoids, are major portions of the Mahra population found still in the extremities of Arabia."

It is not possible to suppose that the recognition of the unity of God was introduced among the Arabs for the first time by Muhammad. For the word Allah, containing as it does the definite article, is a proof that those who used it were in some degree conscious of the Divine Unity. NOW MUHAMMAD DID NOT INVENT THE WORD (ALLAH), BUT...FOUND IT ALREADY IN USE AMONG HIS FELLOW COUNTRYMEN AT THE TIME WHEN HE FIRST CLAIMED TO BE A PROPHET.[69]

Samuel M. Zwemer, in his *The Moslem Doctrine of God*, says also:

But history establishes beyond a shadow of doubt that even the pagan Arabs, before Muhammad's time, knew their chief god by the name Allah and even, in a sense, proclaimed His unity. In pre-Islamic literature...*ilah* is used for any god and *Al-ilah*, contracted to *Allah*...was the name of the Supreme. Among the pagan Arabs this term denoted the chief God of their pantheon...As final proof, we have the fact that centuries before Muhammad the Arabian Kaaba, or temple at Mecca, was called *Beit-Allah*, the house of God.[70]

The *Beit-Allah* or House of God goes back 6,000 years to the time when only Black people populated Arabia. At this time the Black Arabians worshipped only the one God. Drusilla B. Houston, in "Ethiopians in Old Arabia" notes that *"The ancient inhabitants of Arabia Petraea and Yemen (South Arabia) believed in one god and a future life."*[71] As foreigners migrated into Arabia and brought their foreign ideas, and as these indigenous Blacks began to stray away from the Law of God, polytheism grew and finally became the dominant characteristic of Arabian theology at the time of Muhammad. The goddess Allat, along with 359 other idol deities,

---

[69] W.C. Tisdall, *The Original Sources of the Qur'an* (London: Society For Promoting Christian Knowledge, 1905)34.

[70] Samuel Zwemer, *The Moslem Doctrine of God* (New Delhi: Oriental Reprint,. 1932, 1979) 24-26.

[71] Sertima, *African Presence*, 56.

were worshipped as intermediaries between man and Allah. In fact, Allat, together with the pagan goddesses *Manah* and *Al-Uzza*, were called by the pagan Arabs the "Daughters of Allah."[72]

In the ancient ruins of Southern Arabia, which became the center of Black rule in Arabia, the name Allah is found in the Himyaritic[73] inscriptions. Philip Hitti, in his exhaustive *History of the Arabs*, notes:

> Allah...was the principle...deity of Makkah. THE NAME IS AN ANCIENT ONE. It occurs in two South Arabic inscriptions, one a Minaean found at al-Ula and the other Sabean (South Arabia), but abounds in the form HLH in the Lihyanite inscriptions of the fifth century BC. Lihyan, who evidently got the god from Syria, was the first center of the worship of this deity in Arabia. The name occurs as *Hallah* in the Safa inscriptions five centuries before Islam.[74]

Evidence of the worship of Allah in ancient Arabia has been found in both the Northern and Southern portions of the peninsula. It is most documented among the Lihyan in Northern Arabia. Four hundred Lihyanite and Dedanite inscriptions dating back to the fifth century B.C. were found in the area of al-Ulah. In these inscriptions are invocations to Allah. F.V. Winnet, who has translated these inscriptions, list some of them in his article, "Allah Before Islam." Some examples are:

> *O Allah, permit me to accomplish salvation...*
> *O Allah, God without offspring, greeting*
> *O Allah, guide me that I may attain prosperity...*
> *O Allah, God without offspring, knower of men...*[75]

---

[72] P.K. Hitti, *History of the Arabs* (London: Macmillian, 1970)98.

[73] "Himyaritic" comes from "Himyar" meaning "Dusky" and was the name of the Black ruling class of ancient South Arabia. See Drusilla Houston, *Wonderful Ethiopians of the Ancient Cushite Empire* (Baltimore: Black Classic Press, 1926) 113.

[74] Hitti, *History of the Arabs*, 100.

[75] F. Winnet, "Allah Before Islam," *The Moslem World* 28 (1938): 243.

Allah is called in these inscriptions "The Exalted."

*Give favor to this rock, O Exalted Allah.*[76]

The Lihyanites were not the first Arabian worshipers of Allah, only the oldest which are so documented. They were a division of the ancient tribe Hudhayl in the northern vicinity of Mecca and al-Ta'if. Their origin, however, is in Southern Arabia. According to the *Encyclopedia of Islam,* Lihyan was a descendant of Djurhume, who came from Yemen (South Arabia). The *Encyclopedia* thus describes them: *"Their skins were black and shinning; their looks...were not hollow but round and teeming."*[77]

The name Allah derives from the proto-Semitic *al.*[78] According to Ivan van Sertima, *Al* was the name of God throughout the whole Afro-Asiatic world.[79] Parkhurst, in his Lexicon, says *Al* is *"the very name the Heathens gave to their God Sol (Sun)."*[80] Godfrey Higgins says of this name:

> I must now beg my reader to review what has been said respecting the celebrated name of God, Al, Ale, Aleim; and to observe that THIS WAS IN ALL THE WESTERN ASIATIC NATIONS THE NAME OF GOD AND OF THE SUN. This is confirmed by Sir W. Drummond and Mr. Parkhurst...and by the names given by the Greeks to places which they conquered.[81]

As we have before noted, the whole region of the Western Asiatic nations was populated by Blacks.[82] These ancient Black peoples called on Allah as God.

---

[76] F. Winnet, *A Study of The Lihyanite and Thamudic Inscriptions* (Toronto: University of Toronto Press, 1937) 27.

[77] "Hudhayl," *Encyclopedia of Islam,* 3:540.

[78] See True Islam, *Truth of God,* 156.

[79] Ivan Van Sertima, *Golden Age of the Moors,* (New Brunswick: Transaction Books, 1992) 139.

[80] Higgins, *Anacalypsis,* I: 67.

[81] Ibid., 80-1.

[82] See Sertima and Houston.

In *The Truth of God: the Bible, the Qur'an, and the Secret of the Black God* (2007) I have demonstrated that the Pre-Islamic Allah of ancient Arabia was a Black God.[83] This sheds light on a particularly interesting yet enigmatic Islamic tradition, which, itself, further confirms that the Pre-Islamic Allah was the Black God of antiquity. The tradition concerns Khalid ibn al-Walid, the famous Companion of Prophet Muhammad and 'Warrior for Islam.' As noted above, the primary gods of the pagan Arabs at the time of the Prophet were the goddesses Al-Uzza, Allat and Manah, all three considered the "Daughters of Allah" by the Arabs. At the time of Muhammad, Al-Uzzah received the most worship. Her shrine was located in Nakhla, a few miles north of Mecca. In the eighth year after the Hegira (Muhammad's flight from Mecca to Medina) Muhammad dispatched the zealous and valiant Khalid with thirty horsemen to destroy the goddess's sanctuary. While Khalid was putting the sanctuary to the sword, a naked black woman "with flowing hair" approached him. The lady's priest, who was also present, cried out: *"Be courageous, Al 'Uzza, and protect yourself!"* Khalid, it is written, "shook with terror."[84] After regaining his composure and courage, Khalid cleft the Black woman's head and killed her. Khalid reported the deed to Muhammad, expressing doubt that he had actually slain Al-Uzzah herself. He suggested that the Black woman was just a priestess. The Prophet replied, however, *"Of a truth, it was Uzza herself whom thou hast destroyed."*[85]

This is extremely significant. If the Prophet and the Arabs in general accepted Al-Uzzah as a Black woman, and the Arabs saw Al-'Uzzah as the "Daughter of Allah," how do you suppose they saw the Father? We no longer have to speculate. The Pre-Islamic Allah was a Black God, which is why His alleged 'daughter' was Black. Though Muhammad and the *Holy Qur'an* condemn the Arabs' belief that these goddesses are Allah's daughters, they both fail to condemn the anthropomorphism implied. In fact, though Al-Uzzah is not a "Daughter of Allah" in the sense the Arabs

---

[83] Chapter VI.

[84] Tor Andrae, *Mohammed: The Man and His Faith*, 18.

[85] Washington Irving, *Mahomet and His Successors*, 185.

believed, the name is the feminine of *Al-Aziz*, which is one of the 99 Names of Allah.[86]

## 2.5. *Who is that Mystery God?*

As we have noted, the worship of God as a formless spirit floating someplace in the sky did not originate with the Original Man nor was it taught by the Prophets of God.[87] This way of viewing God began with the Greek philosophers. In the fifth century B.C., Anaxagoras reacted against the anthropomorphic God of the ancients and instead proclaimed that God was an *"infinite self-moving mind...not enclosed in any body."*[88] But it was his successor Xenophanes who launched a full fledged attack on the gods of the Greek pantheon and of the original peoples. He condemned the God of the Ethiopians, for example, because He had a *"snub nose and black hair."*[89] Xenophanes said this way of understanding God was wrong because God is properly *"one and incorporeal, in substance and figure around, in no way resembling man; that He is all-sight and all-hearing, but breaths not..."*[90]

This incorporeal God was standardized by Plato (427-347 B.C.). He is given credit as the one who perfected the concept of the Immaterial Reality. Jantzen notes:

> According to a Platonic system of thought, it would be utterly inconceivable that God should have a material body. For a...Platonist, the idea of divine corporeality could be dismissed by a simple syllogism:
>
> *God is Supremely Real and Supremely Good.*
> *Matter is least real and least good.*
> *Therefore God must be immaterial.*[91]

---

[86] "Al-Uzzah," *The Encyclopedia of Islam*, 617.

[87] See below and further: True Islam, *Truth of God*.

[88] Hall, *Secret Teachings of All Ages*, XIII.

[89] E. Schoen, "Anthropomorphic Concepts of God," *Religious Studies* 26 (1990): 124.

[90] Hall, *Secret Teachings of All Ages*, XIV.

[91] Jantzen, *God's Word, God's Body*, .23.

Aristotle (384-322 B.C.) named this Immaterial Reality the "Unmoved Mover." This Unmoved Mover "*was pure being and as such, eternal, immobile and spiritual...Since matter is flawed and mortal, there is no material element in God.*"[92] Plotinus (A.D. 205-270) said this ultimate reality was "*not 'a' thing but is distinct from all things.*" In the sixth century A.D. a Greek Christian wrote a mystical treaty and ascribed it to Denys the Areopagite, St. Paul's first Athenian convert. God is here described as "*a mystery beyond being*" who should more appropriately be called "Nothing."[93] In the treaty, *The Divine Names*, "Denys" says God "*is not to be understood, nothing can be said of him, he cannot be named. He is not one of the things that are.*" This is that Mystery God. Thomas Aquinas would later take up the banner of Plato's Immaterial Reality with the words:

> In this way...God and prime matter are distinguished: one is pure act, the other is pure potency, and they agree on nothing.

The later Greeks introduced the Mystery God to the world as an object of worship. But the Original Man knew better. God is Spirit that manifests Himself in a material body - a black material body.

## 2.6. The 'Great Spirit' of African Traditional Religions

John Mbiti's **African Philosophy and Religion** is a very important work on the religious/spiritual history of our people. Mbiti clearly shows that, far from being limited to certain groups in Africa, the belief in One Supreme God permeates throughout all African societies which have never been touched by Christianity or Islam. This One Supreme God has not, however, always been "the Great Spirit" as Mbiti's work might suggest. Though this is found through out Traditional African Religious expression today, it is not found in Ancient Africa (e.g. Egypt), as we have shown. The "Great Spirit" conception of God is actually

---

[92] Armstrong, *A History of God*, 38.
[93] Ibid., 126.

discontinuous with the Ancient African conception of the Anthropomorphic God. Animism or so-called spirit worship supplanted the worship of the ancient Anthropomorphic God. An example of this transition can be found among the Zulu nation of Southern Africa. The Creator according to the Zulus was *Unkulunkulu*, who was also the First Man. However, today Unkulunkulu is despised and worship has been transferred to the *Amatongo*s or ancestral spirits.[94]

The African belief in the "Great Spirit" developed more and more as we traveled further and further from the centers of civilization. Though "Romantic Afrocentrists" will probably take offense to this statement, it is historically accurate. As we have shown, in all of the original man's ancient centers of civilization - Egypt, Sumer, Mohenjo Daro, Arabia, Persia, ect. - God was not understood simply as a "Great Spirit" but as a spiritual being that manifest itself in the body of a Black man. As groups of Original people left these centers for nomadic reasons or due to Exile some fell away from Civilized Life. This is a fact. The notion of God as a "Great Spirit" in the sky grew more defined the further we strayed.

But some of these populations retained their original understanding of God. Many so-called "primitive" cultures continued to hold on to the God of Our Fathers. In Andrew Lang's *The Making of Religion,* he notes:

The...Supreme Being (of the indigenous peoples), with added power, omniscience, and morality, is the idealization of (themselves)...minus the 'fleshy' body...and minus Death. He was not necessarily a 'spirit'...When we call the Supreme Being of the (indigenous peoples) a 'spirit' we introduce our own animistic ideas into a conception where it may not have originally existed. The Gippsland (of Australia)...believe the Creator was a GIGANTIC BLACK, living among the stars.[95]

---

[94] E.O. James, *History of Religions* (New York: Harper & Brothers, 1957) 226-7.

[95] Andrew Lang, *The Making of Religion* (New York: Longmans, Green, and Co., 1898) 203.

Lang calls the High God of these so-called low races a "magnified non-natural m(a)n." Such a one was referred to by the so-called low races with the same language as Christians refer to their God: the Ancient One, our Maker, our Father. E.O. James, in *History of Religions*, describes this "magnified non-natural man":

> This unique and remote figure stands in sublime majesty as the highest expression of supernatural power and will, primeval and benevolent, the giver and guardian of the good and the right, the supreme originator and upholder of the laws and customs whereby society is maintained as an orderly and ordered whole. So lofty in fact is the conception of the tribal All-Father that at first it was dismissed as having been imported by Christian missionaries or other foreigners acquainted with the higher conceptions of Deity. It has now been established, however...the belief in (the) High (God) among low races is a genuine and characteristic feature of uncontaminated primitive religion recurrent among such aboriginal people as the Australians, the Fuegians in South of America, the California tribes in North America, and certain negritoes and other negroids in Africa and elsewhere.[96]

## 2.7. *Give Me that Old Time Religion*

The belief in One All-Powerful, All-Wise, yet anthropomorphic Creator is the trade mark of the "Old Time Religion" of the Black man and woman. It was this "old time religion," and the God which inspired it, which provided us with the thought processes and world-view allowing us to build marvelous civilizations which baffle scholars and scientists to this very day. These civilizations were built on righteous law. Long before Moses received the Ten Commandments we displayed our righteousness in the 42 Negative Confessions in Egypt and the Code of Hammurabi in Ancient Babylon. This is the same God who appeared to all the prophets, from Abraham to

---

[96] James, *History of Religions*, 8.

Muhammad.[97]    Since we have abandoned the God of Our Fathers, we have been unable to build so much as a Tee Pee for ourselves, by ourselves. We have turned our backs on the God which we worshipped when we were world rulers, and now wonder why we can not rule even our own homes.

Thus we have shown that the world at one time knew that God was a Black man, but the "God of our Fathers" has been abandoned and the god of the enemy has been adopted. It is my conclusion and belief that if Black people are to be truly liberated from our oppressors, and a Black Liberation Theology is going to be the catalyst of this liberation, then we need to pick back up the "God of Our Fathers" and "render unto Caesar what is Caesar's."

---

[97] See True Islam, *Truth of God*.

# CHAPTER III

## *The Black God and Scripture*

3.1. *The God of the Bible is a Man*

Zecharia Sitchin, a scholar of ancient Near East religions observes:

> In all ancient pictorial depictions of gods and men, this physical likeness is evident. Although the biblical admonitions against the worship of pagan images gave rise to the notion that the Hebrew God had neither image nor likeness, not only the Genesis tale but other biblical reports attest to the contrary. The God of the ancient Hebrews could be seen face-to-face, could be wrestled with, could be heard and spoken to; he had a head and feet, hands and fingers, and a waist. The biblical God and his emissaries looked like men and acted like men-because men were created to look and act like the gods.[98]

Reference is made above to the famous passage of Gen.1:26 where Eloheim (God) proclaims, *na'aseh 'adam beselmenu kidemutenu - "Let us make man in our Image after our Likeness."* Here Adam is said to be made in the image and after the likeness of God.[99] The current orthodox interpretation of this passage renders the image and likeness here referred to as a 'spiritual' likeness, therefore eliminating any possibility that God "looks" like man. However, those who understand Hebrew know that this is a most inappropriate interpretation of that passage. The Hebrew words *selem* (image) and *demut* (likeness) denotes the

---

[98]Sitchin, *12TH Planet*, 338.

[99] On this passage see further True Islam, *Truth of God*, 208-217.

*"outward form, not (the) attributes."*[100] According to Helmer Renggren in his ***Israelite Religion***, *"the meaning of the words 'selem' and 'demut,' hardly allows this statement to refer to anything but CORPOREAL SIMILARITY."*[101] Maryanne C. Horowitz, in her article "The Image of God in Man - Is Woman Included?" affirms also that the "image," *selem*, is a Hebrew term which *"contained anthropomorphic corporeal imagery."*[102] These same Hebrew words are used throughout the Old Testament and always have this meaning of corporeality.[103] Thus, to apply any meaning here other than Adam's physical, corporeal similarity to God is to violate the principle of contextual exegesis.

The Prophets, when they saw God, indeed saw a man. Ezekiel, describing his vision of God, says,

> And above the firmament that was over their heads was a throne, as the appearance of a sapphire stone: and upon the likeness of the throne was the likeness as the appearance of a MAN above it. (v27) And I saw the color of amber, as the appearance of fire round about within him, from the appearance of his loins even upward, and from the appearance of his loins even downward (Ez. 1:26-7).

The Prophet Daniel also beheld God. He saw Him as *"the Ancient of Days...whose garment was white as snow, and the HAIR ON HIS HEAD LIKE PURE WOOL (DAN. 7:9)."*

The Hebrew word for man is *'ish*. This is used in reference to God several times.[104] The author of Exodus states emphatically *YHWH 'ish milhamah, YHWH semo, "The Lord is a MAN of war. The Lord is his name. (15:3)."* Also in Isa. 42:13 it reads,

The Lord (*YHWH*) goes forth as a mighty man (*gibbor*),

---

[100] F.J. Dake ***Dake's Annotated Reference Bible*** (Lawrenceville, Georgia: Dake Bible Sales, Incorporated, 1961) 1 ft. y, z.

[101] H. Ringgren, ***Israelite Religion*** (Philadelphia: Fortress Press, 1966) 70.

[102] M.C. Horowitz, "The Image of God in Man - Is Woman Included?" ***HTR*** 72 (1979): 190

[103] For example: Ex.20:4; Lev.26:1;Isa. 40:18; Ezec.1:5

[104] See further True Islam, ***Truth of God***, Chapter II ("The Man-God of Biblical Tradition").

as a man of war (*'ish milhamah*) he stirs up his fury.

In Gen. 18 we read,

> And the Lord appeared unto him (Abraham) in the plains of Mamre: and he (Abraham) sat in the tent door in the heat of the day; (v2) And he lifted up his eyes and looked, and, lo, THREE MEN stood by him: and when he (Abraham) saw them, he ran to meet them from the tent door, and bowed himself toward the ground, and said, 'My Lord, if now I have found favor in thy sight, pass not away...(v4) Let a little water, I pray you, be fetched, and wash YOUR FEET, AND REST YOURSELVES UNDER THE TREE.'

Of these three men that appeared unto Abraham, one of them was Yahweh.[105] The prophet Joshua (5:13) also sees a *"man ('ish) over against him with his sword drawn."* The prophet Joshua drops down on his face and *"did worship* (v14)" this man, who was God. George Fohrer, in *History of Israelite Religion*, says:

> The statements that no man can see him (Ex.33:20) and that he is spirit, not flesh (Isa.31:3) of course do not mean that he is formless or invisible, but rather that man cannot endure the sight of him (cf. Judge. 13:22) and that, in contrast to transitory 'flesh,' he possesses an eternal vitality...All the evidence suggest that *from the outset Yahweh was conceived in human form.*[106]

## 3.2. *The Black God of Israel*

In *The Truth of God* I have demonstrated that the God of ancient Israel and the Bible, Yahweh-El, was not just a man, but a Black man - the same Black God that we have encountered

---

[105] See further True Islam, *Truth of God*, 46-51 ("The Man-God of Biblical Tradition. § 2. 3.1. Genesis 18").

[106] G. Fohrer, *History of Israelite Religion* (New York: Abingdon Press, 1972) 169.

throughout the ancient world.[107] The Bible describes his appearance as *'arapel*, 'thick blackness' and associates him with the Black Bull, the universal symbol of the Black God.[108] According to the esoteric theology of the priests responsible for the final editing of the Torah (Pentateuch or Five Books of Moses) the blue-black robe worn by the high priest symbolized the blue-black body of Yahweh.[109]

## 3.3. *The Anthropomorphic God of Israel*

The Hebrews and Jews[110] believed in the anthropomorphic God all the way up until the time of Jesus and beyond. Gedaliahu G. Stroumsa states,

It must first be pointed out Jewish anthropomorphism seems to have been notorious in the first centuries C.E.[111]

The Church Father Justine Martyr, writing in the second century, said in *Dialogue with Trypho* that the Jewish teachers *"imagine that the Father of all, the unengendered God, has hands, feet, fingers and a soul, just as a composite being."*[112] Origen (A.D. 185-253),[113] Basil of Cesarea (A.D. 330-379) and Arnobious of Sicca all speak of the Jewish belief in an anthropomorphic deity.[114] An example of how the God of Israel was viewed in the fifth century can be found in

---

[107] Chapters VI ("The Bible, the Qur'an and the Black God") and VII ("The Bible and the Secret of the Black God").

[108] See discussion and references in True Islam, **Truth of God**, 163-70 ("The Bible, the Qur'an and the Black God. § 6.3. Yahweh-El, Black God of Israel" and "§ 6.4. Black Bull of Israel").

[109] Ibid., 224-229.

[110] Hebrews and Jews are not the same. The Hebrews are the ancient Black followers of Moses out of ancient Kemet. Jews are the white followers of Moses out from the caves of Europe.

[111] G.G. Stroumsa, "Form(s) of God: Some Notes on Metatron and Christ," *HTR* 76 (1983):: 271.

[112].Ibid.

[113] Paulsen, "Early Christian Belief," 110.

[114] Stroumsa, "Form(s) of God, 271-3.

the Jewish (rabbinic) text *Genesis Rabbah*, ca. A.D. 400-450. Rabbi Hoshaiah is reported as saying:

> When the Holy One (Yahweh), blessed be he, came to create the first man, the ministering angels mistook him [for God, since man was in God's image,] and wanted to say before him, 'Holy, [holy, holy is the Lord of hosts].[115]

There is a legend among the Jews that when the High-Priest Simon the Just on his last Day of Atonement was ministering in the Temple, his usual companion, an old man adorned in white, entered the Holy of Holies with Simon, yet did not leave with him. This raised an eye of surprise in the circle of Rabbi Abbahu, for it is written in Leviticus xvi. 17 that no one could be in the Tent of Appointment during the time when the High-Priest is atoning in the Sanctuary; not even one of the angels. Rabbi Abbahu concluded that surely that venerable old man that entered the Holy of Holies with Simon was no mere mortal - he was God.[116]

## 3.4. *The Rise of Jewish Hellenism and the Mystery God of Judaism*

Influenced by Greek philosophy a number of Jews began interpreting the Biblical passages concerning God in a figurative sense. These new Jewish converts to Hellenism* reacted against the God of their fathers. By the second century B.C., Platonic thought was wide spread and his "Immaterial Reality" began having a powerful influence on the Jewish understanding of God. Aristobulus, in 150 B.C., *"basing himself on Greek thinkers and poets,"*[117] applied an allegorical interpretation to the anthropomorphic descriptions of God in the Bible. But it was the Jewish philosopher Philo Judaeus (20 B.C.-A.D. 40) who, being educated in Alexandria where Platonic thought flourished, systematically applied allegorical interpretations to the Bible, thus

---

[115] J. Neusner, *The Incarnation of God* (Philadelphia: Fortress Press, 1988) 15.

[116] Artur Marmerstein *The Old Rabbinic Doctrine of God: Essays in Anthropomorphism* (New York: Ktav, 1937) 49.

[117] "Anthropomorphism," *Encyclopedia Judaica*, I:55

pushing the God of the ancient religious traditions further out of the Temple. *The Jewish Encyclopedia* says,

> The God of Philo, owing to the influence of Platonism, is not only essentially different from man and the world...but he is entirely devoid of attributes. Philo opposes not only the literal understanding of the anthropomorphic and anthropopathic* passages in the Bible, but also the doctrine of God as an active worker, in as much as activity can not be predicated of a Being devoid of attributes.[118]

The issue of God's corporeality was raised again in the third century. In the Medieval period, Saadia Gaeon (882-942), Bahya (wrote in 1040), and Judah ha-Levi (1075-1141), influenced by Greek Philosophy that was resurrected through the Muslim translation of Greek texts into Arabic, did their part in pushing the God of the Prophets out of the Synagogue and replacing him with the God of the Philosophers. But it was Moses ben Maimon, a.k.a. Maimonides (1138-1204), who planted his foot firmly on the backside of the God of Religion and closed the door of the Temple behind him. "The greatest of the Jewish philosophers," as Maimonides was called, was the first to set up the incorporeality of God as dogma and declared any person who denied this doctrine as an idolater and heretic who will be denied entry into the Here-After.[119] It was

> his 'Guide' (that) determined what was to become the Orthodox concept of God within Judaism for a long time. There is evidence...to show that it was the writings of Maimonides which finally did away with all anthropomorphic notions among the Jews.[120]

Baruch Spinoza (1632-1677) was denounced and banished from the community by the rabbis because he rejected Maimonides principles of exegesis and declared that the scriptural

---

[118] "Anthropomorphism," *The Jewish Encyclopedia*, I:623

[119] Ibid, I:624

[120] "Anthropomorphism," *Encyclopedia Judaica*, I:56

anthropomorphisms were originally meant to be taken literally.[121] Spinoza's ousting from the community of the Jews indicates that the God of Israel was also officially ousted.

### 3.4.1. *The Jews Alter the Bible*

> Do you then hope that they would believe in you, and a party from among them (Jews) indeed used to hear the world of Allah, then altered it after they had understood it, and they know this.
>
> *Holy Qur'an* 2:75

The *Holy Qur'an* accuses the Jews of altering the scriptures of God. Far from being Islamic "anti-Semitism," this fact is a matter of recorded history. John H. Hayes, professor of Old Testament at Candler School of Theology, Emory University, in his book *An Introduction to Old Testament Study*, observes,

> Rabbinical references provide evidence that the pre-Masoretic scribes not only guarded and preserved the text but at times WENT SO FAR AS TO ALTER THE TEXT ITSELF.[122]

Toy, in *Judaism and Christianity*, says also,

> Manuscripts were copied and recopied by (Jewish) scribes who not only sometimes made errors in the letters of the words, but permitted themselves to introduce new material into the text...

These alterations made by the Jewish scribes, called *tiqqune sopherim* or "emendations of the scribes," were not random or casual but were theologically motivated. Hayes observes:

---

[121]Ibid.

[122] John H. Hayes, *An Introduction to Old Testament Study* (Nashville: Abingdon Press, 1979) 55.

Many of the changes assumed seem to have the purpose of making the text more theologically acceptable by changing expressions which seem to lack proper reverence. Some examples...:Gen 18:22 originally read 'YHWH still stood before Abraham' rather than 'Abraham still stood before YHWH'; II Sam 20:1 read 'to his gods' rather than 'to his tents'; Ez 8:17 read 'my God's nose' rather than 'their nose'; and Job 32:3 read 'they condemned God' rather than 'they condemned Job.'[123]

These "emendations of the scribes" were made to conceal the true reality of God. As shown, the God of the Old Testament was a so-called anthropomorphic God - a man. Jewish scribes, now sensitive to the Hellenistic critique of anthropomorphism, corrupted the scripture in an attempt to hide that fact. E.O. James, in *The Concept of Deity* observes that,

In post-exilic Judaism...efforts were made by the scribes to remove some of the more crude anthropomorphisms, or to paraphrase and SPIRITUALIZE them. Thus, in the Targums (i.e. Aramaic translations of the Old Testament) the finger of God of Ex viii. 19 was rendered 'this is a *plague* from before Yahweh' and when He was said to abide in, come to, or depart from a place, the phrase was made to read 'God caused his presence (*shekinto*) to abide there, and the like, just as seeing God, or God manifesting Himself to man, was interpreted as 'the glory (*yekara*) of God.' When the earlier anthropomorphisms were retained (e.g. in references to God having eyes, ears, hands and feet) the term '*memra*,' meaning the 'divine self manifestation,' was introduced as a reverend circumlocution for God as active in the affairs of men.[124]

Robert Dentan, in *The Knowledge of God in Ancient Israel*, acknowledges also "*in later times...older texts were changed to modify*

[123] Ibid.

[124] E.O. James, *The Concept of Deity* (New York: Hutchins University Library, 1950) 81-2

*or eliminate some of the cruder passages (of anthropomorphism)."*[125] *The Jewish Encyclopedia* says,

> For it is obvious that there is a definite method and purpose in the consistent efforts of the nomistic writers to substitute new terms for those found in the ancient authorities (scriptures), or to REMODEL ENTIRE ACCOUNTS. Such revision is to be seen, for example, in the so-called 'priestly code' where ALL THEOPHANIES ARE CONSISTENTLY OMITTED, and the 'word' or the 'presence of God' substituted for them.[126]

When the "Seventy Jews of Alexandria" produced the Greek Septuagint translation of the Bible, the corruption efforts to conceal the God of the Patriarchs continued. *The Jewish Encyclopedia* says again,

> The 'fathers' of the Septuagint went much further than the 'Soferim' (scribes) or the 'Meturgemanim' (translators into Aramaic) in their employment of interpretative expressions, by paraphrasing or spiritualizing ... the anthropomorphic...phrases of the Bible. The 'image of God' becomes in the Septuagint 'the glory of God'...'the mouth of God' (becomes) 'the voice of the Lord'.[127]

In translating the famous Gen. 1:26, Maryanne C. Horowitz says,

> In the translation of 'image' from the Hebrew 'zelem' to the Greek 'eikon,' a term which contained anthropomorphic, corporeal imagery was transformed into an abstract term for which there was a previous Greek philosophic tradition.[128]

---

[125]R. Dentan, *The Knowledge of God in Ancient Israel* (New York: Sealury Press, 1968) 141.

[126] "Anthropomorphism," *The Jewish Encyclopedia*, I:622

[127] Ibid., I: 623

[128] Horowitz, "Image of God in Man,"190.

The Jews also sought to remove references to the Black children of that Black God, called in the scripture "Gods." These divine descendants of the Creator are mentioned in the opening verses of the Bible under the name *Eloheim*. Though it is mistranslated as "God," Finis J. Dake correctly points out:

> The Heb. Eloheim is the word for God in Gen. 1:1 and in over 2700 other places in the O.T. It is a uni-plural noun meaning <u>Gods</u> and is so translated 239 times (Gen. 3.5;Ex 22:28; I Sam 4:8).

*Eloheim* is sometimes used in conjunction with plural pronouns, such as in Gen 20:13 which originally read, *"The Gods they caused me to wander"* and Gen 35:7 which read, *"there the Gods they appeared unto me."* Both verses were changed to read, *"when God caused me to wander"* and *"there God appeared unto him."*

The *Jewish Encyclopedia* not only acknowledges this corruption of the scripture, BUT IDENTIFIES THE GUILTY PARTY (*"a party from among them"*).

> Tannaitic sources mention several passages of Scripture in which the conclusion is inevitable that the ancient readings must have differed from the present text. The explanation of this phenomenon is given in the expression...'Scripture has used euphemistic language', i.e. to avoid anthropomorphism...In Masorectic works these changes are ascribed to Ezra; to Ezra and Nehemiah; or to Ezra, Nehemiah, Zechariah, Haggai and Baruch. All these ascriptions mean one and the same thing: that the changes were made by the Men of the Great Synagogue.[129]

"The Great Synagogue" was reputed to be a "council of elders" of sorts. Little information about them is known, but most scholars agree that the Great Synagogue was instituted during the Persian period. Consisting of anywhere from 85 to 120 Jews, their leader was reputed to be the scribe Ezra. Ezra was a priest-scribe from Babylon who, backed by the royal might of the Persian king

---

[129] "Masorah," *Jewish Encyclopedia*, 366.

Artaxerxes I (465-424 B.C.), traveled to Jerusalem and instituted a major reform among the Jews there.[130] He and his "Great Synagogue" are credited with being the "party from among" the Jews who altered the Bible in an attempt to conceal the reality of the Black God Yahweh.[131]

### 3.4.1.1. *Jews Remove the Name Allah from Bible*

Not only did the Jews alter the Bible in an attempt to conceal the true nature of their Black God, they also removed the true Name of that God, *Allah*. YHWH is one of the many names of God used in the Scripture. But His most perfect name, Allah, which represents the synthesis of All of His beautiful Names, was CONSCIOUSLY REMOVED FROM THE BIBLE. Such names as *El Shaddai* (Ex. 6:3), *El 'Elyon* (Gen. 14:18-24), *El 'Olam* (Gen. 21:33) and *Eloheim* (Gen 1:1) are all purposeful corruptions of the name Allah.

The above names are compound names composed of the name of God prefixed to an attribute. *El* is the presumed name of God, and *El Shaddai* is God Almighty; *El 'Elyon* is God Most High; *El Olam* is God Everlasting, ect. *El* or *Eloh* is the singular of *Eloheim*. Herein lays the deception. The fact is, *El*, *Eloh*, and *Eloheim* are purposeful corruptions of *Al*, *Allah*, and *Alheim*.

The Hebrew words translated "*El*" and "*Eloheim*" are אל and אלהים. The Hebrew letter א written as an "e" is actually the first letter of the Hebrew alphabet called Aleph which is an "a," not an "e." Godfrey Higgins observes:

> I must now beg my reader to review what has been said respecting the celebrated name of God, Al, Ale, Aleim; and to observe that this was in ALL THE WESTERN ASIATIC NATIONS THE NAME OF GOD and the Sun...I must also beg my readers attention to the observation...relating to the

---

[130] Bright, *A History Of Israel*, 385-391.

[131] *The Jewish Encyclopedia* "Anthropomorphism" (I: 622) says again: "Aversion to Anthropomorphism exercised a great influence upon the men of the 'Great synagogue,' who undertook to establish a sacred canon. For the more the belief in the letter increased (literalism), the more zealously did the leading spirits of Israel endeavor to bring the Scriptures into harmony with their purer religious and ethical views".

word El...In the Asiatic languages, the first letter of the word is the first letter of the alphabet (A) and not the fifth (E)...But we don't just increase difficulties (by such errors), WE DISGUISE AND CONCEAL ABSOLUTE FACTS. Thus, it is a fact that the Sun and the God of Moses had the same names; that is, the God of Moses was called by the same word which meant sun, in the Asiatic language: BUT BY CALLING ONE OF THEM EL (NAME OF GOD) INSTEAD OF AL, THE FACT IS CONCEALED.[132]

This fact was concealed by a group of Jewish scribes called Tiberian Massoretes who developed the current vowel system. The Hebrew language is consonantal, possessing no written vowels. Occasionally some consonants, called the *matres lectionis*, were used to indicate vowel sounds.[133] The Hebrew first letter Aleph was one of those consonants. Chomsy, in *Hebrew: The Eternal Language*, notes:

> eventually the Aleph was taken as a long 'A,' as in 'far,' and was employed as a vowel-letter pure and simple. Hence, when one wants to signify in Hebrew the sound 'a' in such words as Paris, Bialik, and the like, the Aleph is employed for the purpose.[134]

When the Greeks took over the Semitic alphabet from Phoenician traders around 800-900 B.C., the Old Hebrew Aleph, written [ ✕ ],[135] became their "A," shape and all.[136] H.W.F. Gesenius, in his *Hebrew-Chaldee Lexicon to the Old Testament*, has a "Comparative Table of Ancient Alphabet," in which the Hebrew Aleph is synonymous with the first letter, which represents "A," in thirteen other ancient languages.[137]

---

[132] Higgins, *Anacalypsis*, 80-81.

[133] Hayes, *Introduction to Old Testament Study*, 50.

[134] William Chomsky, *Hebrew: The Eternal Language* (Philadelphia: Jewish Publication Society of America, 1957) 99.

[135] As opposed to the latter Square Aleph [ א ].

[136] Chomsky, *Hebrew: The Eternal Language*, 79.

[137] H.W.F. Gesenius, *Hebrew-Chaldee Lexicon to the Old Testament*, Appendix.

It was the Tiberian Massoretes who concealed this fact. Massoretic scribes were scribes who added critical notes (*masora*) to the external form of the Biblical text. During the fifth through the eleventh centuries, the Massoretic scribes resurrected the Hebrew language, which had been dead since around 400 B.C., being replaced by Aramaic as the popular language among the Jews.[138] To fix the pronunciation of words and denote vowel sounds, the Tiberian Massoretes (as opposed to the systems developed by the Babylonian and Palestinian Massoretes) introduced the vowel system in which a number of dots and dashes are placed under the letter to represent vowel sounds. By

placing five dots [⸪] under the letter Aleph the letter is changed from an "A" to an "E," and the words Al, Alah, and Alheim are changed to El, Eloh, and Eloheim; thus, the name of God in popular Hebrew. MacGregor Mathers, in *The Kabbalah Revealed*, notes that "Eloh" is written in Hebrew as ALH or Allah.[139] In Synagogue Hebrew, according to Higgins, 19th century Jews still used Allah and Alheim.[140] Lloyd Graham, in *Deceptions and Myths in the Bible*, speaking on *Eloheim* observes: "*The word comes from Alheim and means a council of the Gods.*"[141] Scholars Albert Churchward[142] as well as Gerald Massey[143] confirm that the originals of the Hebrew El and Eloheim possessed an "A" as the first letter, not an "E."

As a side note, the name of God in the sister languages of Hebrew is Allah as well. In Arabic (which is its mother), Aramaic[144] (which was the language Jesus spoke), and Syriac, the name of God is Allah. These three languages are of considerable importance to the development of Hebrew theology. Aramaic is

---

[138] J.T. Sunderland, *The Origin and Character of the Bible*, 60.

[139] MacGregor Mathers, *The Kabbalah Revealed* (London: Arkana Books, 1991) 22.

[140] Higgins, *Anacalypsis*, I: 64.

[141] Lloyd Graham, *Deceptions and Myths in the Bible* (Bill Publishing Co., 1976) 36.

[142] *Origin and Evolution of Religion* (1924; New York: E.C.A. Association, 1990) 317.

[143] *Ancient Egypt: The Light of the World* (1907; New York: E.C.A. Association, 1990) 435.

[144] Bergstrasser, *Introduction to the Semitic Languages* (Winona Lake, Indiana: Eisenbrauns, 1928) 80.

the language used throughout Palestine at the time of Jesus, who used this language himself, along with his followers.[145] Some of the Old Testament texts were written in Aramaic and Arabic. The Oldest and most valuable New Testament codex (A.D. 350) was written in Syriac.

This all means that the Black God of Israel and the Bible was originally Allah, the Black God of ancient Arabia.

## 3.5. *Jesus, Prophet of the Black God*

Jesus was a Hebrew and believed in the Black God of Israel. As Arthur McGiffert in *The God of the Early Christians* explains:

> Jesus was a devout and loyal Jew, and the God whom he worshipped was the God of his people Israel - the God of Abraham, Isaac, and Jacob...So far as we can judge from the Synoptic Gospels and from his attitude reflected there, he did not regard it as his mission to promulgate a new God or to teach new ideas about God, but rather to summon his fellows to live as God - his God and theirs - would have them live...
>
> Jesus' idea of God indeed is quite naïve and anthropomorphic...Jesus' idea of God was wholly Jewish. At no point, so far as we can judge from the Synoptic Gospels, did he go beyond his people's thought about God.[146]

In *The Truth of God* I have demonstrated that indeed the God of Jesus and the Early Church was a man.[147] As I demonstrate there as well, the change in how the God of Jesus and the Church was understood was stimulated by Christian involvement with Greek philosophy. As Robert P. Casey points out:

---

[145] " Who Do Men Say That I Am?" *The Humanist Magazine*, May/June 1991, 8

[146] A. McGriffert, *The God of the Early Christians* (New York: Charles Scribner's Sons, 1924) 3,17.

[147] Chapter III ("God the Father in Early Christian Tradition").

The period in which (the) revival of Platonism took place saw the beginning of Christianity, and in the second century it became apparent that Christian theology, if it were to survive, must justify itself philosophically. In doing so it had to make choices between the materialism of Stoa and the immaterialism of Plato. That it ultimately chose the latter may in part be attributed to the influence of men like Philo and Numenius...[148]

## 3.6. *The Black God of the Qur'an*

A.S. Trittin, in his *Islam*, observes:

> The Koran and tradition (sayings of the Prophet and his companions) often speak of God as if He were a man; to take two examples only, 'When God created the world He wrote with His Hand for Himself, 'My mercy precedes My anger,' and, 'He opens the gates of heaven in the last third of the night, stretches out His hand and says, 'Is there none to ask of me that I may give?' He stays like this till dawn.' In consequence many thought of God as (having) a body; they asked if the throne supported Him and did He fill it. He had the limbs of a man, He was a...light in the form of a man and His hair was black light; He was a body but not like other bodies.[149]

In *The Truth of God* I have demonstrated as well that the God of the Qur'an and Sunnah of the Prophet was a man – in Arabic *shakhs* (corporeal person) and *shabb* (young man).[150] I have also demonstrated that this God is the same Black God of ancient Israel and the ancient Near East generally. [151] The Qur'an in fact narrates God's own incarnation within a Black earthly body called

---

[148] R.P. Casey, "Clement of Alexandria and the Beginnings of Christian Platonism," *Harvard Theological Review* 18 (1925): 45.

[149] A.S. Tritten, *Islam*, (London: Hutchinsons University Library, 1951) 36.

[150] Chapter IV, "Allah the Original Man: God in the Qur'an and Sunnah."

[151] Chapter VI, ("The Bible, the Qur'an and the Black God, § 6.2: *Surat al-Ikhlas and the Black God*.)

'Adam.'[152] Again, it was Muslim intercourse with Greek philosophy that stimulated a change, resulting ultimately in the God of Philosophy replacing the God of the Qur'an and Sunnah in Muslim theology.[153]

---

[152] See discussion and references in True Islam, *Truth of God*, § 7.3.2. Adam, the Qur'an and the Black Body of God, 218-224.

[153] See True Islam, *Truth of God*, § 4.7. The Dogmatic Crises, 117-22.

# CHAPTER IV

## *How Came the Black God, Mr. Muhammad?*

How came the Black God, Mr. Muhammad? This is the way he was born - in total darkness. There was no light no where. And out of the orbit of the universe of darkness there sparkled an Atom of Life. Long before there was a where and a when, He (the Black God) was God. A little small Atom of Life rolling around in darkness...building up itself...just turning in darkness, making its own self...How came the Black God, Mr. Muhammad? He is Self-Created.

> - Excerpts from Muhammad's 1969 Saviors Day Address.

The Hon. Elijah Muhammad did not declare that God was a Black man and stop there. Rather, he proceeded to describe, in broad outline, the process by which God *became* a Black man. The 'Beginning' began, Muhammad teaches, with limitless darkness. This primordial darkness was not simply the absence of light. It was a material darkness, an aqueous (watery) darkness, a *triple-darkness*. Within this triple-darkness there was God as a divine force. This force was powerful but had remained latent and motionless for untold trillions of years. With this divine force in the still darkness was an atom. How the atom first emerged in the darkness is unknown, but at some point the divine force entered the atom and caused it to move. This first motion, a spiral-type motion resembling the number 6, was the beginning of Time. This, Muhammad teaches, occurred seventy-six trillion years ago.[154]

---

[154] See Muhammad, *Theology of Time*, 90-112 and Elijah Muhammad, *Our Savior Has Arrived* (Chicago: Muhammad's Temple of Islam No. 2, 1974) 39-40.

This primordial atom became the root of God's physical body, which God took 6 trillion years to build up - atom by atom, cell by cell. From that first atom 9, 999 others developed. When these original 10, 000 atoms came together by some 'Affinit Energy' God became One, which likely means He developed into the first DNA molecule or what Muhammad calls the 'atom of life.'[155] Once becoming 'One' Allah (God) evolved into the 'Six,' which is to say He evolved from that first DNA molecule into a living human being, called God's 'complete making.'[156] The 'six' represents God's complete, though imperfect human form.

> The Atom out of which Man was created came from space. It was out in space where He originated. An Atom of Life was in the darkness of the space and He came out of that Atom...What came out of space was a Human Being.[157]

> The figures (1) and six (6) are the most outstanding figures that we have. One represents the God who created the Heavens and the Earth and the other one represents the same, the "6". Why is that? He didn't stop growing![158]

> How did the Original Man Himself become "6" instead of being a "1"...He made Himself revolve and then He caused whatever comes into the darkness to revolve like Himself. That He has done. We can't help from revolving. We are not a perfect human being because our form is not perfect.[159]

The evolution from One to Six took six trillion years. Even though this form was not perfect, its creation is a marvel.

> our First Father formed and designed Himself. Think over a Man being able to design His own form and He had

---

[155] See below.
[156] Muhammad, *Theology of Time*, 95
[157] Ibid., 95, 97, 105.
[158] Ibid., 98-99.
[159] Ibid., 108-109.

never seen another Man before He saw Himself. This is a powerful thing.[160]

What did that first human being, God, look like? There is actually a tension in Muhammad's teaching regarding this question. A tension, however, that can be easily resolved if we consult the ancient traditions that also describe the self-creation of the Black God.[161]

According to the Hon. Elijah Muhammad God used the material darkness as the substance of his body. He thus emerged as a total dark being.

> He came out of total darkness and He was dark. He proved that He came out of darkness, because His own color corresponds with the conditions of what is now the Heavens and the Earth, that was nothing then but total darkness. A totally dark man came out of total darkness…[162]

But was this 'totally dark' God 'totally dark' from the beginning? As I have demonstrated in *The Truth of God*, ancient Egyptian, Indian, and Israelite (Biblical) texts describe this same 'self-creation of the Black God' as presented by Muhammad.[163] According to this ancient and widespread tradition, though, when God first emerged from darkness he possessed a body of light. The luminous body was incomparably brilliant. In fact, the sun was set in the sky just as a sign, a pale reflection, of the luminous body of the anthropomorphic 'sun-god.' This brilliantly luminous body, we are told, was counter-productive to the creator's attempt to make a material creation. The divine luminosity was too powerful, keeping matter unstable and, as said in Kemet, 'scorching the cosmos.' Thus each creation was successively destroyed inadvertently by the divine luminosity. The creator thus decided to veil his luminosity in a body made out of the primordial black substance (Kemetic *Nun*; Sumerian *Apsu-Tiamat*;

---

[160] Ibid., 119.
[161] See True Islam, *Truth of God*, 138-54.
[162] Muhammad, *Theology of Time*, 107.
[163] Chapter V, "The Black God and the Ancient Mysteries."

Indic *Nara*; Biblical *Hosek*). As this substance originally contained the divine luminosity (the latter emerging out of the former as the first act of creation), it therefore was the only material substance strong enough to refract the luminosity without itself being destroyed. The brilliantly luminous creator-god thus 'incarnated' in a black, material cosmic body that veils and refracts the divine light as a mercy to the cosmos. The new black body became the 'Temple' of the luminous body of God.[164]

Are there any indications of such a divine luminous body prior to the 'totally dark' body in Muhammad's teaching? There are indeed at least two. Firstly, Muhammad says explicitly, in apparent contradiction to what he said above, that when God first emerged from the darkness He was luminous, not 'totally dark.'

> He (God) created Himself and was Light[165] of Himself. He emitted light from the live atom of Self.

This statement may shed some light (no pun intended) on another statement by Muhammad, which otherwise would be difficult to comprehend.

> Allah is a Warrior from the beginning. He was such a warrior from the beginning, that when He made Himself to appear out of darkness, He then went to war with the darkness, by raising up Light to lighten up darkness, so that darkness could not triumph over Him. He made a Great Light for Himself. He made his own house rotate so that it will stay in and out of the light, so that it would be a sign for us here today. Praise be to Allah.[166]

Without assuming a 'luminous' stage prior to the 'totally dark' stage this statement is difficult to reconcile with Muhammad's teaching on the Black God. Is He here going to war with his own dark self? 'War' implies hostility toward that which one is 'warring' with. Is the dark God hateful of His own somatic (from *soma*, 'body') darkness or is He just hostile toward the cosmic

---

[164] True Islam, *Truth of God*, 146-53.
[165] Abass Rasoul's transcription has "Like of Self," which is clearly an error.
[166] Muhammad, *Theology of Time*, 146.

darkness from which He came? But the cosmic darkness is the substance of His own darkness. How could He be hateful of the one and not the other? In what way was this darkness unsuccessful in 'triumphing' over Him, being that He is presumably already covered in darkness?

All of these questions find ready answers if we assume the ancient tradition of the original luminous body of the Black God as lying behind Muhammad's assertion that, after creating Himself God was a "light unto Himself" and that He "emitted light." Thus, when Allah first emerged from the darkness he was luminous. He then went to 'war' with the darkness by dispersing fiery stars throughout the universe pushing the edge of darkness ever further and further back. The mightiest of the stars, the Sun, was a sign not only of the God's 'work'[167] but, as in the ancient tradition, of the God's own luminosity as well. It would thus have been at a later stage, unspecified by Muhammad, that the God assumed His black body.

This History of Origins taught by the Honorable Elijah Muhammad may sound strange to those who know only the orthodox Christian dogma. However, any student of world religions should immediately see that Mr. Muhammad's basic teachings are in complete agreement with the History of Origins as presented by the ancient religious literature of the Black man and woman found all over the Earth. For those who aren't such students, I will present those parallels hereafter.

---

[167] Ibid., 111.

# CHAPTER V

# A.T.O.M.
## (Allah The Original Man)

5.1. *The Atom and the Origin of the Cosmos*

It may be hard for most people to grasp the fact that this sub-microscopic entity called the Atom is the root of God and Man. As we will see, however, this was understood perfectly by our ancestors. Because this Atom is so important, a detailed description is in order.

The Atom, as discussed previously, is a "bundle of energy." The Standard Dictionary defines the Atom as *"a center of force, a phase of electrical phenomena, a center of energy active through its own internal make-up."* Though the Atom was believed to be the "basic building block" of all things, it is now known to be composed of several "sub-atomic" particles. In the nucleus of the Atom, which accounts for approximately 98% of its mass (as the Sun accounts for approximately 98% of the mass of the Solar System), there is the positive proton and the neutron which has no charge. Revolving around the nucleus (as the planets revolve around the Sun, at least in Newtonian physics) are the negative electrons. The electrons travel at close to (but never at) the speed of light (186, 000 m/sec.) around the nucleus. There are an equal number of protons and electrons in the Atom giving it divine balance.

The proton, neutron and electron are themselves composed of smaller "a-toms" called quarks and leptons. Described as "balls of fire" and "points of congealed energy"[168] these are actually thought to be the building blocks of matter.[169] They are the manifestation of that original 'force' that existed in the universe before the 'sparkling' of the atom. That force became somehow polarized like electricity, producing the quark (positive) and lepton (negative). There are six types of quarks and six leptons.

---

[168] Frank Close, Michael Martin, and Christine Sutton, *The Particle Explosion* (New York: Oxford University Press, 1987) 8.
[169]Leon Lederman, *The God Particle* (New York: Dell Publishing, 1993) 47.

These twelve are the basis of all in existence. Leon Lederman, 1988 Noble Prize winning physicist, says in his book, *The God Particle:*

> We can make anything in the past or present universe, from chicken soup to neutron stars, with just twelve particles of matter. Our a-toms come in two families: six quarks and six leptons.[170]

These twelve "a-toms" are known in religious language as the 12 Sons of God. They are the twelve great gods created by *Brahma* to assist him in the work of creation.[171] They are also the twelve *Tien-Hoang* of China; the twelve *Aesars* of Scandinavia[172]; and the twelve *"sons born into the light"* of the Bank Islands.[173] The quarks never exist individually but as a unit of three called a hadron or occasionally as a unit of two called a meson.[174] Thus, that Primordial Electric Force formed the quarks and leptons, which formed the protons, neutrons, and electrons. Brought together by an Affinit Energy or Magnetic Energy (Power of Attraction), these sub-atomic particles formed the Atom.

When the three quarks came together to form the hadron, the first Divine Quaternary (*quarter* = four) was produced. Because the hadron is composed of three inner ciphers (quarks) and one outer cipher (the shell) (Figure 8), it was referred to as the Sacred Four, the foundation. Ancient Indian literature refers to the hadron as the "Four sons who are One *and become Seven.*"[175] Beyond the hadron (quaternary) formed the three major component parts of the Atom: the proton, neutron, and electron (a type of lepton). These three constitute the Divine Trinity. Together, the hadron (quaternary) and the three major particles (trinity) make up the Atom: the first Septenary or Divine Seven - Allah in His first complete make. Seven, as we will later show, denotes God in physical creation. This Seven usually appears as a Quaternary with a Trinity (4 + 3). The Atom with its seven

---

[170]Ibid., 62.
[171]Blavatsky, *Secret Doctrine*, II: 90
[172]Ibid., 26.
[173]Virginia Hamilton and Barry Moser, *In The Beginning* (New York: H.B.J, 1988) 9.
[174]Lederman, *God Particle*, 335.
[175] Blavatsky, *Secret Doctrine*, I: 82.

Atom

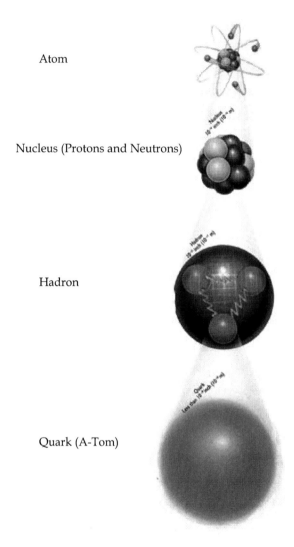

Nucleus (Protons and Neutrons)

Hadron

Quark (A-Tom)

Figure 8
Component Parts of the Atom (From Ronan, *The Universe Explained*,
166)

constituent parts was the first "mature" manifestation of Allah. The Seven were called the "Primordial Seven," "the Seven Sublime Lords," the "Seven Sons of Fire" and the "Seven Eloheim."

How did it all begin according to modern cosmological (scientific) theory? Daniel C. Matt relates:

> In the beginning was the big bang...The primordial vacuum was devoid of matter, but not really empty. Rather, it was in a state of minimum energy, pregnant with potential, teeming with virtual particles. Through a quantum fluctuation, a sort of bubble, in this vacuum, there emerged a hot, dense seed, smaller than a proton, yet containing all the mass and energy of our universe. In less than a trillionth of a second, this seed cooled and expanded wildly, faster than the speed of light, inflating into the size of a grapefruit.
>
> During the inflation, the potential mass and energy could not yet manifest as particles; space was expanding too fast for any particles to congeal out of the vacuum. But as the expansion slowed down, energy latent in the vacuum precipitated as particles and antiparticles...
>
> In its first few seconds, our universe was an undifferentiated soup of matter and radiation. It took a few minutes for things to cool down enough for protons and neutrons to form into simple nuclei of heavy hydrogen and helium. But it was still far too hot for entire, stable atoms to hold together...
>
> For the next 300, 000 years, the universe was somewhat like the interior of a star, filled with protons – radiant particles of energy...The radiation was so turbulent and energetic that electrons could not stick to nuclei to form full-fledged atoms. As soon as an atom began to form, it was immediately ripped apart by radiation...
>
> As the universe continued expanding, its temperature and energy gradually fell...Having lost a critical amount of energy the photons could no longer tear away electrons from circling around nuclei. Relieved of the photon's constant harassment, the electrons were now free for the

first time to settle into orbit around nuclei, forming stable atoms of hydrogen and helium...[176]

The Atom is born. The 'universe' at 300, 000 years that was 'like the interior of star' and filled with such radiant particles that matter could not develop recalls the luminous body of the so-called 'sun-god' of ancient tradition, which kept inadvertently destabilizing material creation with its radiation until God cloaked it with His Black body.

Just as Muhammad stated, this was the beginning of Time. Lederman stumbles over evidence that this Big Bang (which Muhammad agrees happened[177]), was not a random, unguided occurrence. The evidence pointed to the fact that, before the explosion, the Laws of Nature already existed. He observes:

> Let's go back to the prenatal universe again. We live in a universe about which we know a great deal...We are aided by the laws of physics emerging from the laboratories of the world. We are convinced...that only one sequence of events, played backward, can lead via the laws of nature from our observed universe to the beginning and 'before.' The laws of nature must have existed before even time began in order for the beginning to happen...
>
> The concept of time is tied to the appearance of events. A happening marks a point in time...The Great Event, the Big Bang, was a formidable happening that created, among other things, time...
>
> We can try to imagine the pre-Big Bang universe: timeless, featureless, but in some unimaginable way beholden to the laws of physics...What happens as space and time tend toward zero is that the equations we use to explain the universe break down and become meaningless. At this point we are just plumb out of science...What remains? What remains must be the laws of physics.[178]

---

[176] Daniel C. Matt, *God and the Big Bang* (Woodstock, Vermont: Jewish Lights Publishing, 1996) 19-20.
[177] He says in *Theology of Time*, 105: "The history of space teaches us that at one time it was nothing but darkness...BEFORE THE ATOM EXPLODED."
[178] Lederman, *God Particle*, 401-2.

## 5.2. *The Atom of Modern Science and the Egg of Ancient Myth*

The Atom was indeed recognized by the ancients as the physical beginning of God. They universally referred to it as the *Mundane* or *Golden Egg* because of its shape. As the Hon. Elijah Muhammad says:

> Take a magnifying glass and start looking at these little atoms out here in front of you. You see they are egg-shaped and they are oblong. You crack them open and you find everything in them that you find out here.[179]

This Egg was the key to the mystery of Origins. As Manley P. Hall observes:

> The whole mystery of origin and destiny is concealed in the symbolism of that radiant gold egg...It was declared that such as understood this mystery had risen above all temporal limitations.[180]

Two different Eggs were recognized in ancient tradition. The first, the Universal Egg, was the black womb of Space in which existed that Primordial God Force - The Supreme All. The Sanskrit *Book of Dzyan* refers to it as the Eternal Egg.[181] Within this Universal Egg, the Supreme All (God Force) self-fecundated and produced the Mundane or Golden Egg[182]; called "Golden" because the sparking of the Atom was the first visible manifestation of Light.

Proof that in fact the Golden Egg is a symbol for the Atom from which God physically emerged is found everywhere. The *Egyptian Ritual* speaks of the "*egg conceived at the hour of the great one of the Dual Force*" (Sec. V., 2,3). The "Dual Force" is reference to the positive/negative polarity of the Primordial Energy which gave birth to the protons (+) and electrons (-) of the Atom. Occult philosophy depicts this Golden Egg with two poles, a positive on

---

[179] Muhammad, *Our Savior Has Arrived*, 73.
[180] Hall, *MAN - The Grand Symbol of the Mysteries*, 69.
[181] Blavatsky, *Secret Doctrine*, I: 28.
[182] Hall, *MAN - The Grand Symbol of the Mysteries*, 72.

top and a negative on bottom.[183] The ancient Persians depicted two serpents, labeled Good and Evil, contending for the Mundane Egg (Figure 9). Hall notes that the ancients used the serpent to represent Electricity or Force.

> Electricity was commonly symbolized by the serpent because of its motion. Electricity passing between the poles of a spark gap is serpentine in its motion. Force projected through the atmosphere was called The Great Snake. Being symbolic of universal force, the serpent was emblematic of both good (positive) and evil (negative).[184]

From Maurice's *Indian Antiquities*.

Figure 9
Mundane Egg of the ancient Persians

The two serpents contending for the Egg are therefore symbolic of the contending protons (+) and electrons (-) within the Atom. The Orphic Mysteries depict the Egg with the Great Serpent coiled around it (Figure 10) like a mother snake coiled around its recently laid egg. This Great Serpent, Hall informs us, represents the "Fiery Creative Spirit," the God Force from which the Atom or Egg sparked.

[183] Blavatsky, *Secret Doctrine*, I: 556.
[184] Hall, *Secret Teachings of All Ages*, LXXXVIII.

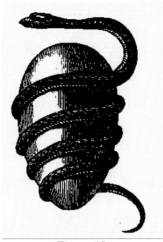

Figure 10
Orphic Egg

Muhammad says again: *"You crack them (egg-shaped atoms) open and you find everything in them that you find out here."* The ancient Mysteries taught the same. The Creator and every morsel of creation were initially contained within the Egg (like the 'seed' or singularity of modern cosmological theory). In The *Vishnu Puranas*, we read:

> Intellect (*Mahat*)...formed an egg...and the Lord of the universe himself abided in it...In that egg, O Brahma, were the continents, and seas and mountains, the planets and divisions of the universe, the gods, the demons and mankind (Book I, ch. 2).

The Egg was said to be composed of seven parts which are the seven constituent parts of the Atom. The Mysteries taught that *"the Absolute All creat(ed) or even evolv(ed) the 'Golden Egg,' into which it (the Absolute All) is said to enter in order to transform himself into...the Creator, who expands himself later into gods and all the visible Universe."* All of the Creator gods are said to have emerged or evolved from the Golden Egg or Atom; *Ra* or *Atum* of Egypt,

*Brahma* of India, *Ahura Mazda* of Persia, *Chumong* of the Coresians, and *Yahweh* of the Israelites.[185]

## 5.3. *The Atom and the Mind of God*

The study of the Atom, nuclear physics, is the scientific study of Allah. It is one of the most revealing theological pursuits. The mind and the power of Allah were first observable in the Atom. It was the first "observable" entity which displayed rudimentary "mind" or "intelligence." That Primordial Electric Force that existed before The Beginning was not just "brute" or unintelligent energy. It was imbued with Divine Intelligence (*Mahat*). It was rudimentary intelligence then but grew to Supreme Intelligence when the Spirit evolved into Man. Most people are not aware of the fact that energy is not "brute" but possesses rudimentary intelligence. The famous scientist Thomas Edison, however, in February of 1890, acknowledged the intelligent atom in an interview in **Harpers Magazine.** He stated:

> I do not believe that matter is inert, acted upon by an outside force. To me it seems that every atom is possessed by a certain amount of primitive intelligence. Look at the thousands of ways in which atoms of hydrogen combine with those of other elements, forming the most diverse substances. Do you mean to say that they do this without intelligence? Atoms in harmonious and useful relation assume beautiful and interesting shapes and colors, or give forth a pleasant perfume, as if expressing their satisfaction...(G)athered together in certain forms, the atoms constitute animals of the lower order. Finally they combine in man, who represents the total intelligence of all the atoms.[186]

This suggestion was scientifically demonstrated in experiments using a maser, a gun that fires atoms one Atom at a time. The experiments were based on earlier ones done by the English

---

[185] See True Islam, **Truth of God.**
[186] Quoted from Alice Bailey, **Consciousness of The Atom** (New York: Lucis Publishing, 1961), 38-39.

physicist Thomas Young in 1803. In the maser experiment, scientists cut two slits in a plate. Beyond the plate was a screen with photographic emulsion. With only one slit open (the second one closed up), an Atom is shot at the plate from the maser. If the Atom hits the plate, it is stopped and seen no more. If it happens to pass through the open slit, it will strike the emulsion and produce a spot on the film. The scientists continued to fire one Atom at a time. They waited an hour between each shot. After a while, a large number of spots accumulated on the emulsion. The edges of this accumulation are the fuzzy diffraction pattern which is characteristic of waves passing through a narrow opening. If the first slit is closed and the second opened, the same results appear (Figure 11). If the scientists open both slits and fire one Atom at a time as in the previous experiment, something very perplexing occurs. A pattern of light-bands separated by dark regions are produced (Figure 12). This is the well-known interference pattern associated with waves. The dark regions are the product of the crest (High) of one wave meeting a trough (Low) of another wave. They cancel each other out. This interference appears as dark bands.

Figures 11 and 12
(From Schroeder, 1997, 15 1)

69

The reason this is perplexing in this maser experiment is because only one Atom is shot at a time and shots are separated by an hour. Thus, there is nothing for the Atom to "interfere" with. Dr. Gerald Schroeder, in his *The Science* of *God*, noted the implications of this experiment:

We already noted that atoms going through the single slit fall everywhere within the diffraction pattern with none of the alternating light and dark bands that result from the interference of waves at the screen. Although we opened both slits, we are still only firing only one atom at a time. It must travel to only one of the two slits and go through that slit. If the other is closed it lands anywhere within the diffraction pattern. If the other slit is open, it never lands in the dark (forbidden) regions originally seen in the interference pattern which developed when we had the two slits open.

The atom is a single entity, with a fixed locality. In its passage through one slit, why should opening or closing the other slit have any effect upon its passage? How can it 'know' if the second slit is open or closed. But it does. Somehow it is aware of its environment . . . This is bizarre.[187]

Now modify the experiment a little. Put a particle detector near one of the slits and leave the other slit unaltered. As we fire the maser, we can monitor through which slit the atom passed. If it is detected, it passed through the monitored slit. If not detected, it passed through the unmonitored slit. Schroeder notes:

With the monitor in place, something very annoying happens. The pattern that accumulates on the screen as the experiment proceeds is the sum of two fizzy patterns as if the first slit was open and the second closed, and then the second opened and the first closed...There are no dark 'forbidden' regions even though both slits are now open and the banded interference pattern should

---

[187] Schroeder, *Science of God*, 154,155.

appear...Particles passing through the second slit (the one with no detector) should follow the usual two-slit pattern. But they don't. They too somehow know about the detector at the other slit.

Not only do the particles know if the second slit is open, they know is someone is looking over their shoulders with a detector!

These double-slit experiments strongly suggest intelligence being displayed by the Atom: the ability to choose. As we have shown, the Atom is the first mature manifestation of Allah, the First Divine Septenary. Inherent in the Atom is the Divine Intelligence of Allah.

Ernst Hackle, another scientist and ally of Darwin, says the Atom also possesses soul:

The recent contest as to the nature of atoms...seems to be capable of easiest solution by the conception that these very minute masses possess - as centers of force - a persistent soul, that every atom has a sensation and a power of movement.[188]

This was understood by our ancestors as well. The words "atom" and "soul" were synonymous with the Initiates of the Great Mysteries.[189]   Valentinus says in *Esoteric Treatise on the Doctrine of Gilgul*:

Light becomes heat, and consolidates into fiery particles (quarks); which, from being ignited, become cold hard particles, round and smooth (atom).  And this is called a Soul, imprisoned in its robe of matter.[190]

5.4. *Atom - A.T.O.M. – ATUM - ADAM*

After six trillion years, enough atoms and cells had formed and coalesced to form the macro-A.T.O.M., Allah The Original

---

[188]Blavatsky, *Secret Doctrine,* II: 673.
[189]Ibid., I: 568.
[190]Ibid., I: 568,

Man.  The first Man in several traditions is therefore named Atom or some variation thereof.   In Egypt, the Creator God Atum was also the first Man.  In fact, George G.M. James, in his monumental *Stolen Legacy*, says the "atom" of science was named by the Greeks after this Egyptian God-Man that evolved therefrom.  He says the name Atum means *"SELF-CREATED; EVERYTHING AND NOTHING; COMBINATION OF POSITIVE AND NEGATIVE PRINCIPLES;ALL-INCLUSIVENESS...THE ALL..."*[191]   These of course are all attributes of Allah The Original Man, the Self-Created All in All (Allah means All In All).[192]

Figure 13
Atum, Black Creator God of Kemet

---

[191]George G.M James, *Stolen Legacy* (San Francisco: Julian Richardson Associations, 1976) 147.
[192]Muhammad, *Theology of Time*, 134.

72

The Supreme God of the Sumerians was called *Anu*, which means in Sanskrit "atom."[193]    The first Man of the Greeks, Hindus, and Buddhists was called Atum or Adam.[194] The Self-Creation of the macro-A.T.O.M. (Allah The Original Man) was presented in scripture under the guise of the creation of Adam, the First Man.[195] Charles Finch, in his *Echoes of the Old Darkland*, confirms this by showing the Biblical Adam to be rooted in the Egyptian Atum. As Adam was the first man made in the image of God and the Father of mankind, Atum was the first God made in the image of Man and the Father of mankind. Finch says:

> The root of ATM is TM (TEM/TUM) which has several meanings, among them 'people' and 'completion' (Adam represented the completion of God's work on the 6th day). Atum is no less the COMPLETE OR PERFECT DIVINE MAN. A cognate root of TEM is DEM and this means 'to name' (Adam was the namer of all the animals). Thus, the most elementary and indisputable etymological analysis demonstrates that ALL THE ATTRIBUTES OF THE EGYPTIAN DEITY ATUM ARE EMBRACED IN THE HEBREW ADAM.[196]

Godfrey Higgins confirms this analysis. He tells us the word "Adam" is a compound of AD and AM. "AD" is the Syrian name of God and also means "Holy." "AM" is the ancient "mystic OM," the unspoken name of God. It was never uttered unless suffixed or prefixed to another word. Ad-AM is thus "God Am" or "Holy God."[197]

---

[193]From *"aniyamsam aniyasam"* meaning "smallest of the small," Blavatsky, *Secret Doctrine*, I:357.

[194]Higgins, *Anacalypsis*, I: 478.

[195] See especially True Islam, *Truth of God*, 208-24.

[196]Charles Finch, *Echoes of the Old Darkland* (Decatur, Georgia: Khenti, Inc., 1992) 144.

[197]Higgins, *Anacalypsis*, II: 202.

# CHAPTER VI

## *Evolution of the Black God*

### 6.1. *Three Lines of Divine Evolution*

The Evolution of God happened on three planes: the Spiritual, Mental and Physical. Each of these "planes of evolution" had its own laws, yet they were "inextricably interwoven and interblended at every point." This Triple Evolution of God is represented in the ancient traditions by a Triangle [Δ], the mental evolution being the bottom bar because it was the last to be completed. This Triple Evolution of God is referred to in the *Rig Veda* (ancient Hindu scripture) as the "Three Strides of Vishnu." The *Zohar* of the Qaballists likewise calls it the "Three Steps of Jehovah."

### 6.2. *Three Stages of God's Physical Evolution*

In the beginning of Madame Blavatsky's **The Secret Doctrine,** she quotes from an archaic manuscript written on a collection of palm leaves allegedly made impermeable to water, air, and fire by some process which is now lost.[198]  On the first page of this manuscript there is a white disc surrounded by a black background.  On page two the same disc appears but now possessing a central point. On the third page the central point had become a diameter of the disc. These three symbols [◘], [☉],[⊕] are some of the oldest religious symbols.[199] They represent the three primary stages of Allah's (God's) bodily evolution.  The first illustration, the white disc surround by a black background, represents Allah (God) in His Primeval State as the Absolute All, the "still slumbering Energy."[200]

---

[198]Blavatsky, *Secret Doctrine*, I:1
[199]Ibid., II: 554.
[200]Ibid., I: 1

# Three Stages of God's Physical Evolution
## Figure 14

God as the All (Energy) – The O

God as the Point (Atom) – The 1

God as the Diameter (Man) – The 6

Blavatsky says:

The Circle was with every nation the symbol of the Unknown...the abstract garb of an ever present abstraction - the Incognisable Deity. It represents limitless Time in Eternity.[201]

The black background represents the Black womb of Space called 'Mother,' which existed before The Beginning. In the Norse cosmogony we read:

In the beginning was a great abyss, neither day or night existed; the abyss was Ginnungagap, the yawning gulf, without beginning, without end. ALL Father, the Uncreated, the Unseen, dwelt in the depth of the Abyss and willed, and what was willed came into being.[202]

The uncreated All Father, which existed in the Black womb, was a hidden light. This is why It is represented by the bright circle or disk. The Bible refers to it as the "Spirit of God" which "moved upon the face of the Deep." The Hebrew *ruah* (Spirit) implies luminosity.[203] Sometimes instead of just a plain circle, a fiery serpent with its tail in its mouth was used to represent the Spirit of God within the Deep. In ancient Egyptian cosmo-theology, the Eternal Unrevealed God *Kneph* was represented by a snake encircling a water urn. This snake identifies the true nature of the Spirit of God. As we have previously shown, the serpent represented electricity. This is, according to ancient tradition, the nature of Allah (God) "before the Beginning." And these traditions use the [◘] as the geometrical symbol of the All.

This agrees with what Mr. Muhammad teaches. He says in *Theology of Time*:

Elijah (you ask), Why did you make the zero round? Because that's the way the Universe was before the Creation of Man....He (God) made Himself in a Circle so

---

[201]Ibid., I: 113.
[202] Ibid., I: 426.
[203] See True Islam, *Truth of God*, 30-31.

that the Wisdom of His Self -Creation could keep going to give knowledge, wisdom, and understanding to you and me."[204]

Muhammad later refers to it as the "Darkened Circle."[205] This Abstract Deity represented by The Circle is called *Parabrahm* by the Hindus; *Zeruana Akerne* by the Zoroastrians; *Kneph* by the Egyptians; and *Ain Soph* by the Jews. God existed in this state, according to these traditions, before The Beginning.

Allah laid dormant in that state for an unrecorded number of years. But all the while, a desire for self-manifestation was building up. The ancient *Book of Dzyan* refers to this desire as the "chief cause of existence."[206] This desire grew stronger and stronger until, we are told, it caused an explosion. The explosion caused the electric force to differentiate into tiny balls of fire called quarks and leptons. This stage is represented by The Circle with the Central Point [☉]. According to physicist Leon Lederman, in his *The God Particle*, the quark is scientifically referred to as a "point-atom," a "geometrical point" which has no dimensions except mass and charge. It has no size, radius, or spatial extent.[207] The Jews referred to this Central Point as the "luminous point" or *Kether*. The ancient (East) Indians refer to it as *Nara*. Scientists simply call it *Quark*.

After the explosion and the manifestation of the quark, it underwent an evolutionary development which lasted six trillion years. It grew into a man, symbolized by the Diameter within The Circle. This is the third evolutionary stage. The Diameter or straight line represents Allah The Original Man.[208] The straight line represents a Man because Man is distinguished from all other beings by his erect posture.[209]

---

[204]Muhammad, *Theology of Time*, 103.
[205] Ibid.
[206] Blavatsky, *Secret Doctrine*, 44.
[207] Lederman, *God Particle*, 103, 125, 142.
[208]Blavatsky, *Secret Doctrine*, I:391.
[209]Ibid., II: 574.

## 6.2.1. *The Descent of Spirit into Matter*

The Spiritual and Physical lines of evolution are parallel but go in opposite directions [ ↑↓ ]. As it is stated of in *Five Years Theosophy:*" *A descent of spirit into matter (is) equivalent to an ascent in physical evolution.*" When Pure Spirit becomes gross matter, this is a "Fall" or descent. Thus, this first theological "Fall of Man" was the fall of spirit into matter. The diagram below (Figure 15) shows the evolutionary path of this "Fall." This is the First Stride of Vishnu or Step of Yahweh.

This Fall or Descent of Spirit into Matter is septenary (Figure 15) as described in the *Vision of Thoth-Hermes*. Thoth was the Egyptian god of wisdom and also the Messenger of the Gods. In his vision, Osiris grants Thoth's request to see "the path of souls (atoms) from which man comes and to which he returns."[210] Osiris opened up the starry heavens for Thoth and showed him the Seven Heavens as seven luminous globes enveloping Thoth. These seven regions, through which is accomplished the "fall and ascents of souls," comprise the "visible and invisible world."[211] Thoth asked: "*O, master, how does mankind journey through these worlds?*" Osiris replies:

Dost thou see a luminous seed (quark) fall from the regions of the Milky Way into the seventh sphere? These are the germs of souls (atoms). They live like faint vapors in the region of Saturn, gay and free of care, knowing not their own happiness. On falling from sphere to sphere, however, they put on increasingly heavier envelopes. In each incarnation they acquire a new corporeal sense, in harmony with the surroundings in which they are living. Their vital energy increases but in proportion as they enter denser bodies they lose memory of their celestial origin. Thus is effected the fall of souls which come from the divine Ether...The soul is the daughter of heaven, and its journey is a test. If it loses the memory of its origin in its unbridled love of matter, the divine spark which was in it and which might have become more brilliant than a star,

---

[210]Edouard Schure, *Hermes And Plato* (London: William Rider & Son, Rp: 1972), 46.
[211]Ibid., 47-8.

# Spirit's Descent into Matter

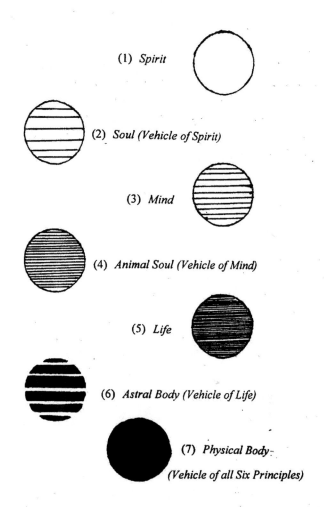

(1) *Spirit*

(2) *Soul (Vehicle of Spirit)*

(3) *Mind*

(4) *Animal Soul (Vehicle of Mind)*

(5) *Life*

(6) *Astral Body (Vehicle of Life)*

(7) *Physical Body*
*(Vehicle of all Six Principles)*

Figure 15

returns to the ethereal region, a lifeless atom, and the soul disintegrates in the vortex of gross elements.[212]

## 6.2.1. $E=mc^2$ and the Reality of God

Since the time of Anaxagoras, the issue of God's nature has been hotly debated. The argument at times centered on the question of whether God was an immaterial, spiritual being, having no connection with matter, or was He in fact a corporeal* being with a material body. This debate has raged now for 2,500 years. In 1905, the answer to this most important question was mathematically notated on the chalkboard of one of the greatest minds the Western World has ever produced. Albert Einstein's famous equation, $E=mc^2$, revolutionized the world of physics. Its significance to the world of theology is equally as tremendous, though most people perceive not.

Without a doubt, $E=mc^2$ is one of the most important discoveries, and its relevance to theological speculation is profound. When properly understood, this mathematical equation provides the Key to the nature of God. The $E$ in this equation stands for energy. What is important to know is that all energy is conserved. This means there is a set amount of energy in the universe and this amount is always constant. This energy cannot be destroyed and no new energy can be created. The energy can simply transform into different "types." This is the Law of Conservation of Energy or the First Law of Thermodynamics. Science recognizes five "forms" or "types" of energy: mechanical, thermal, chemical, electrical and nuclear. The fundamental sources of this energy are the four forces of nature: the Strong

---

Force, the Weak Force, the Electro-magnetic Force, and Gravity. Scientists have now suggested that, in the Beginning, these four forces were merged into one primordial Super Force.

The $m$ in the equation is reference to the mass of an object. Mass and matter are here used interchangeably. Mass is defined as the measure of an object's resistance to acceleration. When you try to push a big car, and can't, its "resistance" to your push is called mass. The $c^2$ is the notation for the speed of light (186, 000 m/sec.) times itself. The significance of this famous equation is that it shows how energy and matter are the same. Trying to avoid as much technical jargon as possible, this is what Einstein is saying: When energy is accelerated, it gains mass. The higher the velocity (rate of acceleration), the greater the mass. It becomes "heavy." Additional weight or mass caused by acceleration is called "energy of motion."[213] All objects and particles acquire mass when traveling at high velocities. A car gets heavier when in motion and an astronaut, traveling at high speeds, gains weight.[214]

The same is true for energy. As the velocity of this energy approaches the speed of light, $c$, it becomes subject to what is called the "Gamma Factor." This principle can best be understood by the use of an illustration. Picture an astronaut traveling in a high-speed spaceship weighing 100 tons. As the space ship accelerates, both the ship and the astronaut increase in mass and gets heavier. By the time the ship reaches 99.999 % of the speed of light, $c$, it now has an effective mass of 2, 237 tons. Because the ship has picked up an enormous amount of additional "mass," it becomes increasingly more difficult to accelerate. It comes to a point where, the more the ship (or particle of energy) approaches the speed of light it becomes too massive to accelerate anymore, so it appears to stop but the energy continues to pile on. An object will always stop before it reaches the speed of light. This is called the "light barrier" and it describes the "gamma factor." This is how energy is converted into matter. As it approaches the speed of light, it acquires more and more mass. By the time it has reached "gamma factor" or the light barrier, it has acquired so much mass its acceleration appears to have stopped (though it is still accelerating very "sluggishly"). The energy becomes "frozen in

---

[213] Nigel Calder, *Einstein's Universe* (New York: Penguin Books, 1979) 34.
[214] Ibid. 164, 165.

matter." The *c* of the equation shows that there is an enormous amount of energy that goes into the creation of the tiniest particle of matter.

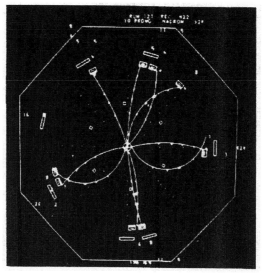

Figure 17

"The Creation of matter is recorded at the Stanford Linear Accelerator Center. From the head-on collision of an electron and anti-electron there emerges a swarm of newly created particles that are intrinsically far heavier. Energy of motion is converted into the rest-energy of matter in accordance with $E=mc^2$." Quote and photo from Calder, 1979, middle.

This is how matter is produced. All matter is "frozen energy" and has an enormous amount of energy inherent within it. While this energy is "frozen" in matter it is called "Rest Energy." I stress again the enormity of the amount of energy that is "frozen" in the tiniest piece of matter. The nuclear bomb is a perfect illustration. The goliath explosion caused by the nuclear bomb is the result of the release of the latent energy stored in the nucleus of the Atom. The question may then be asked, if energy traveling at the speed of light becomes "massy," what about light? Einstein learned that, in agreement with $E=mc^2$, light possesses mass and is heavy. Light is so heavy, in fact, it is subject to Gravity. Of the four forces of nature, Gravity is the weakest and only manifests itself in the macroscopic world. This means it only affects massy objects. It is totally irrelevant in the microscopic world of atoms. Yet, light is subject to Gravity because it is so massive due to its energy of motion. Gravity "bends" the path of light and causes it to fall towards the earth like any other massive body.[215] Light of sufficient energy, such as gamma rays (gamma = "infinite"), can produce material particles.

Now what does all this have to do with God? $E=mc^2$ settled the age-old question of whether God was an unbound spirit or had a material manifestation. As we have shown throughout this text, Energy and Spirit are interchangeable terms. What scientists call Energy, theologians call Spirit, and vice versa. The Spirit of God, with all of the ancient Sacred Traditions, was symbolically represented as a serpent with its tail in its mouth. This is the Primordial Electric Force. The key ingredient in converting energy (Spirit) to matter, according to $E=mc^2$, is motion – high-speed motion. Genesis opens with the words,

> In the beginning God created the heavens and the earth, and the earth was without form and void and darkness was upon the face of the deep. AND THE SPIRIT OF GOD MOVED UPON THE FACE OF THE WATERS.

When the Spirit of God "moved," it began its process of materialization. This initial movement of the Spirit of God is called the "Primum Mobile" or First Motion. The Hindus call it the "Churning of Space." "Churning" is to spin in a spiral-type motion. This spiral is called in mathematics the "Exponential Spiral" and is represented by the small "e" in the formula ($r=e^{ah}$). As the value of Pi (3.14159...) is basic to descriptions of all circles, so "e" is basic to all spirals.[216] This graceful curve occurs in nature more often than any other shape. It is seen in the Nautilus seashell, the Ammonite fossil, the distribution of seeds in a sunflower and the spread of stars in the galaxies (Figure 18). This spiraling motion was the first motion of the Spirit of God, the *Primum Mobile*. This is also the motion of the number 6 (Six), the number of physical creation. Again, the Hon. Elijah Muhammad says:

---

[215] Ibid., 84.
[216] Schroeder, *Science of God*, 63.

This is our number '6'. He (God) made Himself revolve and then He caused whatever comes into the darkness to revolve like Himself.[217]

Figure 18

The Exponential Spiral found throughout the universe: the Nautilus from Capetown; the Ammonite fossil from England, 270 million years; and the spiral galaxy (Photo from Schroeder, 1997, 64)

As the Spirit increased in velocity, It acquired more and more mass and became more and more dense. As It reached gamma

---

[217] Muhammad, *Theology of Time*, 109.

factor, It became "frozen" in matter. Every particle of matter is imbued with an enormous amount of the Spirit, which is "frozen" within it. This is why the Eastern religions teach that the Infinite All pervades everything and is in every-thing. The greatest concentration of the Spirit of God is in matter. This is also why we said earlier that matter is the conveyer of the Spirit: $E=mc^2$.

### 6.3. God's Self-Creation: Ancient East Indian Tradition

Unbeknownst to most, India is one of the great lands of the Black Man. Scholars such as Sertima,[218] Baldwin,[219] Houston,[220] and others have conclusively shown that the original inhabitants of that continent were Black. The early Indus Valley Civilization displayed the high level of civilization possessed by the aboriginal Black Indians. The religious texts of India, the *Rig-Veda*, the *Puranas*, the *Laws of Manu*, the *Bhagavat Gita*, and the *Upanishads*, all spring from the wisdom of these early Blacks.[221]

The scriptures of the East Indians detail the early history and development of God. The Eternal All with them was an abstract, indefinable "Causeless Cause" called *Parabrahm* or *Vishnu*. The Supreme All, at this stage, is not yet God. In the Beginning, according to the *Laws of Manu*, Vishnu existed within the Womb of Space. At a certain time Vishnu made a concentration into itself and produced a Central Point called *Nara*. This Point is described as the *Navel* of Vishnu. It is also described as the Mundane Egg. Brahma the Creator issued forth from this Egg or Navel of Vishnu, the Atom. Manley P. Hall, in **MAN-The Grand Symbol of The Mysteries**, recounts the Indian History of Origins:

> From the old records we gather the following: *Narayana*, an epithet of Vishnu, contemplating the creation of the universe, first generated the 'waters of causation.' Then, moving upon the face of the waters, he dropped the seed of the world (Atom) into the deep. Within the egg was born *Purusha, the heavenly man, resplendent as the sun* (italics

---

[218] *African Presence in Early Asia.*
[219] John Baldwin, *Pre-Historic Nations* (New York: Harper & Brothers, 1869).
[220] Houston, *Wonderful Ethiopians*.
[221] Ibid., 215-221.

mine – TI). Within the egg (Atom) also are all the *lokas*, or worlds, by which is meant all aspects of existence which can be sensed by the perceptions of created things...The egg was originally described as being without consciousness, but the Creator, having entered into the consciousness of time, destiny, and law, the egg became alive and *Purusha*...issued forth...[222]

From out of the 'egg' or atom the Creator–god emerges as a brilliantly luminous man. When the Egg or Atom became alive, it was invested with *Mahat*, Divine Intelligence. Issuing from that first Egg or Atom, according to the *Laws of Manu*, were nine others making the "*ten lords of Being*" or "*ten creative forces*" or the "*Ten Prajapatis*." These Ten are the 10,000 Atoms of Muhammad. The *Commentary to the Book of Dzyan* confirms this:

> The Spheres of Being, or centers of life, which are isolated nuclei breeding their men and their animals, are numberless...The nucleoles (i.e. components of the Atomic nuclei) are eternal and everlasting; the nuclei periodical and finite. The nucleoles form part of the absolute...The nuclei are the light of eternity escaping therefrom...It is that Light which condenses into the forms of the 'Lords of Being'

From the Atom issued forth *Purusha*, the Heavenly Man, who is identified in Indian literature with Brahma the Creator. Brahma is the first Man as well as the Creator. Monier Williams, in *Indian Wisdom*, observes:

> When the universal and infinite being (*Parabrahm*/Vishnu) - the only really existing entity, wholly without form, and unbound...wished to create for his own entertainment the phenomena of the universe, he assumed the quality of activity and BECAME A MALE PERSON, AS BRAHMA THE CREATOR."[223]

---

[222] Hall, *Man-Grand Symbol of the Mysteries*, 73.
[223] Monier Williams, *Indian Wisdom*, 324.

86

Even though Brahma initially emerged as a brilliantly luminous divine man (Figure 19), ancient Indian texts record that he wrapped this body with the black primordial matter, producing the God's black body.[224] The *Puranas* thus take notice of *"the quality of darkness pervading Brahma's assumed body."* Because of this "quality of darkness" which pervaded his new body, Brahma was called *Kali Hamsa*, the Black Swan. We recall that in the *Laws of Manu*, Vishnu is then called *Hansa-vahan* meaning "he who uses the swan as His vehicle." Brahma is the conveyer of Vishnu just as Adam Qadmon was the conveyer of *Ain Soph* and Allah The Original Man was the conveyer of that Primordial Electric Force - all three being the same God.

Figure 19

Indic Creator-god Brahma emerging as a luminous man from the Lotus Plant (DNA molecule) attached to the Naval (Atom) of Narayana

---

[224] See discussion and references in True Islam, *Truth of God*, 150 n. 524.

### 6.3.1. *The Book of Dzyan*

The *Book of Dzyan* is an ancient Sanskrit book of scripture made known to the West primarily through the writings of Madam Helena Petrovna Blavatsky and the Theosophical Society. This ancient book of revelation is illuminating on several points.

There are seven Stanzas or chapters translated from the *Book of Dzyan*, which deal with Cosmic Evolution. Stanza I begins:

> 1: The Eternal Parent (Mother Space) wrapped in her ever invisible Robes (undifferentiated Cosmic Substance) had slumbered once again for seven eternities.
> 2: Time was not, for it lay asleep in the infinite bosom of Duration...
> 5: Darkness alone filed the Boundless All, for Father (Energy), Mother (Space) and Son (Atom) were once again One (undifferentiated), and the Son had not yet Awakened (sparked) for the New Wheel (Cycle of Existence), and His Pilgrimage thereon (discussed below)...
> 8: Alone the One Form of Existence (The All) stretched boundless, infinite, causeless, in dreamless sleep; and Life pulsated unconscious in Universal Space (as latent energy)...
> (II:3)The Hour had not yet struck: The Ray had not yet flashed into the Germ...

"Ray" and "Germ" are two very important terms in the vocabulary of Origins. The solitary Ray flashing into the Germ is the hidden divine luminosity concentrating itself at a single point (Seed or Ray) within the primordial matter, the Germ. The Ray is Father and the Germ is Mother. The Son is the Atom that forms from their union. But as of now, that had not happened. The "Hour" had not yet struck and so Father, Mother, and Son are still One, i.e. undifferentiated. The Beginning takes place in Stanza III:

> 3. Darkness radiates Light, and Light drops one solitary Ray into the waters, into the Mother Deep. The Ray shoots through the Virgin-Egg (Circumference of Space); the Ray

causes the Eternal Egg (Space) to thrill, and drop the non-eternal Germ, which condenses into the World-Egg (a-tom) 4. Then the Three (Quarks) fall into Four (Hadron)...The Luminous Egg (Hadron), which in itself is Three (Quarks), curdles and spreads in milk-white curds throughout the depths of Mother (Space).

Here we have the creation of the quark and hadron from the Ray or spark of Light impregnating the Primordial Substance or Germ lying latent in the Womb of Space. The "Luminous-Egg" here is the Hadron, which resulted from the bonding of three quarks (the Three) making the fourth (hadron). The three quarks are said to "Fall" into the four or the hadron because it is part of Spirit's Decent into Matter discussed above. These hadrons "curdled and spread in milk-white curds throughout the depths of Mother." Ronan, in *The Universe Explained*, uses the same language to describe the actions of these primordial a-toms after the Big Explosion. He says: *"Soon the universe was filled with swirling, primordial gas clouds that gradually curdled into long, thin strands separated by dark voids."*[225]

The period shortly after the Big Explosion[226] that cosmologists call the Big Bang and Muhammad calls simply the "explosion" of the Atom[227] is called the Period of Annihilation. During this period, rudimentary particles of matter and anti-matter annihilated each other. Just as every action has an equal and opposite reaction, every particle has an equal yet oppositely charged anti-particle. Thus, for every negatively charged electron, there is a positron that is positively charged. The same is true for quarks (anti-quarks), leptons (anti-leptons), protons (p-bars), etc. Anti-particles are called anti-matter. Immediately after the explosion, rudimentary particles of matter and anti-matter canceled each other out, a process called Annihilation. Left in its wake was nothing but radiation or energy. Some matter survived annihilation, however, because of an imperfection in the nature of Allah which manifested itself in the created world. This imperfection is called by science the Violation of CP Symmetry

[225]C. Ronan, *The Universe Explained* (New York: Henry Holt & Company, 1994) 178.
[226]Ibid. 178.
[227]Muhammad, *Theology of Time*, 105.

and resulted in there being slightly more matter than anti-matter (for every 100 million quark - anti-quark pairs there is one extra quark).[228] The tiny surplus of matter over anti-matter is the material from which our universe was created. The *Commentary to the Book of Dzyan* refers to this activity of the primordial particles as "fighting."

> From One Life, formless and uncreate, proceeds the universe of lives. First was manifested from the deep cold luminous fire which formed curds in space (quarks)...These fought, and a great heat was developed by the encountering and collision, which produced rotation.

300,000 years after the Big Explosion, according to cosmologists, the temperature of the universe cooled enough for electrons to bond with atomic nuclei and form atoms. Verse 7 of Stanza III thus proclaims:

> Behold, Oh Lanoo![229] The radiant Child of the Two (Atom); The unparalleled Refulgent Glory, Bright Space, Son of Dark Space, who emerges from the depths of the Great Dark Waters. It is Oeaohoo, The Younger...He shines forth as The Sun...

The Atom is here called the Child of the Two - the Two being the Positive and Negative Electricity (Quark and Lepton); the Ray and the Germ; and the Father (Energy/Spirit) and Mother (Space). He is Bright Space (Light), the Son of Primordial Darkness. He is later called in verse eight "the white brilliant Son of the Dark hidden Father." Of course we know the Dark Hidden Father is the *Ain Soph, Parabrahm* or the Abstract Deity. The Son is called *Oeaohoo, The Younger.* Oeaohoo is the name of the Abstract All, the Father.[230] He now emerges as Oeaohoo, The Younger or The Son. The same is found in Egyptian theo-cosmology. The God Ptah becomes his own son, Imhot-pou.[231] We also recognize this from

---

[228]Lederman, *God Particle*, 286.
[229] Lanoo is a student that studies practical Esotericism
[230]Blavatsky, *Secret Doctrine*, 68.
[231]Ibid. I: 353.

our Christian orientation in which God the Father comes to earth as the Son.

The Son is now ready to begin his Pilgrimage mentioned in Stanza I. This Pilgrimage is described in Stanza VII verse 5:

It journeys trough the Seven Worlds of Maya.[232] It stops in the First (Kingdom) and is a metal and a stone (mineral); it passes into the Second, and Behold - a Plant; the Plant whirls through seven forms and becomes a Sacred animal (Third Kingdom). From the combined attributes of these, MANU (MAN), the Thinker, is formed.

Alice Bailey, in *Consciousness of the Atom*, describes this Hajj or Pilgrimage with a little more detail. Bailey says:

We have seen that the atom of chemistry...demonstrates the quality of intelligence; it shows discriminative mind, the rudiments of selective capacity...The atom is then built into all the different stages, and each time it gains according to the force and life of the entity that insoles that form...(T)he atom that goes to the building of the mineral kingdom; it shows not only discriminative selective mind, but elasticity. Then in the vegetable kingdom these two qualities appear, but a third is also found which we might call sensation of a rudimentary kind. The initial intelligence of the atom has acquired something during the transition from form to form and from kingdom to kingdom...Next we have the animal kingdom, in which animal forms show not only the above qualities, but to them is added instinct, or that which will some day blossom into mentality. Finally, we come to the human being (Manu), who shows all these qualities to a far greater degree, for the fourth kingdom is but the macrocosm of the three lower.[233]

---

[232] These are equivalent to the Seven Creations or Evolutions, which we will describe shortly.
[233]Bailey, *Consciousness of the Atom*, 68-9.

The Atom is the Divine Pilgrim and His Journey through all the various kingdoms up into the macro - A.T.O.M. (Allah The Original Man) took 6 trillion years, so teaches the Honorable Elijah Muhammad. More on this below.

## 6.4. *Atum: The Self-Created God of Kemet (Egypt)*

Gerald Massey, through his various writings,[234] has shown conclusively that the Hebrew religion with its Old Testament is a reworking of ancient Egyptian wisdom. The Egyptians, like the Indians, made a point to narrate not only the history of creation but the history of the Creator as well.

According to the priests of Annu, one of the earliest Egyptian cites, the Beginning began with the Primeval Waters called *Nun*. Nun was the "*primeval watery mass from which all the gods were evolved.*"[235] Within Nun was the Hidden God *Kneph* who is equivalent to the Indian Vishnu and Hebrew Ain Soph, all of whom represent the Primordial Electric Force. Coexisting with Nun was *Maa*, Divine Intelligence (Indian *Mahat*). According to Egyptian theo-cosmology, the waters of Nun produced the World Egg, the Atom. Dr. Brugsh, in his **Religion and Mythology**, narrates the Egyptian History of Origins as such:

> there was in the beginning neither heaven nor earth, and nothing existed except a boundless primeval mass of water which was shrouded in darkness and which contained within itself all the germs or beginnings, male and female, of everything which was to be in the future world. The divine primeval spirit (*Kneph*) which formed an essential part of the primeval matter felt within itself the desire to begin the work of creation, and its word woke to life the world, the form and shape of which it had already depicted to itself. The first act of creation began with the formation of an egg (Atom) out of the primeval matter, from which broke forth (*Atum*), the immediate cause of all

---

[234] *Ancient Egypt: Light of The World; Historical Jesus and the Mythical Christ; The Book of Beginnings.*
[235] E.A. Wallace Budge, *The Egyptian Book of The Dead* (New York: Dover Publications, 1967) CXII.

life upon earth...The birth of light from the waters (explosion of the Atom), and of fire from the moist mass of primeval matter, and of (*Atum*) from Nu, formed the starting point of all (religious) speculations, conjectures, and theories of the Egyptian priest.[236]

The Seven Glorious Ones or the Seven Constituent Parts of the Atom were called the *Seven Ali* by the ancient Egyptians. These Seven came together and produced the god *Atum*. Albert Churchward says the Ali *"are the companions, seven in number...who were afterwards absorbed in Atum as constituents of his body."*[237] Atum here is the Atom. From this one, nine other gods issued making the Ten. In the *Book of Knowing the Evolutions of Ra*, an ancient Egyptian theological text, the bursting forth of the 10,000 atoms, the Ten Original Gods of theology, is described. The First God is found saying:

I am he who evolved himself...I, the evolver of the evolutions evolved myself, the evolver of all evolutions, after many evolutions and developments which came forth from my mouth. No heaven existed, and no earth...I found no place whereon to stand...I was alone...there existed none other who worked with me. I laid the foundations off all things by my will, and all things evolved themselves therefrom. I united myself with my shadow, and I sent forth *Shu* and *Tefnut* out from myself; thus from being one god I became three, and *Shu* and *Tefnut* gave birth to *Nut* (4) and *Seb* (5), and *Nut* gave birth to *Osiris* (6), *Horus-Khent-an-maa* (7), *Sut* (8), *Isis* (9) and *Nephthys* (10), at one birth, one after the other...[238]

The Ten Gods would come together to produce the first God-Man, also called *Atum*. Atum, according to Charles Finch in his ***Echoes of the Old Darkland***, was the first God made in the image

---

[236] Ibid., XCVIII-XCVIX.

[237] Churchward, ***The Origin and Evolution of Religion*** (New York: E.C.A. Association, 1924, 1990) 243.

[238] Budge, ***Egyptian Book of The Dead***, XCIX-C.

of a Man.[239] As the Creator, he is always depicted as a Man.[240] He is called in the *Book of the Dead* the "Self-Created."[241] He was also called *Kemu-tef*, which means "he who is his own father." Gerald Massey, in *The Historical Jesus and The Mythical Christ*, shows that the tale of the Immaculate Conception of Christ was in fact a symbolic picture of the Self-Creation of the god Atum. He says:

> In one version of the Gospel according to John, instead of the 'only begotten son' of God, the reading is the 'ONLY BEGOTTEN GOD'...(T)he 'only begotten God' was an especial type of mythology, and the phrase involves the divinity whose emblem is the beetle. This was *Khepr-Ptah* who, like Atum, was reborn as his own son, Iu-em-hept, the Egyptian Jesus. 'To denote the only begotten or a father...the Egyptians delineate a scarabaeus (beetle). And they symbolize by this an only begotten because the scarabaeus is a creature SELF PRODUCED, BEING UNCONCEIVED BY A FEMAL.

Massey concludes,

> This god is the express image of the Christ of John's Gospel, who begins in the first chapter, without father or mother, and is the Word of the beginning, the opener and architect, the light of the world, THE SELF-ORIGINATED AND ONLY - BEGOTTEN GOD.

### 6.5. *The Biblical Six Days and the Evolution of God*

God's spiritual Descent ran parallel with a physical Ascent. The Second Stride of Vishnu or Step of Yahweh is the physical evolution of the "shell" or body of Man (The Temple). This evolution is described in the Bible and the *Holy Qur'an* as senary or going through six stages. The Biblical Six Days of Creation or Six Successive Periods of Evolution are really a picture of the growth of the Atom (First Manifestation of God) into the A.T.O.M.

---

[239] Finch, *Echoes of the Old Darkland*, 144.
[240] Budge, *Egyptian Book of The Dead* CXI.
[241] Ibid., CX.

(Grand Manifestation of God). The Biblical Adam (and Quranic Adam) "created" or evolved on the Sixth Day is therefore A.T.O.M.[242]

This may sound far fetched to those who are only familiar with the orthodox Christian interpretation of the Biblical Six Days, but the Hebrew authors knew better.[243] The real meaning of Genesis is a part of the Secret Tradition of the Jews called *Qabbalah*. The word *Qabbalah* means "secret or hidden tradition." The doctrines that make up this secret tradition came to the Jews by way of Musa (Moses) 4,000 years ago. After years of oral transmission the Secret Doctrine of Israel was codified in books that were to be kept out of the reach of the masses. A picture of this development is given in the apocryphal *Book of II Esdras* 14. Written probably in the first half of the second century AD, it describes the Jewish scribe Ezra's (of the Great Synagogue) supposed divine command to codify the Secret Doctrine. In this account, Ezra was allegedly commanded by God to take five scribes and writing utensils into a field. Ezra was to dictate God's words to the scribes who would write without knowledge of the characters they were writing.

> So during the forty days ninety-four books were written. And when the forty days were ended, the Most High spoke to me, saying, "Make public the twenty four books that you wrote first (the O.T. has twenty four books) and let the worthy and the unworthy read them; but keep the seventy that were written last, in order to give them to the wise among your people. For in them is the spring of understanding, the fountain of wisdom, and the river of knowledge." And I did so. (*II Esdras* 14:44-48).[244]

The "Seventy Books" were reportedly passed down from the Great Synagogue to certain Jewish sages from generation to generation, being always kept out of the reach of the masses. In the 14th century the *Zohar*, Qabbalah's central text (today) was published anonymously in France.

---

[242]Hall, *Secret Teachings of All Ages*, CXXI.
[243] See True Islam, *Truth of God*, Chapter VII, "The Bible and the Black God."
[244] Hayes, *Introduction To Old Testament Study*, 32.

One of the secrets of Qabbalah is the real meaning of Genesis I. Maimonides, for example, the most famous Jewish philosopher, went on record concerning Genesis admitting:

> Whosoever shall find the true sense of it ought to take care not to divulge it. This is a maxim which all our sages repeat to us, and above all respecting THE MEANING OF THE WORK OF THE SIX DAYS. If a person should discover the meaning of it, either by himself or with the aid of another, then he ought to be silent: or if he speak of it, he ought to speak of it but obscurely, and in an enigmatical manner as I do myself; leaving the rest to be guessed at by those who can understand me.[245]

What is the meaning of the Six Days that some Jews know but keep secret? S.L. MacGregor Mathers, in his *The Kabbalah Revealed*, concerning one of the three great Qaballistic writings called the *Siphra Dtzenioutha* or Book of Concealed Mystery, reveals:

> This and the immediately following sections (of the Book of Concealed Mystery) are...to trace the gradual development of the Deity from negative into positive existence; the text is here describing the time when the Deity was just commencing His manifestation from His primal negative form...The view which the Siphra Dtzenioutha here follows is that the beginning of Genesis describes not only the creation of the world, BUT THE DEVELOPMENT OF GOD.[246]

The biblical Six Days of Creation gives detailed accounts of the Self Creation of God. The Genesis tale starts off with the famous yet grossly misunderstood words, "In the beginning, God created the heavens and the earth." The Hebrew reading is *bere'shit bara 'elohiem 'et hashshamayim we'et ha'arez*. The first word *bere'shit*, translated as "In the Beginning," can have two different meanings

[245] Higgins, *Anacalypsis*, 98.
[246] Mathers, *Kabbalah Revealed*, 43, 77.

according to Qabbalah. The first is "From that which was first."[247] This implies that there was already some material in the beginning from which God created Himself and the world. Godfrey Higgins notes:

> The word...'*bara*' in the singular number...does not mean that the Aleim created, but that he formed, '*fecit*,' as the Septuagint says, out of matter previously existing.[248]

Mr. Muhammad says the same.

> The God created Himself out of matter...that he took out of the darkness of space...It made Itself out of a fine Atom of Water that It found there with It in the darkness of the universe.[249]

In Egypt, the Creator God Atum emerged from the already existing Primordial Waters of Nun.[250] Egyptologist Theophile Obenga observes:

> In the beginning there was matter – water - which, though weak, obscure, and abysmal, was powerful, dynamic, capable of creation and innovation, begetter of the gods themselves and the rest of creation...This matter would become consciousness itself, and manifest itself as creation...The ancient Egyptians posited a material state before God and His creation. What is more, God the Creator and Engineer Himself came out of this primordial, uncreated matter.[251]

In the Bible we read:

> In the beginning, God created the heavens and the earth. And the earth was without form and void and darkness

---

[247] Manely P. Hall, *Old Testament Wisdom*, (Los Angeles: The Philosophical Society, 1987), 96.
[248] Higgins, *Anacalypsis*, 79.
[249] Muhammad, *Theology of Time*, 108, 97.
[250]Sertima, *Egypt Revisited*, 292,296.
[251] Ibid.

was upon the face of the deep AND THE SPIRIT OF GOD MOVED UPON THE FACE OF THE WATERS (Gen. 1:1-2).

The word *bere'shit* could also be read as *bara shit* which means in Hebrew "He (God) created the Six."[252] According to Mathers "the Six" is a reference to the six physical manifestations of God on each of the Six Days of Creation, culminating with Man on Day Six – The Grand Manifestation of God.[253]

The next word of the opening sentence of Genesis that needs to be understood is the word mistranslated as "God." The Hebrew word *Alheim* or Eloheim does not mean "God." As Finis J. Dake points out in his **Annotated Reference Bible** regarding this Hebrew word,

> The Heb. <u>Eloheim</u> is the word for <u>God</u> in Gen. 1:1 and in over 2700 other places in the O.T. It is a uni-plural noun meaning <u>Gods</u> and is so trans. 239times (Gen. 3.5; Ex 22:28; I Sam. 4:8;Dan.2:11; 4:6-9;5:11,14, ect.).[254]

Hall says the Eloheim represents "*a host, or a least a group, of powers, symbolically described as SEPTENARY, and not under any condition a single personal deity.*"[255] These Seven "Powers" or "Creators" which constitute the Eloheim or Alheim are the same as the Seven Sublime Lords or Seven Creative Spirits, the *Dhyan-Chohans*, of the Indians. They are the seven constituent parts of the Atom.

"The *Spirit* of Eloheim" in v.2 of the opening chapter of Genesis we have shown is the Electric Force that pre-existed Creation and was represented by the ancients as a serpent with its tail in its mouth making a circle. This Serpent, in the beginning of Creation, grows seven heads. These seven heads of the serpent are the seven constituent parts of the Atom that developed from the Primordial Electric God Force. Hall observes:

---

[252] Mathers, *Kabbalah Revealed*, 46.
[253] Ibid., 41.
[254] Dake, *Annotated Reference Bible*, 280 (N.T.).
[255] Hall, *Old Testament Wisdom*, 95.

The seven-headed snake represents the Supreme Deity manifesting through His Eloheim, or Seven Sprits, by whose aid He established His Universe.[256]

The first Creation Story of Genesis 1 (as opposed to the story of Genesis 2 which is a different Creation) is the story of the creative evolution of the Atom, Allah's First Complete Manifestation. It is the story of Allah's Pilgrimage, as the Atom, through the various kingdoms in search of the Perfect Form for His Divine Theophany or Manifestation. This Pilgrimage lasted Six Days or Six Trillion Years and is described in a Hermetic fragment translated by Strobaeus:

> From one Soul (atom), that of All, spring all the Souls (atoms), [257] which spread themselves as if purposely distributed throughout the world. These souls undergo many transformations; those which are already creeping creatures turn into aquatic animals; from these aquatic animals are derived land animals; from the latter the birds. From these beings who live aloft in the air men are born. On reaching that status of men, the Souls receive the principle of immortality, become Spirits, then pass into the choir of the gods.

The Biblical story of Creation in Chapter 1 traces the same history of God according to the secret tradition of Judaism - His journey from an Atom to His destination as A.T.O.M., Allah The Original Man.

### 6.5.1. Day One

The first act of Creation on Day One was the act of separating the Light from the Darkness.

> And Alheim said, Let there be Light: and there was light. And Alheim saw the light, and it was good: and Alheim divided the light from the darkness (v. 3-4).

---

[256] Hall, *Secret Teachings of All Ages*, LXXXVIII.
[257] Remember the ancients used the words "soul" and "atom" interchangeably.

These are very revealing words. This speaks of the explosion that caused the Primordial Energy, which was hidden in Triple Darkness, to differentiate into balls of fire, quarks, and manifest itself as light. Now the light, no longer hidden in darkness, could be seen ("And Alheim saw the light"). Muhammad says:

> The history of space teaches us that at one time there was nothing but darkness...BEFORE THE A-TOM EXPLODED.[258]

The Qaballistic History of Origins agrees completely with the Hon. Elijah Muhammad. As noted above, the Jewish Qaballists called the Infinite All *Ain Soph*. In the Qaballah, the Cosmic Egg or Womb of Darkness was divided up into three states symbolized by three concentric circles (Muhammad's Triple State Darkness): *Ain*, which is the vacuum of Pure Spirit; *Ain Soph* which is the Limitless and Boundless; *Ain Soph Aur* which is the Limitless Light.[259]

At a certain time, Ain Soph made a concentration into ITS center and produced The Point within The Circle [ ⊙ ]. That Point is the Quark that sparked from the latent Energy. The *Zohar* says:

> When the Concealed of the Concealed wished to reveal Himself, He first made a single point: the Infinite was entirely unknown, and diffused no light before this luminous point (a-tom) violently broke into vision.

It reads also:

> In the beginning was the Will of the King, prior to any other existence...And there went forth as a sealed secret from the head of Ain Soph A NEBULOUS SPARK OF MATTER...

This "luminous Point" or "nebulous spark of matter" is the a-tom that sparked 76 trillion years ago. This a-tom is the "quark" of nuclear physics. The quark is a "spark of fire" which is the basic

---

[258] Muhammad, *Theology of Time*, 105.
[259]Hall, *Secret Teachings of All Ages*, CXVII.

building block of the conventional atom. As we have shown above, "point" is the same name scientists give to the quark ("point atom"). This Primordial Point is represented by the Qaballists by the Hebrew letter *Yod* [ י ]. The *Yod* is a picture of a tiny flame,[260] which is the quark. This Point, represented by the Hebrew letter *Yod,* is God. Blavatsky, on the origin of the term "God," notes:

> The attempt to derive God from the Anglo-Saxon synonym 'good' is an abandoned idea...To the Latin races it comes from the Aryan 'Dyaus (the Day); to the Slavonian, from the Greek Bacchus (Bagh-bog); and to the Saxon races directly from the Hebrew 'Yodh' or 'Jod.' The latter is [ י ], the number-letter 10...hence the Saxon 'Godh,' the Germanic 'Gott,' and the English 'God.'[261]

The Masons symbolize the Deity as an equilateral triangle (Triple Darkness) within which is the *Yod*.[262] *Yod* is the ninth letter of the Hebrew alphabet, the letter "I." The Point is therefore called *Eheyeh* meaning "I AM." Manley P. Hall, in his ***The Secret Teachings of All Ages*** notes:

> the unmanifested AIN SOPH established His first point or dot in the Divine Sea-the three spheres of X (triple darkness-TI). This dot...contains all creation within it, but the first divine and uncontaminated state of the dot, OR FIRST MANIFESTED GOD, was not considered as a personality...but rather as a DIVINE ESTABLISHMENT OR FOUNDATION.[263]

He didn't become a personality until after the emergence and coming together of the TEN, which we discuss below.

---

[260] Hall, ***Secret Teachings of All Ages,*** XLIX
[261] Blavatsky, ***Secret doctrine,*** I:347.
[262] Hall, ***Secret Teachings of All Ages,*** XLIX.
[263] Hall, ***Secret Teachings of All Ages,*** CXVIII.

Figure 20
Kavod, the Luminous Form of God/Adam Qadmon on Day One, depicted by the Kabbalists by the Hebrew letters of the name YHWH.

According to Qabbalah Day One or the first trillion-year period saw both the sparking of the atom and its growth into the first human form God assumed, the brilliantly luminous form. This form consisted of pure light or fire (Figure 20) and is called by the Qabbalists God's *Kavod* or "Glory." This is that dangerously luminous form of God that the ancient traditions said kept scorching the material creation. The accounts regarding this Form reminds one of Matt's above description of the universe shortly after the Big Bang:

> the universe was somewhat like the interior of a star, filled with protons – radiant particles of energy...The radiation was so turbulent and energetic that electrons could not stick to nuclei to form full-fledged atoms. As soon as an atom began to form, it was immediately ripped apart by radiation...

The Qabbalists associate this fiery form of God with Adam Qadmon in his first of four manifestations (see below). The association of the light of Day One with a 'Day One' Adam is found in several Jewish sources. According to the Nag Hammadi tractate *On the Origin of the World* 117:29ff,

> the first Adam is spirit-endowed (*pneumatikos*) and appeared on the first day. The second Adam is soul-endowed (*psychikos*), and appeared on the sixth day, which is called Aphrodite. The third Adam is a creature of the earth (*choikos*), that is, the man of law, and he appeared on the eighth (*sic*, the seventh) day...

The *pneumatikos* or spirit-endowed First Adam, born on the first day, is associated with both the Spirit of God that hovered over the pre-mundane waters (Gen 1:2) and, more commonly, the light of Gen. 1:3. The latter reading is based on a pun on the Greek word *phōs*, meaning both "light" and "man," and used in the Septuagint (Greek) translation of Gen. 1:3. Thus, the product of God's command, "Let there be light (*phōs*)," was a divine Light-Man, an *anthropos* enveloped within and consisting of light. On Day Six this Adam became *psychikos*. Now his body, consisting of all the various anatomical parts of a material body, is yet made of a psychic or ethereal substance (more on this below). The third Adam is the man molded from the earth (Gen 2:7), possessing now an earthly material body. These are all the same Adam during three different stages of his somatic (bodily) development. We will discuss the latter two below.

In Man's first state, He did not possess a body of flesh and blood. The earthly body, we are told, developed on the Sabbath (Seventh Day) from the "dust of the ground" and the 'fleshy body' still later. The body of the Man that emerged on Day One was composed of "luminous ether" or fire. Blavatsky notes,

> Finally, it is shown in every ancient scripture and Cosmogony that man evolved primarily as a 'luminous incorporeal form'.[264]

---

[264] Blavatsky, *Secret doctrine*, II: 112.

In Man's first state, He is described as being *"aerioform, devoid of compactness, and mindless."* His body was not yet material as we know it today, but was "etherial." According to the *Commentary of the Book of Dzyan* Man's Inner, Spiritual Self was at that time the "outer man."[265] This body is said to be "luminous," glowing with "effulgent light." The *Zohar* says of this first (of four) Adam Qadmon,

> When Adam dwelt in the (Heavenly) Garden of Eden, He was clothed in the celestial garment, which is the garment of heavenly light...light of that light which was used in the Garden of Eden."

Manley P. Hall, in *Old Testament Wisdom*, notes:

> Most of the ancient philosophers of the world have taught that life descended onto the physical planet from a sphere of superphysical energy which encloses the earth...According to the *Zohar* and other commentaries, the Heavenly Man emerged from the highest primordial obscurity...Originally, this...man dwelt in a luminous atmosphere above the earth. His body was composed of a kind of radiance like the world in which he lived...[266]

The Honorable Elijah Muhammad said Allah *"Emitted light from the live Atom of Self."*[267] The Persian Prophet Zara Thustra (Zoraster) said, *"God, in His body, resembles light."*[268] This 'Day One' Adam Qadmon is God in his luminous form, *Kavod*. .[269]

## 6.5.2. Day Two

> And Alheim said, Let there be a firmament in the midst of the waters, and let it divide the waters from the waters... And Alheim called the firmament Heaven (v. 6, 8).

---

[265] Ibid., II: 181.

[266] Hall, *Old Testament Wisdom*, 107-8.

[267] Muhammad, *Our Saviour Has Arrived*, 46.

[268] Higgins, *Anacalypsis*, 102.

[269] N. Moshe Lewis, *Ancient Mysteries of Melchizedek* (Queens, New York: D & J Books, 1993), 7, 44.

The words translated "firmament" and "Heaven" are the Hebrew *raqia* and *shamayim*. "*Raqia*" means space, air, but not empty space. The *Holy Qur'an* describes the early Heavens as a primordial cloud.

> Moreover, Allah turned to the Heaven WHEN IT WAS SMOKE and said to it and the earth…(Sura 41:11)

The Arabic word translated "smoke" is *dhukhan*, which means a "gaseous mass with fine particles."[270] What was this primordial gas cloud that became the Heavens?

Shortly after the Period of Annihilation, a dense cloud of hydrogen and radiation formed. According to astrophysicists Hydrogen (actually hydronic nuclei; electrons had not yet developed) was the very first element that developed in the Universe, being composed of just one proton and neutron.[271] Shortly thereafter, helium, with only two protons and neutrons, formed from hydrogen. These two account for 99% of all the matter of the universe. The remaining 100 elements make up only 1%.[272] Hydrogen is the basis of all other matter. Two trillion years after the Explosion, the temperature of the universe dropped and these hydrogen clouds produced the first generation of stars. In the core of these stars, other atoms were produced by nuclear fusion in which extremely high temperatures (minimum temperature of 10 million K)[273] melded protons and neutrons into the hydrogen atom, producing the Periodic Table of Elements. Stars are the factories of matter and hydrogen is the "raw material" from which matter is produced. The lives of some of these first generation stars ended in a huge explosion called a supernova, which blasted the newly formed heavy atoms into space.

The Universe on Day Two was a dense cloud of hydronic nuclei and radiation. This cloud is called "firmament" and "Heaven" in the Bible. This is appropriate because 90% of all

---

[270] Maurice Bucaille, *The Bible, The Qur'an, And Science* (Paris: Seghers, 1987), 145.
[271] Colin A. Ronan, *The Universe Explained* (New York: Henry Holt & Company, 1994), 167.
[272] Ibid.
[273] Ibid.

matter of the 76 quintillion miles of space is Hydrogen.[274] This gaseous mass was likely the Hydrogen cloud.[275] Pressure in the Universe caused the Hydrogen to condense and liquefy,[276] producing liquid hydrogen, the "Mystic Ocean" of the ancients.[277] This liquid hydrogen could also be the "waters" of the firmament developed on Day Two (Gen. 1:6-8).

### 6.5.3. Day Three

> And Alheim said, Let the waters under the heaven be gathered together unto one place, AND LET THE DRY LAND APPEAR...
> And Alheim called the dry land Earth...
> And Alheim said, Let the Earth bring forth vegetation, THE PLANT YEILDING ITS SEED...(v. 9-11)"

Day Three was a very important Day in the Story of Creation. What developed on Day Three was "dry land," Earth, and "plant yielding seed." This is extremely important to understand.

The dry land here called Earth is reference to the development of the material world as we know it. "Earth" here does not mean the globe. It simply means "matter."[278] It was on Day Three that the electrons attracted to the hydronic nuclei and formed the First Septenary, the Atom - the building block of matter. At this stage, via fusion in that first generation of stars, Oxygen had developed and, after joining with Hydrogen, produced water ($H_2O$). Now, life could start. The *Holy Qur'an* says: *"We made from water every thing living (21:30)"*

In this Primordial Ocean Hydrogen, Nitrogen, Oxygen and Carbon came together and produced the DNA molecule, the 'Atom of Life,' if you will. This was the Second Divine Septenary - the Second Complete Make of Allah and the first biological manifestation of Allah. DNA, Deoxyribonucleic Acid, is, like the Atom, encoded with Allah's signature Seven (Figure 21). Called

---

[274] Ibid.
[275] Ibid., 150.
[276] Ibid, 120.
[277] Higgins, *Anacalypsis*, 335.
[278] Hall, *Old Testament Wisdom*, 95-6.

the "very secret of Life"[279] it is composed from four nucleotides (Quaternary) - nitrogenous bases adenine (A), thymine (T), guanine (G), and cytosine (C). Each nucleotide is made up of three parts (Trinity): deoxyribose, which is a five-carbon sugar; a phosphate group; and a nitrogen-containing base.[280]

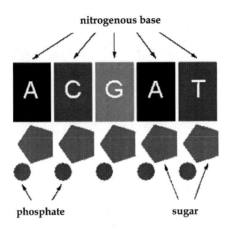

Figure 21
DNA, the Second Divine Septenary

Above we noted that, according to the Hon. Elijah Muhammad 10, 000 atoms came together making Allah the One. I suggested that this was the birth of the DNA molecule. I found powerful confirmation of my suggestion in Dr. Jeremy Narby's *The Cosmic Serpent: DNA and the Origins of Knowledge.* On page 103, he makes the observation: "*DNA IS ONLY 10 ATOMS WIDE*"[281] This is very powerful. All DNA is 10 atoms wide. They vary in length. The human DNA is 2 yards long and 10 atoms wide. The DNA of the primordial prokaryotic cell (simple unicell) is much shorter but 10 atoms wide as well. The length is determined by how many rows of 10 are "stacked" on top of each

[279] W. Davis and E. Soloman, *The World of Biology* (Philadelphia: Saunders College Publishing, 1986), 201.
[280] K. Arms and P. Camp, *Biology, A Journey Into Life* (Philadelphia: Saunders College Publishing, 1988), 144.
[281] Narby, *Cosmic Serpent*, 103.

107

other. So all DNA is composed of a number of atoms, which is an exponent of 10.

According to Qabbalah or the Secret Tradition of the Jews, out of that one "globe" or "shinning sapphire"- as the first atom is called - nine other globes or atoms emerged making TEN (read: 10,000), the *Ten Seppherot* or Sapphires, as they are called. These are the Ten Prajapatis of the East Indian *Vedas*, the Ten Gods of Egypt, and thus the 10, 000 atoms that made Allah The One, that first DNA molecule. Just as that DNA molecule made up of the 10,000 atoms was the foundation of all life, the Ten *Seppherot* of the Qaballah are called "the foundations of all creations" and the "ten roots of the Tree of Life".[282]  The Qaballah says they were "*the numbers or emanations of the Heavenly Light.*"[283] The Pythagoreans represented these 10, 000 a-toms by the *Tetractys*, an equilateral triangle consisting of 10 Yod's or tiny flames - quarks (Figure 22). The Pythagoreans taught that the *Tetractys* was the "symbol of the Creator."[284] These TEN Great Circles of Light or globes represent the 10, 000 atoms Allah (God) used to make Himself One. At this point He became a personality (an actual organism) and not just a "divine establishment or foundation" as He was when He was just the Point or Atom.

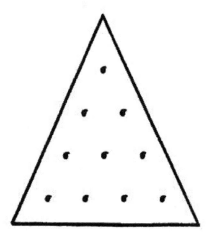

Figure 22
*Tetractys*

---

[282] Hall, *Secret Teachings of All Ages*, CXVIII.
[283] Blavatsky, *Secret Doctrine*, II:37.
[284] Hall, *Secret Teachings of All Ages*, CXCIII.

6.5.3.1. *DNA and the Secret of God*

Rensberger, in his ***How The World Works***, describes the DNA as:

> a chemical that can store information. Living organisms rely on the information stored in the DNA to control how they grow from a single cell to a complex, fully developed adult. The information in the DNA tells each cell what specialized features to develop (making one cell a nerve cell, another a liver cell, and so on), and what on going process to engage in. DNA, in words, IS THE MASTER MOLECULE OF LIFE.[285]

This "Master Molecule" operates from a blueprint that is inherent in its nature. Dr. Robert Gange, in his ***Origins and Destiny*** notes:

> to explain the origin of life we must explain the origin of a particular sequence of nucleotide bases in the DNA blueprint that instructs the cells to manufacture proteins, including the production of three thousand vastly complex enzymes that supply the 'workmen' responsible for doing the actual assembly.
> The blueprint also contains detailed specifications that produce the heart, stomach, kidneys, and gall bladder, along with every other organ and gland in the body. It also instructs the manufacture of muscles, nerves, and skin, together with the myriad of body parts including the eyes, ears, and brain. And if that isn't enough, the blueprint contains additional instructions responsible for the manufacture of reproductive organs that perpetuate the blueprint by producing new human beings![286]

DNA is a long, twisting chain made of two interwoven ribbons that are connected by the four bases adenine, thymine, guanine, and cytosine. This forms a Double Helix (Figure 23). The four nucleotides are designated by the four letters that begin each

---

[285] B. Rensberger, *How The World Works,* 112.
[286] Gange, ***Origins and Destiny,*** 85-6.

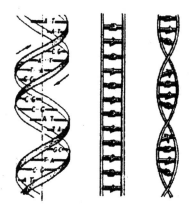

Models of DNA double helix

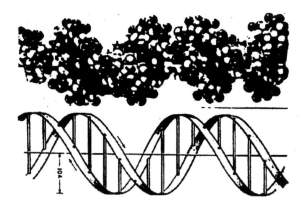

Figure 23
DNA Double Helix

name (A, T, G, C). These four letters make up the alphabet of the genetic language. The molecular instructions that come from the DNA are conveyed by words that are composed of just three letters, such as ATG. Thus the genetic alphabet is composed of four letters (Quaternary) and the "words" are composed of three letters (Trinity). We have again the Divine Septenary.[287]

The nature of the genetic language has led researchers to conclude that it is the result of intelligence, not random chemical activity. Linguist Ramon Jacobson has pointed out that the coding system displayed by the genetic language was originally thought to be an "exclusively human phenomena" which requires the presence of intelligence to exist.[288] Biologist Robert Pollack notes that *DNA is not merely an informational molecule, but is also a form of text, and therefore it is best understood by analytical ways of thinking commonly applied to other forms of text, for example, books.*[289]

DNA is an acronym for Deoxyribonucleic Acid. Here, we find the Secret of God. Dr. Alim Muhammad[290] suggested in 1988 an interesting etymological breakdown of the word. He suggests that "Deoxy" is related to the Latin root "Deus" meaning "God"; "Ribo" is related to the Arabic "Rb," written "Rob." This means "the Lord which nourishes a thing stage by stage, during its evolutionary development towards perfection"; "Nucleic" meaning center. Thus, Deoxyribonucleic means that at the center of every cell there is God, the Lord which nourishes stage by stage our (human) development towards the perfection of our being. This (too) is the great Hajj. The Muslim Holy Pilgrimage is only a sign of the true journey; Man's journey from a single cell to a fully developed human who, after evolving mentally and spiritually, has achieved the perfection of his being. This august stage of development is called in Islam *mutma'innah*, meaning "soul at rest."[291] The ancient Egyptians called this stage "*Summum Bonum*."

---

[287] The Cosmic Senary (The Six), being the number of physical creation, is also inherent in the cell. There are six billion base pairs of chromosomes in each cell (Narby, 183). The two ribbons of DNA wrap around each other 600 million times in the human cell. Almost all biomolecules are made of six elements: hydrogen, carbon, oxygen, nitrogen, phosphorous, and sulfur...

[288] Narby, *Cosmic Serpent*, 135

[289] Ibid., 144.

[290] Lecture, 'AIDS in the Black Community," 1988, Final Call Building, Chicago, Illinois.

[291] Yusef Ali, *Holy Qur'an*, p. 472 ft. 1239.

Man at this stage can then proclaim: *"Labbaika Allahumma labbaika* (Here I am, O Allah, in Thy August Presence)."

Dr. Alim's suggestion is given powerful support by Gregg Braden in his *The God Code: The Secret of Our Past, the Promise of Our Future*.[292] Braden first demonstrated the correlation between the alchemical elements Fire, Air, Earth and Water and the chemical substances of DNA – nitrogen, hydrogen, carbon and oxygen. Then, by using the Hebrew science of *gematria* (the science of letters as numbers), Braden was able to correlate the simple atomic mass of these chemicals to Hebrew letters thus:

| *Alchemical Element:* | Fire | Air | Water | Earth |
|---|---|---|---|---|
| *DNA Chemical:* | Hydrogen | Nitrogen | Oxygen | Carbon |
| *Simple Atomic Mass:* | 1 | 5 | 6 | 3 |
| *Heb. Letter Equivalents:* | Y | H | V | G |

The first two Hebrew letters, YH, spell the eternal name of God in Hebrew (*Yah*). The third and forth letters, VG, gematrically indicate the Hebrew word *gav* which carries the meaning "interior of/within the body." Braden thus announces:

A remarkable discovery linking the biblical alphabets of Hebrew and Arabic to modern chemistry reveals that a lost code – *a translatable alphabet* – and a clue to the mystery of our origins, has lived within us all along. Applying this discovery to the language of life, the familiar elements of hydrogen, nitrogen, oxygen, and carbon that form our DNA may now be replaced with key letters of the ancient languages. In doing so, the code of all life is transformed into the words of a timeless message. *Translated, the message reveals that the precise letters of God's ancient name are*

---

[292] Carlsbad, Ca.: Hay House, Inc., 2004.

*encoded as the genetic information in every cell, of every life. The message reads: "God/Eternal within the body"*...These substitutions now reveal that the ancient form of God's name, YH, exists as the literal chemistry of our genetic code...[293]

God is thus in our very genetic makeup. Thus we understand better the Qur'an's statement that Allah is "closer to (man) than (his) jugular (50:16)."

*6.5.3.2. DNA: The Throne of God*

The DNA molecule is the Throne of Allah. Inside the very genetic makeup of the Original Man Allah Ta'ala (God Most High) sits enthroned. Thus, the Qur'an makes the curious statement, *"His (Allah's) Thrown of Power is ever on water (11:7)."* The cell in which the DNA lives is around 90% water. From there, Allah (God) sends down instructions, like revelation, on the production of every organ of every life form. These "instructions" or "scriptures" are conveyed to the ribosomes by another nucleic acid called "Messenger RNA." Like the Prophets and Messengers of God, this Messenger RNA is responsible for communicating God's Word to the ribosomes.

Genesis 1:11 says, *"Let the earth* (atom) *bring forth vegetation: plants yielding seed."* The DNA molecule or "Atom of Life" within the cell was symbolized by the ancients as the Lotus plant. The Lotus plant is a seed plant (*"plant yielding seed"*) which functions like the DNA molecule within the cell.

This plant grows in the water, and amongst its broad leaves puts forth a flower, in the center of which is formed a seed vessel, shaped like an inverted cone, and punctured on top with little cavities or cells, in which the seeds grow. The orifices of these cells being too small to let the seeds drop out when ripe they shoot forth into new plants, in the places where they were formed: the bulb of the vessel serving as a matrix to nourish them, until they acquire

---

[293] Ibid., xiv, 134.

such a degree of magnitude as to burst it open, and release themselves...This plant, therefore, (is) productive of itself, and vegetating from its own matrix, without being fostered in the earth...[294]

Concerning the seeds of the lotus, Sir W. Jones notes that

they contain - even before they germinate - perfectly formed leaves, the miniature shape of what one day, as perfect plants, they will become, nature thus giving us a specimen of the preformation of its production...the seed of all phanerogamous plants bearing proper flowers containing an embryo plantlet ready formed.[295]

The Lotus, being the ideal seed plant, perfectly represented the DNA molecule, the seed of life. The ancients recorded that the Creator evolved out of the Lotus and sat enthroned on the Lotus. Such was the case with Brahma of India and Ra of Egypt.[296]

Figure 24
Horus emerging from Lotus Plant

[294] Higgins, *Anacalypsis*, I:339.
[295] Blavatsky, *Secret Doctrine*, I:57.
[296] See True Islam, *Truth of God*.

The Lotus Plant/DNA is the Throne of Allah (God). The Indian *Upanishads* make this very point, noting with regarding to man's divine Self:

This Self, who understands all, who knows all, and whose glory is manifest in the universe, lives within the lotus of the heart.

The 10,000 atoms that came together to produce the first DNA molecule are written of by the Indians and the Qabbalists. The *Zohar* reads:

We have learned that there were Ten who entered into the Sod ('mysterious assembly'), and that SEVEN ONLY CAME FORTH.

It reads again,

The Deity manifests itself through the Ten Sepphiroth (10,000 atoms) which are the radiating witnesses...From the basin, like Seven channels, issue the Seven Sepphiroth...For TEN EQUAL SEVEN.

In the Indian *Laws of Manu*, the "Ten Lords of Being (Prajapatis)" produce "Seven other Manus."[297] This, I believe, is all reference to the 10,000 atoms coming together and forming the first DNA molecule - the Second Divine Septenary of Allah.

6.5.3.3. *Say: He Allah is One*

Dr. Charles Price, former president of the American Chemical Association, stated his belief in 1971 that the fact that

DNA language in the simplest one-cell organism is exactly the same DNA language that duplicates a human being...suggest(s) that one original cell became the progenitor of all life on earth.[298]

---

[297] Blavatsky, *Secret Doctrine*, I:449.
[298] T. Howard and J. Rifkin, *Who Should Play God?* (New York: Delacorte Press, 1977), 18.

In 1986, 285 scientists from 22 countries who participated in the landmark eighth Conference on the Origin of Life held at Berkley in California, agreed that *"all life on earth, from bacteria to sequoia trees to humans, evolved from a single ancestral cell."* The first cell to develop was the prokaryotic cell (Figure 25), the simplest of all cells containing only a circular molecule of double-stranded DNA folded up in a nuclear area. This cell lacks the nucleus surrounded by the nuclear envelope, which all other cells possess. This is the simple single-celled moneron from the Kingdom Monera.[299]

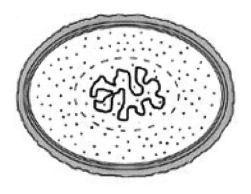

Figure 25
Prokaryotic Cell

What is most interesting about the conclusions and current thinking of modem science is the suggestion that this primordial, ancestral cell did not originate on earth but in interstellar space. Lynn Margulis, in her summation of the fourth Conference on the Origin of Life, said,

> The central problem inspiring these conferences, perhaps slightly better defined, is as unsolved as ever. DID OUR ORGAMIC MATTER ORIGINATE IN INTERSTELLAR SPACE? The infant science of radio-astronomy has

---

[299] Arms and Camp, *Biology, A Journey Into Life*, 326.

produced evidence that some of the smaller organic molecules are there.

In 1986, The *New York Times* headline story read, "NASA to Probe Heavens for Clues to Life's Origin on Earth" (September 6, 1986). Sandra Blakeslee summed up the current thinking of the scientific community at the time:

> Driving the new search for clues to life's beginnings is the recent discovery that comets, meteors and interstellar dust carry vast amounts of complex organic chemicals as well as the elements crucial to living cells.
>     Scientists believe that Earth and other planets have been seeded from space with these potential building blocks of life.[300]

The suggestion that the ancestral cell and life originated, not on earth, but in space is only confirming what the Honorable Elijah Muhammad said twenty years ago:

> The Atom out of which man was created came from space. It was out in space where He originated. An Atom of Life was in the darkness of the space and He came out of that Atom...What came out of space was a Human Being.[301]

### 6.5.3.4. *DNA: Making Fire to Live in Water*

The DNA molecule, like the light particle, is paradoxical in nature. It brings together two mutually exclusive elements, Water and Fire. DNA exists in water, which makes up 90 percent of the cell. This water is salt water and its concentration of salt is remarkably similar to that of the world ocean. *"We sweat and cry what is basically seawater"* according to biologists Lynn Margulis and Dorion Sagan. [302] While this DNA lives in water, it spits fire like a dragon. It has been discovered that the DNA of all living

---

[300] Sandra Blakeslee, "NASA to Probe Heavens for Clues to Life's Origins on Earth, " *The New York Times*, September 6, 1986, A1.
[301] Muhammad, *Theology of Time*, 105.
[302] Ibid., 184.

beings emit tiny balls of fire called photons (tiny charged particles of energy). These photons are emitted at a rate of 100 units per second per square centimeter. The wave-length of these emissions correspond to that of visible light. They are emitted so regularly that researchers have compared it to an "ultra weak laser." These coherent photon emissions are said to produce luminous holographic images, which the cells use to communicate with each other and with other organisms.[303]

One of the most exciting experiments in this field consists of placing two lots of unicellular organisms in a device that measures photon emissions and separate them with a metal screen. Under these circumstances, the graph of one lot's photon emissions is completely different from the others. When the metal screen is removed, however, both graphs coincided "to the highest degree."[304] Divine Intelligence is inherent in the DNA.

The ancients recognized the divine nature of DNA. As we have shown, they symbolically represented it as the Lotus Plant. They also represented it, however, as Twin Snakes. At the beginning of several ancient cosmogonies* that Primordial Electric Force (Spirit of God) was represented as the Great Invisible Serpent with its tail in its mouth making a circle. After creation began, the Great Invisible Serpent produced the visible Twin Serpent. This image of the Twin Snakes is a *double entendre*: it has two significances. On one level it can represent the polarization (positive/negative) of that original divine force. On the other hand, Dr. Jeremy Narby has shown that the Twin Snake motif, found all over the world, also represents the ancient's knowledge of DNA.[305] In fact, these Twin Snakes were often depicted entwined like the Double Helix of DNA. DNA is said to wriggle in the cell *"like two small snakes slithering through mud."*[306] Molecular biologist Chris Wills says the *"two chains of DNA resemble two snakes coiled around each other in some elaborate courtship ritual."*[307] He even represents the DNA Double Helix as two entwined serpents (Figure 26).

---

[303] Ibid., 204.
[304] Ibid.
[305] *Cosmic Serpent*.
[306] *Science News* 145 (May 7,1994): 293.
[307] Quoted from Narby, *Cosmic Serpent*, 92

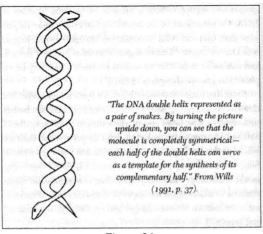

"The DNA double helix represented as a pair of snakes. By turning the picture upside down, you can see that the molecule is completely symmetrical — each half of the double helix can serve as a template for the synthesis of its complementary half." From Wills (1991, p. 37).

Figure 26
DNA Double Helix as Twin Snakes. From Wills, 1991, 37

As in the case with the Lotus Plant symbolism, God the Creator (as opposed to God the Infinite All) is identified with the Twin Serpents. The *Dictionary of Symbols* says under the heading "serpent":

It makes light of the sexes, and of the opposition of contraries...it is...a twin to itself; like so many of the important creator gods who are always, in their first representation, cosmic serpents...Thus the visible snake (DNA) appear as merely a brief INCARNATION OF A GREAT INVISBLE SERPENT (SPIRIT OF GOD), which is causal and timeless, a master of the vital principle and of all the forces of nature. It is a primary 'old god' found at the beginning of all cosmogonies...

The Creator God of South America is the Black God *Quetzalcoatel*. Quetzalcoatel was born from the Invisible Cosmic Serpent named *Coatlicue*. Quetzalcoatel is called "The Plumbed Serpent." Claude Levi-Strauss notes:

In Aztec, the word *coatl* means both 'serpent' and 'twin.' The name *Quetzalcoatel* can thus be interpreted either as 'Plumed serpent' or 'Magnificent twin.[308]

Most DNA is linear and thus the Twin Serpents motif pictures two linear serpents intertwined. However, the oldest cell, the prokaryotic cell, direct descendent of the Primordial Ancestral Cell, has one double helix with its ends joined making a circle.[309] This single circular DNA of the simple prokaryotic cell is represented by the *Ouroboros*, the Serpent Dragon. The Serpent Dragon Ouroboros is depicted, like the Great Invisible Serpent, with its tail in its mouth making a circle (Figure 27).

Figure 27
Ouroboros

The **Dictionary of Symbols** says the Dragon, one of the elders of the reptilian family, represents *"the union of two opposed principles."* What are the two opposed principles that this Serpent Dragon symbolizes? Narby says,

---

[308] Ibid. 62. "As the creator of life, the cosmic serpent is a master of metamorphosis. In the myths of the world here it plays a central part, it creates by transforming itself." Narby, **Cosmic Serpent**, 86.
[309] Arms and Camp, **Biology, A Journey Into Life**, 145.

Sometimes the winged serpent takes the form of a dragon, the mythical and double animal par excellence, WHICH LIVES IN WATER AND SPITS FIRE.[310]

He lives in water and spits fire, just like the paradoxical DNA. When DNA is symbolically represented as the Lotus Plant, it represents the Throne of God, the Holy Seat from which He issues divine decrees (instructions). When it is represented as the Twin Serpents, it represents the Creator Himself who creates by transforming into its creatures, just as the DNA does.

### 6.5.4. *Day Four*

> And Alhiem said: Let there be lights in the firmament of heaven to separate the day from the night...(v., 14)

Day Four saw the birth of the Sun (and a moon, but not necessarily *our* current moon). The sun was not among the first generation of stars born on Day Two. Muhammad said it was created 72 trillion years ago; that is to say 4 trillion years (Day Four) after the explosion of the atom. However, the sun seems not to have been put into use until six trillion years after the explosion, i.e. on Day Six (for the reasons see below).[311]

### 6.5.5. *Day Five*

Day Five saw the birth of the Animal Kingdom. The fish or aquatic animals were the first to develop from the Primordial Waters.

> And God said, Let the waters bring forth abundantly the moving creatures that hath life, and fowl that may fly above the earth in the open firmament of heaven. And God created great whales, and every living creature that moveth, which the waters hath brought forth...(vv. 20-21)

From aquatic animals, land animals formed.

---

[310]Narby, *Cosmic Serpent*, 83.
[311] Muhammad, *Theology of Time*, 96, 108.

And God said, Let the earth bring forth every living creature after its kind, cattle, and creeping thing, and beast of the earth after his kind…(v. 24)

The Atom had to go through all the following stages (Inmetallization, Inherbbation, and Inzoonization) before it could develop the physical shell of Man (Incarnation). Agassiz, in *Principles of Zoology* makes the same observation. He says the progress in the succession of beings,

> consist in an increasing similarity of the living fauna, and, among the vertebrates, especially, in the increasing resemblance to man. Man is the end towards which all animal creation has tended from the first appearance of the Paleozoic fishes.[312]

### 6.5.6. *Day Six*

And Alheim said, Let Us make Man in Our Image, after Our Likeness…(v. 26)

Finally the material, or rather semi-material shell or human body of God/Man emerges on Day Six. This Man/body is different from the Man of Genesis 2 that was made from the "dust of the ground (2:7)" on Day Seven. This Man/body was made in the Image (*selem*) and Likeness (*demut*) of the Alheim or Eloheim. The Eloheim, we recall, were the Seven constituent parts of the Atom - the Seven Sons of Fire. The Eloheim were "balls of fire" themselves, and the Man/body that developed on Day Six was likewise of a fiery nature. Not, however, of white fire but, as the Qabbalaists say, "of black fire," which enveloped the "white fire."[313]

According to Jewish, Gnostic and Christian sources the human form of God/Man itself went through four different 'compositional' stages. That is to say, the composition or substance of the body changed four times. These 'bodies' are

---

[312]Agassiz, *Principles of Zoology*, p. 206.
[313] Idel, *Absorbing Perfections*, Chapter Two.

stages during Spirit's descent into matter. We recall that Nag Hammadi tractate *On the Origin of the World* 117:29ff mentions three of these bodies or stages: the *pneumatic* or luminous, spiritual body of Day One, the *psychic* body of Day Six, and the earthly body of the Sabbath Day (or some say eighth day). The fourth body is the body of flesh which resulted from Adam's/God's 'fall' and exile from the Garden of Eden. As the Church Father Origen describes this 'descent':

> all rational creatures, incorporeal and invisible, if they be negligent, gradually slip to lower levels and take to themselves bodies according to the quality of the places into which they descend; that is, first ethereal (spiritual) bodies, and then aereal (*psychic*). And when they reach the vicinity of earth they are enclosed in denser bodies (earthly), and finally are bound to human flesh (Jerome, *Con. Joh. Hieros.* 16).

The *psychic* body or the body of Man on Day Six is said to be made of an *aereal* substance. That is to say, substance of the black, sub-lunar air or air below the moon.[314] This was therefore a black body. See for example Porphyry's description of the descent of the astral body:

> Originally of an ethereal substance, in the course of its descent the (spirit) is progressively darkened and thickened as it absorbs moisture from the air, until it finally becomes fully material and even visible.[315]

In Man's first three states (spiritual, psychic, earthly) his body is said to get progressively denser, but it lacked flesh. Flesh is a substance the body acquired only after the fall, we are told. In his *psychic* or *areal* state, the Original Man was called a *Dyooknah* or "divine phantom." This black, semi-material body is also called God's "Shadow" because it 'shades' creation from the intense heat

---

[314] See e.g. Philo, *Spec.* I.85.
[315] Quote from E.R. Dodds, "Appendix II: The Astral Body in Neoplatonism" in idem, *Proclus: The Elements of Theology* (Oxford: Clarendon Press, 1963): 318. Cf. Porphyry, *On The Cave of the Nymph* 62-66.

of the 'sun,' i.e. the luminous body. The body density of this 'shadow-body' was halfway between the complete spirituality of the Day One luminous form and the earthly, material form of Day Seven. This shadow-form is illustrated by the satirist Lucian of Samosata (AD 120-AD 180) in his *True History*. Describing the inhabitants of the "Island of the Blessed Ones" Lucian says:

> They have no bodies, but are intangible and unsubstantial—mere form without matter; but, though incorporeal, they stand and move, think and speak; in short, each is a naked soul, but carries about the semblance of body; one who did not touch them would never know that what he looked at was not substantial; they are shadows, but upright, and black (II, 12).

The Black God has now emerged. Occultist Eliphas Levi, in his *History of Magic*, describes the emergence of this Man-God called Adam Qadmon:

> The Synthesis of the world formulated by the human figure, ascended slowly and emerged from the water, like the sun in its rising. When the eyes appeared, light was made; when the mouth was manifested, there was the creation of spirits and the world passed into expression. The entire head was revealed, and this completed the first day of creation. The shoulders, the arms, the breast arose, and thereupon work began. With one hand the Divine Image put back the sea, while with the other it raised up continents and mountains. The Image grew and grew; the generative organs appeared, and all beings began to increase and multiply. The form stood at length erect, having one foot on land and one upon water...Such is Adam Qadmon, the primordial Adam of the Kaballists. Such is the sense in which he is depicted as a giant; and this is why Swedenborg, haunted in his dreams by reminiscences of the Kabalah, says the entire creation is only a titanic man and that we are made in the image of the universe...The face of God, crowned with light, rose over the vast sea and was reflected in the waters thereof.

His two eyes were manifested, radiating with splendor, darting two beams of light...The brow of God and His eyes formed a triangle in heaven, and its reflection formed a second triangle in the waters. So was revealed THE NUMBER SIX, BEING THAT OF UNIVERSAL CREATION.[316] (Figure 28)

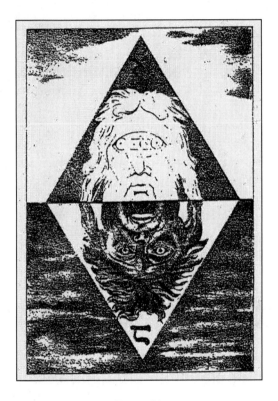

Figure 28
Levi's 'Head of the Zohar' depicting the luminous Adam Qadmon (God) and his black reflection in the waters, which will become his black body.

This Black God's number is Six, emerging on Day Six, six trillion years after the explosion of the atom. This Black God, Allah The Original Man, went through a Six Trillion Year development taking him from a moneron to a plant (vegetable

---

[316] E. Levi, *History of Magic* (York Beach, ME.: Samuel Weiser, Inc., 1970) 50-51.

kingdom), to an animal (animal kingdom) to finally, the God/Man. As the Qaballah says regarding Adam Qadmon "the All became *"a stone (atom), a stone becomes a plant; a plant a beast; a beast a man,"* and this man, the Qaballah says, becomes *"finally God. Thus accomplishing his cycle or circuit…"*[317] The *Zohar* says:

> As soon as man appeared, everything was complete…for everything is comprised in man. He unites in himself all forms (iii, 48a)."

The Divine Pilgrim has reached His Destination. Six Days or Six Trillion Years later, Allah The Original Man emerges in all His Splendor.

The Black Man has touched down. This Black Adam (A.T.O.M), created or evolved on the Sixth Day, is God in His most Complete and Evolved form. He started as an Atom (1) and grew to be A.T.O.M. (6). Mr. Muhammad teaches:

> The figures one (1) and six (6) are the most outstanding figures that we have. One represents the God that created the Heavens and the Earth, and the other one represents the same, the "6". Why is that?, He didn't stop growing! He grew into the scientific knowledge of '6' and when He got into the '6' he still had us puzzled. We didn't know how to overtake Him because the '6' came 6 trillion years after the '1'… [318]

This Black Adam (A.T.O.M.) is called *Qadmon* (God-Man) by the Jewish Qaballists, *Ahura Mazda* by the Zoroastrians, *Marduke* by the Babylonians, *Atum* by the Egyptians, *Yahweh* by the Hebrews, and *Brahma* by the Hindus. These Creator Gods are one and the same with the Black Man who emerged from Triple Darkness 70 Trillion years ago. Eliphas Levi thus proclaims the secret of the Qaballah: *"Man is God on Earth, and God is Man in Heaven."*

[317] Blavatsky, *Secret Doctrine*, II:186.
[318] Muhammad, *Theology of Time*, 98-9.

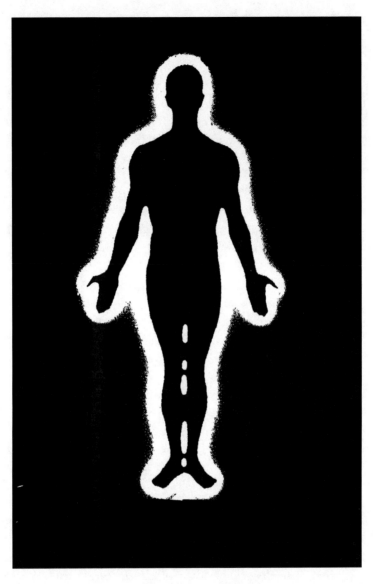

Figure 29
Black God surrounded by aura of Light.

*6.5.7. The Sabbath Day*

> These are the generations of the heavens and of the earth
> when they were created, in the day that YHWH Alheim
> made the earth and the heaven...
> And YHWH Alheim formed man of the dust of the
> ground, and breathed into his nostrils the breath of life:
> and man became a living soul (2:4-7).

Manley P. Hall, in *Old Testament Wisdom*, observes:

> There are two distinct accounts of what at first appears to
> be the production of the human being. The first is
> contained in (Genesis) 1:26-28...In the second chapter of
> Genesis, there is another description of the human
> creation. The context indicates definitely that this second
> process of generation is not merely a restatement of the
> first, for it occurs after God has blessed the seventh day,
> and the first creation took place on the sixth day.[319]

Two very important developments occurred on the Sabbath
Day: God's body materializes further and His brain matures. The
"dust of the ground" is reference to the hard material that Allah
adorned on Day Seven. The atoms condensed. This is called
God's Descent to Earth and the new body is called God's "Earthly
Garment." The *Zohar* says: *"The Soul* (atom) *and the Form*
(shadow-body), *when descending on earth, put on an earthly
garment."* The *Zohar* specifically describes this earthly garment the
God adorns as His material body. Allah's (God's) descent onto
earth is described in the *Divine Pymander of Thoth*, an Egyptian
Gnostic text. It describes the ethereal God, called 'Man,'
incarnating within the 'shadow-body' (Day Six) and then being
wrapped in a material cloak called 'nature' (Day Seven)

> The Man (God) longed to pierce the circumference of the
> (Seven) circles...Having already all power, He stooped
> down and peeped through the seven Harmonies

---

[319] Pp. 104-5.

and...showed to lower Nature the form of God. The Man, looking into the depths, smiled, for He beheld his shadow upon the earth and a likeness mirrored in the waters, which shadow and likeness were a reflection of Himself. The Man fell in love with His own shadow and desired to descend into it. At once with the wish it became a reality, and he came to inhabit the (shadow-)form...Nature, beholding the descent, wrapped herself about the Man whom she loved and the two mingled. For this reason, earthly man is composite. Within him is the Sky Man (God), immortal and beautiful; without is Nature, mortal and destructible.

After "inhabiting" or incarnating within the 'shadow-form' Nature, that is to say earthly matter, embraced him in that form. This is just a picturesque way of saying the shadow-body now materialized. Eliphas Levi, in his *History of Magic*, presents an image he calls "The Grand Symbol of the Qabbalah" (Figure 30). A white male supposed to represent, in Levi's ethnocentric way, the luminous form of God stands erect and a Black woman is upside down, her legs passing under the extended arms of the male. Their hands join and around the image are the Hebrew letters, YHWH, i.e. Yahweh, the sacred name of God. This picture, we are told, is Yahweh in his luminous form and Nature or the black material body that he wears as a garment. Matter, by the ancients, is represented as feminine.

As noted this materialization process occurred in four graduated stages. The first "fire God" gave way to a form slightly more dense and compact (shadow-form), which gave birth to an even more compact body, the earthly or natural body. This body is material, but the matter, as Philo put it, was a 'pure' matter. It was not 'flesh.' The fourth or fleshy body developed after and is

Figure 30
Levi's 'Grand Man of the Zohar'

a mark of the 'Fall' of Adam and his exile from Eden. These Four Stages are referred to as the Four Root Races. The Commentary to the *Book of Dzyan* describes the first three:

> (*I.*) Man in the First Round and First Race on Globe D, our Earth, was an ethereal being, non-intelligent but super-spiritual...
> *II.* Round. He is still gigantic and ethereal but growing firmer and more condensed in body, a more physical man. Yet still less intelligent than spiritual, for mind is a slower and more difficult evolution than is the physical frame...
> *III.* Round. He has now a perfectly concrete or compacted body...He has now reached a point where his primordial spirituality is eclipsed and overshadowed by nascent mentality

In the Qaballah, these Four Stages are called the Four Men of the Zohar. The *Zohar* notes:

> the first being (was) 'the perfect, Holy Adam'...that disappeared'...the second is called the protoplastic androgen Adam of the future terrestrial and separated Adam; the third Adam is the man made of 'dust'...'The fourth Adam'...'was clothed with skin, flesh, nerves, etc. "

The Third Adam, God with a black material body, was supremely wise. The Mental Evolution reached its climax with Him. Man in His First State was 'mindless,' or, better, his intelligence was there but rudimentary in comparison to how it will evolve. The final (Third) Stride of Vishnu (mental evolution) or Step of Yahweh had not progressed too far. Slokas IV of the *Book of Dzyan* says:

> 17. The Breath needed a form; the Fathers (atoms) gave it. the Breath needed a gross body, the Earth molded it....But Breath needs a Mind to embrace the Universe; 'We can not give that,' said the Fathers. 'I

never had it,' said the Spirit of Earth...Man remained an empty, senseless Bhuta (phantom)."[320]

Both the Bible and the *Holy Qur'an* concur with the said above. It was after this creation of Man's body from dust that Allah (God) "breathed into him of My Spirit," making Man a "Living Soul." The body became a Living Soul after He developed mentally. This is the Third Stride of Vishnu and it took place on Day Seven, the Sabbath. Muhammad says also: *"In the making of God Himself, He could not have a Will until He had brains capable of thinking."*[321] He is now Complete. The Three Strides of Vishnu and Steps of Yahweh have all been finished.

In Genesis 1, God is always called Eloheim. In Genesis 2, which begins with Day Seven, God is always called Yahweh Eloheim. In the Qaballah, it is affirmed, *"Yahweh is Eloheim."* This is to assure the people that the two are in fact the same God. But the question is then raised, *"How is Yahweh Eloheim?"* How is it that that the two, Eloheim of Chapter I and Yahweh of Chapter 2, are the same God when their creations were different? How did they become the same God? The answer is given by the Qaballah, *"By Three Steps."* The Three Steps are the same as the Three Strides of Vishnu-the Spiritual, Physical, and Mental Evolution which took God from a simple Atom (Eloheim) to a fully grown Man (Yahweh).

## 6.6. *Evolution of the Black God in Esoteric Islam*

Islamic theology, like all others, has an exoteric or public dimension as well as its esoteric or hidden dimension. While the masses know only the outer dimension or "garment" of the doctrine, the learned few are initiated into the "Qaballah," or secret tradition. The "Qaballah" of Islam is called *Sufism*. Sufism traces the same historical development of God. According to this hidden tradition of Islam, in the beginning God existed as a single, immaterial essence called *'ayn*, similar to the Ain or Ain Soph of Jewish Qabbalah. This Single Essence is described as The

---

[320]Blavatsky, *Secret Doctrine*, II: 17.
[321]Muhammad, *Theology of Time*, 371.

Absolute, called also *Haqq*, Truth.[322] How long The Absolute existed in this state is unrecorded. At a certain point, The Absolute began feeling the Desire to manifest Itself in concrete form. This Desire for Self-Manifestation is called *Mashi'ah*, the Divine Wish. The process by which The Absolute's Desire for Self Manifestation in Concrete Form is actualized is called *Tajalli*.

This *tajalli* or process of self manifestation of the Deity occurred, according to Esoteric Islam, in Seven Stages or Strata (*maratib*), comparable to the biblical Seven Days. These strata or *maratib* are the Seven Densities of Matter starting with the First which is The Absolute - totally immaterial and incomprehensible – to the Seventh which is the created world of matter. It was on the Fourth Strata that the Single Essence (Absolute) differentiated into the various Names and Attributes of Allah. Toshihiko Izutsu, in his comparative study of Sufism, notes:

> What is generally known as 'Names' and 'Attributes' is nothing but a theological expression of this infinite variety of the possible forms of self-manifestation of the Absolute.[323]

These, as we have shown, are the atoms. The Names are later described as the infinite ways the Absolute manifests Itself *"in the world of concrete Being."*[324] The concrete stages of The Absolute's Self Manifestation are called the *tajalli shuhudiy* or "self manifestation in the visible world." On the Seventh Strata, all of the Names or Attributes (atoms) came together and formed the *Insan Kamil* or The Perfect Man. This Perfect Man has the sole distinction of being the only being which possesses in its nature all of the Names. Everything else in the universe manifests one single Divine Name. The *Insan Kamil*, however, manifests every one of them. He is thus called *Al-Kawn Al-Jami'*, "The Comprehensive Being."

---

[322] Toshihiko Izutsu, *A Comparative Study of the Key Philosophical Concepts In Sufism And Taoism* (Tokyo: The Keio Institute of Cultural And Linguistic Studies, 1966) 144.
[323] Ibid., 35.
[324] Ibid., 147.

Those discrete things and properties that have been diffused and scattered all over the immense universe become united and unified into a sharp focus in Man. The structure of the whole universe with all its complicated details is reflected in him in a clear and distinctly articulated miniature. [325]

At this stage, The Absolute becomes God. The Original Man or Perfect Man is Allah, the All In All who synthesizes all of the Divine Names of The Absolute.

Man on a cosmic level, or the Perfect Man, is endowed with a perfect 'comprehensiveness.' And because of this 'comprehensiveness' by which he synthesizes in himself all the existents of the universe not individually but in their universality, the Perfect Man shows two characteristic properties which are not shared with anything else. One is that he is the only being who is really and fully entitled to be a perfect 'servant' ('abd) of God. All other beings do not reflect God because each actualizes only a single Divine Name; they cannot, therefore, be perfect 'servants. ' The second characteristic feature of the Perfect Man consists in his being in a certain sense the Absolute itself...The Absolute, in its self-revealing aspect, reaches perfection in the Perfect Man. In the latter the Absolute manifests itself in the most perfect form, and there can be no self-manifestation more perfect than this. The Perfect Man, in this respect, IS THE ABSOLUTE, while at the same time a creature.[326]

According to Esoteric Islam, Allah manifested Himself as the Perfect Man in a "luminous, fiery form." This Perfect Man is the same as the Adam Qadmon of Esoteric Judaism. This Perfect Man, Allah, was made of light. Some early Muslim scholars described Allah in this state as such: "*He had the limbs of a man, He was a...light in the form of a man and His hair was black light ...*"[327] The

---

[325] Ibid., 211.
[326] Ibid., 231.
[327] A.S, Tritten, *Islam* (London: Hutchinsons University Library, 1951) 36.

Light from which the body of *Insan Karnil* was formed is called *Nur Allah* or the Light of Allah.[328] The Body of Light is called *Al-Surah Ai-Ilahijyah*, The Divine Form. This Divine Form is the same as the *Kavod* or Form of Esoteric Judaism (Qaballah). The Form is named Muhammad ('One worthy of praise').

The First Man is Esoteric Islam was not named Adam, but Muhammad. Not Muhammad ibn Abdullah of Arabia (P.B.U.H.). This Muhammad is Allah as the Divine Form. The Arabic letters of the name Muhammad produce a human figure (Figure 31), which is liken unto the Divine Form of Allah. According to a Tradition of Ibn 'Abbas, the Prophet's cousin,

> He (Allah) brought about (human) creation through the form of the name Muhammad...The head is shaped round like the letter *Mim*, and the hands like the letter *Ha*: the belly like the letter *Mim*, the feet like the letter *Dal*.[329]

Allah as the Divine Form, the Man of Light, is called Muhammad. When the Divine Form cloaks itself in matter, It is called Adam. This process is symbolically described in the Holy Qur'an. There are three different accounts of the "Creation" of Adam that will concern us and they each reveal an important detail. The first mention of the formation of Adam is in 2:30.

> *30. And when thy Lord said to the angels, I am going to place a ruler in the earth, they said: Wilt Thou place in it such as make mischief in it and shed blood? And we celebrate Thy praise and extol Thy holiness. He said: Surely I know what you know not.*
> *31. And He taught Adam all the names...*

---

[328] John Macdonald, "Islamic Eschatology-1," *Islamic Studies*, 3 (1964): 285-308.
[329] Ibid., 294.

# The name Muhammad in Arabic. Read from right to left.

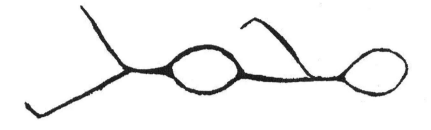

## The Secret of the name Muhammad

Figure 31

The word translated as "ruler" is often translated as "vicegerent." However, neither translation captures the true meaning of the Arabic word here used. The word *Khalifah*, according to Maulana Muhammad Ali, comes from *khalafa* which means "*he came after or succeeded another that had perished or died.*"[330] The One that Adam succeeded is Allah. How is it said that Allah perished or died? Prior to Adam, Allah existed as the Divine Form - a man of Light with no material body. Adam represents Allah in His material state. Once Allah's body materializes in Adam, He no longer exists as the Divine Form. It exists as the Inner Man of this Adam, but has no independent existence. This is why the word used here for man is *insan*. According to Ibn Arabi, one of the greatest Sufi scholars, this word *insan* has the meaning of 'pupil' as well as 'man.'

Furthermore, (he deserves to be named Man - *insan* - because) he (Adam) is to God as the pupil (*insan*) is to the eye as the instrument of vision, i.e. seeing. Thus he is called *insan* because God (The Divine Form) beheld His creatures through man, and had Mercy upon them.[331]

The Divine Form wrapped itself in a material cloak and viewed the world through the material eyes of this material cloak called Adam. Thus Prophet Muhammad (P.B.U.H.) said, "*Allah created Adam in His Form.*" The Form is the Divine Form. This Adam represents the sum total of all the Names of Allah. This is why it is said in verse 31, "*And He taught Adam all the Names.*" According to Ibn Arabi, this means Adam "actualizes all Divine Names."

The second narrative we will look at in the Qur'an treating Adam's creation is in Sura (Chapter) 15:28.

26. *And surely We created man of sounding clay, of BLACK MUD fashioned into shape.*
27. *And the jinn, We created before of intensely hot fire.*

---

[330] Maulana Muhammad Ali translation of the *Holy Qur'an*, 17, n. 48
[331] Izutsu, *Comparative Study*, 218.

*28. And when thy Lord said to the angels: I am going to create a
mortal of sounding clay, of Black Mud fashioned into shape.
29. So when I have made him complete and breathed into him of
My spirit, fall down making obeisance to him.
30. So the angels made obeisance, all of them together-
31. But Iblis (did it not) . . .*

Here Adam is described as being made from "black mud (*hama*)
fashioned into shape." (15:26) After being made "complete," Allah
"breathed into him of My Spirit." This Black Mud represents the
primordial material darkness mixed with the primordial waters
from which Allah created Himself. This is the black material that
Allah adorned. In Abu Layth's tenth century collection of Ibn
Abbas's Traditions, this "Black Mud" is described as "flesh, blood,
veins and sinews."[332] This is why the angels and everything in the
earth are ordered to "make obeisance (*sajada*)" to this Black Adam,
while at the same time the Qur'an says: "And *to Allah makes
obeisance every living creature that is in the heavens and earth, and the
angels too (1 6:49).*" And also: "*Whoever is in the heavens and the earth
makes obeisance to Allah ONLY, willingly or unwillingly (13:15).*" This
again is a picture of Allah's Self-Creation out of Triple Darkness 76
trillion years ago.

The final narrative is Sura 38:71-88. The important detail here
is in verse 75. After Iblis refused to make obeisance to this Black
Adam like the rest of the angels, Allah says: "*0 Iblis, what prevented
thee from submitting to him whom I have created with BOTH MY
HANDS?*" According to Esoteric Islam, the "Two Hands" of Allah
by which Adam was created represent the Spiritual and Material
Nature of Adam/God.

> You must have understood by now the real nature of
> Adam's body, i.e. his outward 'form,' as well as the real
> nature of his spirit (*ruh*), i.e. his inward 'form.' Adam is the
> Absolute (in view of his inward form) and (represents) the
> creatures (in view of his outward form)...God joined His
> two hands for (creating) Adam. This He did solely in order
> to show his high position ... The (joining of His two hands)
> symbolizes nothing other than the fact that Adam joins in

---

[332] Macdonald, "Islamic Eschatology," 297.

138

him two' forms '; the form of the world and the form of the Absolute. These two are the 'hands' of God.[333]

The Inner Man of this Black Adam is Allah Himself, according to Esoteric Islam. Thus the Prophet said again, "*He who knows himself knows his Lord.*"[334] Adam's body is thus called *Ruhiyyah-badabiyya*" meaning "spiritual-bodily." This is why it is written in the Qur'an that Allah is the Manifest and the Hidden (57:3). He is the Hidden Spiritual Body and the Manifest Material Body.

*6.7. Seven, the Name of God*

The sacred cosmologies of the great religions of antiquity say the same basic thing:
    1. In the beginning, God the Father existed as an Abstract Deity in the Womb of Space called Mother. The Abstract Father God, represented by the Circle [◘], lay latent, unmanifested, for an unspecified amount of time.
    2. At a certain period, called The Hour, The Circle produced The Point [☉], which means the Abstract Father manifested Himself as an A-tom, the manifest Son. This Son grew until he became the Diameter [⊕], at which point He becomes Man, the Creator.    The Prophet Zara Thustra from Persia (Zoraster), to whom God revealed the *Zend Advesta*, taught that the Abstract Father, the Boundless Circle, was called *Zeruana Akerne*. From Zeruana issues *Ahura Mazda*, the Creator, who was a Man.[335] The Abstract Father of Egypt was *Kneph*,[336] the Manifest Son, *Atum*.    The Abstract Father of India was *Parabrahm*, the Manifest Son, *Brahma*. And so on.  In every case, the Son is the Vehicle through which the abstract Father manifests Himself and the Son is also the Creator.  They are actually the same God during two different stages of development. Thus Jesus could proclaim, "I and my Father are One"

---

[333] Izutsu, *Comparative Study*, 219, 222.
[334] Ibid., 33.
[335]Bramely, *Gods of Eden*, 114-5.
[336]James B. Pritchard, *The Ancient Near East, Volume I & II* (New Jersey: Princeton University Press, 1958) I:1.

Another trait that is consistent in these great religious traditions is that God The Father is represented by a Three Lettered Name, and God The Son is represented by a Four Lettered Name. In India, the Abstract Deity is attributed the ineffable mystic AUM (Figure 32).[337] Ain Soph, according to the *Sepher Yetzirah*, is represented by the three Hebrew letters *A, M, Sh* called the Mother Letters. The Jews also use the letters IAO to represent the Hidden Deity, just as the Chaldeans did.

Figure 32
The Mystic *AUM* of Hinduism

The Infinite All is designated by three letters and symbolized by the triangle.[338]Three is the Spiritual Number because the spiritual nature of Man is threefold.[339] Three thus best represents God as the Infinite Spirit. As Maurice, in his *Indian Antiquities*, says: *"Nearly all the Pagan (non-Christian) nations of antiquity, in their various theological systems, acknowledged a trinity in the divine nature."*[340] The Three represents God as "indivisible in essence and indivisible in action".[341]

---

[337]Higgins, *Anacalypsis*, I:106.
[338]Blavatsky says, *"The triangle being a symbol of Deity everywhere."* **Secret Doctrine**, .I: 113.
[339]Hall, *Secret Teachings of All Ages*, XLIV.
[340]Maurice, *Indian Antiquities* VI: 35.
[341]Doan, *Bible Myths*, 369.

God The Son is designated by the Four Lettered Name or the Tetragrammaton. Blavatsky observes:

> Every anthropomorphic god (god in human form), in old nations, as Marcelinus Vicinus well observed, has his name written with four letters. Thus with Egyptians, he was Teut; the Arabs, Alla; the Persians Sire; the Magi, Orsi; the Mahometans, Abdi; the Greeks, Theos; the ancient Turks Esar, the Latins, Deus; to which J. Lorenzo Anania adds the Germanic Gott; the Sarmatian Bouh, etc., etc.[342]

The quaternary always represents the physical nature of Man,[343] which is made from the Four Elements: Hydrogen, Oxygen, Nitrogen and Carbon. Henry Drummond, in his *Natural Law in the Spiritual World*, explains:

> If we analyze this material point at which all life starts, we shall find it to consist of a clear structureless, jelly-like substance resembling albumen or white of egg. It is made of Carbon, Hydrogen, Oxygen and Nitrogen. Its name is protoplasm and it is not only the structural unit with which all living bodies start in life, but with which they are subsequently built up. 'Protoplasm', Huxley says, 'simple and nucleated, is the formal basis of all life. It is the clay of the Potter.[344]

These Four, also representing Fire (Hydrogen), Earth (Carbon), Air (Nitrogen) and Water (Oxygen), were termed the "four sons of God" by the Egyptians and the "four Maharajahs" by the ancient Indians. Thus, the Four Lettered Name of God designated the physical nature of God, God as The Diameter, the Manifest Son. Brahma, in the *Vishnu Purana* (Book I, ch. V), is described as the manifest quaternary or fourfold. The Jewish Adam Qadmon is called "He of the Four Letters."[345] Those Four

---

[342]Blavatsky, *Secret Doctrine*, .II:602-3.
[343]Hall, *Secret Teachings of All Ages*, XLIV.
[344]Ibid., CV.
[345]Blavatsky, *Secret Doctrine*, II: 596.

letters are the Tetragrammaton, which is the Hebrew letters Y [י],

H [ה], W [ו], H [ה]. This is Yahweh, the anthropomorphic god of the Hebrew Bible. ADAM QADMON IS YAHWEH. Called the Grand Man of the Zohar, Adam Qadmon is the grand manifestation of Ain Soph. This Black God is described as the *mercabah* or throne-chariot of Ain Soph, who *"used the (heavenly form, Adam Qodman) as a chariot through which to descend, and wished to be called by this form, WHICH IS THE SACRED NAME YAHWEH (Zohar)."* This, we are told, is the key to the Riddle of God: *"Whosoever acquaints himself with…the* mercabah *and the* lahgash (secret speech), *will learn the secret of secrets."*

God's Full Name is thus composed of the Three and the Four Letters, or the Seven Letters. Thus the Greek poets said: *"Seven sounding letters sing the praises of Me, The immortal God, the Almighty deity."*[346] The union of the Three Letters and the Four Letters is MAN, called the Third Septenary.[347] Hall explains:

The 3 (Spirit, Mind and Soul) descend into the 4 (the world) the sum being the 7, or the mystic nature of man, consisting of a threefold spiritual body and a fourfold material form.[348]

The Occultists call MAN *Saptaparna* meaning the "seven leafed plant." He is represented by the Triangle (His Spiritual nature) over the Square (His material nature). This MAN is called the "Seven Lettered God"[349] and is the answer to the Great Riddle of the Seven Vowels. In the Gnostic text *Pistis Sophia*, Jesus says,

No mystery is more excellent than they (the seven vowels): for they shall bring your souls unto the Light of Lights…Nothing, therefore, is more excellent than the mysteries which ye seek after, saving only THE MYSTERY OF THE SEVEN VOWELS.

---

[346]Ibid., II: 603.
[347]Ibid., II: 590.
[348]Hall, *Secret Teachings of All Ages*, LXXII.
[349] Blavatsky, *Secret Doctrine*, I:410.

142

Hall refers to the Seven Vowels as *"the unwritten vowels, which together make up the name of the manifested deity."*[350] The Secret of the Seven Vowels, the Secret of the Tetragrammaton, the Secret of the Masonic Word (see below), the Secret of the Riddle of the Sphinx, are all one and the same - MAN, the Black Man.

While Seven (7) is the number of God as the Divine Man, Six (6) is the number of Man's imperfect physical creation, as Mr. Muhammad teaches.[351]  Madam Blavatsky says in *The Secret Doctrine*:

> Now, the number six has been regarded in the ancient mysteries as an emblem of physical nature.  For six is the representation  of the six  dimensions of all bodies (top, bottom, front, back, right, and left)....Therefore, while the 'senary' was applied by the sages to 'physical' man, the 'septenary' was for them the symbol of that man 'plus' his immortal soul.[352]

The Third Septenary is thus referred to as the "Perfect MAN" by the ancients. The Triangle is invisible while the Square is on the plane of objective perception. The following diagram shows the breakdown of the Third Divine Septenary-Man (Figure 33).

And as would be expected, the septenary manifests itself throughout the nature of MAN.  Nearly all ancient theologies (at least, the Indian, Egyptian, Hebrew, Druid, etc.) acknowledged the Seven Souls or Principles of MAN.  The Indian and Egyptian are thus:

|  | Indian | Egyptian |
|---|---|---|
| 1. | *Atma* – Pure Spirit | 1. *Kha* – Spirititual Double |
| 2. | *Prana* – Breath of Life | 2. *Ba* – Ancestral Soul |
| 3. | *Astral Body* | 3. *Sheut* - Shadow |
| 4. | *Buddhi* – Spiritual Soul | 4. *Ib* - Heart |
| 5. | *Manas* – Intelligence | 5. *Akhu* - Intelligence |
| 6. | *Kama* – Animal Soul | 6. *Ren* - Name |
| 7. | *Rupa* – body or form | 7. *Ha* - Body |

---

[350] *Old Testament Wisdom*, 98.
[351]Muhammad, *Theology of Time*, 109.
[352]Blavatsky, *Secret Doctrine*, II: 591.

# The Triune Nature of God (Man)

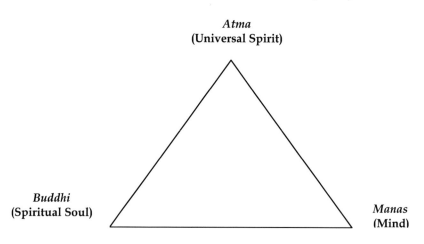

*Atma*
(Universal Spirit)

*Buddhi*
(Spiritual Soul)

*Manas*
(Mind)

## Quaternary Nature (Body) of God (Man)

| | | |
|---|---|---|
| Oxygen | **Water** **Fire** | Hydrogen |
| Nitrogen | **Air** **Earth** | Carbon |

Figure 33
God, the Divine Septenary

144

The septenary is also manifested in MAN's physical composition, as Hall observes in *MAN: Grand Symbol of the Mysteries:*

> physiology, as imperfect as it is, shows septenary groups all over the exterior and interior body: the seven orifices, the seven 'organs' at the base of the brain, the seven plexuses...the seven sacred organs about the heart, the seven layers of the epidermis, the seven ductless glands of first importance, the seven methods by which the body is vitalized, the seven sacred breaths, the seven body systems (bones, nerves, arteries, muscles, etc.), the seven layers of the auric egg, the seven major divisions of the embryo, the seven senses...and the seven-year periods into which human life is divided.[353]

MAN, the great Septenary or Seven Lettered God, was recognized by our ancient forefathers and mothers as the *"summation of all the possibilities immanent in the Universe,"* according to de Lubicz in *The Temple In Man*.[354] MAN was the "Key to the Riddle of Life" and thus the answer to the Great Riddle of the Sphinx.[355] And as such, the ancients erected a statue of the Grand MAN in the midst of their Temples as a "textbook." This statue was covered with hieroglyphics and opened showing the internal organs. By studying this textbook, man could obtain 360 degrees of knowledge. The ancient Egyptians thus proclaimed "Know Thy Self." The Grand MAN, The Black Man, is God.

---

[353]Hall, *Man: Grand Symbol of the Mysteries*, 63.
[354]de Lubicz, *Temple in Man*, 25.
[355]Hall, *Secret Teachings of All Ages*, LXXIII.

## CHAPTER VII:

# *The Black Woman: God's Co-Creator*

*7.1. The Black God and his Black Goddess*

Another important aspect of the ancient understanding of God was that the male God was always balanced with the female Goddess. You did not find the God without a feminine expression of that God. They always came in pairs as the Ma'atic Balance demanded. Thus, in ancient Kemet (Egypt), there was in the very beginning the pairs: *Nun* and *Naunet* (primeval water and counter heaven); *Hugh* and *Hauhet* (the boundless and its compliment); *Kuk* and *Kauket* (darkness and its compliment); and *Amun* and *Amaunet* (the hidden and its compliment).[356] This was true in Ancient Babylon, Ancient Canaan, and throughout the Ancient World. They came as a couple: Anu/Antu, Asar/Asat, El/Elat, Allah/Allat, ect.

But today, in Western Judaism, Western Christianity, and Western Islam, the Goddess, feminine expression of the God, has been buried. It is the Honorable Elijah Muhammad who brought her back and taught that the Black Woman was the "CO-CREATOR" with God. He said there was never a time when the Black God Allah was without his Goddess, the Black Woman.

The Western World understands the origin of Woman according to the narrative in the second chapter of Genesis. Adam, so the story goes, was made to go to sleep by God. During his rest, God took one of Adam's ribs and made from it Eve, his help-meet. This tale, though essentially rooted in truth, has been interpreted through the sexist eyes of Western Man and, as such, has been the springboard for many of his discriminating and abusive ways toward women. The actual history which is at the root of this narrative, however, completely reverses the interpretation and precludes any condescending outlook on womanhood.

---

[356] Nobles, *African Psychology*, 41.

Muhammad teaches that after Allah created Himself, His first feeling was that of loneliness and His first desire was to reproduce Himself. He began to scientifically study Himself and found within Him a second self: the X chromosome. Allah The Original Man proceeded to give that Second Self an independent form. Because He had so much love and respect for the Womb from which He sprung, He put that same womb in the Second Self that He created. Thus was born Womb-man or Woman. The Black Woman was, according to the Honorable Elijah Muhammad, the very first creation of God after He created Himself. Before there was a sun, moon, or star, Muhammad says, there was the Black Woman. These two, Allah The Original Man (God) and His Second Self became the first man and woman, the progenitors of the whole human family. She is the Co-creator with God. This is what Muhammad teaches.

This is also what the Black man and woman of antiquity taught. According to the *Law of Manu*, after Brahma emerged out of darkness, he created from his own body *Vach*, his female self. Brahma and Vach were thus the first man and woman in existence. Through Vach, Brahma reproduces himself as *Viraj*. Viraj is Brahma again,[357] just as the Egyptian god Ptah is reborn as his own son, *Iu-em-hept*. Vach is described as the "Queen of the Gods" and the Earth "who yields us nourishment and sustenance."[358]

## 7.2. *Holy Mary, Mother of God*

The ancient theo-cosmologies called the Primordial Space 'the Virgin Mother' and the Universal Egg. Mother Space is always represented as the Mother Goddess, the most famous being the Egyptian Aset or Isis. The Christian world got their Virgin Mary from this Holy Virgin, who gave birth to the Son (Man-God) without ever knowing man.[359] As the Eternal Matrix of Space, she is rightfully called the Virgin Mother of God. Once the Spirit fecundates in her (i.e. when it begins its movement toward self-creation) and they conceive the Son (i.e. the Male Creator God),

---

[357] Blavatsky, *Secret Doctrine*, I: 137.
[358] Ibid., I:434.
[359] Hall, *Secret Teachings of All Ages*, XLV.

the Creator God then goes back into the Womb of Darkness to create the cosmos. The Mother of God then becomes, metaphorically, the Wife of God. After he creates from himself the woman and places in her the Womb, the metaphorical 'Mother of God' becomes the physical Wife of God. Thus, in Egypt, the Father God called Amun (The Hidden) was called "the husband of his mother," meaning the Goddess Mut. Mut was hailed as the "queen of Heaven," "the Earth" and "Mother." The Indian God Brahma, as Prajapati, was called "His mother's husband."[360]

One of the oldest religious symbols is that of the Virgin Mother with the infant Son in her arms (Figure 34). This is Isis and Osiris of Egypt. Osiris the Father God is reborn as his own son Horus through his wife/mother Isis.[361] This religious symbol, found all over the earth, represents the Eternal Virgin Mother Space and the Manifest Son who is the Creator and Father Incarnate. The Virgin Mother (Space) is Black and thus the God (Son) is Black. Paul Boyd observes:

> The representations of the Goddess Mother and Child in the respective countries have in general been recorded as being Black in complexion. In India, the Goddess Mother and Child, Isi and Iswara; in China, Shing-Moo or Ma Tsoopo with child in her arms; In Asia, Cybele and Deoius; and in Mexico, Ciuacoatl and Quetzacoatl, all had Black complexions."[362]

And the same is true for the Virgin Mary and Jesus. In all the Roman countries of Europe, the Virgin Mother and Child are Black; in the Cathedral at Mouins; the Church of St. Stephen at Genoa; the Church of St. Francisco at Pisca; the Church at Brixen in Tyrol and all over.[363] This universal icon represents Mother Space and the Manifest God (Son). (Figure 35)

---

[360]Blavatsky, *Secret Doctrine*, I: 91.
[361]Boyd, *African Origin of Christianity*, 66.
[362]Ibid., 90.
[363]Higgins *Anacalypsis*, II: 137-139.

Figure 34
Isis and infant Horus

Figure 35
The Fedorovo Virgin, 18th century Russia


The Goddess was the conveyer of Allah's Mercy. The Quranic chapters begin *"Bishmillah ir'Rahman ir'Rahim,"* meaning "In the Name of Allah, the Beneficent, the Merciful." The *Rahim* or Merciful nature of God is manifest in the Woman.[364] A stern father disciplines his child with a rod of iron. But God put the quality of mercy, His Mercy, in the nature of Woman. Thus, Paul C. Boyd notes in *The African Origin of Christianity*:

(The Mother Goddess) was the light and the hope of the world and she was named the Mylitta in Babylon. Under

---

[364]Louis Farrakhan, Madison Square Garden, Oct. 1985 lecture.

that title she was 'The Mediatrix' or in other words, 'the Mediator', which suggests that she was the most virtuous and COMPASSIONATE of women....(U)dner the title of 'The Mediatrix,' the Aphrodite was in reality 'the wrath-subduer.' It is a Chaldee expression and comes from the words 'aph' meaning 'wrath' and 'Radah' meaning 'to subdue'....In Athens, she was Amarusia, 'the Mother of Gracious Acceptance'; and, finally, in China, she was the goddess, Kuayin, 'the goddess of mercy'."[365]

## 7.3. *The Divine Secret in Woman*

The Honorable Louis Farrakhan, in his historic "WHO IS GOD?" lecture delivered at Christ Universal Temple, Chicago, Illinois on February 24, 1991, says these most profound words:

The woman is made after the womb out of which God created Himself, and in the woman is the Secret of God. The reason you are far away from God is because of your attitude towards women. You will never find God and you will never grow to honor God, as long as you are a mistreater and disrespecter of women. THE WOMAN IS THE SECRET AND SHE CONTAINS THE SECRET....The riddle has been with God, but the secret of the riddle is in woman, and unless and until we become better acquainted with who <u>she</u> is, you may never see who <u>you</u> are.

The Secret of God is revealed in the Womb of Woman during the Nine months of pregnancy. Mr. Muhammad teaches that the whole Self Creation of God is re-enacted during those Nine months a child develops in its mother's womb. Thoth Hermes, the Egyptian god of wisdom, said the same thing when he addressed his son Tatian thousands of years ago:

If thou will contemplate the Creator even in perishable things, in things which are on earth, or in the deep, reflect,

---

[365]Boyd, *African Origin of Christianity*, 76.

O my son, ON THE FORMATION OF MAN IN HIS MOTHER'S WOMB.[366]

The Ray of light of the *Book of Dzyan*, which falls into the Mother-Deep and impregnates the Germ, is the Sperm (Spirit or Ray) entering the Mother-Deep or Womb of the Woman and impregnating the Egg or Germ.[367] From the union of these two polar opposites (Ray/Germ, positive/negative electricity, Spirit/Matter) the Son (Atom) is produced in the Womb of Space as the Son (Cell) is produced in the Womb of Woman. From the One Atom came many millions of atoms to form the Body of God; and in the Womb of Woman, the One Cell divides (mitosis) into millions of cells and forms the Body of Man.

God's physical evolution, The Six Days of Creation, are reenacted in the Womb of Woman. The initial Cell, representing the Mineral Kingdom, proceeds through the higher kingdoms until it reaches MAN. Blavatsky describes the process:

> At the end of three or four weeks the ovum has assumed a plant-like appearance, one extremity having become spheroidal and the other tapering like a carrot. Upon dissection it is found to be composed, like the onion, of very delicate laminae or coats, enclosing a liquid. The laminae approach each other at the lower end, and the embryo hangs from the root of the umbilicus almost like fruit from the bough. The stone (mineral) has now become changed, by 'metempsychosis,' into a plant. Then the embryonic creature begins to shoot out, from the inside outward, its limbs, and develops its features. The eyes are visible as two black dots; the ears, nose, and mouth form depressions...before they begin to project. The embryo develops into an animal-like fetus-the shape of a tadpole-and, like the amphibious reptile, lives in water and develops from it.[368]

---

[366]Hall, *Man: Grand Symbol of the Mysteries,* 39.
[367] Mircea Eliade, "Spirit, Light, and Seed," *History of Religion* 11 (1971); 1-30.
[368]Blavatsky, *Secret Doctrine,* II: 188.

The "tadpole" then becomes human in the "fourth hour." Lefevre, in *Philosophy* also acknowledged the said above. On page 484 he says:

> A very strong argument in favor of variability is supplied by the science of Embryology. Is not a man in the uterus...a simple cell, a vegetable with three or four leaflets, a tadpole with branchiae, a mammal with a tail, lastly a primate and a biped (man)? It is scarcely possible not to recognize in the embryonic evolution a rapid sketch, a faithful summary, of the entire organic series.

The Secret of God in Woman.

# Chapter VIII:

# *The Secret of All Ages*

8.1. *The Secret of God and the Ancient Mysteries*

The knowledge of God has been a closely guarded secret for over 50,000 years. The secret was held by The Mysteries and the secret societies. Manley P. Hall says of the Great Mysteries of ancient Egypt:

> there was...a secret theological system in which God was considered as the Grand Man and, conversely, man as the little god."[369]

In Edouard Schure's **Hermes and Plato**, a hierophant (teacher) from the Mysteries is quoted instructing his student:

> Remember that there are two main keys to knowledge. This is the first: 'The without is like the within of things, the small is like the large; there is only one law and he who works is One...And this is the second:' **MEN ARE MORTAL GODS AND GODS ARE IMMORTAL MEN.'** Happy the man who understands these words, for he holds the key to all things.[370]

Nesta Webster, in her **Secret Societies and Subversive Movements**, says:

> The war now begins between the two principles: the Christian conception of men reaching up to God and the secret society conception of MAN AS GOD.[371]

---

[369]Hall, *Secret Teachings of All Ages*, CXXIII.

[370]Schure, *Hermes and Plato*, 53.

[371]Nesta Webster, *Secret Societies and Subversive Movements* (The Christian Book Club of America, 1924) 30.

154

U.S. Anderson, who has spent almost all of his adult years studying secret societies and esoteric learning, reveals their secret in his book, *The Three Magic Words*:

> YOU ARE GOD. THE VEIL REMOVED. This is the ineffable secret, the ultimate illumination, the key to peace and power. You are God...Though this knowledge is not new, IT HAS BEEN EXCEEDINGLY RARE AND HELD AMONG A VERY FEW MEN.[372]

U.S. Anderson sounds very much like Mr. Muhammad who said:

> You are walking around looking for a God to bow to and worship. YOU ARE THE GOD.[373]

One of the most famous ancient Mysteries patterned after the Egyptian Rites were the Eleusinian Mysteries from Greece, 1400 BC. Allegedly founded by Eamolopas, these Mysteries instructed her white initiates into the Secret of the Black God. Eliphas Levi, in *The History of Magic*, says:

> It was only after the initiate of the Eleusinian mysteries had passed victoriously through all the tests, had seen and touched the holy things, that, if he were judges strong enough to withstand the last and most dreadful secret, a veiled priest passed him at flying pace and uttered in his ear the enigmatic words: OSIRIS IS A BLACK GOD. [374]

8.2. *Masonry and the Secret of God*

The secret of Masonry, the most popular of all secret societies, is: Man is God and God is a Black Man. This is the secret of the WHITE LODGE. Our Prince Hall brothers have a different

---

[372]U.S. Anderson, *The Three Magic Words* (New York: Thomas Nelson & Sons, 1954) 313, 317.

[373]Muhammad, *Our Saviour Has Arrived*, 35.

[374] Page 25.

Masonry from the whites, which is why whites keep the Lodge and the Shrine segregated.

The Nature of God is revealed through the Symbols of Masonry. Harold Waldon Percival, a Master Mason, says in his book for Masons entitled *Masonry and its Symbols* that the culmination of the Masonic purpose is represented by a Temple (Lodge) filed with effulgent light.[375]   This is Man as God.   He says Man's physical body is:

> the...lodge in which all the degrees are worked...The Ground floor is the pelvic section. The Middle Chamber is the abdominal section. The Sanctum Sanctorium is the thoracic section.   The Royal Arch is the physical body in its atmosphere, complete. The top of the head represents the keystone.[376]

The Effulgent Light which fills the Temple or Lodge is the Three Great Lights of Masonry (Bible, Square and Compass) which represent the Triune Self of Man.[377]   This Triune Self is divided into the Doer, Thinker, and Knower and is represented by the three degrees: Apprentice, Fellowcraft and Master Mason. The Master Mason is the Knower, which represents God.   Allah introduces Himself in the *Holy Qur'an*: "I, Allah, am the Best Knower."   Percival says:

> After the candidate has been raised to the degree of Master Mason, he represents the Doer, Thinker, and Knower, each developed to its capacity and coordinated so that they are a trinity, the Triune Self.   This trinity is in Masonry represented by a right-angled triangle in the lodge.[378]

---

[375]Harold Waldin Percival, *Masonry and its Symbols* (Dallas: The Word Foundation, Inc., 1980) 45.

[376]Ibid., xxii.

[377]Ibid., 10.

[378]Ibid., 36.

We quote Blavatsky again: *"the triangle being a symbol of Deity everywhere."*[379]

The pathway to God is represented by the Seven Stairs which lead up to the Sanctum Sanctorium where the Master Mason Degree is given. Percival, on the meaning of these stairs, says:

> The body as a whole is King Solomon's Temple....The entrance or first step is the prostate, the second step symbolizes the kidneys, the third the adrenals, the fourth the heart, the fifth the lungs, the sixth the pituitary body AND THE SEVENTH THE PINEAL GLAND.[380]

These Seven Stairs which lead to the Hall of the Master Mason (God) sound like the Seven Chakras which are MAN's 'internal' stairs to Godhood (see below).

The Word of the Mason is the Name of God. As we saw earlier, The Name of God is composed of a First Name possessing Three Letters and a Last Name possessing Four Letters. Percival says the first Name is found in the last letters of the names of the Three Ruffians who murdered Hiram Ablif: Jubela, Jubelo, and Jubelum. Percival says:

> Each has a part of the Word. If their parts were combined they would be AUM or AOM or three of the four parts of the word.[381]

AUM, we remember, is the First Name of God in East Indian tradition as the Absolute, Incorporeal All. The second part of the Masonic Word was revealed by Albert Pike, head of the Supreme Council of 33 in 1889, in his *Morals and Dogma*:

> The True Word of the Mason is to be found in the concealed and profound meaning of the Ineffable Name of Deity (YHWH) communicated by God to Moses...The true pronunciation of that name was in truth a secret, in which,

---

[379]op. cited.
[380]Percival, *Masonry and its Symbols*, 19.
[381]Ibid., 29.

however, was involved the *far more profound secret of its meaning*. In that meaning is included all the truth that can be known by us, in regard to THE NATURE OF GOD.

The Word of the Masons is thus the Full Name of God: the Seven Letters which represent the Septenary Nature of MAN. What is the Secret of the Name, or Nature, YHWH (God) alluded to by Pike? Manley P. Hall, another world renowned Mason, reveals the Secret:

By placing the four letters of the Tetragrammaton in a vertical column, a figure closely resembling the human body is produced, with the *Yod* [ ׳ ] for the head, the first *He* [ ה ] for the arms and shoulders, *Vau* [ ו ] for the trunk of the body, and the final *He* [ ה ] for the hips and legs."382

The Name of Yahweh (YHWH) in Hebrew

Figure 36

The Secret of the Name YHWH

---

382 Hall, *Secret Teachings of All Ages*, CXXIV.

The figure produced is not just that of a human body, *but of a Black Body*.

Once a Mason has earned his 32nd Degree he has the option of joining the Mystic Shrine where he would earn the honorary 33rd Degree. He then leaves the Square (Bible) and starts to use the Compass (Qur'an). It is in the Shrine where the secrets of Masonry are revealed. The Reality of Allah The Original Man is made fully manifest to those whites who are so privileged to receive the Honorary Degree. They then begin calling themselves 'Muslim Sons.'

During initiation into the Shrine, according to former Shriner Jim Shaw, the Grand Puba says these words to the candidate:

> By the assistance of Allah and the Creed of Muhammad; by the legendary sanctity of our Tabernacle at Mecca, we greet you and in commemoration of the Arabs faith as sincere you will now be permitted to proceed in the rites and ceremonies of the Mystic Shrine.[383]

After marching the candidates to a designated area in the temple the gong sounds. The Grand Puba and the Assistant Reban proclaim:

> Who is he who has professed to have conversed in person with the Supreme and maketh himself mightiest of his Muhammad...

[Gong]

(Ass. Reban):

> What shall the (men) who have reflected with adherence that which the Prophet Muhammad hath revealed? Wherefore their works shall not prevail. Do they not travel the earth and see the end of those who went before them?

[Gong]

---

[383] Jim Shaw, "The Mohammadean Rite of the Mystic Shrine," Tape.

(Priest):

Why do unbelievers indulge themselves and eat as beasts. Shall not their portion be a torment. Appeal to the Prophets for Truth…

These are wealthy, influential white men proclaiming that Allah, the Black Man, is God! Such is the Secret of Masonry.

## 8.3. *The Secret of the Vatican*

The Church has many secrets. One of the most important and closely guarded was revealed during an incident connected with a relic of the Apostle Peter. Peter is considered the "beloved of Jesus" and as such was he upon whom Jesus founded his church. The Papal See is supposed to be the legacy of St. Peter. The Vatican claims him as the founder and the Pope his successor. Peter had a particular chair he sat in that would later become the property of the Vatican who celebrated a festival in its honor every January 18th. The chair was exhibited for the adoration of the people. In 1662, however, the festival was abruptly terminated.

That year, upon being cleaned, it was discovered that engraved on it was a god thought to be Hercules because he is pictured with what is thought to be representations of the Twelve Labors of Hercules. Giacomo Bartolini, who was present at the discovery, stated that Pope Clement X rewarded an author for his attempt to come up with a cover story .[384] But the most remarkable discovery was made some years later by the French. Godfrey Higgins recounts:

> When the wicked French got possession of Rome, they did not fail to examine this celebrated relic, and lo! In addition to the labours of Hercules, they discovered engraved upon

---

[384] Higgins, *Anacalypsis*, I:691-2.

it, in Arabic letters, THE MOHAMEDAN CONFESSION
OF FAITH."[385]

The so-called "Mohamedan confession of faith" is *Ashadu-an-la-illaha-illa-Allah* meaning "I bear witness there is no God but Allah." That god, Black God, is not Hercules: it is Allah The Original Man. Higgins concludes:

> I can scarcely conceive a more marked proof of the nature
> of the secret doctrine of the Conclave (Vatican).[386]

---

[385] Ibid.
[386] Ibid.

# CHAPTER IX:

# *Ye Are Gods*

9.1. *Gods of Old*

God the Originator's physical body had to return to its earthly source just as ours will. But He did not die. His spirit lives on through His Children, the Black Man and Woman, who everyone should now know as the Original People of the Planet Earth. We sprung directly from God Himself. These "Original People" have been described by all the ancient writings as a Divine People with great powers. The Mexican scripture *Popol-Vuh* describes the Original People as a people *"whose sight was unlimited, and who knew all things at once"*. The *Popol-Vuh* as well as the *Book of Dzyan* attribute to these primordial Black folk the ability to *"fly as well as they could walk."*[387]

These ancient Blacks were recognized as the Family of God. These are the "gods" of ancient history. Prehistoric Egypt and Chaldea are said to have been the "Land of the Gods." In Egypt these gods were called *Neteru,*[388] and in Chaldea the *Anunnaki,* meaning "Those Who from Heaven to Earth Came."[389] Zecharia Sitchin, scholar of ancient Near Eastern civilizations, says in his ***The 12th Planet*** concerning these "ancient gods":

> They were the "olden gods" of the epic tales, and, in the Sumerian belief, they had come down to earth from the heavens.
>
> These were no mere local deities. They were national gods-indeed, international gods... They were powerful, capable of feats beyond mortal ability or comprehension. Yet these gods not only looked like humans but ate and drank like them and displayed virtually every human

---

[387]Blavatsky, *Secret Doctrine,* II: 55.

[388] Budge, *Egyptian Book of the Dead,* lxxxiii.

[389]Zecharia Sitchin, *Genesis Revisited* (New York: Avon Books, 1990) 19.

emotion of love and hate, loyalty and infidelity.[390]

The ancient Cannaanites called them *Banu 'ili*, "the Sons of El (God)," and the Hebrews *Bene'elyon* (Sons of the Most High).[391] We meet with them in the enigmatic verses of Chapter 6 of Genesis:

> And it came to pass, when men began to multiply on the face of the earth, and daughters were born to them,
> 2 That the Sons of God (*bene'eloheim*) saw the daughters of men (Caucasian Adam) that they were fair; and took them wives of all which they chose....
> 4 There were giants in the earth in those days; and also after that, when the Sons of God came in unto the daughters of men, and they bare children to them, the same became mighty men which were of old, men of renown.

Mr. Muhammad teaches us that this is the beginning of miscegenation. It happened in Arabia when the Adamic[392] Caucasians lived among the Righteous, here called Sons of God, six thousand years ago. Rabbi Yonah N. Ibn Ahron, Hebrew and Near Eastern scholar who speaks over twenty Middle Eastern and Eurasian languages, seems to agree with Mr. Muhammad. He says:

> the earliest Biblical reference to GENETIC VARIATION within the human family is in the sixth chapter of Genesis, where we read :'And it came to pass when Man began to multiply on the face of the earth and daughters were born unto them and the Sons of Those on High (Sons of God) saw the daughters of Man[393]

---

[390]Sitchin, *12th Planet*, 89.

[391]E.T. Mullen, *The Assembly of the Gods* (Chico, California: Scholar Press, 1980) 117.

[392]I must clear up the "Adamic" confusion". The Adam of Genesis has two meanings, for there are two Adams described. One is the A.T.O.M., God Himself. The other, born 4004 B.C., is the Caucasian who is known among historians as the "Adamic race".

[393]Ivan Sanderson, *Abominable Snowman*, 377.

Michael Bradley, in his *Chosen People from the Caucuses*, agrees:

> Without resorting to either mystical or extraterrestrial conjectures, we can say, at least, that 'those from on high' (Sons of God) and 'men' presumably down below were of the same species. Women bore children to them. The two groups were 'inter fertile,' the same species. It is equally certain, however, that 'those from on high' on the one hand, and 'men' on the other hand were of markedly different races (emphasis original).[394]

The word translated "giants"(Gen.6:4) is *Nephilim*. According to Rabbi Yohan the Sons of God were called such "because men would fall (*nophel*) on their faces with fright at the sight of them."[395] By the use of this term to describe the Sons of God, the Bible connects them with the "gods" (*Anunnaki*) of Sumner. In Numbers 13:33, the Nephilim are called the "sons of Anak". "Anak" or "Anakim," according to Zecharia Sitchin, is the Hebrew rendering of Anunnaki.[396]

These ancient Black gods were called "the Children of Heaven" by the *Book of Jubilees*[397], "Sons of the God of Heaven" and "Holy Ones" by the *Book of Noah*.[398] Madame Blavatsky says of these "Sons of God":

> This race could live with equal ease in water, air, or fire, for it had an unlimited control over the elements. These were the 'Sons of God'...It was they who imparted Nature's most weird secrets to men, and revealed to them the ineffable, and now lost 'word'.[399]

---

[394]Michael Bradley, *Chosen People from the Caucasus* (Chicago: Third World Press, 1992) 121.

[395]Ibid., 120.

[396] Sitchin, *Divine Encounters*, 74.

[397]Ibid., 75.

[398]Ibid., 81-2. The *Book of Jubilees* and *Book of Noah* are apochraphal scriptures.

[399]Blavatsky, *Secret Doctrine*, II: 220.

Creuzer says of them:

> Those Children of Heaven and Earth were endowed at their birth by the Sovereign Powers, the authors of their being, with extraordinary faculties both moral and physical. They commanded the Elements, knew the secrets of heaven and the earth, of the sea and the whole world, and read futurity in the stars...It seems, indeed, as though one has to deal, when reading of them, not with men as we are but with Spirits of the Elements sprung from the bosom of Nature and having full sway over her...all these beings are marked with a character of magic and sorcery[400]

The *Holy Qur'an* also attributes to the Black Adam (A.T.O.M., as opposed to the Caucasian Adamites) and his children control over the forces of nature.[401] These are the Gods of Antiquity: The Black Man and Woman. It is not enough to teach that "We were Kings." We were (are) Gods. But this all begs the question, WHAT HAPPENED? Today we are not controlling ourselves much less the forces of nature. How did we lose that glory?

*9.2. The Fall of Man (God)*

One of the most revealing, and neglected, verses of the Bible is Psalms 82:6-8. It reads:

> I have said, YE ARE GODS; AND ALL OF YOU ARE CHILDREN OF THE MOST HIGH.
> 7. But ye shall die like men (*Adam*), and fall like one of the princes.
> 8. ARISE, O GOD, judge the earth: for thou shalt inherit all nations

This is the Fall of Man that the ancient writings recognize. As we mentioned earlier, there were actually Three Falls - Spiritual,

---

[400]Ibid., II:285.
[401]Ali, *The Holy Qur'an*, 19, ft. 56;31:20.

Mental and Physical. The first was the Spiritual Fall or Descent which began 76 trillion years ago and culminated with the Spirit's descent into fleshy matter. The Second was the Mental Fall. This took place 50, 000 years ago. This is when our Higher Selves, due to rebellious living, went to sleep, and the All Seeing Eye of MAN closed. The *Book of Dzyan* says *"Then the Third Eye acted no longer"."* Once the Third Eye closed, the Immortal MAN became mortal god.

The Fall mentioned in Psalms 82:7 is the Mental Fall which occurred 50,000 years ago. This is confirmed by the Hebrew text. J. Morgenstern, in "The Mythological Background of Psalm 82" says the verse "But ye shall die like men" is properly translated as "ye shall become mortal," thus the gods are sentenced to the loss of immortality. He says:

> That 'ye shall become mortal' is the precise meaning of *'temutun'* here, rather than 'ye shall die", may well be inferred from the context, for there is nowhere the slightest implication that these gods were to die at that very moment and actually the second half of punishment imposed upon them, viz. that they must fall as one of the (princes) implies that this was an additional detail...which must...be visited upon them before the stage of their doom, viz. death, could befall them. This necessitates the conclusion that there must have been some interval between the imposition of this sentence upon them and the execution of the final detail thereof. Accordingly we are compelled to translate *'temutun'* here not 'ye shall die' but '...ye must become mortal...[402]

In Sam. 14:14 that same phrase (*mutun*) is translated "For we are mortal" instead of "For we must surely die". Thus, when the gods "died" and "fell," we became mortal.

As stated above, this "Fall" consisted of the closing of the Third Eye: MAN's pineal gland or Ureaus. Called in medical terminology the "epiphysis cerebri," it is recognized by occultism

---

[402]J. Morgenstern, "The Mythological Background of Psalm 82", *Hebrew Union College Annual* XIV (1939): 73, f80.

as the seat of God-Consciousness in Man. It has been called the All Seeing Eye, the Eye of Siva, the Eye of Osiris, and the Eye of the Gods.

The pineal gland is a cone shaped body joined to the roof of the third ventricle in the brain by a "flattened stalk" called the hebenula or pituitary body. These two (pineal gland and pituitary body) have been called the "head and tail respectively of the Dragon of Wisdom."[403] The pineal gland is so placed that it forms a little door between the third and fourth ventricles, closing the contents of the third (heavenly water) from the fourth.

The third ventricle is the reservoir, so to speak, of a cerebral fluid secreted by the epithelial cells of the chorioid plexuses. This fluid was known by the ancients as the "nectar of life", "divine fluid" and "heavenly water".[404] Hall says of it:

> Is not this 'dew' the lux or light fluid, the pure akasa, the fiery mist, the heavenly luminous water, the Schamayim, or fiery water, the sea of crystalline before the throne of God, the fountain from which flows the four ethereal rivers that water the whole earth?[405]

The pineal gland is the seat of the seventh *chakra* (meaning "wheel of force") or energy center in MAN. According to East Indian tradition there are seven chakras which exist along the spinal column. These energy centers or chakras are stimulated into operation by a "serpentine or twisting force" called in Sanskrit *Kundalini.* Kundalini lies coiled in the sacral plexus, where it rest upon the triangular bone at the bottom of the spine *"in three and one half circles, as does the sleeping serpent over the head of Shiva."*[406]

---

[403]Hall, *MAN: Grand Symbol of the Mysteries,* 214.
[404]Ibid., 140.
[405]Ibid., 143.
[406]Ibid., 192.

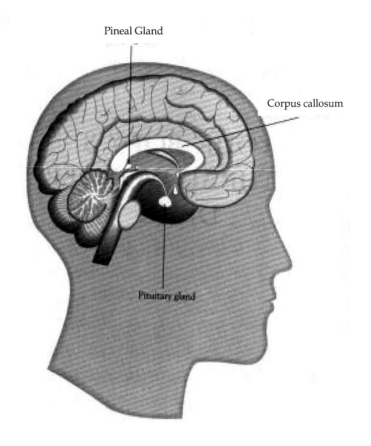

Figure 37
Pineal Gland

   While the Kundalini is at the bottom, the place of the lowest chakra called *Muladhara*, the carnal, animal nature of Man is stimulated and His *kama-manas* or animal-mind is Lord. When that serpentine force or Kundalini is at the pineal gland, the Seventh Chakra called *Sahasrara* is activated and the Third Eye is opened. Man is thus in union with His Higher Self which is God. His *buddhi-manas* or divine mind is then Lord. When the Black Man and Woman "fell" 50,000 years ago and we lost our immortality, the Kundalini "fell" from the seventh (Divine) chakra to the first (animal) chakra. It is said to have "entered the Nether World." This descent of the Kundalini is one of the meanings of the ancient Summerian tale of The Descent of Ishtar to the Nether World.[407]

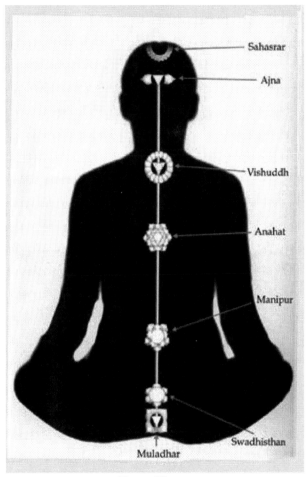

Figure 39
The Seven Chakras

We have been living a terrestrial and carnal existence since then. The reclaiming of our former glory and immortality would then require us to raise the Kundalini back up the spinal column,

[407]See Pritchard, *The Ancient Near East,* I: 80-85.

operating the intermediate chakras (2-6) in the process, until it reaches its destination in the Holy City Mecca which is the brain. There it will stimulate the pineal gland and the Third Eye, the All Seeing Eye, will once again be opened. Manley P. Hall, in *Man: Grand Symbol of the Mysteries*, describes the process:

> The psychical and occult currents moving in the brain in their ascent through the spinal cord must pass through the cerebral aqueduct which is closed by the trap door of the pineal gland. When this body - the ibis of the Egyptians - 'lies backwards' as it were on its haunches, it closes the opening into the fourth ventricle and forms a sort of stopper. It thus seals the contents of the third ventricle (heavenly water), dividing them from the fourth. When stimulated by Kundalini, the gland stands upright, lifting itself like the head of a cobra snake to strike and, like the head of this snake, the gland increases in size and its little finger-like protuberance (pituitary body) moves with the rapidity of a serpents tong. The pineal gland, having removed itself as an obstruction to the passage between the ventricles, permits the essences in the brain to mingle in a spiritual alchemy.[408]

This, then, was the second Fall of Man. There was a small population of 'gods' who did not transgress divine law and therefore maintained their immortal existence. These few in turn set up a secret school system designed to train fallen man to raise that Kundalini up and open the Third Eye. This "secret school system" was called The Mysteries. Manley P. Hall says in his *Secret Teachings of All Ages*:

> The Mysteries were organized for the purpose of assisting the struggling human...to reawaken the spiritual powers which, surrounded by the flaming ring of lust and degeneracy, lay asleep within the soul. In other words, man was offered a way by which he could regain his lost

---

[408]Hall, *MAN: Grand Symbol of the Mysteries*, 214.

estate.[409]

Richard King, in *African Origin of Biological Psychiatry* says also:

> The Egyptian Mystery System had as its most important object, the DEIFICATION OF MAN (emphasis mine. TI) and taught that the soul (mind) of man, if liberated from it's bodily fetters, could enable him to become godlike, attain vision and hold communion with the immortals...[410]

In the Egyptian Mysteries referred to by King, the novice or student studied seven levels of Arts and Sciences for 42 years. After completing this study, he would have reached his "Summum Bonum" and, according to George G.M. James, *"advanced from the level of a mortal to that of a God."*[411] Of the powers learned by these graduates of the Mysteries James says:

> According to Herodotus, the Egyptian Priests possessed supernatural powers, for they had been trained in the esoteric philosophy of the Great Mysteries, and were experts in Magic. They had the power of controlling the minds of men (hypnosis), the power of predicting the future (prophecy) and the power over nature (i.e. power of Gods)...(inserts original, TI)[412]

This is all of our potential as the Children of God, i.e. Gods. The prophets Moses and Jesus were trained in this system but never graduated (See works of Yosef ben Yochannan and others). Master Fard Muhammad, the teacher of Elijah Muhammad, completed the 42 years of study in the worlds best Mystery and non-mystery schools. After reaching his "Summum Bonum" or

---

[409]Hall, *Secret Teachings of All Ages*, XXI.

[410]Richard King, *African Origin of Biological Psychiatry* (Germantown: Seymour-Smith) 28.

[411]G.G.M James, *Stolen Legacy* (San Francisco: Julian Richardson Associations, 1976) 1.

[412]Ibid., 134.

Greatest Good, He came to North America, by Himself, and brought with Him a teaching which contains the essence of them all. Why? The Hon. Elijah Muhammad taught:

> The Father is our own kind. He wants to make you and me, not just believers, but Gods. Everyone of you, according to what He (Master Fard Muhammad) has taught me, will be Gods...There is no doubt that we are really Gods, but we lost our power and knowledge as shown in the parable of the Jesus. "Salt is good as long as it has saving power. When it no longer has saving power it is not good for anything, but to be thrown out and trampled under people's feet." This is referring to us. We had knowledge and we will be powerful when we are restored to what we originally were. But, we have been robbed of power through depriving us of the Knowledge of Self....

> Allah has taught me that He would like to restore you. You have lost everything of self. Now He wants to restore you back to Self...He didn't come here just to show us who He was. He came here to show us who He was, who we are, and then to make us rulers.[413]

The third or physical Fall came 6, 000 years ago. The seed of this fall was, according to Mr. Muhammad, the miscegenation which took place in Arabia described in the enigmatic verses of Genesis Chapter Six. As a result, the Lord says, *"My Spirit shall not always strive with Man (Original Man) for that he is ALSO flesh: and his days shall be an hundred and twenty years. (6:3)"* MAN's life span was reduced from the length of the Original Adam, 936 years according to Genesis 5:5, to 120. Man has suffered his complete fall and God has withdrawn Himself into hiding. This was done so the Caucasian (Satan) could rule the earth unhindered in accord with the Divine Plan of the Most High. The Caucasian, according to Mr. Muhammad, was given six thousand years to rule the earth. After that time, God would reawaken and reclaim the land. This is why the Bible says that God comes "after the

---

[413] Muhammad, *Theology of Time*, 118-119.

workings of Satan". It says Satan will have six days ("a day unto the Lord is as a thousand years") to do his work, but on the seventh day or seventh thousandth year, God will come back and sit Satan down. In Siam in the East Indies, there is a system of religious temples called *Par-cha-di* or *Dagoba*, which means "roof of the Lord". One of these temples is dedicated to the god *Kiakiack* which means "The God of Gods". In this temple, the god Kiakiack is pictured asleep and the people of Siam say the God of Gods is to SLEEP FOR SIX THOUSAND YEARS.[414] The Black Man is Kiakiack, the God of Gods who slept for six thousand years.

The Black Man has fallen asleep. He is the Lion found asleep in Juda, and the Lion (Sphinx) found lying in the desert of Egypt. Even though, however, the Black Man suffered a fall on all three levels, there has always been a tiny population of gods that maintained their paradisacle state, even after the final fall six thousand years ago. The governing body of these gods is a Supreme Council of Twelve. This Council is described in detail in the next chapters.

---

[414]Higgins, *Anacalypsis*, I: 639.

# CHAPTER X:

# *The Twenty Four Scientists*

## 10.1. *God and His Council*

The Honorable Elijah Muhammad taught that Allah was a Man. He presided over a Divine Council which consisted of twenty-three other Black Men who are gods like Him but of a lesser degree. The twenty-four of them make up a Secret Order, the most secret of all Secret Orders. They are variously referred to as the Twenty Four Scientists, the Twenty Four Elders or the Council of The Gods. Muhammad teaches that these twenty-four men govern the universe. Of the twenty-four, there are Twelve Major Scientists and Twelve Minor Scientists. They constitute the best minds of the Original Nation. Of the Twelve Major Scientists, One of them sits as Judge above all the others because He is the Best Knower. This One is called Allah.

These twenty-four men, who are gods, are the wisest Black Men anywhere on earth. They represent every tribe and color of the Nation of Islam. The inner circle of Twelve is the real power behind the universe. They hold within their circle all knowledge and they pass their wisdom down from Father to Son. The language of these men is Arabic and their way of life is Islam. Collectively, they are called Allah as the One Judge among them is called Allah.

These Twenty Four Scientists have nine main duties. Their first duty is to write history. But writing history for these Gods does not mean recording events after they happen. These Gods write the history of the world BEFORE it transpires. The Honorable Elijah Muhammad teaches that at the beginning of every 25,000 Year Cycle, twenty three Scientists would go out from the root of civilization to all four corners of the Earth; to every nation, among every kindred and tongue, and live among the people for a period of time studying the culture of that people. They would "tune in" to the thinking of the people. By tuning in on the thinking of the people, they could look down the line of time, and according to the dissatisfaction in the minds of the people, could predict exactly what the people would do and the time in which it would happen, for the next 25, 000 years.

These Gods could look down the line of time to the fruition or fulfillment of yearning of this seed of dissatisfaction, and write the history: what will be, when it shall be, how it shall be, why it shall be. After they had tuned in on the earth, the Gods would reassemble back at the Root of Civilization. After sitting down and predicting what shall be allowed to transpire, the Twenty Fourth Scientist, the Judge and sole authority, would decide on what would be and what would not be. He, Allah, has the final decision and will ultimately give the command of 'Kun'-Be! He has the power to stop any of the predicted developments and cause it to develop a different way. But when He feels it is necessary for the history to be written as the Gods presented, it is guaranteed to transpire on the earth, for He has said 'Kun.'

This 25,000 Years of Prophetic History is put in a book that is kept by the Gods. They then make sure that history is fulfilled. They exacerbate the conditions on the earth to make sure it develops just as it was prophesied. When ever a segment of the History is about to be fulfilled, one of the Twelve Major Scientists raises up a man from the midst of a particular people and informs that man of the coming events. That man is made a "Prophet" and he then begins to prophesy. His prophecies are written down and are called "scriptures." Scriptures are writings that are portions of a greater writing. The scriptures of the world - the Bible, the Qur'an, the Zend-Avesta, and others - are portions of the Greater Writing, also called Qur'an or Umm al-Kitab, the Mother Book. As we will show later, Abraham, Moses, Jesus, Muhammad, and all of the prophets were approached by one of these Gods from the Circle of Twelve (Majors).

The number of Gods on this Divine Council being twenty-four is not arbitrary. Muhammad teaches,

There is a significance to the number 24 Scientists and the 25,000 years. The number 24 Scientists used is in accordance with the hours in our day and the measurement of the circumference of our planet...Our

175

planet is not exactly 25,000 miles in circumference, it is 24, 896 and we, according to astronomy, don't have a full 24-hour day but near that - 23 hours, 56 minutes and 46 seconds. The change made in our planets rotation at the Poles is about one minute a year and takes 25,000 years to bring about a complete change in the region of the poles. The actual poles are inclined 23 1/2 degrees to the plane of its orbit. The original nation uses 23 Scientists to write the future of that nation for the next 25,000 years, and the 24th is the Judge or the One God, Allah.

These Scientists write the Prophetic History to equal our home (Earth) circumference of approximately 25,000 square miles; thus, a year for every mile.

These Scientists are also responsible for governing the Mother Ship and piloting it. More on that later. They destroy evil on the earth through the science of nature, by controlling the weather, rain, hail, snow and earthquakes. The Son of Man does all of this.

The Scientists' duty is to guide the History of the earth in accord with the 25,000 Year Prophetic History and to fulfill the scriptures. The Bible is a book of prophecy which describes events that take us all the way into the Apocalypse. As the History is written, the Twenty Four Scientists make sure it happens just as it is written. They are also responsible for imparting Wisdom, Knowledge, and Understanding to Allah's prophets and ministers. The Scientists are responsible for collecting and preserving the wisdom of the universe. When the Caucasian was released from the caves, he went all over the earth destroying the Black civilizations that he found. One of the things he did in the process was burn down the libraries that we stored divine knowledge in. This was repeated when whites invaded Egypt, Chaldea, India and elsewhere. Today writers mourn the loss of such works as the Egyptian *Book of Thoth* or *Histories* written by Manetho, or the *Chaldean Histories* written by Berosus. Scholars assume they were destroyed during the invasions. But in fact, it is the duty of the Gods to secure such wisdom and make sure it is not destroyed.

The Scientists serve as the "Heads" of the Black Nation. The Honorable Elijah Muhammad taught that there were originally five billion members of the Black Nation on the earth that were divided into 12 Nations. The Head of each of these 12 Nations was one of the Twelve Major Scientists. They were each represented by one of the twelve constellations.

As stated in the beginning, this is a Secret Order. These Twenty Four constitute a fraternity of wise men, a grand order of adepts. Whites are aware of this Secret Order of God and have patterned their own secret orders after it. Giuseppe Mazzini, lord of the Alta Vandita which was the highest lodge of the blackest Freemasonry in France, Germany, and England, said in 1871 in a letter to his comrade Dr. Breidenstine a few years before his death:

> We form an association of brothers in all points of the globe. We wish to break every yoke. Yet, there is one unseen that can be hardly felt, yet it weighs on us. Whence comes it? Where is it? No one knows...or at least no one tells. This association is secret even to us the veterans of secret societies.[415]

This "secret association" that weighs on them is the Secret Association of the Gods: The Twenty Four Scientists. It has come to be known in secular circles as "The Hierarchy," "The Great Brotherhood," or "The Hidden Directorate." It is said to rule all of the secret societies and Mysteries through its adepts. According to *The Trail of the Serpent*,

> the higher grades of all hermetic societies 'require that the adept be enslaved by some astute mind or group of minds which, it would seem, seek to rule the nations through hypnotically controlled adepts...for one and all of these modern Mysteries are ruled by some unknown hierarchy[416]

One of the secret societies that is reported to have received guidance from the Gods is the Golden Dawn Society of Germany. Samuel Liddell Mathers, reformer of the Golden Dawn in 1892, claimed that he received the Order's *four ascending Adeptus Grades*

---

[415]William Guy Carr, *Pawns In The Game* (USA. 1958), XVII.

[416] Ernest Scott, *The People of the Secret* (London: Octagon Press, 1983) 156.

degrees from the Gods whom he called "The Secret Chiefs." In a meeting with his fellow initiates, he described his encounters with the Gods:

> As to the Secret Chiefs of the Order...from whom I have received my wisdom of the Second Order...I can tell you NOTHING (emphasis original). I know not even their earthly names, and I have rarely seen them in their physical bodies...My encounters with them have shown me how difficult it is for a mortal, however advanced, to support their presence...the sensation was that of being in contact with so terrible a force that I can only compare it to the continued effect which is usually experienced by any person to whom the flash of lightning passes during a violent storm; coupled with a DIFFICULTY OF RESPIRATION SIMILAR TO THE HALF STRANGLING EFFECT PRODUCED BY THE ETHER. As tested as I have been in occult work, I cannot conceive a much less advanced Initiate being able to support such a strain, even for five minutes without death ensuing...the nervous prostration after each meeting being terrible and accompanied by cold sweats and bleeding from the nose, mouth, and ears.[417]

## 10.2. *The Gods as al-Ghayb (The Hidden)*

This Divine Council of Twelve has for trillions of years been the Supreme Government of the Black Nation with God (the Judge) as its King. Until 66 trillion years ago, the King and His Host ruled the Nation openly and publicly. God was then known among the people. 66 trillion years ago, however, God went into hiding. After a Great God tried to destroy the planet with high explosives, God, along with His Council, "went underground." No more were they to rule the Nation openly. Instead, they became a secret order and governed the Nation clandestinely.

This withdrawing of God is a pivotal aspect of many aboriginal traditions which teach that at one time God was on

---

[417] Ravenscroft, *The Spear of Destiny* (York Beach, Maine: Samuel Weiser, Inc., 1973) 116.

earth but has since "gone away."[418]  E.O. James, in his *History of Religion*, notes:

> In all these widely separated groups (aboriginal tribes)…the Supreme Being…is thought to have existed before death came into the world, and having made Himself, He lived on the earth, could 'go anywhere and do anything.' After a time, for one reason or another, He retired to the seclusion of the sky where He has lived ever since as the Great Chief.[419]

God and His Entourage were to stay in hiding for a pre-determined number of years and then reveal their identity to the masses once again.  In ancient Egypt, as we have shown, the Creator was a Black Man named Atum which means "the Self-Created."  He was said to have been assisted by a "paut" or Council of Gods called the Ali.  After time, Atum and his Ali hid themselves from the people. Atum's name was changed to Amun which means "the Hidden."  Dr. Albert Churchward, in *Origin and Evolution of Religion*, says:

> The word Amen…means 'what is hidden,' 'what is not seen,' 'what cannot be seen.'  The hymns to Amen often state that he is 'HIDDEN TO HIS CHILDREN,' 'HIDDEN TO GODS AND MEN.'…In the Hymns to Amen-Ra he is adored as one and the same as Atum, which shows that Amen is a later name for Atum: AND HE IS REPRESENTED AS 'THE HIDDEN GOD' OF AMENTA, OR 'THE SECRET EARTH.'

God and His Divine Council were said to have hidden themselves in a secret subterranean kingdom called variously *Amenta, Shamballah, Shangri-La*, and *Agarthi*.  From this hidden kingdom, God and His Host are said to direct the affairs and the future of nations and individuals.

10.2.1. *The Hidden Civilization*

---

[418] K. Armstrong, *History of God* (New York: Ballantine Books, 1993). 3.

[419] E.O. James, *History of Religions* (New York: Harper & Brothers, 1957) 8.

This Hidden Kingdom is said to be populated by a hidden civilization of Original People here on earth, the remnants of that original "God Tribe." They are reputed to reside in subterranean communities scattered around the globe. In Eastern Mysticism, these subterranean communities are collectively known as *Agarthi* or *Shamballah*. Agarthi, according to Buddhist tradition, was established over sixty thousand years ago (some say 66 trillion) by one of these Holy Men (gods) who took his tribe underground. The name of this Holy Man is lost to history, but he reputedly possessed incredible wisdom and power which he used with the labors of his tribe to make the paradisical Agarthi.[420] Millions of "holy men and women" are said to reside there where no evil or suffering can penetrate.

According to Ancient Egyptian tradition, the Man-God named Atum-Ptah tunneled through the Earth and constructed a subterranean paradise called *Amenta* or "the Hidden Earth."[421] Atum-Ptah, along with his family of helpers called the Ali, disappeared into Amenta. His name was then changed to *Amun*, "The Hidden One."

Agarthi and Amenta are very similar. Agarthi is reputed to be a vast subterranean kingdom located underneath the surface of Central Asia. Like Amenta, Agarthi is enclosed by a circle of subterranean mountains, in the center of which is the fabled Mount Meru where the king of the world sits enthroned. This king is the King or Judge of the Twelve Major Scientists called in these traditions the Twelve Goros of Agarthi or the Twelve Princes of Shamballah.[422] In 1922 Ferdinand Ossendowski, a Polish scientist from Russia, published a chronicle of his travels in Central Asia. An immediate best-seller, **Beasts, Gods, and Men** detailed discussions Ossendowski had with certain lamas in Mongolia concerning Agarthi and the World King. He notes:

On my journey into Central Asia I came to know for the

---

[420] Walter Kafton-Minkel, *Subterranean Worlds* (Port Townsend, Washigton: Loompanics Unlimited, 1989), 170.

[421] Albert Churchward, *Origin and Evolution of Religion* (New York: ECA Association, 1924), 264.

[422] Kafton-Minkel, *Subterranean Worlds*, 188.

first time about "The Mystery of Mysteries," which I can call by no other name...The favorite Gelong Lama of Prince Chultun Beyli and the Prince himself gave me an account of the subterranean kingdom...

No one knows where this place is. One says Afghanistan, others India. All the people there are protected against Evil and crimes do not exist within its bounds. Science has there developed calmly and nothing is threatened with destruction. The subterranean people have reached the highest knowledge. Now it is a large kingdom, millions of men with the King of the World (the Judge) as their ruler. He knows all the forces of the world...

The capital of Agharti (Shamballah) is surrounded with towns of high priests and scientists...The throne of the King of the World is surrounded by millions of incarnated Gods. They are the Holy Panditas. The palace itself is encircled by the palaces of the Goro, who possess all the visible and invisible forces of the earth, the inferno, and the sky and who can do everything for the life and death of man. If our mad humankind should begin a war against them, they would be able to explode the whole surface of our planet and transform it into deserts. They can dry up the seas, transform lands into oceans and scatter the mountains into the sands of the desert...In cars strange and unknown to us they rush through the narrow cleavages inside our planet.[423]

One gains entrance into the kingdom of Agharti through tunnels and cave passages. Dr. Raymond Bernard, in his *The Hollow Earth*, notes

It is claimed that the earth's crust is honeycombed by a network of tunnels passing under the ocean from continent to continent and leading to subterranean cities in

---

[423] Ferdinand Ossendowski, *Beasts, Men, and Gods* (New York: E.P. Dutton & Company, 1922), 300-304.

large cavities in the earth. The tunnels are especially abundant in South America, especially under Brazil.

The most famous of these tunnels is the "roadway of the Incas," passages which stretch for several hundred miles south of Lima, Peru, and under Cuzeo, Tiahuanaco and the Three Peaks, proceeding to the Atacambo Desert. Another is in Arica, Chile.

> It is claimed that the Incas used these tunnels to escape from the Spanish conquerors and the Inquisition, when entire armies entered them, carrying with them their gold and treasures on the backs of llamas, which they did when the Spanish Conquerors first came. Their mysterious disappearance at this time, leaving only the race of Quechua Indians behind, is also explained by their entering the tunnels…It is claimed that these tunnels had a form of artificial lighting and were built by the race that had constructed Tiahuanco long before the first Inca appeared in Peru. Since the Incas who entered these tunnels…were never seen since and disappeared from the earth's surface, it is probable that they continued to live in the illuminated subterranean cities to which these tunnels led.[424]

Many of these mysterious tunnels exist under Brazil and open into the Roncador Mountains of northeast Matto Grosso. This opening is guarded by a fierce dark-skinned tribe of Murcego and Chavantes Indians. They are known to kill anyone who dared to enter the tunnel uninvited.

These gods or Holy People are Supreme Scientists and as such their subterranean Kingdom is said to possess astonishingly advanced technology. According to Edwin Bernbaum in *The Way to Shambalah,*

> According to descriptions of the King's palace…special skylights made of lenses act like high-powered telescopes to reveal life on other planets and solar systems. The King

---

[424] Raymond Bernard, *The Hollow Earth* (New York: Carol Publishing Group, 1969) 216.

also possesses a glass mirror in which he can see scenes of whatever is happening for miles around; lamas familiar with modern technology explain it as a kind of television screen that enables him to monitor the events of the outside world.

Nicholas Roerick, a mystic and artist of whom we shall have more to say later, traveled through out Asia searching for signs of the Hidden Kingdom. During his travels he was told of occasions when the Subterranean dwellers came above ground:

> Long ago people lived there; now they have gone inside; they have found a subterranean passage to the subterranean kingdom. Only rarely do some of them appear again on earth. At our bazaar such people come with strange, very ancient money, but nobody could even remember a time when such money was in usage here...Through all Asia, through the spaces of all deserts, from the Pacific to the Urals, you can hear the same wondrous tale of the vanished holy people.[425]

## 10.2.2. *The World King*

One of the groups who are said to have had contact with Allah and His Emissaries are the Lamas of Central Asia. One entrance to the hidden, subterranean Kingdom of God is said to be located North of the Gobi Desert. From there, "the Hidden Directorate" or "Inner Circle of Humanity" governs the affairs of men. This Inner Circle, according to the Lamas, is a Circle of Twelve God-Men called the Princes of Shamballah or the Goros of Agarthi. These Twelve owe allegiance to One Man who is Supreme in Power, Wisdom and Holiness. This One Man is called the King of the World or World-King or *Brahytma*. From the Hidden Kingdom the Brahytma or World King judicates. Brahytma, like Allah, is not a person but a position or office like the presidency. The Best Knower among the Gods is He who sits enthroned for a

---

[425] Nicholas Roerich, *Shambhala: In Search of the New Era* (Rochester, Vermont: Inner Traditions International, 1930), 215.

designated term.  One Lama said of the World-King,

> He knows all the forces of the world and reads all the souls
> of humankind and the GREAT BOOK OF THEIR
> DESTINEY.  Invisibly he rules eight hundred million men
> on the surface of the earth and they will accomplish his
> every order.[426]

"The Great Book of their destinies" is probably the *Umm Al-Kitab*
or Mother Book which contains the destiny of the world for 25,000
Years.

There have been reports of this World King making Himself
known to a selected group of initiates.  Dr. Ossendowski asked
one of the lamas, "Has anybody seen the King of the World?"
The lama replied

> Oh yes!  During the solemn holidays of the ancient
> Buddhism in Siam and India the King of the World
> appeared five times.  He rode in a splendid car drawn by
> white elephants and ornamented with gold, precious
> stones and the finest fabrics; he was robed in a white
> mantel and red tiara with strings of diamonds masking his
> face.  He blessed the people with a golden apple with the
> figure of a Lamb above it…He also appeared five hundred
> and forty years ago in Erdeni Dzu, he was in the ancient
> Sakkai Monastery and in the Narabanchi Kure."

In another account, Dr. Ossendowski noted that one night, in a
small Mongolian town called Narabanchi, he was lead into a
temple by a Lama who told him a very interesting story.  One
night in 1890, a group of horsemen arrived in Narabanchi and
demanded that all Lamas enter the Temple in which sat the
Throne of the World King.  As the Lamas were gathered in the
temple,

> one of the strangers mounted the throne, where he took off
> his 'bashlyk' or cap-like head covering.  All of the Lamas

---

[426] Ossendowski, *Beasts, Men, and Gods*, 302.

fell to their knees as they recognized the man who had been long ago described in their sacred bulls of Dalai Lama, Tashi Lama, and Bogdo Khan. He was the man to whom THE WHOLE WORLD BELONGS and who has penetrated into all the mysteries of nature. He pronounced a short Tibetan prayer, blessed all his hearers and afterwards made predictions for the coming half century. This was thirty years ago and in the interim all his prophesies are being fulfilled. During his prayers before the small shrine in the next room this door opened of its own accord, the candles and lights before the altar lighted themselves and the sacred braziers without coals gave forth great streams of incense that filled the room. And then, without warning, the King of the World and his companions disappeared from among us. Behind him remained no trace save the folds in the silken throne coverings which smoothed themselves out and left the throne as though no one had sat upon it.[427]

The King of the World is known to travel the globe in the humble garb of a novice and communicate in the language of the land He is in.

Tradition has it that a number of individuals have been privileged to penetrate into the Kingdom to view it and come back to tell us about it. Sakkia Mouni, Undur Gheghen, Paspa, and Khan Baber are some of these blessed ones. One lama was able to give a very detailed account of an immensely profound ritual which the World King performs in the Hidden Kingdom.

throughout the whole year the King of the World guides the work of the Panditas (gods) and Goros (Twelve Great Gods) of Agarthi. Only at times he goes to the temple cave where the embalmed body of his predecessor lies in a black stone coffin. This cave is always dark, but when the King of the World enters it the walls are stripped with fire and from the lid of the coffin appear tongues of flame. The eldest Goro stands before him with covered head and face

[427] Ibid, 178-9.

and with hands folded across his chest. This Goro never removes the covering from his face, for his head is a nude skull with living eyes and a tongue that speaks. He is in communion with the souls who have gone before.

The King of the World prays for a long time and afterwards approaches the coffin and stretches out his hand. The flames thereon burn brighter; the stripes of fire on the walls disappear and revive, interlace and form mysterious signs from the alphabet *vatannan*. From the coffin transparent bands of scarcely noticeable light begin to flow forth. These are the thoughts of his predecessor. Soon the King of the World stands surrounded by an aureole of this light and fiery letters write and write upon the walls the wishes and orders of God (Most High). At this moment the King of the World is in contact with the thoughts (tuning in) of all the men who influence the lot and life of all humankind: with Kings, Czars, Khans, warlike leaders, High Priests, scientists, and other strong men. He realizes all their thoughts and plans. If these be pleasing before God (Most High), the King of the World will invisibly help them; if they are unpleasant in the sight of God, the King will bring them to destruction…

After his conversation with his predecessor the King of the World assembles the 'Great Council of God' (Twelve or Twenty Four Scientists), judges the actions and thoughts of great men, helps them or destroys them…Afterwards the King of the World enters the great temple and prays in solitude. Fire appears on the altar, gradually spreading to all altars near, and through the burning flame gradually appears the face of God (Most High). The King of the World reverently announces to God (Most High) the decisions and awards of the 'Council of God' and receives in turn the Divine orders of the Almighty. As he comes forth from the temple, the King of the World radiates with Divine Light.[428]

Many very significant observations were made in this narrative.

---

[428] Ibid., 308-9.

The World King is said to, on occasion, view the thoughts of His predecessor (The World King who ruled before Him) whose body was embalmed. A highly placed minister in the Nation of Islam and aid to the Honorable Louise Farrakhan once said that there are three embalmed bodies which are closely guarded secrets of the world. One is the body of Jesus (to be treated elsewhere). Another is the body of the first white Jew who listened to Musa's civilizing teachings as he attempted to raise the cave dwelling Caucasians 4,000 years ago. That Jew's body was embalmed. The third body, according to this minister, is the body of the Judge who ruled the last Cycle of 25,000 Years which ended *circa* 13,086 B.C. This is the "predecessor" of the World King here. The King, by reading the Akasic Record or thought-forms of His predecessor, is able to discern the Will of the Most High, the Spirit of the Creator. The Great Gods are always obligated to pay homage to the Creator. Though He is no longer physically present, His Sprit and Mind permeates All. The World King or Judge is He who best manifests the Spirit and Mind of the Most High.

In the following, we will see that, though it sounds blasphemous today, the existence of this Secret Order of God was acknowledged by the whole of the ancient civilized Black World; the world that gave the present world all of it's major religious concepts.

# CHAPTER XI:

# *The Council of the Gods in Ancient Tradition*

11.1 *The Divine Assembly*

E. Theodore Mullen, in his very enlightening book, *The Assembly of The Gods: The Divine Council In Canaanite and Early Hebrew Literature* observes,

> The concept of the divine assembly, or the assembly of the gods, was a common religious motif in the cultures of Egypt, Mesopotamia, Canaan, Phoenicia, and Israel.[429]

With these may also be added the Indians, Hittites, Persians, and Arabians. We will attempt to analyze these various concepts in comparison with what the Honorable Elijah Muhammad has taught.

11.1.1. *The Sumerian Anunnaki*

Sumer is the name of the ancient civilization that preceded the Akkadian and Babylonian civilizations of the area now called Iraq. It is believed by many scholars to be the oldest civilization. Others contend that such honor should be given to Kemet (Egypt). I will not engage in that debate here. However, I will point out that Sumer was a Black civilization. Ivan Van Sertima, in his *African Presence in Early Asia*, as well as other scholars, has shown beyond dispute that the indigenous people of Sumer were not a so-called Semitic people, but were Black. The oldest and Chief God of these Black Sumerians was called *Anu* and his council was called the *Anunnaki*. Samuel N. Krammer, in *History Begins at Sumer*, says,

> From as far back as our written records go, the Sumerian

---

[429]Mullen, *Assembly of The Gods*, 113.

theologian assumed as axiomatic the existence of a pantheon consisting of a group of living beings, MANLIKE IN FORM but superhuman and immortal, who...GUIDE AND CONTROL THE COSMOS IN ACCORDANCE WITH WELL-LAID PLANS AND PRESCRIBED LAWS. Each of these anthropomorphic but superhuman beings was deemed to be in charge of a particular component of the universe and to guide its activities in accordance with established rules and regulations.[430]

Through the Cuneiform Texts (CT), which are the ancient writings of the Sumerians, we learn a great many details of this Divine Assembly. In these writings, it was referred to in many ways, but primarily as *puhur ilani* ("council of the gods") or the *Anunnaki*.[431] The Anunnaki was composed of an inner circle of the higher and lower region Gods. According to Zecharia Sitchin the number of these heavenly gods was twelve. He says,

This emphasis on the number 12 can be traced to the fact that the Solar System has twelve members, and each of the leading Anunnaki was assigned a celestial counterpart, FORMING A PANTHEON OF TWELVE 'OLYMPIANS' who were each assigned a constellation AND A MONTH.[432]

This Sumerian Anunnaki, consisting of twelve gods, each assigned to a constellation and a month, is the root and origin of the Latin *annum* ("year"), French *anne* ("year") and English *annual* ("yearly").[433] Sitchin says again,

There were many other gods in Sumer-children, grandchildren, nieces, and nephews of the Great Gods; there were also several hundred rank-and-file gods...who were assigned...'general duties.' But only TWELVE made

---

[430] S.N. Krammer, *History Begins At Sumer* (London: Thomas & Hudson) 129

[431] Mullen, *Assembly of the Gods*, 117; Sitchin, *12th Planet*, 19

[432] Sitchin, *Genesis Revisited*, 208

[433] Ibid., 209

up the Great Circle (emphasis orig.)[434]

This Circle of Great Gods was also referred to as the "*Exalted Court.*"[435] This is exactly as is taught by the Honorable Elijah Muhammad. He said the Twelve Major Scientists were represented by the Twelve Constellations. The "Lower Region" Gods undoubtedly consisted of Twelve also. These were also called "The Gods of Heaven and Earth."

The Head God or Judge of the Anunnaki was called the *Lugaldimmerankia*, which means "The King of the gods of the heavens and earth."[436] Anu, the "Father of the Gods" was always the Lugaldimmerankia, until he was replaced by the Anunnaki with Marduk the Young God. The way this transition takes place is a perfect example of how the Sumerian Council functions. In the *Enuma Elish*, the old Babylonian Creation epic, the Anunnaki Gods were looking for a champion to slay the evil Tiamat. The young god Marduk approached them saying

I will accomplish all that is in your hearts. I will be your avenger and slay Tiamat. But you must make me supreme. From now on, my words will fix the destinies of the gods. And whatever I create will remain unchanged.[437]

The Anunnaki first tested Marduk. They spread the starry canopy in the sky and challenged Marduk to remove it by his word. After succeeding in this and the challenge to make it reappear, the Gods prostrated themselves before Marduk and proclaimed joyfully "*Marduk is King.*" The tablet reads,

They erected for him a princely throne...'Thou art most honored of the great gods, thy decree is unrivaled...From this day unchangeable shall be thy pronouncement. To raise or bring low-these shall be (in) thy hand. Thy

---

[434] Sitchin, *The 12th Planet*, 126
[435] Ibid., 92
[436] Pritchard, *Ancient Near East*, 37, n.1
[437] V. Hamilton, *In The Beginning* (New York: H.B.J., 1988) 83.

utterance shall be true, thy command... unimpeachable. No one among the gods shall transgress thy bounds![438]

The office of Lugaldimmerankia was not a permanent position. Just as the President sits in that seat for a specific term, so did the Judge or King of the Anunnaki Gods hold that office for a specific term called *bala*. The term or period was named after the particular incumbent, just as we refer to the "Reagan Administration" or the "Bush Administration." This is exactly as the Honorable Elijah Muhammad teaches. He says,

> The planet Earth was governed by 24 wise scientists. The wisest of these scientists was He that was the Supreme Being, and the name of His great Office was Allah, just as the name of the Office of the leader in this country is President. And just as the man who is called by the name President may die and another man take his place, so it is with He that is called by the name Allah. But the name remains forever.[439]

The Sumerian Council met on a mountain court called *Ubshuukkinna*. As the Gods arrive at the court, there is embracing between them and they first have a banquet. They joyfully ate and drank before the meeting moved to more serious matters. A very interesting example of the proceedings of the Assembly is here given from one of the tablets:

> All the great gods who decree the fates entered before Ansar; they filled Ubshuukkinna. They kissed each other when they met together in the assembly. They conversed as they sat in the banquet. They ate bread, they poured [sweet drink], they made their throats flow with sweet drink...Quickly they became carefree as the spirit rose. For Marduk, their avenger, they fixed his decree[440]

---

[438]Ibid., 31

[439] Muhammad, E. *AL AKHIRAH*, UNPUBLISHED.

[440] Mullen, *Assembly of the Gods*, 176-7

This shows the astonishingly human-like nature of this Council. Here before a meeting, all the participants greet each other with kisses and conversation. They are then entertained with a banquet. Only after the eating and drinking does the Assembly get down to business. This is like a typical executive board meeting. In these meetings the Gods make such decisions as to send a flood down to drown mankind,[441] or to establish kingships in the land. In the Creation Epic of Mesopotamia, there is described a meeting with the Council under King Marduke to pass judgment against Kingu. Marduke places the call to the Gods to assemble:

> Let the great gods be here in Assembly, Let the guilty be handed over that they may endure.' Marduke summoned the great gods to Assembly; Presiding graciously, he issues instructions. To his utterance the gods pay heed. The king addresses a word to the Anunnaki:'...Who was it that contrived the uprising, and made Tiamat rebel, and joined the battle? Let him be handed over who contrived the uprising'...The Igigi, the great gods, replied to him, to Lugaldimmerankia, councilor of the gods, their lord: 'It was Kingu who contrived the uprising[442]

The ancient Sumerians and Babylonians acknowledged the existence of this Council of Gods. This Divine Assembly was divided up into the Twelve Higher Region or Heavenly Gods and the Lower Region or Earthly Gods. The Judge or Lugaldimmerankia was to serve an appointed term called the *bala*. This Council had total control over the workings of the universe and the affairs of men. It must be remembered that these Gods were human in form. T. Jacobsen, in his article "Primitive Democracy in Ancient Mesopotamia," notes,

> The Sumerians and Akkadians pictured their Gods as human in form, governed by human emotions, and living

---

[441] Pritchard, *Ancient Near East*, I: 30
[442] Ibid., 36-7

in the same type of world as did men.[443]

The main difference is that these humans are Supreme in Knowledge and Power.

## 11.1.2. *Ancient Egyptian 'Paut Neteru'*

So too did the Black inhabitants of Ancient Kemet (Egypt) believe in the existence and power of this Council of The Gods. E. Wallis Budge, in his translation of the so-called *Book of the Dead,* says,

> The priest of Ainu (oldest city of Kemet) at a very early period grouped together the...greatest gods of Egypt, forming what is called the 'paut neteru'...or 'company of the gods,' or as it is written in the pyramid texts, 'paut aat..., 'the GREAT company of gods'; the text also show that there was a second group of...gods called 'paut net'eset'... or 'lesser company of the gods'.

Budge says again, in his *The Gods of the Egyptians,*

> The Egyptian word here rendered 'company' is PAUTI or 'paut'...and the meaning usually attached to it has been nine...But the last quoted passage proves that a 'paut' of the gods might contain more than nine divine beings...Again, in a litany to the gods of the Great company given in the Unas text (line 240 ff.) we see the 'paut' contains...ten gods...In the text of Mer-en-Ra (line 205) the 'paut' contains nine gods, and it is described as the 'Great paut which is in Ainu'...whilst in the text of Pepi II...the same 'paut' is said to contain Tem, Shu, Tefnut, Seb, Nut, Osiris, Osiris-Khent-Amenti, Set, Horus, Ra, Khent-maati, and Uatchet, i.e., TWELVE GODS.[444]

---

[443]T. Jacobsen, "Primitive Democracy In Ancient Near East," *Journal of Near Eastern Studies* II (1943): 167

[444] Budge, *Gods of the Egyptians*, 87-88

Sometimes, the Great Gods and the Little or Lesser Gods are mentioned together as *paut neteru aat paut neteru netchest*, meaning "the Great Company of the Gods and the Little Company of the Gods."[445] That the true *paut neteru*, both Great and Little, was composed of twelve gods is shown by Albert Churchward in his *Origin and Evolution of Religion*. He observes,

> In the papyrus of Ani and of Nunefer we see depicted the Judges of Maat as twelve in number, sitting on Twelve Thrones. The earthly representation was TWO CIRCLES, ONE NORTH (HIGHER REGION) AND ONE SOUTH (LOWER REGION), DIVIDED INTO TWELVE DIVISIONS EACH.[446]

The fact that these twenty-four Judges are each sitting on thrones is an important feature which we will elaborate on later. As Sitchin says,

> The head of the Egyptian pantheon was Ra...who presided over an Assembly of the Gods that numbered twelve.[447]

James Bonwicks, in *Egyptian Belief and Modern Thought*, affirms:

> The TWELVE GODS may be more readily identified with Mazzaroth, or the twelve signs of the Zodiac, through which the sun passed every year...Proclus calls them the 'twelve super-celestial gods.[448]

The Great and Lesser Companies of the Gods were also, like Sumer, called the Gods of Heaven and the Gods of Earth.[449] The Gods of Heaven are the Twelve Major Scientists that the Honorable Elijah Muhammad refers to, and the Gods of Earth are

---

[445] Ibid., 87

[446] Churchward, *Origin and Evolution of Religion*, 134.

[447] Sitchin, *12th Planet*, 82

[448] J. Bonwicks, *Egyptian Belief and Modern Thought* (Colorado: Falcon's Wing Press, 1956) 99-100

[449] Budge, *Gods of The Egyptians*, 91

the Twelve Minor Scientists.

There are a few very interesting pictures given of this *paut neteru*. In the *Text of Pepi I*, Budge describes Pepi being made King of the Council:

...The king is said to sit on an iron throne and to weigh words at the head of the Great Company of Gods in Ainu; the two companies of the gods lift up the head of Pepi...and he takes the crown in the presence the Great Company...he sits at the head of the two companies...and in their boat...;and he stands between the two companies.[450]

In the *Legend of Ra and Isis*, Isis seeks to make herself Queen of the heavens. She does so by coercing Ra, through poisoning him with a serpent, into revealing to her his sacred name. In the legend, we get a picture of Ra's *paut neteru*. It reads:

Now behold, each day Ra entered AT THE HEAD OF HIS HOLY MARINERS and established himself upon the THRONE of the two horizons...

Ra calls the Gods to council,

Let there be brought before me THE CHILDREN OF THE GODS with healing words and with lips that know, and with power which reacheth unto heaven.[451]

This is a very interesting picture of Ra and his *paut neteru*. Here, they are referred to as "his holy mariners" and "children of the Gods." This last appellation is most significant, for it is a description of the members of the Council that reoccurs in the Divine Assembly motif. In another picture of the Divine Assembly, called *The Deliverance of Mankind from Destruction*, Ra fears that mankind has conspired against him. Thus he turned to his God and maker, Nun, for a solution to this menace. It reads;

---

[450] Ibid.

[451] Budge, *Egyptian Book of The Dead*, XC.

195

Then his majesty perceived the things which were being plotted against him by mankind. Then his majesty said to THOSE WHO WERE IN HIS RETINUE: "Pray, summon to me my Eye, Shu, Tefnut, Geb, and Nut, as well as the fathers and mothers who were with me when I was in Nun, as well as my god Nun also…Thou shalt bring them secretly…Thou shalt come with them to THE GREAT HOUSE, that they may TELL THEIR PLANS…

Then these GODS WERE BROUGHT IN, and these gods [came] beside him, PUTTING THEIR HEADS TO THE GROUND IN THE PRESENCE OF HIS MAJESTY…Then they said in the presence of his majesty: 'Speak to us, so that we may hear it.

In this picture, Ra calls the *paut neteru* his "retinue" which has military implications. Similar designations to describe the members of a god's court is common. Also, the god's were called to assemble at the "Great House." Later, we will develop the motif of the sacred meeting place of the Council, for there is always a specific place where the Gods are called to assemble. In Sumer, the meeting place was in a large mountain court called *Ubshuukkinna*. The gods are also shown here prostrating before the Head God. This too is a recurring picture of the Divine Assembly.

The ancient Kemetians were aware of this Holy Council of The Gods. The Head God was the Judge of this council which is divided into two groups, the Great Company and the Lesser Company, both of which were composed of Twelve Great Gods and Twelve Lesser Gods. It must be pointed out here that these "Gods" were human in form, as they are in Sumer. The *Book of Phylons* clearly shows these Twenty Four Gods to be human beings, for the Gods of the early Egyptians were human in form and supreme in power.[452]

---

[452]See Budge, *Gods of The Egyptians,* 40, 57.

### 11.1.3. *The Hittite Company of Twelve*

Around 2,000 B.C., a group of unknown origin migrated into the mountain area of Anatolia. This people have become known to history as the Hittites. In Yazilikaya, the ancient Hittite capital, there sits a religious gallery. In this Hittite gallery is a depiction of the Hittite pantheon inscribed on rocks arranged in a semicircle (Figure 39).

Figure 39
The Twelve Gods, ancient Temple of Yazılıkaya

Sitchin observes,

(I)t is clear that the Hittite pantheon, too, was governed by the 'Olympian' twelve. The lesser gods were organized in groups of twelve, and the Great Gods on Earth were associated with twelve celestial bodies.[453]

In the Hittite description of this Divine Assembly are to be found all the characteristics that are found in the Sumerian and Kemetic descriptions. They are referred to as the "Gods of Heaven and Earth."[454] In a Hittite epic entitled *"Kingship in Heaven,"* the recounter lists the twelve "mighty olden gods" who are the "forbearers." He proceeds to tell a very interesting history of the

---

[453] Sitchin, *12ᵗʰ Planet*, 64
[454] Ibid.

Judgeship of the Council:

> Formerly, in the olden days, Alalu was king in Heaven;
> He, Alalu, was seated on his throne.
> Mighty Anu, the first among the gods, stood before him,
> Bowed at his feet, set the drinking cup in his hand. For
> nine counted periods, Alalu was king in Heaven.
> In the ninth period, Anu gave battle against Alalu.
> Alalu was defeated...On the throne sat Anu.[455]

It continues:

> For nine counted periods Anu was king in Heaven;
> In the ninth period, Anu had to do battle with Kumarbi.

These excerpts highlight some very important aspects of the Divine Assembly motif. First, the King or Judge of the Council is almost always pictured sitting on his Throne. His Kingship is in fact represented by the Throne. The significance of the Throne can be seen in practically all the cultures we will examine in connection with the Divine Assembly and the Anthropomorphic God. We learn here in fact that the Throne is the position. The King who sits in it changes, and those vying for the position do so by going after the Throne. It is like the Oval Office. The Oval Office, like the Throne of the President, represents the position. He who sits in the Office changes constantly, but the Oval Office represents an idea and position that is consistent and seemingly permanent. This is exactly as the Honorable Elijah Muhammad described the Kingship of the Gods.

Another significant aspect highlighted by this epic is the fact that the position of the King is to last only a designated time period. *"For nine counted periods"* is how long Alalu sat on the Throne before he was challenged by Anu. And *for nine counted periods* did Anu sit before he was challenged by Kumarbi. The fact that they are "counted" periods implies that the term is pre-determined. Again, this is as the office of President. The one who holds that position can only do so for a pre-determined period of 4

---

[455] Ibid., 69

years. Afterwards, he is challenged by others for that position. This is the concept of the *bala* of the Sumerians.

This, too, is in accord with what the Honorable Elijah Muhammad taught.

> Once every 25,000 years a new God has been coming up in the past, so God taught Me. Their Wisdom would always run through about 25,000 years and then they would change and bring in another One...From the year '1' of the Calendar Time of 25,000 years, it would be another 25, 000 years before we allow a new God to rule, so God taught me.[456]

Not that the God actually physically lived for 25,000 years, but His wisdom will be the Rule of that particular Cycle.

### 11.1.4. *The Canaanite Adat 'El*

It is with the Canaanite writings that we begin to get a clearer picture of this Divine Council and its function. Canaan is the ancient name of the area, which is today called Palestine (Israel). The ancient Black Canaanites contributed greatly to the religion of the Hebrews. The God of these ancient Black people was named 'El/Al. He was always depicted as an aged man with gray hair and beard sitting on a Throne.

'El was the Head or King of a Divine Council called *Adat'El* or "Council of 'El/God." F.M. Cross, in ***Canaanite Myth and Hebrew Epic***, says: "*In Canaan the original image of 'El is as Judge in his assembly.*"[457]

Probably the most revealing picture of 'El and his Council is given in a text which describes a conflict between the gods Bal and Yam. Yam has received kingship through the Decree of 'El. As part of his kingship, Bal, a member of the Council and second only to 'El, is to be turned over as a servant to Yam. Bal refuses and rebukes Yam, invoking his destruction. Yam then sends two

---

[456] Muhammad, *Theology of Time*, 113-114.

[457] F.M. Cross, *Canaanite Myth and Hebrew Epic* (Cambridge: Harvard University Press, 1973) 37.

messengers to the gathered Council to affirm his kingship. Yam instructs his two messengers:

> Arise, Lads, do not tarry! Verily set face
> Toward the appointed assembly to midst of Mount Luli.
> To the feet of 'El do not fall, Do not prostrate yourself
> To the appointed assembly.
> Arise! Constantly stare! Repeat your message
> and say to Bull, his father, 'El
> Repeat to the appointed assembly: 'Message of Yam your master...
> The lads arise, they do not tarry. Verily they set face
> To the midst of Mount Luli, toward the appointed assembly.
> Now the gods were seated to eat. The Sons of Qudsu to dine.
> Bal' was standing beside 'El.

We learn much about the *Adat' El* from this text. It is clear that they, like in Sumer, met on a mountain, in this case Mount Luli. Those that are privileged to enter into the midst of the gathered Assembly are required to prostrate themselves before the Gods. We know this is the tradition because, Yam, in rebellion, instructs his messengers "not" to bow down before the Gods.

We see another parallel with the Sumerian concept of the Divine Council in the "banquet" motif. The Gods were seated to eat as the messengers arrived. As we noted, the gathering of the Sumerian Council commenced with a banquet. This is true of the Canaanite Council also. In the so-called *Banquet Text*, we read that:

> El prepared game in his palace,
> Provisions in the midst of his temple.
> He summoned the gods 'to mess.'
> The gods ate and drank...
> 'El sits enthroned in his shrine,
> 'El sits enthroned at his banquet.

The Banquet of the Gods of 'El's/Al's Council was called

*marzihu.*[458]

As well as being designated *Adat'El*, this Divine Council was more often referred to as *puhur 'ilm*, "assembly of the Gods" or *phr m'd*, "the gathered assembly." Other times it is referred to as *phr bn 'ilm*, "the assembly of the sons of 'God/'El," and the gods referred to as *banu 'ili*, the "sons of El" or *banu qudsi*, "the sons of Qudsu (Atirat)." This designation of the gods becomes extremely important as we analyze the Hebrew Divine Assembly.

One of the most significant features of the Divine Assembly that begins to emerge from the Canaanite writings is its militaristic nature. 'El's kingship is the result of his ability as a warrior-god.[459] Likewise in Sumer, "*the investiture of kingship (was) to the warrior-god of the cosmos.*"[460] Marduk was granted kingship over the Council only after he defeated the dragon Tiamat. We saw in the Hittite description the necessary military prowess of the god who would be King. In one of the Ugaritic (Canaanite) texts, the Assembly is referred to as *talituha (tlth)*. Mullen says,

> The final term 'tlth' presents an important clue to the identities of *'ilm* (gods) who constitute the council. We have followed P. Millers interpretation of the noun 'tlt,' taking it from the Hebrew 'salis,' 'officer,' translating it here 'retinue.' As we shall show, 'tlt' does designate a military retinue...(I)t is the retinue of the divine council...The council members are to be seen as members of a military company surrounding their aged leader, 'El.[461]

The members of the Council sit on *kahtu zubulu*, "princely thrones." Mullen says again,

> As we noted...'zubulu,' in Ugaritic (Canaanite language), designates the victorious warrior-gods Ba'l and Yamm...As

[458]Mullen, *Assembly of the Gods*, 264

[459] Ibid., 146

[460] Ibid., 177

[461] Ibid., 181

a title, it was applied only after victory in battle. So here, the designation of the thrones of the council members by the term 'zubulu' must also be seen as a reference to the military exploits of these gods who were once active military personnel alongside their mighty leader 'El.[462]

In the Phoenician writings of 'El, he is a warrior-god that is surrounded by "allies" who go to war along side him. In Kemet, we found the members of Ra's council called "mariners," and "those who were in his (Ra's) retinue." It is important to keep this military nature of the council in mind as we examine the Hebrew description of Yahweh's Council.

From the gathering of the Council, 'El issued his *tahumu* or "Decree." Mullen observes:

> 'El's decree is taken for granted as a prerequisite for any important matter influencing the realm of the gods...Whenever the need arose to decide an important matter relevant to order in the cosmogonic realm, the gods would journey...to the dwelling of 'El to receive the decree or permission of the aged patriarch.[463]

The Honorable Elijah Muhammad taught that it was the Judge who issued decrees and had the final say. That Twenty Fourth God was He who said "Kun," Be, and It Is. The other gods made no decisions what so ever. It was the Head God, in this case 'El, that was the author of all decrees. As we shall see, the other gods' duty was to carry out the decrees issued by their Lord.

I shall take this time to recount the main points that have been made thus far. The belief in a "Council of the Gods" is to be found among practically all the nations of the Near East: the Sumerians, Egyptians, Hittites, Persians, Phoenicians, Arabians, Syrians, Indians, Greeks, and Canaanites. Though there are some differences in the various beliefs, there is also great similarity. In all of them, the Council consisted of Twelve Major Gods and Twelve Minor or Lesser Gods. The head of the Council was the

---

[462]Ibid., 186
[463]Ibid., 146

Supreme God of the pantheon: Anu, Ra, Ahura Mazda, 'El, etc. This Head God was the Supreme authority. He is usually depicted as a warrior-god, and the Council as his retinue.

We have learned that the Head God was more of an office than an actual god. A particular god served in that post for a pre-determined period, then a new god takes his place for that same period. The Council gathered at a central point to make decisions affecting the cosmos and man. Before such decisions are pronounced, however, there is usually a Banquet in which the Gods eat, drink, and be merry. The gods in all of these cultures are human in form and deed, but super human in power and wisdom.

## 11.1.5. *Persians, Indians, Greeks*

The ancient Persians believed that their God, *Ahura Mazda*, was the Head of a group of "Creators"[464] that equaled twelve in number.[465] And like the ancient Arabians, each of the twelve were assigned a month.[466] The Phoenicians spoke of *mphrt 'il gbl qdsm*, "the assembly of the holy gods of Byblos." The Syrians had *Alaheim*, "gods" or "Council of the Gods."

In the Hindu *Vedas* of India, mention is made of Twelve Gods who made up one family. These Gods are called the Twelve *Adityas* or *Devas* ("shining ones"). The King of the Twelve Adityas was Kash-Yapa, which means "he who is the Throne." Again, the significance of the Throne is here seen. The Twelve Adityas were each assigned to a zodiac sign and celestial body.[467] The Greeks worshipped the Twelve Gods of Olympus. Here, as with the Hindus, the Twelve Gods and Goddesses were of one family. These Gods, as in the other civilizations we have seen, were human in form and Black.

---

[464] Blavatsky, *Secret Doctrine*, I:436
[465] Higgins, *Anacalypsis*, I: 781.
[466] Ibid., 5
[467] Sitchin, *12th Planet*, 61

# CHAPTER XII:

# *The Divine Council in Scripture*

## 12.1. *Yahweh and the Elohim*

The Hebrews, learning much from the Canaanites as well as the Kemetians, would of necessity have much in common with the religious beliefs of these cultures. F.M. Cross, in a chapter entitled "Yahweh and the Council of the Gods" observes,

> Like 'El, Yahweh may be seen as Judge of his council, as King in his court, or as Divine Warrior surrounded by the heavenly hosts. In Canaan the original image of 'El is as Judge in his assembly. In Israel also, the dominant image is that of Yahweh judging in his divine assembly.[468]

I would say that the Hebrews give the most detailed account of this Divine Assembly. We first meet with this Council in the opening verse of the Bible, *"In the beginning GOD created..."* The word here translated "God," as we have shown, is the Hebrew *Alheim* or *Eloheim* meaning "Gods." Who are these Gods? On one level of reading they are the component parts of the Atom. But the term *Eloheim* has another significance as well. The suspense is heightened more with the use of first person plural pronouns when Eloheim speaks. The now infamous Gen. 1:26 *"Let US make man in OUR image after OUR likeness."* We find such usage of plurals again in 3:22, after Adam ate of the Forbidden Tree, God says, *"Behold, the man is become as ONE OF US..."* In the eleventh chapter, after God realized that the people spoke one language, he says, *"Go to, LET US go down, and there confound their language..."*

Contrary to traditional orthodox Christian interpretation, these plurals do not refer to the Catholic Trinity. These are references to the Hebrew Council of The Gods. Lloyd Graham, in

---

[468] Cross, *Canaanite Myth and Hebrew Epic*, 190

his **Deceptions and Myths in the Bible**, says again: *"The word (Eloheim) comes from Alheim and means a Council of the Gods."*[469] These Gods are men. The ***International Standard Bible Encyclopedia*** notes that "Eloheim" was a title designating *"a position of honor and authority of men."*[470] R. A. Finlayson, Professor of Systematic Theology, observes in ***The New Bible Dictionary*** that the word Eloheim *"is applied in the Old Testament to men."*[471]

The historical Yahweh who gave Moses his mission (as opposed to the archetypal Yahweh who represented the Original Man) was not God Most High, the Creator. He was one of the Alheim or Eloheim. Thus in Deuteronomy 7:5-6, Moses says to the Israelites,

> For you are a people consecrated to YAHWEH YOUR ELOHEIM; it is you that YAHWEH OUR ELOHEIM has chosen to be his very own people out of all the peoples in the earth.

Each god (*eloheim*) was responsible for a "nation"; they were his people and he was their Eloheim. The biblical account is the history of Yahweh establishing his kingship in the Council, just as Marduk had to establish his kingship in the Anunnaki years earlier. A glimpse at Yahweh's bid for the Throne is recorded in Psalms 82:

> <Yahweh> stands in the Council of 'El/Al to deliver judgment among the gods.
> No more mockery of Justice
> No more favoring the wicked!
> Let the weak and the orphan have justice,
> Be fair to the wretched and the destitute…
> I once said, 'You too are gods, sons of El Elyon, all of you.'"

---

[469] op. cited.

[470] James Orr, *The International Standard Bible Encyclopedia*, Vol. I, "God," 1254.

[471] J.D. Douglass, *The New Bible Dictionary*, "God," 474.

Here, the Assembly of the Gods is referred to as *Adat'El/Al*, just as in Canaan. Yahweh is seen standing in the Council of Al (Allah) condemning the other Alheim, accusing them of failing to meet the social challenge of the day. Thus, Yahweh asserts his authority. But as Karen Armstrong argues, this was easier said than done.

> Yahweh's victory was hard-won. It involved strain, violence and confrontation...Yahweh did not seem to be able to transcend to older deities in a peaceful, natural manner. He had to fight it out.[472]

This is why Yahweh is depicted in the Old Testament as such a ferocious warrior. In Exodus 15:3, it is written "*Yahweh is a MAN OF WAR. Yahweh is his name.*" Here he is explicitly described as a MAN (*'ish*) of war (*milhamah*). Isa. 42:13 reads,

> The Lord (YHWH) goes forth as a mighty man (*gibbor*),
> as a man of war (*'ish milhamah*) he stirs up his fury;
> He cries, he shouts aloud,
> He shows himself mighty against his foes.

The most graphic description of Yahweh as a warrior is in Duet. 32:39-43

> See now that I, even I, am he,
> and there is no god with me:
> I kill, and I make alive; I wound, and I heal:
> neither is there any that can deliver out of my hand...
> (41) If I whet my glittering SWORD,
> and mine hand take hold on judgment;
> I will render vengeance to my enemies,
> And reward them that hate me.
> (42) I will make mine arrows drunk with blood,
> and my sword shall devour flesh;
> And that with the blood of the slain and the captives,
> from the beginning of revengers upon the enemy.

---

[472] Armstrong, *History of God,* 31.

In Psalms 89:6, Yahweh has secured victory among the Gods.

> The heavens praise your wonders, O Yahweh,
> And your truth in the council of the holy ones
> (*qehal qedosim*).
> For who in the skies can compare to Yahweh?
> Who is like Yahweh among the sons of God  (*bene 'elim*)?
> A dreadful god in the council of the holy ones
> (*sod-qedosim*)
> Great and terrible above all those around him.
> Yahweh, God of the host (*elohe seba'ot*), who is like you?
> Mighty Yah(weh), your faithful ones surround you.

In Jerimiah. 23:18,22, the prophet distinguishes between true and false prophets by asking the question, *"Who has stood in the council of Yahweh <sodh YHWH>, and has perceived and heard his word?"* Yahweh goes on to say of the false prophets,

> But if they had stood in my council *<sodh>*, then had they caused my people to hear my words.

Here the term *sodh YHWH* is used to designate the Council. In Job 15:8, it is referred to as *sodh eloah*, meaning "council of God," though it is now translated "secret of God."

The members of the Council are referred to with many designations. We have seen Eloheim, simply meaning "the Gods" (also Ps. 95:3, 96:4, 97:7b, 148:2).[473] In other places they are referred to as *bene 'eloheim* (Duet 32:8), *bene ha'eloheim* (Gen. 6:2, 4; Job 1:6; 2:1), and *bene 'elyon* (Ps. 82:6), all of which mean "sons of God," "sons of the Gods," or "sons of the Most High." This, too, finds it parallel with both Kemet and Canaan. The members of Ra's Divine Assembly, in the *Legend of Ra and Isis*, which we examined earlier, were called "children of the gods." In Canaan, as we noted, the gods of El's Council were often called *bani 'ili*, as in

---

[473] Morgenstern, "Mythological Background of Psalm 82," 39 f.66

this text which reads,

> Let it be born to the assembly of the sons of 'El, to the council of the sons of 'El.[474]

Reflective of this is Job 38:7,

> When the morning stars sang together, and all the sons of God (*bene 'eloheim*) shouted for joy.

*Qedosim*, meaning "Holy Ones," is another designation for the gods of Yahweh's Assembly. This designation shows that these are gods like Yahweh, though of inferior rank, because Yahweh himself is referred to as the "Holy One," *qedes* (Lev. 20:26; Isa.6:3; Ps. 99:3, 5, 9). In Isa. 54:5, Yahweh is the "Holy One of Israel."

One of the few good examples of an actual court proceeding, when Yahweh gathers his Council together for deliberations, is reported by the prophet Micaiah ben Imlah (I Kings 22:19-23). Micaiah actually was brought into the proceedings in a vision. Ahab of Israel and Jehoshaphat of Judah, after receiving favorable oracles from the four hundred prophets (22:5-6), summoned Micaiah. His oracle was different from that of the four hundred prophets. Micaiah's vision of the proceedings of the Divine Assembly revealed the reason for the discrepancy. I Kings 22:19-22 reads:

> And he (Micaiah) said, Hear thou therefore
> the word of the Lord: I saw the Lord
> SITTING ON HIS THRONE,
> and all the host of heaven
> standing by him on his right and on his left.
> (20) And the Lord said, Who shall persuade Ahab,
> that he may go up and fall at Ramoth-gilead?
> And one said of this manner, and another said of that manner.
> (21) And there came forth a spirit, and stood before the Lord,

---

[474] Mullen, *Assembly of the Gods*, 270

and said, I will persuade him.
(22) And the Lord said unto him, Wherewith? And he said,
I will go forth, and be a lying spirit
In the mouth of all his prophets. And he said,
Thou shalt persuade him, and prevail also:
Go forth, and do so.

The first thing we notice in this description of Micaiah's vision is that he saw Yahweh sitting on "his Throne." Again we see the significance of the Throne. Around the Throne are the *seba' hassamayim*, "the host of heaven." These are the same as the Eloheim, *bene 'Eloheim*, and *qedosim*.[475] "Host of Heaven" is another designation of the gods who, like the Canaanite *talituha*, emphasizes the militaristic character of the Council.

Yahweh then proceeds to address the Council: "*Who will entice Ahab...?*" (v20). Yahweh is asking which one of the Gods will volunteer to go and entice Ahab. This is reminiscent of 'El convening with his council for the purpose of healing the ailing Kirta. 'El sits enthroned and addresses his council,

Who among the gods will cast out the illness,
Who will drive out the sickness?
No one among the gods answered him.

In 'El's proceeding, none of the gods answered his request. In Yahweh's, the gods at first discussed it among themselves: "*One said one thing and another said another*" (v20). The council reached a decision, and afterwards one of them approached and addressed the enthroned Yahweh (v21). This one is referred to as *haruah*, "the spirit." For clarity, I must point out that even though this individual is referred to as *haruah*, here translated as "the spirit," we are not dealing with a literally immaterial spirit. The members of this Council, like Yahweh himself, are men.

This *ruah* that stands before Yahweh and volunteers himself tells Yahweh his idea of placing a "lying spirit in the mouth of the four hundred prophets (v22)." Yahweh agrees, and commissions the god with an imperative "*Go forth and do so*" (v22).

---

[475] Morgenstern, "Mythological Background of Psalm 82," 40 [12]

A similar description of the proceedings of the Divine Court was witnessed by Isaiah. Whereas Micaiah only saw the proceedings in a vision, Isaiah actually was allowed to attend. In the sixth chapter, we read,

> In the year that the king Uz-zi-ah died
> I saw also the Lord sitting upon a throne,
> high and lifted up, and his train filled the temple.
> (2) Above it stood the seraphim: each one had six wings...
> (3) And one cried to another, and said,
> Holy, holy, holy is the Lord of Host.

Here again Yahweh is seen on a throne "high and lifted up." We note here that the assembly takes place in a Temple (v1). What catches our attention most, though, is how Isaiah describes those around the Throne: *seraphim*. *Seraphim* literally means "flames." He describes them as having six wings, two covering their face, two covering their feet, and two they fly with. These are not, however, members of the Divine Council. Isaiah then cries out because he is one of unclean lips (v5). He says, *"for mine eyes have seen the King, the Lord of Hosts."* At that point one of the *seraphim* comes over to him, and with coal from the altar, purifies Isaiah (v7). Then Isaiah hears Yahweh address the Council:

> Also I heard the voice of the Lord saying, Whom shall I send, and who will go FOR US? (v8)

Compare this with Micaiah's vision and El's address to his council. In this case, Isaiah steps up and volunteers as opposed to one of the divine attendants of the Council. H.W. Robinson, in his article, "THE COUNCIL OF YAHWEH," observes,

> The order of events should be noted, for their right understanding depends on this order. It is only AFTER the cleansing of Isaiah's lips that he is able to participate in the council of Yahweh, and to address Yahweh Himself. Yahweh calls upon His council for a decision as to His messenger, and asks for a volunteer (as in Micaiah's vision) who will go 'for us,' i.e., for the whole body of

councilors. Naturally, the cleansing of the lips (as the local organ employed in delivering the message) equips the prophet for his future task; but its first and immediate result is to enable him to join in the deliberations of the council.[476]

This reflects the holiness of the Divine Council. It should be noted here that both scenes portray the prophet as the Messenger for the Council. F.M. Cross observes,

> More concretely, the prophet is the Messenger of the Divine Court or Council, and his authority rest upon the absolute authority of the council, its great Judge or great King who pronounces the judgment, which the prophetic messenger is to transmit.[477]

This is true to the teachings of the Honorable Elijah Muhammad. He teaches that the Prophet is in fact the messenger to the whole Council of Twelve.

Micaiah's and Isaiah's descriptions of the proceedings of the Divine Assembly are basically similar. In Job 1:6-12; 2:1-7 a picture of the proceedings is given which introduces two new and important details. In Job, we read,

> "(6) Now there was a day when the sons of God
> came to present themselves before the Lord,
> and Satan came also among them.
> (7) And the Lord said unto Satan,
> Whence cometh thou? Then Satan answered the Lord,
> And said, 'From going to and from in the earth,
> And from walking up and down in it.'

Here, the *bene ha'eloheim* came to present themselves before Yahweh. What is important is that they came on an appointed day (*hayyom*) and Satan was among them. Morgenstern asks and

---

[476] H.W. Robinson, "THE COUNCIL OF YAHWEH," *Journal of Theological Studies* 45 (1944): 154

[477] Cross, *Canaanite Myth and Hebrew Epic*, 189.

answers a very important question concerning the time in which these proceedings take place. He asks,

> precisely when and upon what occasion did Yahweh hold His divine court and pronounce judgment upon mankind (?) Was it at any indeterminate moment in the year, when and as often as the spirit moved Him, or was it upon some particular occasion, at some fixed moment of the year, specifically appropriate for this peculiar, divine function?

He answers,

> (T)raditional Judaism has known, seemingly from fairly early times, of an annual Day of Judgment, judgment by God Himself, judgment not only of Israel but also of other nations and even of all mankind...And this annual Day of Judgment by the Deity has always been identified with the New Years Day. [478]

Morgenstern observes that the word *hayyom*, here translated as "a day," really means "the day." In the Targum of the Jews, they write that verse of Job *hayyom, beyoma' dedina' bere's satta'* meaning, *"On the Day of Judgment, upon the New Years Day."*[479] In I Sam. 1:4 *hayyom* means the New Years Day, the eighth and culminating day of the Asif festival.[480]

Morgenstern points out the significance of the fact that in both 1:6 and 2:1, the *bene ha'eloheim* are not summoned by Yahweh to gather, but come of their own accord upon a certain day. *Hasatan* (Satan) too comes. It is clear that, because he travels up and down the earth, he was not with the other *bene ha'eloheim* in the preceding days. Thus his appearance on that same day could not have been based on an agreement with them. *Hasatan* has been busy roaming the earth monitoring the sinful deeds of men. They all appeared together because it is routine to convene on that particular Day, which Morgenstern suggests is New Years Day.

---

[478] Morgenstern, "Mythological Background of Psalm 82," 43.
[479] Ibid., 44
[480].Ibid.

Edwin Kingsbury, in his article "The Prophets and The Council of Yahweh," agrees that the Day of Convening for the Council of Gods was New Years Day. He says, referring to the time of Micaiah's vision,

> There is reason to believe that the scene at the 'threshing floor' connects this experience with some agricultural feast. It is possible that the time of the chapter may be fixed even more closely by noting that in the Septuagint ch.22 follows immediately after ch. 20 (having excluded ch. 21 which deals with the Elijah legend and disrupt the chronology). The given (date) in ch. 20 is 'the turn of the year.' If the events in ch.22 take place just three years after the events recorded in ch. 20, then the time of the events in ch.22 is also 'at the turn of the year.' This would place the events at the time of the spring agricultural festival and of the New Year of Israel.[481]

Kingsbury, like Morgenstern, places all of the Conventions on the New Years Day, the Annual Day of Judgment.

Yahweh in v8 asks Satan has he considered his servant Job, a perfect and upright man. Satan suggests that Job is faithful only because Yahweh has blessed him. But if Yahweh's "hedge" was removed from around Job, he would certainly be of the sinful. Thus, Yahweh gives Satan a year to do to Job what he will, except harm his person. We read of Satan's works against Job in the rest of chapter 1-the destroying of his flock and the killing of his children. But Job turns humbly to Yahweh and says, "*The Lord giveth, and the Lord taketh away; blessed be the name of the Lord.*"(*v22*) In chapter 2, we read,

> Again there was (the) day (*hayyom*) when the sons
> of God came to present themselves before the Lord,
> and Satan came also among them
> TO PRESENT HIMSELF BEFORE THE LORD.

---

[481]E.C. Kingsbury, "The Prophets and The Council of Yahweh," *Journal of Biblical Literature*, 83 (1964): 280

Again we see, a year later, on the same *yom*, the *bene ha'eloheim* came to present themselves before Yahweh. What is interesting is that, as opposed to chapter 1:6, Satan too came to "PRESENT HIMSELF BEFORE THE LORD." In the first chapter, Satan just came. Though the gods came to "present themselves," Satan did not. But here, in the second convention, Satan shall present himself.

The Honorable Elijah Muhammad teaches that the Gods of the Assembly each go to a particular part of the earth. The twenty-three would, over the course of time, live among every people, nation, kindred, and tongue. They would study that people- tune in to the thinking of the people and study that people's history. The Gods then, by the use of the Law of Cause and Effect, would be able to predict the future of that people. The Gods would then convene back in the Holy City, and present their findings to Allah, the Judge. At which point, He would say either "Let it Be" or "No." This, I believe, is the meaning of the *bene ha'eloheim* "presenting themselves before the Lord."

In the first convening of the Gods with Yahweh, Satan didn't come to present any findings, for it was in that meeting that he was given the "Job Assignment." The next year, however, Satan was to present his findings on Job. And of course, his findings were unfavorable to himself. Thus, he asks for another year to work on Job, with more power, and Yahweh says, "Let It Be."

We have thus presented the evidence that the assembling of the Council of Yahweh, to pass judgment on the world, occurs on New Years Day. The Honorable Elijah Muhammad said that this New Years Day comes every 25,000 years. In ancient Kemet, where the ancient Black Hebrews spent considerable time learning and borrowing the religious ways of the Kemetians, their calendar consisted of one Great Year. This Great Year was determined by the Precession of the Poles, which took 25,897 years. Thus, one Great Year consisted of 25, 897 years, and every 25,897 years they celebrated the New Year. The Hebrews, particularly Moses who was a student of the Kemetic Mysteries, in all probability learned of this Great Year. If so, it is possible to see in the Hebrew Annual Day of Judgment a closing of a 25, 000 Year Cycle, as taught by the Honorable Elijah Muhammad.

The second detail highlighted by the Job narrative is the

position Satan, or *Hasatan* occupies in the Divine Assembly. Satan is not yet viewed as a malevolent being who is the enemy of God. He is one of the *bene ha'eloheim*. Morgenstern says,

> His function is to roam about the world and take notice of the acts of men and at the proper moment to bring to Yahweh a report thereof. Moreover, the import of the name, Hasatan, 'the adversary' or 'the accuser'...indicates that it is sins and crimes of men, rather than their meritorious deeds, of which he takes note and which he reports to Yahweh. It is therefore a role of fixed hostility to mankind and, moreover...a role specifically assigned to him by Yahweh...(H)asatan...while still one of the 'bene ha'elohim,' i.e.,...one of 'the host of heaven,' is that particular divine minister of Yahweh regularly commissioned to seek out the iniquitous deeds of men and report them to Yahweh at His great judgment assembly, His 'adat 'el.[482]

This is why we find Satan coming with the *bene ha'eloheim* in Job. At this point he is a member of the Assembly. The other *bene ha'eloheim* are commissioned to roam the earth also, as we learn in Zec. 1:8-11. They bring back information concerning the nations of the earth to Yahweh. Hasatan is a member with a specifically defined role given to him by Yahweh himself: to bring back the report of the iniquitous deeds of men. He is not yet the enemy of God but one of His ministers. Mullen notes that the name *Hasatan* occurs with the definite article making it a title instead of a name. He says,

> Nowhere in the Old Testament does Satan appear as a demonic figure opposed to God. The name itself is applied in only three passages, all of which are post-exilic. In the Old Testament, the Satan is indeed a divine being, but in each occurrence the name is an appellative -- it defines the role which the member of Yahweh's court performed as the 'adversary.' In post-biblical material,

---

[482] Morgenstern, "Mythological Background of Psalm 82," 42

however, this figure became the source and personification of Evil.[483]

Satan's job is to patrol the earth and make reports of the iniquitous deeds of men and then report them to Yahweh. Thus, in Zeceriah, Satan attempts to bring charges against Joshua the high-priest. It is only in post-biblical times when Satan becomes the epitome of evil. How did Satan go from being one of the *bene ha'eloheim*, one of the gods of the Divine Assembly, to being the antithesis of God and the source of evil?

Biblical and apocryphal writings speak of a rebellion that took place in heaven in the beginning. The leader of this rebellion against God was one of God's brightest shinning angels. The angel wanted to exalt himself above God and therefore, along with his followers, were cast out of heaven and from that point on became the source of all worldly evil: Satan.

12.2. *The Twenty-Four Elders of the Book of Revelations*

References to the Council are scarce in the New Testament. One early Christian text that describes the Council was found at Nag-Hamadi. Entitled, *The Apocryphon of John*, it was written in Coptic and is dated to the third century, though it is a revision of earlier works. This text speaks of God as The MAN. Frederick Borsch, in his **Son of Man in Myth and History**, describes this Man-God according to the *Apocryphon of John*:

> He is to be praised and is seen as a cosmic figure...He is creator, both father and son, the primal, source of all things. He wears the 'aeons' like a crown and rays dart forth from him...He is the Word and savior...The TWELVE THAT SURROUND HIM WEAR CROWNS AND ARE ROBED IN GLORY AS THEY BLESS THE KING.[484]

What we notice here is that "The Man" is the thirteenth member, an extra God. The same curious extra God is found in the Book of

---

[483] Mullen, *Assembly of the Gods*, 276.

[484] F. Borsch, F. **Son of Man in Myth and History** (London: S.C.M. Press, 1967) 62-3

Revelations. In the fourth chapter we read:

(2) And immediately I was in the spirit;
and behold, A THRONE was set in heaven,
and one sat on the throne.
(3) And he that sat was to look upon
like jasper and a sardine stone:
and there was a rainbow round about the throne,
In sight like unto an emerald.
(4) And round about the throne
Were FOUR AND TWENTY SEATS:
And upon the seats I saw
FOUR AND TWENTY ELDERS sitting,
clothed in white raiment's;
And they had on their heads crowns of gold...
(10) The four and twenty Elders fall down
before him that sat on the throne,
And worship him that liveth forever and ever,
And cast their crowns before the throne,
Saying, Thou art worthy, O Lord,
To receive glory and honor and power...
(5:1) And I saw in the right hand of
him that sat on the throne a BOOK
written within and on the backside
sealed with seven seals."

This is a clear description of the 24 Scientists, here called Elders. The Man sitting on the Throne is God. This Throne is the center of activity in Revelations, for it is mentioned 40 times. The other twenty-four are also sitting on thrones like God, showing that they are gods also, but of a lower rank. The Twenty Four Elders are shown prostrating themselves before God and worshipping Him. This seems to be their main duty in Revelations. It is interesting that the Man on the Throne is holding a Book in his hand sealed with seven seals. This picture in Revelations of the Twenty Four Elders is the culmination of the Biblical references to the Divine Assembly beginning with the *Eloheim* of Genesis 1. These are the Twenty Four Scientists that the Honorable Elijah Muhammad taught the world of. It is interesting, however, that the Judge in this picture makes the twenty 'fifth' person, not the twenty fourth as usual. Up 'till now, there were twenty-four gods with the twenty fourth being the Judge. But here, all 24, including the Judge, bows down to a twenty-fifth God. Who is this divine Man? We will answer this question shortly.

12.3. *Islam's Exalted Assembly*

The Muslim world also acknowledges the existence of this Divine Assembly. L.M.J. Garnet, in *Mysticism and Magic in Turkey*, writes,

> According to the mystical canon, there are always on earth a certain number of holy men who are admitted to intimate communion with the Deity.[485]

Manley P. Hall, in his *Mystics in Islam*, observes also,

> "According to certain mystical calculations, the true saints of the Moslem world are...the 'unseen men' who journey to all parts of the world according to the Will of God and are given authority over the affairs of mankind, both Moslem and non-Moslem. Sometimes these saints are collectively referred to as The Owners, or Masters of Destiny. The chief among them is known as the Center, and each morning the saints assemble at Mecca, presumably by some mystical projection of their higher natures, and report all they have done to the Center.[486]

The Center here is thought to be the Judge, Allah. Hall further says of the Center,

> At the head of the hierarchy composing the inner or mystical Dervish Order is a most august sole, who is called

---

[485] As quoted in Manley P. Hall's, *Mystics in Islam* (Los Angeles Philosophical Research Society, 1975) 89

[486] Hall, *Mystics in Islam*, 46.

the 'Axis' or 'Pole' of the universe... (H)e often wanders the earth in the garb of a novice. He is a Master of the power of magic, can make himself invisible at will, and traverse vast distances with the speed of thought...This great body of spiritual mystics, collectively the 'Lords of Souls' and 'Directors,' is an invisible government controlling all the temporal institutions of Islam, and far surpassing in power all earthly monarchs...With ...AN INNER BODY COMPOSED OF GOD-MEN so highly advanced and so superior to ordinary humanity that they seem more mystical than real, it is evident that the Dervishes form a very powerful Order in the Islamic world.[487]

This 'Axis of the Universe' is Allah Himself, the World King or Judge. It is interesting that He often walk's the earth as a novice (which is just a student instead of Master). Master Fard Muhammad, the Axis which we will deal with later, first appeared as a "prophet" instead of the God that He really was. Fazur Rahman, in *Islam*, says,

the world is kept in tack, thanks to the existence of a network of...saints of DIFFERENT RANKS...around which the WHOLE UNIVERSE ROTATES. But for this spiritual structure, the UNIVERSE WOULD GO TO PIECES."[488]

This Divine Assembly is also mentioned in the *Holy Qur'an*. Just as God uses the plural personal pronoun "Us" and "Our" in the Bible, so too does the *Holy Qur'an* use the plural "We" (*nahnu*):

And surely We created man of sounding clay (15:26)
And indeed We have given thee a Reminder from Ourselves (20:99)
And We made the heaven a guarded canopy (21:32)"
And to Us you are returned (21:35)

---

[487] Ibid., 89-90

[488] F. Rahman, *Islam* (New York: Holt, Renehart, Winste, 1960) 136

Who are the "We" and "Us"? Muslim scholars today, having not understanding, attempt to dismiss these plural references by saying this is only Allah using language to express the greatness of His majesty. However, this is a very weak attempt on their part to rectify these clearly plural references with their misunderstanding of monotheism. These references could not be Allah using kingly language, because hard pronouns such as "Ourselves" (21:17; 25:46, ect) necessitate the presence of a group of persons. Also such references to "Our eyes" in 11:37, "Our hands" in 36:71 further prove this point.

Further proof that a plurality of beings is meant here is given in Surah 56:59:"*Is it you that create or are We the CREATORS?*" "Creators" denotes more than one. Also, in 51:47,"*We are the Makers*" and 15:23 "*We are the Inheritors.*" These are clearly references to a plural body. The *Holy Qur'an* mentions this Divine Council in Surah 37:8 where it refers to the "Exalted Assembly" (*al-mala' al-a'la*). Both Yusef Ali and Maulana Ali refer to this as a "heavenly assembly." Remember, in ancient Sumer the Divine Assembly was called the "Exalted Court." Mention is also made in the Qur'an of the "Exalted Chiefs" (38:69). Are these "Exalted Chiefs" members of the "Exalted Assembly"? And if so, are they the Major Scientists?

The *Holy Qur'an* refers to members of this Divine Assembly as *mala'ikah*, translated as "angels." We found the members of Yahweh's Council referred to as *Mal'ak*, "angels." The word actually comes from the Arabic *malaka*, meaning "he controlled" or from *alk*, meaning "to send." These etymologies reveal that the true meaning of the word is not angel, but an emissary or one sent from the Council who has control over the forces of nature.[489] These so-called angels, just as in the Bible, are pictured encircling Allah on His Throne. A.J. Wensinck, in *The Muslim Creed*, describes the duties of these *mala'ikah*:

> In the Kuran the angels are mentioned as the heavenly host side by side with Allah Himself. They are His obedient servants who encircle His Throne, praising Him and prostrating themselves. They are His intermediaries

[489] Maulana Muhammad Ali, *The Holy Qur'an*, 17, n. 47.

with man, and more especially the bearers of His revelation and command. They console the Faithful and implore Allah's forgiveness on their behalf. They also accomplish the separation between body and soul when the children of man die; sometimes they combine this function with that of punishing the infidels. Especially in connection with the resurrection of the dead they are often mentioned: they will bear the throne on that day, they will be ranged in a row with the Ruh, but the intercession of many of them will be of no avail."[490]

In Surah 39:75 it reads,

> And thou seest the angels (*mala'ikah*) going round about the Throne of Power, glorifying their Lord with praise.

We found that one of the duties of the *bene ha'eloheim* was to praise Yahweh in the Council. In Psalms 89:8-9, the heavenly host are referred to as "all those around him" (*al-kol-sebibaw*) and the "faithful ones (who) surround you (Yahweh)" (*we'emunateka sebiboteka*). Also, compare this with the picture in the Book of Revelations 4 of the Elders sitting around God on a Throne praising Him. Such is the case here also. In Surah 42:5, it says the

> (*mala'ikah*) celebrate the praise of their Lord and ask forgiveness for those on earth.

The *mala'ikah* are also said to petition Allah on behalf of men. We find this described in Surah 40:7-9:

> Those who bear the Throne of Power and those around it celebrate the praise of their Lord and believe in Him and ask protection for those who believe.

Here a distinction is made between those "who bear the Throne" and "those around" the Throne, showing that their is a rank. It is possible that this is reference to the Major and Minor Scientists.

---

[490] A.J. Wensinck, *The Muslim Creed* (New Delhi: Oriental Reprint, 1932, 1979), 198

Not all angels are part of the Council. A distinction is made between regular angels and "*the angels who are near to Him (Allah) (al-mukarrabun) 4:172).*" In Zec. 3:4, the gods are referred to simply as "those who stood before Him." The "Exalted Chiefs" are mentioned in Surah 38, entitled "Those Ranging in Ranks." In Surah 78:38, the *mala'ikah* are said to "*stand in ranks*" with *Al-Ruh*, The Spirit, at the forefront. Al-Ruh is the angel Gabriel. He, like the *haruah* of Micaiah's vision, is a member of the Council referred to as The Spirit. Gabriel, or Al-Ruh, is mentioned as leading the *mala'ikah* on two other occasions: in Surah 70:4 ascending to Allah; and in Surah 97:4 descending to earth. Gabriel's role in the Exalted Assembly is discussed in a later chapter.

Men are forbidden to worship these *mala'ikah*. In Surah 34:40, we read,

And on the day when He will gather them all together, then will He say to the angels: Did these worship you? (41) They will say: Glory be to Thee! Thou art our Protecting Friend, not they; nay, they worshipped the jinn; most of them were believers in them.

Compare this with Deut. 4:19 where Yahweh admonishes the people from worshipping "the host of heaven." The members of Allah's Exalted Assembly are not to be worshipped, but are to worship Him.

The members of Allah's Exalted Assembly also accompany Him in battle, just as the members of the Canaanite and Hebrew Assemblies accompanied the God in battle. In Surah 89:21, we read,

Nay, when the earth is made to crumble to pieces, (22) And the Lord comes with the angels (*mala'ikah*), ranks on ranks; (23) And hell is made to appear that day.

These *mala'ikah* go to battle with Allah, "ranks on ranks."

The members of this Exalted Assembly are also referred to as *Hafazah*, "Keepers" (6:61; 82:10). As Keepers, they watch over the affairs of men to "guard the consequences of his deeds."[491] This is compared with the *bene ha'eloheim* referred to as "Guardians of the people" and "Watchers." As Keepers, they are also described as "Honorable Recorders" who "know what you do" (82:11). They are said to have all the deeds of man recorded. We notice that, in the Book of Job, the *bene ha'eloheim* were commissioned to go out in the world and make a record of the deeds of men.

The Exalted Assembly of Islam shares a lot in common with the Hebrew *Adat'el*. Both are composed of the heavenly host encircling God as He sits enthroned. The members of each share the same duties, such as praising the God, serving as messengers or ambassadors, and accompanying the God in battle. Both have a member called *Ruah* or *Ruh*, The Spirit. Another member of the Adat'el was Hasatan. Satan was originally one of the bene ha'eloheim who was driven out of heaven. In the Exalted Assembly, one of the mala'ikah was *Iblis*. Iblis was the rebellious angel who was "driven away" (15:29-36) and later emerged as *Shaiton*, the Devil. Two other angels that they share in common are Gabriel and Michael. Both are mentioned by name in the *Holy Qur'an* (2:98) and both are mentioned by name in the Bible (Dan. 8:16; 9:21;10:13;12:1). The Qur'an, like the Bible, has its "angel of death" (32:11).

### 12.3.1. *Jabril and the Divine Assembly*

The most famous *mala'ikah* written of in the Qur'an as a leader of sorts of the other "angels" is Jabril or Gabriel. It is written that Muhammad would frequently go up into the mountain cave of Hira and meditate and contemplate over issues of the divine. But on one of those sessions, a vision came to him. In the vision, the angel Gabriel came to him and with a loud and authoritative voice said to the Prophet, "Read." After Muhammad replied, "*I am not one who can read*," Gabriel "*took hold to me and pressed me so hard that I could not bear it any more.*"[492] Then after the third repetition of this, Gabriel revealed to Muhammad the first *Surah* (Chapter) and *Ayat* (verse) of the *Holy Qur'an*:

---

[491] Ali, *Holy Qur'an*, n. 1269.

[492] Quotes taken from *A Manual of Hadith*, by Maulana Muhammad Ali.

Read in the Name of thy Lord Who created-He created man from a clot-Read and thy Lord is most Honorable.

It was Gabriel who, over a period of some 22 years, revealed the totality of the *Holy Qur'an* to the Holy Prophet. It has generally been assumed that the angel Gabriel was some spooky being with wings or something that is other than a man. But the Holy Prophet and the *Holy Qur'an* say differently: the angel Gabriel was a Man. The Qur'an says,

Then We sent to her (Mary) Our spirit and it appeared to her as a WELL-MADE MAN (19:17).

Gabriel is known as the Spirit of Truth or the Holy Spirit.[493] We have seen that such a member of the Council described in Hebrew literature was designated as "Ruah," The Spirit.

In describing the way in which he receives revelation, Muhammad mentions two ways as reported by A'isha. The first and the hardest on him is when he only hears Gabriel in his ears but he doesn't see Him. The other is when he does see Him and

the Angel comes to me in THE LIKENESS OF A MAN and speaks to me and I retain in memory what he says.[494]

In the Prophetic Hadith there is a very interesting account of a particular experience that the Prophet had with Gabriel. It is related by Umar, the second Caliph. I will quote it in its entirety:

One day while we were sitting with the Messenger of Allah (may the blessings and peace of Allah be upon him) THERE APPEARED BEFORE US A MAN WHOSE CLOTHS WERE EXCEEDINGLY WHITE AND WHOSE HAIR WAS EXCEEDINGLY BLACK; no signs of journeying were to be seen on him and none of us knew

---

[493] Ibid., 4, ft. #7.
[494] Ibid., 12.

him. He walked up and sat down by the Prophet (may the blessings and peace of Allah be upon him). Resting his knees against his and placing the palms of his hands on his thighs, he said: O Muhammad, tell me about Islam. The Messenger of Allah (may the blessing and peace of Allah be upon him) said: Islam is to testify that there is no god but Allah and Muhammad is the Messenger of Allah, to perform the prayers, to pay the zakat, to fast in Ramadan, and to make pilgrimage to the House if you are able to do so. He said: You have spoken rightly, and we were amazed at him and saying that he had spoken rightly. He said: Then tell me about *iman*. He said: It is to believe in Allah, His angels, His books, His messengers, and the Last Day, and to believe in divine destiny, both the good and the evil thereof. He said: You have spoken rightly. He Said: Then tell me about *ihsan*. He said: It is to worship Allah as though you are seeing Him, and while you see Him not yet truly He sees you. He said: Then tell me about the Hour. He said: The one questioned about it knows no better than the questioner. He said: Then tell me about its signs. He said: That the slave-girl will give birth to her mistress and that you will see the bare-footed, naked, destitute herdsmen competing in constructing lofty buildings. Then he took himself off and I stayed for a time. Then he said: O 'Umar, do you know who the questioner was? I said: Allah and his Messenger know best. He said: IT WAS GABRIEL, WHO CAME TO YOU TO TEACH YOU YOUR RELIGION.[495]

In fact, the name Gabriel, according to *The Encyclopedia Of Islam*, means "Man Of God."[496] He seems to be an angel of special significance, for he is described as leading the other angels in the ascension to Allah (70:4) and descending to Earth (97:4). Surah 78:38,

The day when the spirit (*al-ruh*) and the angels stand in

---

[495] An-Nawawi's *Forty Hadith*, #2.
[496] "Djabra'il," *The Encyclopedia of Islam*, 2:362.

ranks; none shall speak except he whom the Beneficent permits and he speaks right.

This distinction between the *mala'ika* and *Al-Ruh* has perplexed scholars. It is clear, though, that it shows Gabriel to be one of great and special significance among the other *mala'ika*.

Gabriel was a Divine Man, a Scientist. *The Encyclopedia Of Islam* notes that,

> As a rule he appeared as an ordinary strong man...WEARING TWO GREEN GARMENTS and a silk turban, on a horse.[497]

These green garments, as well shall see, seem to be the characteristic dress of the Scientists of Islam.

12.4. *The Unknown Men in Scripture*

We have just outlined the structure of this "secret government" composed of 24 Black Men who are Gods and who control the functions of the universe. This body of Black Gods is known throughout the world under different names: *Eloheim, Adat'El, the 24 Elders, Anunnaki, Aditays, the Judges of Ma' at, The Mystic Order of Dervishes,* etc. It is this body of Black Gods that brings rain, hail, snow, and earthquakes. It is this Council, as outlined, that also imparts knowledge to the world. The identity of the members of this Divine Council is usually unknown. It is only known among the Circle. The Head Judge is called Allah. Every now and then, however, we will learn of this One's personal attribute. *Marduk, Ahura Mazda,* and *Yahweh* were the personal attributes of the Head Gods who ruled at various times. As stated in the previous chapter, whenever an aspect of the Prophetic History is about to be fulfilled, one of the Major Scientists or Gods will raise up one from among the people and that one will teach him and make him a prophet.

---

[497] Ibid., 2:363.

That One would either be the Judge, or He would be one of the Twelve Major Scientists. When it is one of the Scientists that are commissioned for this job, He appears as an Arch-Angel or as an "Unknown Man" of scripture.

## 12.4.1. *Abraham and His Three Visitors*

In the 18th Chapter of Genesis it is written of Abraham:

And the Lord appeared unto him (Abraham) in the plains of Mamre: and he sat in the tent door in the heat of the day; And he lifted up his eyes and looked, and lo, THREE MEN stood by him: and when he saw them, he ran to meet them from the tent door, AND BOWED HIMSELF TOWARD THE GROUND, and said, MY LORD, if now I have found favor in thy sight, pass not away, I pray thee, from thy servant: Let a little water, I pray you be fetched, and WASH YOUR FEET, AND REST YOURSELVES UNDER THE TREE: And I will fetch a morsel of bread, and comfort your hearts; after that ye shall pass on...And they said, So do, as thou hast said. And Abraham hastened into the tent unto Sarah, and said, Make ready THREE MEASURES OF FINE MEAL...AND MAKE CAKES UPON THE HEARTH. And Abraham ran unto the herd, and fetched a calf tender and good...And he took butter, and milk and the calf which he had dressed, AND SET IT BEFORE THEM; AND HE STOOD WITH THEM UNDER THE TREE AND THEY DID EAT...

AND THE MEN ROSE UP from thence, and looked toward Sodom: and Abraham went with them to bring them on the way. AND THE LORD SAID, Shall I hide from Abraham that thing which I do;...And the Lord said, Because the cry of Sodom and Gomorra is great, and because their sin is very grievous; I will go down now, and see whether they have done according to the cry of it...

And THE MEN TURNED THEIR FACES FROM
THENCE, and went toward Sodom: But Abraham stood
yet before the Lord...And the Lord went his way...

I put as much of Chapter 18 in here as possible because an
extremely important fact is revealed here. Of those THREE
MEN that approached Abraham in the plains of Mamre, one
of those men was The Lord (Yahweh). The Lord and the two
other Men that are with him are fed very well by
Abraham and Sarah; fed with regular food that you and I eat:
bread, cakes, meat, butter, and milk. These are three human
beings, but one of them is Yahweh. This man who approached
Abraham with two other "men" is identified by the narrator as
Yahweh, but most scholars generally assume that Abraham
himself is in a fog regarding the identity of his visitors. As we will
later see, this is a recurring phenomenon: Holy figures will
appear but their identity would not be known. This Man
who is Abraham's Lord is in fact Allah, the Head Judge of
the Council of the Gods of Abraham's day. Notice that this
simple designation Adonay ("Lord") seems to be an identifying
mark of the Council members. As we will soon see, almost all,
if not all, of these unidentified figures are referred to as Adonay or
"My Lord."

But who are the other two men with him? The very next
chapter reveals their identity. At the closing of the 18th Chapter,
the two men leave the Lord behind talking to Abraham
and they go on to Sodom. The Lord eventually meets them
there. The opening of Chapter 19 says:

And there came TWO ANGELS TO SODOM at
even...and Lot seeing them rose up to meet them; and
he bowed himself with his face toward the
ground; And he said, Behold now, MY
LORDS...into they servants house, and tarry all
night, AND WASH YOUR FEET, and ye shall rise up

early, and go on your ways...

But before they lay down, the men of the city, even the men of Sodom, compassed the house round...And they called unto Lot and said unto him, 'Where are the MEN which came in to thee this night? Bring them out unto us that we may know them...

But THE MEN put forth their hand and pulled Lot into the house to them, and shut to the door...

And THE MEN said unto Lot, 'Hast thou here any besides? Son in law, and thy sons, and thy daughters, and whatsoever thou hast in the city, bring them out of this place: For WE WILL DESTROY THIS PLACE, because the cry of them is waxen great before the face of the Lord; AND THE LORD HATH SENT US TO DESTROY IT...'

And when the morning arose, THEN THE ANGELS hastened Lot, saying Arise, take thy wife and thy two daughters, which are here; lest they be consumed in the iniquity of the city...

Clearly the two men that accompanied The Lord were two of His Angels, or two other Scientists from the Council. The Head Judge is Allah, the God, while the others are called in scripture His Angels It is these other Scientists or Angels that destroy cities with Allah. The Unnamed Holy Man and the two men with Him represented Allah, the Judge, and two of His Angels or Scientists.

12.4.2. *Daniel and the Black Angel*

There are other times when the Head Judge doesn't go. Instead, He sends one of the other Major Scientists to do the job of conversing with the prophet. In these situations, the identity of the Scientist is usually unknown. In fact, when one appears in scripture, the scholars know not who or what he represents. He is not identified as an angel. He is referred to as one of God's Servants but He is not identified as a prophet. He in fact teaches the prophets. He is no ordinary Servant because he has great power and the prophets bow down in their presence. They are actually one of the Major Scientists.

One appears in the Book of Daniel, Chapter 10. It is necessary that I quote the entire chapter so that the full significance is revealed. It reads:

> In the third year of Cyrus King of Persia a thing was revealed unto Daniel, whose name was called Belteshazzar; and the thing was true, but the time appointed was long: and he understood the thing, and had understanding of the vision.
>
> In those days I Daniel was mourning three full weeks. I ate no pleasant bread, neither came flesh nor wine in my mouth, neither did I anoint myself at all, till three weeks were fulfilled. And in the four and twentieth day of the first month, as I was by the side of the great river, which is Hiddekel;
>
> Then I lifted up mine eyes, and looked, and behold a CERTAIN MAN CLOTHED IN LINEN, WHOSE LOINS WERE GIRDED WITH FINE GOLD OF UPHAZ: HIS BODY ALSO WAS LIKE THE BERYL, AND HIS FACE WAS THE APPEARANCE OF LIGHTNING, AND HIS EYES AS LAMPS OF FIRE, AND HIS ARMS AND HIS FEET LIKE THE COLOUR TO POLISHED BRASS, AND THE VOICE OF HIS WORDS LIKE THE VOICE OF A MULTITUDE.
>
> And I Daniel alone saw the vision: for men that were with me saw not the vision; but a great quaking fell

upon them, so that they fled to hide themselves. Therefore I was left alone, and saw this great vision, AND THERE REMAINED NO STRENGTH IN ME: FOR MY COMELINESS WAS TURNED IN ME INTO CORRUPTION, and I retained no strength. Yet I heard the voice of his words: and when I heard the voice of his words, then was I in a deep sleep on my face, and MY FACE TOWARD THE GROUND.

And, behold, a hand touched me, which set me upon my knees and upon the palms of my hands. And he said unto me, 'O Daniel, a man greatly beloved, understand the words that I speak unto thee, and stand upright: for unto thee AM I NOW SENT.' And when he had spoken this word unto me, I STOOD TREMBLING. Then said he unto me, 'Fear not Daniel: for from the first day that thou didst set thy heart to understand, and to chasten thyself before thy God, and thy words were heard, and I am come for thy words. But the prince of the kingdom of Persia withstood me one and twenty days: but lo, Michael, one of the chief princes, came to help me, and I remained there with the chiefs of Persia. Now I am come to make thee understand WHAT SHALL BEFALL THY PEOPLE IN THE LATER DAYS: FOR THE VISION IS FOR MANY DAYS.' And when he had spoken such words unto me, I set my face towards the ground, and I became dumb. And behold, one like the similitude of the sons of men touched my lips: then I opened my mouth, and spake, and said unto him that stood before me, '0 MY LORD (ADONAY), by the vision my sorrows are turned upon me, and I have retained no strength. For how can the servant of this my lord talk with this my lord? For as for me, straightway there remained no strength in me, neither is there breath left in me.' Then there came again and touched me one like the appearance of a man, and he strengthened me, And said, 'O man greatly beloved, fear not: PEACE BE UNTO THEE, be strong. And when he had spoken unto me, I was strengthened, and said, 'Let my lord speak, FOR THOU HAS STRENGTHENED ME.' Then said he, 'Knowest thou wherefore I come unto thee? and now I will return to fight with the prince of Persia: and when I am gone forth, lo, the prince of Grecia shall come. 'BUT I WILL SHOW THEE WHAT IS WRITTEN IN THE SCRIPTURE OF TRUTH: and there is none that holdeth with me in these things but Michael your prince. (end)

Who is this Divine Man? He is one with great power to strengthen the prophet Daniel, and great authority to cause the prophet to tremble and bow his face to the ground. His identity is made known in the 14th and 21st verse. "Now I am come to make the understand WHAT SHALL BEFALL THY PEOPLE IN THE LATTER DAYS." And also, "BUT I WILL SHOW THEE THAT WHICH IS NOTED IN THE SCRIPTURE OF TRUTH." He is a Black Angel: his body is like beryle, a blue black stone. This Holy Man is one of the 12 Major Scientists who has come to reveal to Daniel the aspect of the Prophesy about to be fulfilled.

### 12.4.3. *Al-Khadir and the Exalted Assembly in Islam*

These Scientists have likewise been written of as "Unknown Men" in the *Holy Qur'an*, the sacred scripture of Islam. One of the most mysterious figures of Muslim tradition is the Unidentified Servant of The Lord found in Surah 18, section 9 and 10, beginning with ayat 65. It begins:

They found one of our servants whom We had granted mercy from Us and Whom We had taught knowledge from Ourselves.

The "We" here is the rest of the Council speaking. It continues:

Moses said to him: May I follow thee that thou MAYEST TEACH ME of the good thou hast been taught? He said: Thou canst not have patience with me. And how canst

232

thou have patience in that whereof thou hast not a comprehensive knowledge? He said: If Allah please, thou wilt find me patient, nor shall I disobey thee in aught. He said: If thou wouldst follow me, question me not about aught until I myself speak to thee about it.

So they set out until, when they embarked in a boat, he made a hole in it. (Moses) said: Hast thou made a hole in it to drown its occupants? Thou hast surely done a grievous thing. He said: Did I not say that thou couldst not have patience with me? He said: Blame me not for what I forgot, and be not hard upon me for what I did.

So they went on until, when they met a boy he slew him. (Moses) said: Hast thou slain an innocent person, not guilty of slaying another? Thou hast indeed done a horrible thing. He said: Did I not say to thee that thou couldst not have patience with me? He said: If I ask thee about anything after this, keep not company with me. Thou wilt then indeed have found an excuse in my case.

So they went on until, when they came to the people of a town, they asked its people for food, but they refused to entertain them as guests. Then they found in it a wall which was on the point of falling, so he put it into a right state. (Moses) said: If thou hadst wished, thou couldst have taken recompense for it. He said: This is the parting between me and thee. Now I will inform thee of the significance of that with which thou couldst not have patience.

As for the boat, it belonged to the poor people working on the river, and I intended to damage it, for there was behind them a king who seized every boat by force. And for the boy, his parents were believers and We feared lest he should involve them in wrongdoing and disbelief. So We intended that their Lord might give them in his place one better in purity and nearer to mercy.

233

And for the wall, it belonged to two orphan boys in the city, and there was beneath it a treasure belonging to them, and their father had been a righteous man. So thy Lord intended that they should gain their maturity and take out their treasure - a mercy from their Lord-and I did not do it of my own accord. This is the significance of that with which thou couldst not have patience (End)."

Who is this Unnamed Servant? Surely he is more than a prophet, for he TEACHES prophets. His identity was in fact revealed in the 80th and 81st verse (ayat). In explaining why he killed the young boy, he says, "*We* feared" and "*We* intended." As we have shown, the "WE" is referring to the Council of Gods. He, this Unnamed Servant, is one of the Council of the Gods; one of the Scientists. He is not the Judge, but one of the Majors.

Muslim tradition has since called him *Al-Khadir* which means "the green one." One can't help but connect this designation with the green garments said to be worn by the Scientists such as Gabriel. His real name, geneologym, or date is unknown. However, much is recorded of him in these traditions. He is said to live on an island, the name of which is unknown. Others say he lives in Jerusalem and makes salat every Friday in the Mosques of Mecca, Medina, Jerusalem, Kuba' and on the Mount of Olives. He makes pilgrimage to Mecca every year, drinks from the Well of Zem Zem every Friday, and washes in the well of Siloam.

Al-Khadir is said to possess great power. As Allah's khalifa (deputy) on sea and wakil on land, he has power over the sky, sea, and all quarters of the earth. He is immortal, can make himself invisible at will, and can speak the language of every people. Al-Khadir was a god to the Syrian sailors and in India he was appealed to as a river-god by the name <u>Kh</u>-w-ad<u>ja</u> <u>Kh</u>idr.[498]

### 12.4.3.1. *The Scientists and Jalal-ud-Din*

In the thirteenth century a Muslim by the name of Jalal-ud-Din became an adept of the Dervish Sufi Order. In A.D. 1260 he was urged by Hasan Husam al-Din to compose the *Mesnevi*, which is a

---

[498] "Al-Khadir," *The Encyclopedia Of Islam*, 4: 902-905.

six volume mystical poem of Islam. Jalal-ud-Din seems to have procured the favor of the Divine Assembly, if we believe the reports, and on occasions had direct contact with the gods on the Council. At the age of 23, Jalal traveled to Aleppo to further his studies. While there, many of his peers were jealous, and thus complained to the governor that this young man left his cell each night at midnight for some mysterious reason that they suspected was immoral. The governor decided to find out the truth for himself and one night hid himself outside the college gate. At exactly twelve, the gate allegedly mysteriously opened of itself and Jalal emerged. The governor attempted to follow and found himself traveling at great speed over a considerable distance.

The journey concluded 350 miles from Aleppo, at the tomb of Abraham at Hebron. Hall describes what happened next:

> The governor then beheld a domed edifice, wherein was congregated a large company of mysterious beings wearing GREEN ROBES, who came forth to meet Jalal-ud-din. They embraced him with affection and then conducted him into the building. The governor became so frightened he fainted. When he awoke, the domed building was gone, and the bewildered magistrate was hopelessly lost in the desert.[499]

Another mysterious interaction with the Divine Assembly was reported by Jalal's widow. She was regarded in her day as a model and virtuous woman. She related that one evening she had seen through the chink in the door her husband and an associate engaging in spiritual communion. Suddenly the wall opened and six strangers dressed in green robes entered, saluted and bowed, placing a nosegay of bright flowers at the feet of Jalal. This was the more odd because it was in the depth of midwinter. The six mysterious strangers stayed until sunrise then departed through the walls again. Jalal gave the nosegay to his wife, saying they were given to her as gifts from the strangers. She sent her servant with the bouquet to the perfumers mart in the city to ask what type of flowers they were. All the merchants were astonished, for

---

[499] Hall, *Mystics in Islam*, 97.

they had never seen such. A spice merchant, though, from India recognized them to be petals of a flower that grows in Ceylon, southern India.[500]

12.5. *The Duties of the Gods*

Thus far, we have seen that the Gods serve a great many functions as members of God's Divine Court. They write the Prophetic History of the Black Nation. They Serve as warriors in God's army and accompany Him in His Holy Wars. The Gods will act as messengers for the Head God. In Deut. 33:2b-3, the functions of the Gods are explicitly stated:

> At his right hand marched the mighty ones,
> Yea, the guardians of the people.
> All the holy ones are at your right hand.
> They prostrate themselves at your feet,
> They carry out your decisions.

In these verses, the military duties of the Gods are reinforced, but other duties are also acknowledged. They are to prostrate themselves before the God (v3c). This is one of their divine duties, to praise and prostrate themselves before the God, for they are not His equal. This point is reinforced in Ps. 29:1-2:

> Ascribe to Yahweh, O sons of the gods (*bene 'elim*)!
> Ascribe to Yahweh glory and honor!
> Ascribe to Yahweh the glory of his name!
> Prostrate yourselves to Yahweh when he appears in holiness!

The Gods are to carry out all the decisions of Yahweh (Deut. 33:3d). Whatever the Judge decrees, the Gods will bring into fruition.

---

[500]Ibid.,98

## 12.5.1. *The Gods as Heads of State*

In Deut. 33:3 the Gods are referred to as the "guardians of the people." The Honorable Elijah Muhammad taught that in the beginning, there were five billion people on the earth divided up into twelve nations. The ruler of each nation was one of the Twelve Major Scientists. This teaching is confirmed in Deut. 32:8-9 where it reads:

> When the Most High apportioned the nations
> When he separated the sons of man,
> He established the boundaries of the peoples
> According to the number of the sons of God.

While the King James Version writes "sons of God" as "sons of Israel," the discovery of the ancient Hebrew texts from Qumram prove that it is properly written "sons of God" or "sons of the gods," *bene ha'eloheim*.[501] The nations were apportioned and the boundaries of the peoples were set based on the number of the *bene ha'eloheim*. What was the number of the *bene ha'eloheim*?
L. Graham, in *Deceptions and Myths of the Bible*, says,

> Eloheim. The word comes from Alheim and means a council, a Council of the Gods...The Eloheim were inferentially twelve in number, since there were twelve Titans and twelve powers of the zodiac.[502]

The number of the Eloheim is Twelve. The nations and peoples were apportioned and each of the twelve Eloheim was placed over a nation. They were to be the guardians of the people. In Deut. 4:19, Yahweh forbids the people from worshipping the sun, moon, stars, or all the "host of heaven" whom Yahweh had *"allotted (halaq) unto all nations under the heavens."* In the apocalyptic Book of Sirac, it states: *"For every nation he appointed a ruler, But Israel is the Lord's portion."*[503]

---

[501] Hayes, *Introduction to The Old Testament Study*, 74.

[502] Graham, *Deceptions and Myths of the Bible*, 36.

[503] Mullen, *Assembly of the Gods*, 203.

The Gods duty as guardians of the people might have been what gave rise to their designation as the *Watchers*. In Dan.4:17, it is written that "*This matter is by the decree of the Watchers, and the demand by the word of the holy ones.*" They are called the Watchers in the apocryphal *Book of Enoch*.[504] In the Kemetic Text *Pepi II*, they are called Watchers.

We have seen that the Gods are often dispatched as messengers for the Council and/or the Judge. When they are in this role, they are referred to as a *mal'ak*, often translated "angel." The word really means "ambassador," "to dispatch as a deputy" or "messenger." This speaks to the gods' role as ambassador to the Council. When reference is made to "angels" in the Bible, the reference is usually to one of the Scientists. We have developed this later in this writing.

### 12.5.2. *The Gods and the Black Death*

Some times one of the Scientists would be dispatched from the Council in order to be a messenger for the Council. Other times, however, Scientists are dispatched not to carry a message to the people, but to bring destruction to a people. These are "Angels of Death" or "Death Angels." When Yahweh destroyed Sodom and Gomorrah he dispatched two angels, i.e. Scientists, to bring about this destruction (Gen. 19).

One of the oft' used methods of destruction is the sending of plagues upon a people. Yahweh sent plagues into Egypt to curse Pharaoh (Ex. 11:1). Because this type of destruction is used so often, there is apparently a god on the Council that is the god of Pestilence and Plague. In Habakkuk 3.3 this god is said to precede the coming of God from Teman. It reads,

> God came from Teman, and the Holy One from Mt. Paran...Before him Pestilence (*Daber*) marched, And Plague (*Resep*) went forth at his feet.

Mullen says,

---

[504] Morgenstern, "Mythological Background of Psalm 82," 88

Here, the designation of the members of the military entourage as Pestilence (*daber*) and Plague (*resep*) shows the terror involved in the theophany of the Divine Warrior. The inclusion of Resep, the god of pestilence and disease, is not surprising. As this god could be invoked in the assembly when the concern was for progeny...so he could also accompany the warrior-god in combat.[505]

*Resep*, the god of Pestilence and Disease, also called *Daber*, was a part of the Divine Council in Canaan. In an ancient Canaanite text, six of the members of the Assembly are mentioned: El, the Judge, and *Aliyan, Ba'l Yarihu, Kotar, Rahmayyu,* and *Rapsu.* Rapsu, like the Hebrew Resep, is the god of Pestilence and Plague.[506] *The Encyclopedia of Religion* observes that the two gods are in fact the same god.[507] We observe this god in I Chron. 21:14-16:

> So the Lord sent Pestilence upon Israel:
> and there fell of Israel seventy thousand men.
> (15) And God sent an angel unto Jerusalem to destroy it:
> And as he was destroying, the Lord beheld,
> and he repented him of evil,
> and said to the angel that destroyed,
> 'It is enough, stay now thine hand.'
> And the angel of the Lord stood by the
> threshing floor of Ornan the Jebusite.
> (16) And David lifted up his eyes,
> And saw the angel of the Lord
> Stand between the earth and the heaven,
> Having a drawn sword in his hand
> stretched out over Jerusalem.

In the thirteenth and fourteenth centuries, Europe was hit with great plagues that wiped out between one-third to one-half of the European population. The plague which so devastated Europe

---

[505] Mullen, *Assembly of the Gods*, 194.

[506] Ibid., 179-80

[507] "Canaanite Religion," *The Encyclopedia of Religion*, 2: 39.

was Bubonic Plague, but it has become known as Black Death. The orthodox history says that the plague was caused and spread by rodents and through the cold air. However, there is more to the story than meets the eye. William Bramley, in *The Gods of Eden*, observes that,

> Troubling enigmas about the Black Death still linger. Many outbreaks occurred in the summer during warm weather in uncrowded regions. Not all outbreaks of bubonic plague were preceded by rodent infestation: in fact, only a minority of cases seemed to be related to an increase in the presence of vermin. The greatest puzzle about Black Death is how it was able to strike isolated human populations which had no contact with earlier infected areas. The epidemics also tended to end abruptly.[508]

The most puzzling phenomenon associated with the Black Death is the curious appearance of mysterious Black Men right before the outbreak of the plague, and their mysterious subsequent disappearance. Johannes Nohl, in his *The Black Death, A Chronicle of the Plague*, chronicles these mysterious appearances. He writes,

> in the year of Christ 1571 was seen at Cremnitz in the mountain towns of Hungary on Ascension Day in the evening to the great perturbation [disturbance] of all, when on the Schuelersberg there appeared SO MANY BLACK RIDERS that the opinion was prevalent that the Turks were making a secret raid, but who RAPIDLY DISAPPEARED again, and thereupon a RAGING PLAGUE BROKE OUT IN THE NEIGHBORHOOD.[509]

These Black riders are reminiscent of the *bene ha'eloheim* in Zec. 1:8-11. They too are pictured mounted on horses. Nohl cites a

---

[508] Bramley, *Gods of Eden*, 180-1

[509] J. Nohl, *The Black Death: A Chronicle Of The Plaque* (London: George Allen and Unwin Ltd., 1926) 63

journal from 1680 which reported:

> That between Eisenberge and Dornberge thirty funeral biers [casket stands] all covered with black cloth were seen in broad daylight, among them on a bier A BLACK MAN WAS STANDING WITH A WHITE CROSS. When these had disappeared a great heat set in so that people in this place could hardly stand it...Whereupon the epidemic set in Thuringia in many places.[510]

Probably the most interesting took place in Germany:

> In Brandenburg [in Germany] there appeared in 1559 horrible men, of whom at first fifteen and later on TWELVE were seen. The foremost had beside their posteriors little heads, the others fearful faces and long scythes, with which they cut the oats, so that the swish could be heard at a great distance, but the oats remained standing. When a quantity of people came running out to see them, they went on with their mowing.[511]

Plague struck Brandenburg right after. Who are these mysterious Black Men whose presence and subsequent disappearance brings pestilence and disease? Bramley theorizes that they are members of a Council of Gods (whom he calls the Custodians). He believes they were engaged in germ-warfare. The "long scythes" carried by the twelve men referred to above, he believes, are instruments designed to spray poison or germ laden gas. The fact that, with all their mowing, no oats were cut, and because these "scythes" emit a loud noise, his theory is not altogether far fetched.

Bramley's theory of germ-warfare is strengthened further by the reports of a "mist" which preceded the epidemic. George Deaux, in *Black Death*, notes that, *"German accounts speak of heavy vile-smelling mist which advanced from the East and spread itself over Italy."*[512] He says in other countries,

---

[510] Ibid., 63.

[511] Ibid., 54.

[512] G. Deaux, *The Black Death, 1347* (New York: Weybright & Talley, Inc., 1969) 4

people were convinced that they could contract the disease from the stench, or even...actually see the plague coming through the streets as a pole fog.[513]

Nohl says,

> During the whole of the year 1382 there was no wind, in consequence of which the air grew putrid, so that an epidemic broke out, and the plague did not pass from one man to another, but everyone who was killed by it got it straight from the air.[514]

Had the god Resep visited Europe?

12.5.3. *The Scientists, the Qur'an and the 25, 000 Year History*

In Surah 45:29, it reads,

> This is Our record that speaks against you with truth. Surely We wrote what you did.

In Surah 36:12, we read, "*We record everything in a clear writing.*" This clear writing is the writing that the Honorable Elijah Muhammad taught contained the prophetic history of the world. This Book contains every thing that will transpire on the earth for a 25, 000 Year Period. In Surah 27:75, it reads,

> And there is nothing concealed in the heaven and the earth but it is in a clear book.

Surah 57:22 says,

> No disaster befalls in the earth, or in yourselves, but IT IS IN A BOOK BEFORE WE BRING IT INTO EXISTENCE-surely this is easy to Allah.

---

[513].Nohl, *Black Death,* 78
[514]Ibid., 63.

This confirms what the Honorable Elijah Muhammad taught.

Prophet Muhammad also taught of this writing of Prophetic History. He said at one point,

> The first thing Allah created was the Pen. He said to it: Write. It asked: Lord, what shall I write? He answered: Write the destinies of all things till the advent of the Hour.[515]

The "Clear book" which contains the record of man's deeds and the prophetic history of the world is referred to as the *Umm al-Kitab*, meaning Mother or Original of the Book. In Surah 43:3-4, it is written,

> Surely We have made it an Arabic Qur'an that you may understand. (4) And it is in the Original of the Book (*Umm al-Kitab*) with Us, truly elevated, full of wisdom.

The Honorable Elijah Muhammad taught that the *Holy Qur'an* and Bible are "scriptures," meaning they are pieces of a bigger writing. That bigger writing is here referred to as *Umm al-Kitab* and is in the possession of the Exalted Assembly.

The Great Pyramid of Kemet, the so-called Pyramid of Ghezah, is the house of that 25, 000 Year Prophetic History. In Kemet, the *Urshi* or "Mystery Teachers of Heaven" were Astronomers. They read the history in the stars and celestial bodies, and then wrote them on the walls of the Great Pyramid.[516] G.G.M. James, in his *Stolen Legacy*, observes that these Kemetic Mystery Teachers, through their rigorous and disciplined 42 year study in the Mystery System, gained not only the power to control the forces of nature, but also to predict the future.[517] These Urshi coded their prophesies in symbol and allegory on the walls of the temples. This prophecy was based on the Cycles of the Great Year. Charles Finch, in his *Echoes of the Old Darkland*, describes this Great Year that the Kemetians

---

[515]Wensinck, *Muslim Creed*, 108.

[516] Massey, *Ancient Egypt: The Light of the World*, 269, 271.

[517] James, *Stolen Legacy*, 134.

calendar of events was based on. He says,

> It (the Great Year) is determined by the Precession of the Equinoxes, itself a function of the 23 1/2 degree tilt of the earth's axis. This tilt gives us two north poles, the magnetic north defined by the earth's tilted northern axis and the vertical north-pole, sometimes referred to as True North or the north pole of the ecliptic...This 23 1/2 degrees of tilt gives the earth a wobbling motion, like a spinning top, as it rotates and revolves around the sun. As a result of this wobble, the magnetic north pole describes a slow, retrograde circle around the north pole of the ecliptic. Over the slow course of time, this means that the position of the equinoxes against the background of the stars gradually shifts in a counter-clockwise movement and the pole-star itself is displaced for another. It takes between 25, 860 to 25, 920 years for the earth's axis to complete this cycle. This is the Great Year and the apparent retrograde movement of the equinoxes relative to the circle of constellations represents the Precession. Once this was discovered...by pre-historic Kamit astronomer-priests, the heavenly circle was divided into 12 arcs, EACH DOMINATED BY A CONSTELLATION associated with a mythic type...Each of the 12 arcs of the Precessional circle represents a 'month' of 2, 155-2, 160 years in the Great Year of nearly 26, 000 years.[518]

In other words, the north-pole which is tilted 23 1/2 degrees, as the earth rotates, transcribes an imaginary "circle" around the heavens. It takes 25, 860 years to complete. As this Precession progresses, the pole passes through the Twelve Constellations which are over the north-pole. It remains in each of the twelve for a "month," which equals 2,155 years. This is the Great Year. Each "month" was presided over by one of the twelve constellations. We have seen that each of the Twelve Judges of Ma'at, or the Twelve Gods of Ra's Council, was represented by one of the Zodiac. The Honorable Elijah Muhammad taught that each of the

---

[518]Finch, *Echoes of the Old Darkland*, 121-2.

Twelve Major Gods was represented by a constellation.

26,000 Year Precession Period

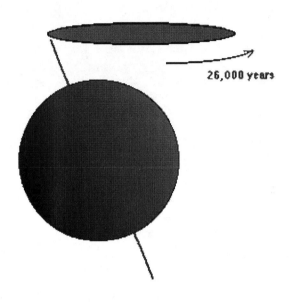

26,000 years

Figure 40
Earth's Precession and the Great Year

This Great Year of 26, 000 years was the Kemetic Calendar. The Urshi based their predictions on this Great Year,[519] just as the Honorable Elijah Muhammad teaches. The Great Pyramid was designed to contain the complete record or "Mother Book" of 25, 000 years of prophetic history coded in its structure and hieroglyphics. Churchward says,

> The Arab traditions affirm that the Great Pyramid of Ghizeh was a 'star-temple' and a treasury of knowledge - the hidden wisdom and the means of keeping chronology

---

[519] Churchward, *Origin and Evolution of Religion*, 152.

from the beginning TO THE END OF TIME.[520]

He quotes a Colonel Green who says that the ascending and descending Passage and Grand Gallery of the Pyramid coincides with the Great Year of 25, 897 years. This is revealing because Richard Noon, in his *5/5/2000* maintains that built into the ascending and descending Passage are mathematical predictions and prophecies which take us to the end of the word. Thus, it contains 25, 000 years of prophetic history. The two diagonals of the base added together equal the Great Year.[521]

The Great Pyramid houses this 25, 000 Years of Prophetic History called Bible or *Holy Qur'an*. Churchward concludes,

> When you have learned the hidden mysteries contained in the symbolism of the Great Pyramid you must arrive at the conclusion that IT IS THE WORD OF GOD WRITTEN IN STONE...It contains the message and gnosis for poor humans for their salvation and way to eternal life...THE GREATEST BIBLE WRITTEN IN STONE.[522]

Gerald Massey has proved beyond all doubt that the whole of the Old and New Testament books are reworkings of the Kemetic Wisdom written in stone which we have learned is prophecy. Thus, the Honorable Elijah Muhammad teaches that the Bible is 75% prophecy. Charles Finch concludes, elaborating on Massey,

> Gerald Massey states that ANCIENT PROPHECY CONSISTED OF KNOWING THE CYCLE OF THE GREAT YEAR, because in knowing, THE CHARACTERISTICS OF EVERY AGE COULD BE REVEALED BEFOREHAND. The Old Testament has come to us as, on the one hand, a book of judgment, and on the other, A BOOK OF PROPHECY...PROPHECY WAS A NATURAL UNFOLDING OF COSMIC FATE TIED TO THE INEXORABLE CLOCKWORK OF CELESTIAL TIME

---

[520]Ibid., 146.
[521]Ibid., 148
[522] Ibid., 158-9

The Judges which preside over the cycles are the Twelve Judges of Ma'at. There could not be any greater evidence of the truth of what the Honorable Elijah Muhammad teaches. The Kemetic Urshi predict history to last a cycle of one Great Year or 25,000 years. This prophetic history was written in symbols on the walls and in the structure of the Great Pyramid.

*12.6. Concluding Note*

In conclusion, Mullen says,

> Our study of the divine council in Canaanite, Phoenician, and early Hebrew sources has revealed a great similarity in the constitution and function of the divine assembly. The council of the gods met to decree the fate of both gods and humans. The assembly was composed of MAJOR AND MINOR DEITIES, whose functions were to aid the high god in warfare, to carry out his decree, to act as the herald of the council, and to honor and adore him. They did not have the power of decree or of life. This belonged only to the high god 'El/Yahweh.[524]

The same can be said of Sumer, Kemet, Persia, India, and all the other traditions we have examined. My conclusion is that these are not all different Assemblies with different gods. The similarities in all of them make it clear this is the same Divine Assembly, with Twelve Minor Gods and Twelve Major Gods, One of which is The God and Judge. Manley P. Hall notes:

> The number twelve frequently occurs among ancient peoples, who in nearly every case had a pantheon consisting of twelve demigods...presided over by the Invincible One.

---

[523] Finch, *Echoes of the Old Darkland*, 170.
[524] Mullen, *Assembly of the Gods*, 278-9

These are all men, the God and the Heavenly Host that surround Him. They control the destiny of the world and the life of individuals. This is the true theophany, for God manifest Himself today as He always has: as a Council of Gods with One being the Supreme Ruler of the Universe. Everything the Hon. Elijah Muhammad said concerning the Twenty Four Scientists, I believe I have shown here, is backed up by the testimony of our ancient mothers and fathers.

# Chapter XIII:

# *The Gods in Secular History*

*13.1. The Scientists and the Birth of the United States of America*

Both the Powers of Good (Council of The Gods) and the Powers of Evil (Council of The Devils) have their agenda for a New World Order. And at the center of both agendas is the United States of America. America is the focal point of both Powers. She was written in the Prophetic History around 15,094 years ago when this current *Qur'an* was written. She appears in the Book of Revelations as "That Mystery Babylon." America is that Mystery Babylon, The Great Whore. She is the most powerful and most wicked nation that has ever existed in the last 6,000 years. Allah actually rose America up so that He can destroy her. It is written in the scripture that God rose up Pharaoh and gave him his power so that, after He destroyed her, the world will see that He Allah is God. So Allah has been developing America to the point where she is now, so that he can destroy her and prove to the world that there is no God but He.

The Devil also had great plans for America. She was established to be the corner-stone nation of the New World Order. Manley P. Hall, in *The Secret Destiny of America* said:

Men bound by secret oath to labor in the cause of world democracy decided that in the American Colonies they would plant roots of a new way of life....Not only were many of the founders of the United States Government Masons, BUT THEY RECEIVED AID FROM A SECRET AND AUGUST BODY EXISTING IN EUROPE WHICH HELPED ESTABLISH THIS COUNTRY FOR A

PARTICULAR PURPOSE KNOWN ONLY TO THE
INITIATED FEW.[525]

Who was that secret and august body and what was the reason
they aided in America's establishment that is only known to the
initiated few? This body was the Council of the Devils.

One of the most closely guarded secrets of this society (2nd
only to the Reality of God) is what is referred to as the Great Plan.
This was the Plan to establish the New World Order with America
as its corner-stone. This Plan goes back 4,000 years to the time of
Musa (Moses). Hall says:

> The explorers who opened up the New World operated
> from a master-plan and were agents of re-discovery rather
> than discovery. Time will reveal that the continent now
> known as America was actually discovered and, to a
> considerable degree, explored more than A THOUSAND
> YEARS BEFORE THE BEGINNING OF THE CHRISTIAN
> ERA. The true story is in the keeping of the MYSTERY
> SCHOOLS, and passed from them to the Secret Societies of
> the medieval world...Plans for the development of the
> Western Hemisphere were formulated in Alexandria,
> Mecca, Delhi, and Lhasa [Tibet] long before most
> Europeans were aware of the great Utopian program.

One is referred to Hall's *The Secret Destiny of America* and William
Still's *New World Order: The Ancient Plan of Secret Societies* for an in-
depth look at this Great Plan.

I have endeavored to show that this nation now known as
America is the product of Divine fulfillment of prophesy. Both
Allah and Shaiton (Satan) had a vested interest in seeing America
developed. The role that the Council of the Devils played in her
development is known to all serious students of secret societies.
The Masonic Publication *New Age* admits,

> It was Masons who brought about the war (Revolutionary
> War), and it was Masonic generals who carried it through

---

[525] Manley P. Hall, *The Secret Destiny of America* (Los Angeles: Philosophical Research
Society,1944, 1991) 133.

to a successful conclusion. In fact, the famous Boston Tea Party, which precipitated the war, was actually a recessed meeting of a Masonic Lodge.

The *Masonic Bible* states,

For well over 150 years, the destiny of this country has been determined largely by men who were members of the Masonic Fraternity.[526]

These Masons were acting in accord with instructions from that "secret and august body" in England. While the governments were seemingly embroiled in war, the secret societies of the two lands were working in cahoots to bring the War about.

What is not so well known is the role that the Council of The Gods played in America's early development. This brings us right back around to our discussion of the Unknown Men of history. We have before noted that the Scientists would often send one under anonymity to a people to teach a prophet. Likewise did they send one of their own into America (and Europe) to help guide the early development of this country.

## 13.1.1. *The Scientists and the U.S. Flag: the Professor*

The Honorable Elijah Muhammad taught us about the "Unknown Man That Designed Our Flag," the Flag of the U.S. It is popularly believed that Betsy Ross designed the flag, but in fact she just sewed it up. It was one of the Scientists, known in history only as "The Professor," that designed the Flag of America. Hall gives the full story of this Scientist called "The Professor" in his book *The Secret Destiny of America*.

According to Hall, the Colonial Congress met in the fall of 1775 and appointed Franklin, Lynch and Harrison to consider and recommend a design for the flag. General Washington was then in camp at Cambridge, Massachusetts, and the Committee went there to consult with him. While there, the committee stayed at the residence of a "patriotic well-to-do citizen." At that time the

---

[526] W.T. Still, *New World Order: The Ancient Plan of Secret Societies* (Lafayette: Huntington House, 1990) 21

best room in this gentleman's residence was temporarily occupied by a *"peculiar old gentleman."*[527] The only other guest room was given to Lynch and Harrison while Dr. Franklin shared the room with the old gentleman. Hall says:

> Nothing is known about the mysterious old man except that he was referred to as 'The Professor'; his name is not preserved. He was beyond SEVENTY YEARS OF AGE but apparently IN THE PRIME OF HIS LIFE. HE ATE NOT FLESH, FISH, NOR FOWL, OR ANY GREEN THINGS, AND DRANK NO LIQUOR, WINE OR ALE. HIS DIET CONSISTED OF CEREALS, WELL RIPENED FRUIT, NUTS, TEA, AND SUCH SWEETS AS HONEY AND MOLASSES. He was well educated, highly cultured, of extensive as well as varied information, and very studious. He spent most of his time pondering over RARE BOOKS AND ANCIENT MANUSCRIPTS, WHICH HE SEEMED TO BE DECIPHERING, TRANSLATING OR REWRITING. THESE HE KEPT CAREFULLY LOCKED UP IN A HEAVY IRON-BOUND CHEST AND NEVER SHOWED THEM TO ANY PERSON..."[528]

The Professor was introduced to everyone on December 13 and subsequently invited to be on the committee. What happened next is very intriguing yet revealing. Hall says:

> After graciously accepting the invitation, the Professor made his first recommendation. He pointed out that the committee now consisted of six persons, George Washington and the host being honorary members. SIX WAS NOT AN AUSPICIOUS NUMBER, and as none of the members could be spared, let the hostess be included THAT THE NUMBER COULD BE INCREASED TO SEVEN. This suggestion was unanimously accepted...[529]

---

[527] Hall, *Secret Destiny of America*, 146.
[528] Ibid.
[529] Ibid.

As we have covered in other writings, six is the scriptural number of the imperfect Black Man and of Beast (devil) while seven is the number of God (Immortal Man). The committee met the following evening in the Professor's room. General Washington opened the proceedings by asking Dr. Franklin for his recommendations. Franklin answered by requesting that the committee listen to the words of his new friend, the Professor. The Professor made the following remarks:

> The sun of our political air, the sun in the heavens, is very low in the horizon-just now approaching the winter solstice, which it will reach very soon. But, as the sun rises from his grave in Capricorn, mounts toward his resurrection in Aries, and passes onward to his glorious culmination in Cancer, so will our political sun rise and continue to increase in power, in light, and glory; and the exalted sun of summer will not have gained his full strength of heat and power in the starry Lion until our Colonial Sun will be, in its glorious exaltation, demanding a place in the governmental firmament alongside of, coordinate with, and in no wise subordinate to, any other sun of any nation upon earth.[530]

The Professor finally submitted the design for the flag, which was as it is now with the exception of the 50 stars. In the original, the British Union Jack was in the blue. However, the Professor said that particular part of the flag was subject to change in the future. On January 2, 1776, Washington, with his own hands, raised the flag given to him by this Muslim Scientist he knew as "The Professor."

The flag this Scientist gave America contained the nature and history of the white man's world because she (America) was to be the pinnacle of the white world. The six white stripes represent the six thousand years the white man was given to rule the earth. The seven red stripes represent the Freedom of the Original Nation, for red symbolized freedom. It begins with a red stripe

---

[530]Ibid., 146-154.

253

and it ends with a red stripe, for As it was in the beginning, So shall it be in the ending. The Original Nation was on top in the beginning exercising freedom, and We will be back on top in the ending of their world (which is happening now). The blue field represents deception, for blue is the color of deceit. As you look up in the sky, it looks blue. But you jump to try and grab that which is blue you will never do it. Or as you look into a deep blue ocean, go put your hand in it and handle the blue water. The blue disappears. This blue is caused by the ether of the sky refracting light, giving off a blue glow. Blue is the color of deception. The white man's world is built on deception and lies. He has lied about everything under the sun. He has lied about God, himself and others. This is the meaning of the Flag of America as designed by one of the Council of The Gods.

13.1.2. *The Scientists and the Declaration of Independence*

The next Scientist that is apparently made an anonymous appearance in secular history and contributed to America's birth is "The Unknown Man Who Swayed The Signers of the Declaration of Independence." On July 4, 1776, a group of men gathered at the old State House in Philadelphia to decide whether they would go ahead and sign the Declaration. It was a heated debate because, if the Revolutionary War failed, every man that signed the parchment would be subject to death for high treason. There were several speeches given. In the balcony of the old State House citizens crowed to listen to the proceedings. Jefferson spoke "with great vigor." John Adams and Ben Franklin spoke, one with great strength and the other in calm, quiet words. The delegates hovered between sympathy and uncertainty as the meeting proceeded for hours. All the doors were locked and a guard was posted to prevent interruption. The talk was of axes, scaffolds and other penalties for their actions. Then, out of nowhere, a *"strong, bold voice"* thundered at the cowardly future fathers saying:

-'Gibbet! They may stretch our necks on all the gibbets in the land; they may turn every rock into a scaffold; every tree into a gallo; every home into a grave, and yet the words of that parchment can never die...Sign that parchment! Sign, if the next moment the gibbet's rope is about your neck!...Nay, do not stare and whisper with surprise! It is truth, your own hearts witness it: God proclaims it...(A) handful of men, weak in arms, but mighty in God-like faith: nay, look at your recent achievements...then tell me, if you can, that God has not given America to be free!

It is not given to our poor human intellect to climb to the skies, and pierce THE COUNCIL OF THE ALMIGHTY ONE. But methinks I stand among the awful clouds which veil the brightness of Jehovah's throne. Me thinks I see the RECORDING ANGEL come trembling up to that throne and speak his dread message. 'Father, the old world is baptized in blood. Father, look with one glance of THINE ETERNAL EYE, and behold evermore that terrible sight, man trodden beneath the oppressor's feet, nations lost in blood, murder, and superstition, walking hand in over the graves of the victims, and not a single voice of hope to man!' He stands there, the Angel, trembling with the record of human guilt. But hark! The voice of God speaks from out of the awful cloud: 'Let there be light again! Tell my people, the poor and oppressed, to go out from the old world, from oppression and blood, and build My alter in the new'...(end)

This speech reveals the identity of this Unknown Man. His reference to The Council of The Almighty One and The Recording Angel makes it plain. This unknown speaker fell exhausted into his seat. The delegates, inspired by his enthusiasm, rushed forward to sign. It was done. The delegates turned to express their gratitude to the unknown speaker for his eloquent words but he was not there. Hall asks:

Who was this strange man, who seemed to speak WITH DIVINE AUTHORITY, whose solemn words gave courage to the doubters and sealed the destiny of the new nation? Unfortunately, no one knows. His name is not recorded; none of those present knew him; or if they did, not one acknowledged his acquaintance. How he entered into the locked and guarded room is not told, nor is there any record of the manner of his departure. Not one claimed to have seen him before, and there is no mention of him after this single episode. Only his imperishable speech bears witness to his presence...In all, there is much to indicate that the unknown speaker was ONE OF THE AGENTS OF THE SECRET ORDER, GUIDING AND DIRECTING THE DESTINY OF AMERICA.[531]

This "Unknown Speaker" was in fact "one of the agents of the Secret Order guiding and directing the destiny of America." However, not an agent of the white man's Order of the Quest (Council of The Devils), as Hall believes. He was an agent of The Council of The Gods, The 24 Scientists. As the Council of Gods controls the "religious affairs" of the world by sending a representative that often hides his identity, so too do they send representatives to guide the destiny of nations. It was their representative that gave America her flag. It was their representative who inspired the doubting delegates to sign to Declaration of Independence so that she could be free from England and grow to be that great nation (not good nation) that it was prophesied she would be when The Scientists wrote the History over 15,000 years ago.

13.2. *Saint Germain and the Twenty-four Scientists*

Before we examine the last and greatest of the Scientists that appeared on the American scene I want to discuss a most enigmatic figure who seems to have some relation to the Circle of Scientists. He is known as Compte Saint Germain. He did not appear in America, but in Europe in the 18th century. Hall says of him,

> During the early part of the eighteenth century there appeared in the diplomatic circles of Europe the most baffling personality of history - a man whose life was so near a synonym of mystery that the enigma of his true identity was

---

[531] Ibid., 171.

256

Figure 41
Portrait of Saint Germain

as insolvable to his identity was as insolvable to his contemporaries as it has been to later investigators.[532]

Biographer James O. Tyron agrees:

> There are romances of real life more cleverly and ingeniously constructed by the hand of destiny than the best works of the trained novelist. There are characters of real life more interesting, amusing, or outlandish than any constructed by the pen of the creator of fiction. Such a character was the Count Saint-Germain.[533]

Count Saint-Germain's origin, nationality, and parentage are as unknown today after a hundred years of research as they were to his closest associates. Some have speculated that he was actually Leopold George, the eldest son of Prince Francis Rakoczi II. The problem is, Prince Francis's eldest son died at the age of four.[534] Another theory alleges that he was the son of a wealthy cloth merchant in Moscow.[535] The Count, on one occasion, gave an ambiguous hint at his origins. The Countess of Genlis, who was governess to the children of Philippe Egalite, Duke of Orleans, engaged the Count in conversation on his origins. She recalls:

> When asked if Germany was really his native country, he shook his head with a mysterious air, and heaving a deep sigh (said),'All that I can tell you of my birth...is that at seven years old I was wandering about the woods with my governor, and that a reward was set upon my head!' These words made me shudder, for I never doubted the sincerity of this important communication...'The evening before my flight,' he continued, 'my mother, whom I was never more to behold...fastened her portrait upon my arm,'....[536]

---

[532]Hall, *Secret Teachings of All Ages*, CXCIX
[533]J.O. Tyron, "Count Saint-Germain," *The Catholic World*, 149 (1934): 42.
[534] Franco, "The Count of Saint Germain," *The Musical Quarterly* 36 (1950): 542.
[535] Birch, "The Comte De Saint Germain," *The Nineteenth Century And After* 63 (1908): 113.
[536] Franco, "Count of Saint Germain," 543.

The Count himself purposely contributed to the mystery that surrounded him. Isabel Oakley-Cooper, a biographer on the life of this amazing personality, says of the various alias' that he used:

> During this time (1710-1822) we have M. de St.-Germain as the Marquis de Montferrat, Comte Bellamarre or Aymar at Venice, Chevalier Schoening at Pisa, Chevalier Weldon at Milan and Leipzig, Comte Soltikoff at Genoa and Leghorn, Graf Tzarogy at Schwalbach and Treisdorf, Prinz Ragoczy at Dresden, and Comte de St.-Germain at Paris, The Hague, London, and St. Petersburg.' It is evident that M. de St.-Germain adopted these various names in the interest of the...secret...work which historians have presumed to be the major mission of his life.[537]

His contemporaries were dumbfounded as to his true origins. French Emperor Napoleon III (r. 1852-1870) ordered a dossier compiled on the mysterious Count, but all the documents were destroyed in a fire that erupted in the house containing them. Many of his contemporaries believed he had lived as much as three hundred years.[538] There is no evidence of this, but it is certain that he lived "*to an unnatural age.*"[539] Frederick the Great, as well as Voltaire, described him as a man *"that never dies."*[540] On one occasion, he said to Louis XV,

> Sire, I sometimes amuse myself, not by making it believed, but by allowing it to be believed, that I lived in ancient times.

On another occasion he said to Baron von Gleichen,

> Those stupid Persians imagine that I am five hundred years old, and I encourage them in this thought, because I

---

[537] Hall *Secret Teachings of All Ages*, CXCIX.
[538] Tyron, "Count Saint-Germain," 43.
[539] Ibid., 42.
[540] Ibid., 45.

see it pleases them. Although in reality I am MUCH OLDER THAN I LOOK.[541]

Birch observes,

> People thought he lived by virtue of some charm, for he was never known (in over forty years of being on the public scene) to eat in public, to confess to illness or fatigue, or to grow perceptibly older in looks.[542]

With regard to eating he gained notoriety as a dinner-guest because he never ate anything. One hostess remarked to him,

> My dear Count, you have been a guest at my house now on three occasions and I have never seen you take a morsel of food. Do you never eat?

The Count replied to his concerned hostess,

> "Never, except in my own house, where the meal is prepared under my directions and for my consumption alone." She answered, "Do you know that you are not very complimentary to the chefs of Paris, including my own?" "On the contrary," the Count responded, "any of these chefs would feel themselves insulted if they were asked to prepare the only sort of meal which I eat..."[543]

Hall says that the Count ate no meat nor drank any wine.[544] Remember, the Professor was noted for his strange diet that consisted on no meat or strong drink.

He spoke fluently German, English, Italian, Portuguese, Spanish, French, Greek, Latin, Sanskrit, Arabic, and Chinese. Hall says the Count spoke these diverse languages so well that *"in every land he visited he was accepted as a native."*[545]

---

[541] Franco, "Count of Saint Germain," 541.
[542] Birch, "Comte De Saint Germain," 114.
[543] Tyron, "Count Saint-Germain," 42-3.
[544]Hall, *Secret Teachings of All Ages*, CXCIX.
[545]Ibid.

One name that was unanimously agreed upon by those who came in contact with him was 'der Wundermann' (the Wonderman). His contemporaries gave him this name because of the display of enormous super-natural power that was accredited to him. St. Germain allegedly had the ability to write the same article with both his hands at once, and when the two were placed together under a light, the writing on one sheet matched exactly the writing on the other.[546] He proved to his associates that the compartments of his brain worked independently by inscribing a love letter and a set of verses simultaneously.[547] The Count's memory was said to be so keen he would often show off by repeating pages of print after just one reading.[548] His knowledge of history baffled his contemporaries, being able to expound in detail on every occurrence of the preceding two-thousand years. Voltaire, in a letter to the King of Prussia, described St. Germain as *"a man who never dies and who knows everything."*[549] Cobenzl, in 1762, said of him also, *"he knows everything and shows an uprightness and a goodness of soul worthy of admiration."*[550] Hall notes,

> This remarkable person also had the surprising and impressive ability to divine, even to the most minute details, the questions of his inquisitors before they were asked. By something akin to telepathy he was also able to feel when his presence was needed in some distant city or state, and it has even been recorded that he had the astonishing habit not only of appearing in his own apartment and in those of friends without resorting to the conventionality of the door but also of departing therefrom in a similar manner.[551]

St. Germain was a multi-talented genius. He played several musical instruments with great skill, including the violin. Some of his most famous pieces are *Six Sonatas for Two Violins* and *Musique*

---

[546]Ibid.
[547]Birch, "Comte De Saint Germain," 115.
[548]Ibid.
[549]Ibid., 118.
[550] Ibid., 123.
[551] Hall, *Secret Teachings of All Ages*, CXCIX.

*Raisonnee*, as well as an opera *L'Inconstanza Delusa*. These and others are catalogued in the old music section of the British Museum.[552]

St. Germain was a profound chemist, we are told. It was said that he could crystallize carbon and also remove flaws from precious stones. The credulous Madame de Hausset of the Court of Louis the Fifteenth tells how Louis showed the Count a large diamond with a flaw, remarking that the stone would be worth double if it were flawless. St. Germain offered to make it flawless within four weeks. He requested that a jeweler be summoned to judge. The jeweler, who had at first priced the diamond at 6000 franks, offered the King 10,000 for the flawless stone.[553]

Another display of his alchemical abilities was allegedly experienced by none other than Chevalier de Seingalt, a.k.a Casanova. He had visited the Count at Tournay. The Count, surrounded by a regiment of bottles and retorts with which he was engrossed in chemical experiments, offered Casanova a mixture for his health, for he had complained of being ill. After Casanova refused, the Count said, *"If I can't be permitted to doctor on you, at least I shall show you something else I can do. Have you a copper coin?"* After taking the coin from his guest, he melted it over a charcoal fire and dipped it in water to cool. *"Here is your money,"* the Count said, *"but note that it is now gold!"* Casanova, in awe, took the coin, and later presented it to Marshall Keith, Governor of Neuchatel.[554]

This remarkable figure first appeared publicly in European society in England in 1743, though he was also known in Venice in 1710.[555] In 1745, the Jacobites invaded Scotland. The British authorities, suspecting that St.-Germain was a spy, arrested him. He was released, with the authorities covering him with apologies. Horace Walpole wrote of his arrest,

> The other day they seized an odd man, who goes by the name of Count St. Germain. He has been here two years, will not tell who he is or whenche, but profess two very

---

[552] Franco, "Count of Saint Germain," 546.
[553] Birch, "Comte De Saint Germain," 116.
[554] Tyron, "Count Saint-Germain," 44.
[555] Bramley, *Gods of Eden*, 268.

wonderful things, the first that he does not go by his right name, and the second, that he never had any dealings, or desire to have any dealings, with any woman-nay, nor any (substitute)...He sings and plays on the violin wonderfully, composes...He is called an Italian, a Spaniard, a Pole...[556]

St. Germain was apparently prepared, like Musa (Moses), the Professor, the Swayer of the Signers of the Declaration of Independence and Fard Muhammad, to be able to go among whites and not be detected. He was clearly the son of one of the dominant Black Scientists who produced him through a white mother to affect the complexion that was needed of him (see portrait above, Figure 41). But his Black ancestry was clearly noted by Madame de Genlis as she described his appearance. She says of him,

He was somewhat below middle size, well made, and active in his gait; his hair was black, HIS COMPLEXION DARK, his face expressive of talent, and his features regular.[557]

An eastern origin may have been the reason for his noted "*love of the East (that was) a passion.*"[558] He came to Europe from the east, being the guest at the Court of the Shah of Persia between 1737 and 1742. His Eastern learning and esoteric knowledge was well known to his contemporaries. Two of his most famous writings are now in the library of Troys: *The Most Holy Threefold Wisdom*, containing elements of Eastern esoteric knowledge such as so-called Hermetic Philosophy; and *The Magic Revealed to Moses, Rediscovered in an Egyptian Monument, and Preserved with great care in Asia under the device of a Winged Dragon.* He had a retreat in the Himalayas where he periodically retired for many years, often found in sitting posture of the Buddha meditating. On one occasion, he declared that he would some day return to the East

---

[556] Ibid., 261; Birch, "Comte De Saint Germain," 114.
[557] Franco, "Count of Saint Germain," 544.
[558] Birch, "Comte De Saint Germain," 114.

for eighty-five years before he appeared again on the European scene.[559]

In June, 1760, the *London Chronicle* ran a series of articles on St. Germain under the title, "Anecdotes of a Mysterious Stranger," which read in part:

Whatever may have been the business of a certain foreigner here about whom the French have just made or have affected to make a great bustle, there is something in his most unintelligible history that is very entertaining; and there are accounts of transactions which bound so nearly upon the marvelous that it is impossible but they must excite the attention of this Athenian age. I imagine this gentleman, against whom no ill was ever alleged, and for whose genius and knowledge I have the most sincere respect, will not take umbrage at my observing that the high title he assumes is not the right of lineage or the gift of royal favor; what is his real name is perhaps one of those mysteries which after his death will surprise the world more than all the strange incidents of his life...

It is certain...he has supported himself always at considerable expense, and in perfect independence, without any visible or known way of living...The country of this stranger is as perfectly unknown as his name; but concerning both, as also his early life, bust conjecture has taken the place of knowledge...All we can with justice say is: This gentle is to be considered an unknown and inoffensive stranger, who has supplies for a large expense, the sources of which are not understood.

Many years ago he was in England, and since that time has visited several other European kingdoms, always keeping up the appearance of a man of fashion, and always living with credit.

He had the address to find the reigning foible always of the place where he was going to reside, and on that he built the scheme of rendering himself agreeable. When he came here he found music was the hobby of the country,

---

[559] Hall, *Secret Teachings of All Ages*, CC.

and took the fiddle with as good grace as if he had been a native player whom true 'virtu' reigns; and there he appeared as a connoisseur in gems, antiques, and medals; in France he was a fop, in Germany a chemist...

The rumor ran that the stranger could make gold. The expense at which he lived seemed to confirm that account; but the minister at that time...ordered an inquiry to be made whence the remittances he received came, and told those who applied to him that he would soon show them what quarries they were which yielded this philosopher's stone...but the fact is that in the space of two years, while he was thus watched, he lived as usual, paid for everything in ready money, and yet no remittance came into the kingdom for him.

The thing was spoken of and none now doubted what at first had been treated as a chimera; he was understood to possess, with the other grand secret, a remedy for all diseases, and even the infirmities in which time triumphs over the human fabric.

In spite of all the mystery surrounding this seemingly Divine Man, he was able to ingratiate himself on the most powerful persons in Europe. Birch says:

The travels of the Compte de Saint-Germain covered a long period of years and a great range of countries. From Persia to France and from Calcutta to Rome he was known and respected. Horace Walpole spoke with him in London in 1745; Clive knew him in India in 1756; Madame d'Adhemar alleges that she met him in Paris in 1789, five years after his supposed death...He was on familiar and intimate terms with the crowned heads of Europe and the honored friend of many distinguished persons of all nationalities. He is often mentioned in the memoirs of his day, and always as a man of mystery. Frederick the Great, Voltaire, Madam de Pompadour, Rousseau, Chatham, and

Walpole, who all knew him personally, rivaled each other in curiosity as to his origin.[560]

As we have noted earlier, one of the duties of the Scientists is to fulfill the scriptures. The history that was decreed when the Gods met at the beginning of the 25, 000 year cycle had to be brought into fruition. Thus, the Scientists are sent out among the people to make sure certain events take place. St. Germain's political activity clearly demonstrates his membership on the august Council. He is reputed to have played a part in *"every occurrence of any importance which had taken place within the past generation."*[561]

After his release from the British authorities, St. Germain departed from England and was for a year the guest of Prince Ferdinand von Lobkowitz, the first minister to the Emperor of Austria. At this time, Austria and England were allied against France and Prussia in the War of Austrian Succession. While in Austria, he was introduced to the Marshal de Belle-Isle, the French Minister of War. William Bramley, in *The Gods of Eden*, observes,

> This is an intriguing sequence of events. Here we have a man arrested as a suspected enemy of England during a time of war, who then immediately went to stay with a top minister of a nation (Austria) which was allied to England. During that stay, this same man befriended the Minister of War of a nation (France) which was an enemy of Austria! St. Germain's political contacts on all sides of a raging war were remarkable.[562]

While in France, St. Germain was the secret agent of King Louis XV. As such, he negotiated with Frederick the Great the alliance between France and Prussia. He also negotiated with General York, commander of the English troops, in 1760 concerning peace with France during the Seven Years War. From Paris St. Germain went to the Russian capital of St. Petersburg. There, he helped Catherine overthrow the monarchy of her

---

[560] Birch, "Comte De Saint Germain," 112.
[561] Tyron, Count Saint-Germain,"43.
[562] Bramley, *Gods of Eden*, 262.

despised husband, Tsar Peter III. In 1762, St. Germain planned with the Russian family Orloffs the coup d'etat which established the thrown of Tsarina Catherine, which lasted twenty-nine years.

The Count was a Russian General while they were fighting the Turks, and was then known to them as Count Soltykoff. He went to Vienna in Austria in 1772. While there, the Treaty of Petersburg was effected partitioning Poland to Russia, Austria and Prussia. In 1775, he traveled to India on board ship with English Commander Robert Clive who was on his way to fight the French. It was reported that St. Germain also played an important part in the French Revolution of 1789. In 1779, he was for five years the guest of Prince Karl of Hesse, the top leader of the Strict Observance Masonic Lodge.

It is clear by the above chronology of events in which the Count played significant roles that He was sent by the Council to fulfill prophecy. He was involved in practically all of the history making events of his time, setting the stage for other occurrences to take place and bring world affairs in accordance with the written Prophetic History.

Many scholars have made the mistake, because of his association with prominent Masons, by asserting that Compte St. Germain was himself a Mason. On the contrary, he was of the Higher Order. He, in fact, taught those prominent Masons of his day. Count St. Germain was known to instruct the whites of Germany at "*illuminist meetings in caverns by the Rhine*" which he conducted.[563] After his mission in Vienna in 1772, Birch notes,

> The next few years he spent in Germany in the society of the...unknown leaders of secret societies. Bieberstein, Weishaupt, Prince Charles of Hesse, and Mirabeau are known to be his friends; he instructed Cagliostro in the mysteries of the magician's craft, and worked in conjunction with Nicolai at securing the German press in the interest of the perfectibilist movement.

Adam Weishaupt was the infamous founder of the Order of the Illuminati in 1776. His tutelage under the Count, as well as that of

---

[563]Birch, "Comte De Saint Germain," 112.

the other prominent Masons noted above, proves that the Count was of a higher Order. He established many Masonic Lodges through out Europe for white people.[564] Why? The Honorable Elijah Muhammad teaches, as noted above, that a small group of white people are allowed to study the Black Man in secret for 35-50 years. In the process, they were to clean themselves up and live upright. By doing this, those particular whites would be allowed to come among the righteous and do trade, without being killed as quickly as would the other whites who have not undertaken this study. They were also allowed to wear the Fez and Flag of Islam, only a sword was placed over the Flag reminding them that if they ever revealed the secret that we gave them this opportunity, their head would be taken by that sword. The sword was the emblem of Justice used by the Original Man in Muhammad's time (1400 years ago).

It was the Half Original Man, Musa, on orders from the Scientists, which set up the first Masonic "Lodge" four thousand years ago. The Count, apparently another Half-Original Man, while in Europe, established more Lodges as a grace to those whites whom the *Holy Qur'an* prophesies will enter the Here-After. The German secret order, the Thule Society, which produced Adolph Hitler, taught that these Scientists initiated whites into the "Higher Mysteries."[565]

In 1784, Dr. Biester, a Mason, declared that St. Germain was dead. The report went out that he died in Schleswig. But Hall observes,

> It is well known that many members of...secret societies have feigned death for various purposes. Marshal Ney, a member of the Society of Unknown Philosophers, escaped the firing squad and under the name of Peter Stuart Ney lived and taught school for over thirty years in North Carolina. On his deathbed, P.S. Ney told Doctor Locke, the attending physician, that he was Marshal Ney of France.[566]

---

[564] Ibid., 123.
[565] T. Ravenscroft, *The Spear Of Destiny* (York Beach, Maine: Samuel Weiser, Inc., 1973) 243.
[566] Hall, *Secret Teachings of All Ages*, CC.

Birch agrees,

> Great uncertainty and vagueness surround his latter days,
> for no confidence can be reposed in the announcement of
> the death of one illuminate by the other, for, as is well
> known, all means to secure the end were in their code
> justifiable, and it may have been in the interest of the
> society that Saint Germain should have been thought
> dead.[567]

It is possible that the Scientists faked the death of Saint
Germain, just as they will do again in America on February 25,
1975 with their chosen representative, the Honorable Elijah
Muhammad. Saint Germain is reported to have attended the 1785
Masonic convention in Paris and the famous Wilhelmsbad
Masonic conference held also in that year.[568]

Countess d'Adhemar of France stated that the Count appeared
there on several occasions in 1789 before the outbreak of the
French Revolution. He met with the King and Queen, warning
them of their impending doom and the unfavorable future of their
country. It is in these conversations that the Count identifies
himself and his purpose. As noted, when ever a part of the
Prophetic History is about to be fulfilled, one of the Scientists will
go among the people and inform one of them of these future
events. This is exactly what the Count did in France in 1789. He
informed the monarchs that:

> The time is fast approaching when imprudent France,
> Surrounded by misfortune she might have spared herself,
> Will call to mind such hell as Dante painted.
>
> Falling shall we see scepter, censor, scales, Towers and
> escutcheons, even the white flag.
>
> Great streams of blood are flowing in each town; Sobs
> only do I here, and exiles I see. On all sides civil discord
> loudly roars...As from the Assembly votes of death arise.
> Great God, whom can reply to murderous judges?[569]

---

[567] Birch, "Comte De Saint Germain," 125.
[568] Bramley, *Gods of Eden*, 268.
[569] Birch, "Comte De Saint Germain," 125.

The Count agreed to meet Madame d'Ahemar in the Church of the 'Recollets to discuss further these prophesies. He said these revealing words to her:

> S.G.: I am Cassandra, prophet of evil...Madame, he who sows the wind reaps the whirlwind...I CAN DO NOTHING; MY HANDS ARE TIED BY A (ORDER) STRONGER THAN MYSELF...The hour of repose is past, THE DECREES OF PROVIDENCE MUST BE FULFILLED (emphasis mine).
> MME.: What do they want?
> S.G.: The complete ruin of the Bourbons. They (the revolters) will expel them from all the thrones they occupy and in LESS THAN A CENTURY THEY WILL RETURN in all their different branches to the rank of simple private individuals. France as Kingdom, Republic, Empire, and mixed Government will be tormented, agitated, torn. From the hands of class tyrants she will pass to those who are ambitious and without merit.[570]

These dialogues are most revealing, for the Count identifies himself as an emissary of a higher power, and declares that "THE DECREES OF PROVIDENCE MUST BE FULFILLED." This confirms his identity as one of the Scientists whose mission was to fulfill the Decrees of God established in the year 1, at the beginning of the 25,000 Year Cycle. Bramley concludes,

> The likely explanation, based on the known facts of St. Germain's life, is that he was not so much a Freemason as he was AN AGENT FROM THE HIGHER BROTHERHOOD.[571]

Hall agrees,

---

[570] Ibid., 126.
[571] Bramley, *Gods of Eden,* 263.

The Compte de St.-Germain...(was one of)...the greatest emissaries sent into the world by the Secret Brotherhood in the last one thousand years.[572]

[572]Hall, *Secret Teachings of All Ages*, CC.

# CHAPTER XIV:

# *Comer By Night*

14.1. *A Stranger in Detroit*

In 1930, an enigmatic figure appeared in Detroit, Michigan. C. Eric Lincoln, in his study of the Nation of Islam called ***Black Muslims in America,*** says of "The Stranger in Detroit":

> Sometime in the midsummer of 1930, an amiable but faintly mysterious peddler appeared in the black ghetto of Detroit. He was thought to be an Arab, although his racial and national identity still remains undocumented...No one knew very much about the founder of this first temple (in Detroit). Usually he referred to himself as Mr. Farrad Mohammad or Mr. F. Mohammad Ali. He was also known as PROFESSOR Ford, Mr. Wali Farrad and W.D. Fard...Inevitably, there was a proliferation of legends about so mysterious a figure. One such legend is that Fard was a black Jamaican whose father was Syrian Moslem. Another describes him as a Palestinian Arab who had participated in various racial agitation's in India, South Africa, and London before moving on to Detroit. Some of his followers believed him to be the son of wealthy parents of the tribe of Koreish-the tribe of Mohammed, founder of classical Islam. Others say that he was on a diplomatic career in the service of the kingdom of Hejaz, but that he sacrificed his personal future 'to bring freedom, justice, and equality' to the 'black men in the wilderness of North America, surrounded and robbed completely by the Cave Man...At the other extreme, a Chicago newspaper investigating the Black Muslim Movement refers to Fard as 'a Turkish-born Nazi agent [who] worked for Hitler in World War II.[573]

---

[573] *The Black Muslims In America* (Beacon Press, Boston. 1961, 1973) 12-14.

Figure 42
Master Fard Muhammad

E.D. Beynon in his 1938 article on Fard and the nascent Nation of Islam stated:

> Although (Fard) lived in Detroit from July 4th, 1930, until June 30th, 1934, virtually nothing is known about him save that he 'came from the East,'...His very name is uncertain...One of the few survivors (Sister Carrie Muhammad) who heard his first addresses states that he himself said: 'My name is W.D. Fard and I came from the Holy City of Mecca. More about myself I will not tell you yet, for the time has not yet come. I am your brother. You have not yet seen me in my royal robes.[574]

Of the 35,000 Blacks from around the country who reportedly followed Fard, none knew exactly "who He was." None, except one.

When Elijah Muhammad, then Elijah Poole, first heard the mysterious stranger speak on September 22, 1931, we are told that he instantly recognized his true identity. When the lecture was over Elijah got in line with others to shake this man's hand. When his turn came, he told the stranger, "You are the One whom the Bible's prophets foresaw coming: The Son of Man." The stranger reportedly confirmed Elijah's insight and then told him, "But you go ahead now brother, that is good."

## 14.2. *God, In Person*

Around the year 13, 086 BC (over 15,000 years ago), the Gods convened at the Holy City Mecca. A new Judge was chosen whose wisdom-rule was to last 25,000 years until around the year AD 11, 914 (or there about, around 10,000 years from now). That convention 15,000 + years ago ushered in a new Cycle of History - the Year 1. The Mother Book was written and the history of the world up until around AD 11, 914 was decreed. Prophesies concerning the birth and work of Yakub, the Great Deluge, and the birth of the Son of Man (God in Person) were all contained in the Umm al-Kitab.

---

[574] Erdmann Doane Beynon, "The Voodoo Cult Among Negro Migrants in Detroit," *American Journal of Sociology,* 43 (1938): 897.

According to Elijah Muhammad, W.D. Fard is none other than the fulfillment of the worldwide scriptural prophecies concerning the coming of God in Person in the Last Days. The eschatological ('end-time') birth of this 'coming God in Person' is actually recorded in the Book of Isaiah 9:6,

> For unto us a child is born, unto us a son is given: and the government shall be upon his shoulder: and his name shall be called Wonderful, Counselor, The mighty God, The Everlasting Father, The Prince of Peace. Of the increase of his government of peace there shall be no end...

This is a man-child born of a woman, but he is the Mighty God. According to the worldwide scriptural prophecies the Mighty God will be born in the East and make his appearance in the West.

> For as lightning cometh from the east, and shineth even unto the west; so shall also the coming of the Son of Man be (Matt. 24:27).

From where in the East will the Son of Man, God in Person, come? The Book of Habakkuk 3:3 said "God came from Teman, and the Holy One from Mount Paran." Both Teman and Mt. Paran are in Arabia. Why does God come into the world? Murray, in his *Jesus And the Kingdom of God*, says,

> The decisive element in the theophany descriptions of the Old Testament...is the concept of the coming of God; the descriptions of the accompanying phenomena in the natural order are to be viewed as parabolic...but the supremely important matter is that God 'comes' into the world...in the future... More important than the place from which the Lord comes is the 'purpose' for which he comes. The passages we have considered provide the answer: the Lord comes for the punishment of the wicked and the deliverance of his people.

Habakkuk 3:13 says of the Lord,

Thou goest forth to save thy people, thou cometh to save thy anointed.

It is written in Revelation that God will himself dwell among a particular people. It says,

And I heard a greater voice out of heaven saying, Behold, the tabernacle of God is with men, AND HE WILL DWELL WITH THEM, AND THEY SHALL BE HIS PEOPLE, AND GOD HIMSELF SHALL BE WITH THEM, AND BE THEIR GOD (21:3).

Who is this people whom God has chosen to dwell among? God made a covenant with the seed of Abraham (who was a Black Man) in Genesis 15:13-15

Know of a surety that thy seed would be a stranger in a land that is not theirs, and shall serve them: and they shall afflict them FOUR HUNDRED YEARS; And that nation, whom they shall serve, will I judge: and afterward shall they come out with great substance.

This covenant was never fulfilled by any white Jews in bondage in Egypt 4,000 years ago. The Jews themselves told Jesus that they were never in bondage to any man (John 8:33). Who fulfills that prophecy of being in bondage in a foreign land for 400 years? It is certainly the Black Man and Woman who were brought from Africa (in the East) to America (in the West). In Isaiah 43:5 God says of this people:

Fear not: for I am with thee: I will BRING THY SEED FROM THE EAST, AND GATHER THEM IN THE WEST.

There is simply no other people on earth fitting this description so precisely. Black people were brought out of the East into the Western Hemisphere in 1555 on a slave ship named Jesus. Blacks have been here now over 430 years in this strange land, among strange people, and have been afflicted for that time. I Peter 2:9-10 says of this people,

276

But ye are a chosen generation, a royal priesthood, A PECULIAR PEOPLE: that ye shall shew forth the praises of him who have called you OUT OF DARKNESS INTO THE MARVELOUS LIGHT: Which in time past WERE NOT A PEOPLE, BUT ARE NOW A PEOPLE OF GOD: Which had not obtained mercy, but now obtained mercy.

No one can deny that the so-called Negroes in America tragically fit this description. No one was in more darkness at the time of the coming of W.D. Fard in 1910 (see below). It is said that if you want to hide it from a Black person, put it in a book. Sadly this is still true today. Blacks in America are a "Peculiar People" made that way by the "Peculiar Institution" of slavery.

The coming of God in the Last Days was prophesied by the world over under different titles. In the apocalyptic writings of Enoch which probably date to the first century, and written in Ethiopic, we find the coming of God mentioned also under the title of Son of Man and Holy One. The opening oracle reads,

The Holy Great One will come forth from his dwelling, And the Eternal God will tread upon the earth...And appear in the strength of his might from the heaven of heavens.

Also,

For the Heavenly One will arise from his royal throne, And he will go forth from his holy habitation with indignation and wrath ON ACCOUNT OF HIS SONS.

Murray notes,

Here the coming of God is motivated 'on account of his sons'-that is, BY REASON OF THE SUFFERING THEY ENDURED AT THE HANDS OF THEIR OPPRESSORS.

According to Jesus' prophecy of the coming Comforter in John 14, the God of the Eschaton will reveal all wisdom to the people he chooses to dwell among:

277

If ye love me keep my commandments, And I will pray the Father, and he shall send you ANOTHER COMFORTER, THAT HE MAY ABIDE WITH YOU FOR EVER... But the Comforter, which is the Holy Ghost, whom the Father will send, IN MY NAME, HE SHALL TEACH YOU ALL THINGS, AND BRING ALL THINGS TO YOUR REMEMBRANCE...

This Comforter whom the Father will send is other than Jesus. Jesus is not here talking about himself coming back. He just said the Comforter would come "in his name." And when he comes, he would reveal "ALL things."

The Holy Qur'an makes two references to the eminent Coming of Allah. In the Surah "The DAYBREAK" it says

And thy Lord COMES WITH THE ANGELS, RANKS ON RANKS (89:22).

The chapter is about the End Days. Thus, at the End Days, we are to expect the Coming of God. Also, in 21:44 it is written

See they not then that We are VISITING THE LAND...?

Allah is a part of that "WE" that will be visiting the lands. Thus, we should expect Allah and His Angels to come in the Last Days and visit the land. He came and has visited the land.

The Ancient Egyptians prophesied the coming of the Great *Iu-em-hept*. He was to reveal all the secrets of the history and future of the world and establish the Universal Kingdom of Peace on earth. The ancient prophesy said that He would make himself known "in the West." The Chinese prophesied that their God Tien would make Himself known in the Last Day in the person of the Holy One. They are waiting for the Holy One to appear "in the West." The Native Americans of Mexico are waiting for the God-Savior Quetzacoatel to come here to the West "FROM THE EAST." The Hindus believe that in the Last Days, "when the fixed stars have all...returned to the point from which they started," their God Vishnu will "appear among mortals, IN THE FORM OF AN

ARMED WARRIOR, riding a white horse." In the Latter Days, the God Buddha "will come again."

Thus, the world's religions are expecting a certain God-Man to come among men in the Last Days as a warrior to destroy the wicked and establish the Kingdom of God. These are not all different personages. They are likely the same Man-God just described by different titles or names. But there is some agreement that He will come from the East and make Himself known in the West.

The Book of Daniel says,

> I saw in the night visions, and behold, with, the clouds of heaven there came one like a son of man, and he came to the Ancient of Days and was presented before him. and to him was given dominion and glory and kingdom, that all peoples, nations and languages should serve him; his dominion is an everlasting dominion which shall not pass away, and his kingdom one that shall not be destroyed. (7:13-14)

The Ancient of Days represents Allah The Original Man, who is God, the Ancient of Days; The originator of the Heavens and Earth. The Son of Man is God Who Comes in the Last Days; he is the New Ruler. His Kingdom will last forever. Borsch, in *Son of Man in Myth and History*, says, "(This) scene portrays the YOUNG GOD TAKING THE PLACE OF THE OLD." In the Book of Enoch also we find:

> And there I saw One who had a head of days, and His head was white like wool, and with Him another being whose countenance had the appearance of a man, and his face was full of graciousness, like one of the holy angels...This is that Son of Man who hath righteousness...And whose lot hath THE PRE-EMINENCE BEFORE THE LORD OF SPIRITS IN UPRIGHTNESS FOR EVER. And this Son of Man whom thou hath seen Shall put down...the kings and the mighty from their seats

Borsch says of this Son of Man,

He is also a JUDGE WHO SITS ON A THRONE, and the throne is identified as THE VERY THRONE OF GOD HIMSELF. This idea is hard to account for unless...we reach back to the ancient conception of THE YOUNG GOD COMING TO THE THRONE OF THE OLD GOD.

According to these traditions, the God who is born and thus comes in the Last Days, the Young God, will sit in the seat and actually replace the Old God, the Creator, as Lord of the World.

14.3. *Early History of Master Fard Muhammad*

The Bible refers to a particular people as the Lost Sheep and Lost Tribe of Israel. It was this people that were to be the cornerstone of God's New World. "The stone that the builders rejected, that same has become the headstone of the corner (I Peter 2:7)." The Scientists, we are told, knew that it was time for the people to be found and redeemed, but the scriptures didn't give the location except in symbolic terms. Thus God says in Ezekiel 34:11-12,

Behold, I, even I, will both search my sheep, and seek them out. As a shepherd seeketh out his flock in the day that is among his sheep that are scattered; so will I seek out my sheep, and will deliver them...

Apparently sometime around AD 1874 the Gods located the Lost Sheep here in America. They then began preparing that one that would be sent to retrieve this sheep lost in America. This one had to have a certain body and body-type. One of the Gods on the Council was Fard's Father who has come to be known in NOI tradition as 'Alphonso'. Alphonso was a wealthy Koreish Arab, the tribe in which Prophet Muhammad of Arabia was born. Fard told Elijah in 1931 that he was from the royal dynasty of the Hashmite *Shariffs* of Mecca who ruled the Hejaz prior to World War I. Alphonso Allah was a pure, jet Black Man from Teman, Arabia. He would have come himself, we are told, but he knew he would be coming into a solid white country. The authorities would have given him too many problems for, at that time, America didn't allow foreign Black Men to come into the country freely without having official business with the government. According to Elijah Muhammad,

> He (Master Fard Muhammad) said His father knew he would not be successful in coming in a solid white country, and he being a solid Black man. So, He taught me that His father said, 'I will go and make me a Son. And I will send my Son among them, looking like them.' Think over that! 'My Son, they will think He is one of them, and He will find our lost people.

This is consistent with the prophecies concerning the Coming God. The Bible says God would come "without observation" as "a thief in the night." Being a jet Black Man, Alphonso would not be able to come to a solid white America "undetected." Thus he had to specially prepare one that could come "undetected." That one had to have a certain complexion to be able to move in certain circles in America "without observation." Also Paul in Romans 8:3 prophesied that God would come "in the likeness of sinful flesh, to condemn sin in flesh." He would come in the likeness of the sinful white flesh of the Caucasian to condemn the Caucasian.

The Coming God thus had to have a certain body prepared for him to come in. Thus, God says in the Book of Hebrews 10:5:

> Wherefore when He cometh into the world, he saith, Sacrifice and offering thou wouldest not, BUT A BODY HAST THOU PREPARED ME.

Fard's mother was a Caucasian woman raised under the Law of Islam in Azerbaijan, a country in the Caucasus region of Eurasia. She "never mixed with her wicked people" because she was kept in Muslim society all of her life.[575] She was taken through a "purification" process so that she could bare this child. This is reportedly the woman that the Bible says had the "seven devils"

---

[575] See Warith Deen Muhammad, *As The Light Shineth From the East* (Chicago: WDM Publishing Co., 1980) 29; Peter Goldman, *The Death and Life of Malcolm X* (Chicago: University of Illinois Press, 1979) 36.

cast out of her. Her name, according to tradition, was reportedly Baby Gee. She was specially prepared to give birth to this special son.

Elijah Muhammad says that "Baby Gee" is the woman referred to in the Book of Revelations (12:1):

> And I saw a great wonder in heaven, a woman clothed with the sun, and the moon under her feet and upon her head a crown of twelve stars.

This lady was a wonder in heaven (Mecca) because she wasn't from heaven yet she gave birth to a child of heaven to be sent out of heaven. The Hon. Elijah Muhammad said:

> The woman that's seen sitting in the sun, in the light of truth and in the midst of the righteous, is a wonder to see sitting, because she is not of that particular family. But what happened? The God cleaned her up. He striped her of the devil and made her fit to give birth to a child, a child He intended to use to go after his people and to redeem that people from her people.

Min. Louis Farrakhan has said that the twelve stars upon her head could mean that the Twelve Major Scientists had approved this woman. Mr. Muhammad says:

> And she was made a perfect, Holy and Righteous woman, though not by nature; yet, made righteous.

The child was born on February 26, 1877 in the Holy City Mecca. He had the appearance of a white man, even thou he was Black. Some have suggested that because Fard's mother was white, he could not be a God. Logically this reasoning is fallacious. If an apple seed is planted in soil somewhere in Africa, it will germinate as an apple tree. If that apple seed is planted in soil somewhere in Asia, it will germinate as an apple tree, and if that apple seed is planted in soil somewhere in Europe, it will still germinate as an apple tree. Point being, regardless to where one plants the apple seed, it will germinate as an apple tree. Fard was the seed of his Father. His mother would have been like the soil. Once the soil was cleaned from its impediments, the seed is theoretically able to germinate as God.

As he grew up Fard reportedly sat in the Circle of the Scientists and was taught the collective knowledge of the Twelve Major Scientists. They individually imparted their knowledge to him, even though they did not know each other's Wisdom. Collectively they reportedly held 360 degrees of Knowledge. Fard broke the Circle and became the first to have the collective knowledge of all 12. He also studied in the library vaults in Mecca. His Father would take him around to the Kings and pay large sums of money for rare, ancient books of Wisdom. Remember also, after Emperor Justinian closed down the Mystery School in Kemet (Egypt) in the 6th century, George James teaches us that the priest fled through out the world and secretly developed those teachings which taught Man how to be God. One of the places they went to and developed those teachings was Mecca. Fard actually traveled the world over and studied "every educational system of the civilized world." He studied a total of 42 years for his mission. Remember also that in the Mystery System of Egypt, after one studied for 42 years he reached his Sunnum Bounum, which meant his Godhood.

Master Fard Muhammad was a world traveler. The Hon. Elijah Muhammad told Buzz Anderson in 1964:

He visited the Isle of the Pacific, Japan, China, Canada, Alaska, the North Pole, India, Pakistan, and all of the Near East and Africa. In fact, He visited every inhabited place on earth. He studied with the wild life in the jungles of Africa and learned the language of the birds. He pictured and extracted the language of the people of Mars.[576]

In preparation for his mission, Fard reputedly calculated the measurements of the universe. Muhammad says:

He stood still and measured the earth, the waters, mountains, hills, deserts, rivers, and weighed them by

[576] 1964 Interview.

283

ounces and pounds and gallons. Even the old earth itself, and did not over look the atmosphere in which our planet rotates in. He measured the air by inches, feet and miles, and weighed the whole contents (11 2/3 quintillion pounds). He also counted the atoms and cracked them to pieces, and told the amount man breaths in from a cubic inch, foot, yard. He did not leave us foolish concerning the great magnificent starry canopy. He counted and measured the distance between the eight inhabitable planets, taught us their days, years, the square mileage of all, another great wonder. He told us how we come to have a moon, by whom...The fiery sun was conquered by His measuring line, and her great mass unfold. YES! His eyes pierce throughout the vast open space and his measuring rod recorded the diameter of the whole (76,000,000,000,000,000,000, 76 quintillion miles).[577]

After he reached maturity, Fard became the Judge of the Council. We get a picture of this in the Book of Revelations 4:10, where a 25th God is sitting on a throne with all of the 24 Elders seated around him giving him praise and worship. Fard Muhammad is reputed to be greater than any God that ever went before him. None of the Judges before his time, we are told, are equal to him in Wisdom. All of the others had wisdom that only covered a 25, 000 year cycle. But this God's Wisdom is written in scripture to last forever.

### 14.3.1. *Detroit History*

W.D. Fard arrived in America in 1910, entering through New York City. "Upon His arrival, Master Fard Muhammad literally sat on a curb and cried when he saw the condition of His father's people."[578] Fard made his way to California where he enrolled at the University of Southern California.[579] While there Fard stayed

---

[577] Elijah Muhammad, 1936 Letter to Detroit Laborers.

[578] Anthony L. Muhammad, in his *Mysteries of the Holy Quran, the Bible, and Minister Louis Farrakhan Revisited* (Los Angeles: Ant Valley Book Company, 1997), page 146, quotes Jabril Muhammad's address in San Diego, California in 1981.

[579] Elijah Muhammad to Hatim A. Shahib in 1951 interview. Hatim A. Sahib, "The Nation of Islam," Masters thesis, University of Chicago, December 1951, 69; Erdmann Doane

in the home of a white family.[580] The Hon. Elijah Muhammad said Fard was educated at USC in Los Angeles for 20 years.[581] He then returned to Mecca, changing his name from Wallace ("stranger") Fard to Wali ("friend") Fard.

Master Fard Muhammad returned to America in 1930 settling in Detroit, Michigan. On July 4 he began teaching in Paradise Valley, an impoverished section of Detroit also called 'Black Bottom.' Posing as a silk-peddler Fard went door to door in this poor Black community ingratiating himself onto the residents. After getting in the peoples' houses Fard began teaching them of their people back East. Word spread quickly throughout Paradise Valley and the Greater Detroit area about this man and his teaching. The residents clamored to hear more about 'life back home' until some of them volunteered what little money they had to rent a hall in which he could to speak to them *en masse* and at length. Soon, even this hall, made into a temple, was unable to accommodate all of the eager listeners. As Hatim Sahid remarks:

> Several persons who witnessed the movement in its earliest phase declared the enthusiasm among the Negro community for the emerging movement and its messenger Fard was the dominant phenomenon among thousands of Negros in Detroit. They were coming to hear Fard speak, though they knew that they would have no chance of hearing him or getting in the temple because the people were crowded in the basement, around the windows, outside the basement, and in the adjacent streets.[582]

By 1931 Fard had organized his followers and appointed a minister, Abdul Muhammad, and a secretary, Ugan Ali. It was in that year, 1931, that a recent migrant from Georgia, Elijah Pool, heard of this man and his teaching through his father who had himself encountered them through Abdul Muhammad. When Elijah first went out to hear this man he could not get in the hall,

---

Beynon, "The Voodoo Cult Among Negro Migrants in Detroit," *American Journal of Sociology*, 43 (1938): 897.

[580] Elijah Muhammad to Buzz Anderson, 1964 Interview.

[581] Elijah Muhammad to Hatim A. Shahib in 1951 interview. Sahib, "The Nation of Islam," 69.

[582] Sahib, "The Nation of Islam," 84.

but he "heard some of his words come out of the window."[583] The crowd kept him again listening from the outside on a second trip to one of Fard's lectures. However, after this second meeting Elijah made it inside to see that Fard was shaking hands with the guests. He got in line and at his turn he told Fard that he knew who he was: "you are that one we read in the Bible that he would come in the last day under the name Jesus." Fard looked at him very serious and said: "Yes, I am the one that you have been looking for in the last two thousand years; I am the one. But you go ahead now brother, that is good."[584]

Elijah went back to Hamtramck where he and his family resided and shared what he heard from Fard with his "poor brothers and sisters." In the fall of 1931 Fard was speaking again, but Elijah stayed home with the children while his wife, Clara, went to the meeting hall. During the meeting, Fard stopped and asked for Elijah. He said to the audience: "Anyone in this hall know the little man who lives in Hamtramck?" Clara answered, "Yes, he is my husband." Fard told Clara to tell Elijah to "go ahead and teach Islam," he will back Elijah up. Shortly after that, Fard and his secretary, Ugan Ali, visited Elijah's home. In a private conversation in the living room Elijah asked him: "Are you the God that's supposed to come and separate the righteous from the wicked and destroy the wicked?" Elijah recalls: "Master Fard's eyes grew small and he changed to a reddish complexion and said to me, with his finger pointed in my face, 'Who would believe that but you?'"[585] Fard went on to say that "he was Mahadiah and that he was Allah who everyone expected to come two thousand years after Christ who was crucified at Jerusalem."[586]

---

[583] Elijah Muhammad to Hatim A. Shahib in 1951 interview. Sahib, "The Nation of Islam," 91.

[584] Ibid. 92.

[585] Ayman Muhammad, Elijah's eldest child, who there on that occasion, recalling his father's words to him. See Steven Barboza's *American Jihad: Islam After Malcolm X* (New York: Doubleday, 1993), 268.

[586] Elijah Muhammad, statement to the FBI September 20, 1942. FBI File on Wallace Fard, September 30, 1942, #100-9129.

## 14.3.1.1. *The Year 1932: Persecution Begins*

The nascent Nation of Islam, or as it was more popularly called, Allah Temple of Islam, was a quiet storm in Detroit until Thanksgiving 1932 when it was thrust into public awareness as the "Voodoo Cult." One of Master Fard Muhammad's followers, Robert Harris, who styled himself "King of Islam," ritualistically murdered his roommate, James Smith. A mentally deranged native Harris "sacrificed" his roommate with a dagger and an automobile axle. The broader community thus was made aware of this movement through headlines such as, "Cult 'King' Kills Man on Alter" and "Leader of Cult Admits Slaying at Home 'Altar'."[587] Harris was actually not a 'leader' within the movement, but simply one of the 8000 members at the time, known to Ugan Ali, the secretary and right-hand man of Fard at the time, but unknown to Fard himself who had by 1932 withdrawn to the shadows, leaving the day-to-day operations in the hands of Ali.[588]

Harris claimed that he killed Smith "on the order of the Gods of Islam,"[589] by which he meant Fard and Ali according to the detectives assigned to the case, Det. Oscar Berry and Det. Charles W. Snyder (Fard was acknowledged even at this stage as 'God'; see below). They initiated a search for the two with Fard as their primary interest.[590] According to *The Detroit Free Press* ("Raided Temple Bares Grip of Voodoo in City," November 23, 1932 A01) detectives Berry and Snyder gained entry into the Temple on Hastings Street after acquiring a "secret password" through a Temple member. On Tuesday, November 22 they entered the Temple and found at the podium Ugan Ali whom they arrested. Wednesday morning the detectives met Fard coming out of his room at the Traymore Hotel 1 West Jefferson Ave. "He did not

---

[587] *Detroit Evening Times* November 21, 1932, A01; *The Detroit Free Press* November 21, 1932 A01.

[588] "Voodoo Killer Tries to Flee From Police," *Detroit Evening Times* November 23, 1932 A02.

[589] "Cult 'King' Kills Man on Altar"; "Cult Killer Bares Plot on Mayor," *Detroit Evening Times* November 22, 1932 A01; "Head of Cult Admits Killing," *Detroit News* November 21, 1932 A01; "Voodoo Slayer Admits Plotting Death of Judges," *The Detroit Free Press* November 22, 1932 A01, 03.

[590] "Leader of Cult to be Quizzed," *Detroit News* November 23, 1932 A07.

# Murder of Judges Plotted by Priest of Barbaric Cult

## Voodoo Leader Also Planned to Kill Dole Worker

Continued from Page One

not been investigated for Voodoo, and it is generally believed that their Mohammeddanism exists only in meaningless but impressive mixture of Allahs, Mohamets and other Mohammedan incantations.

High priestesses and priests of Allah, clad in pseudo Oriental costumes are frequent defendants in Police Court swindling cases. Preying on the superstitions and susceptibility of Negroes, they have robbed families of their savings. Their victims, however, have been gulled mostly through a belief in the high priest's ability to foretell the future, and the cases have not born the marks of the race's fear of Voodoo.

Harris explained that Harris was his slave name. Police believe that the name Karien was sold to him.

Judge Jeffries said Monday night that he does not know Harris and cannot recall having encountered any individual who might be the "King of Islam." Judge Gordon could not be reached.

### Fights Police Desperately

Harris fought desperately with police when they tried to take a fingerprint of his left hand, which was gloved. He refused to remove the glove until forced to do so.

"My right hand belongs to everyone," Harris told the detectives, 'but my left hand belongs to the King."

The forty-four-year-old "King of Islam" paced up and down gesticulating wildly as he told detectives of the zeal which goaded him into murdering Smith before the eyes of

**ROBERT HARRIS**

talked the matter over with Bertha, and suggested Smith as a victim.

When she refused to be a party to the murder, Harris said he pulled her from the bed and beat her, saying he would kill her instead, unless she acquiesced. He also professed himself willing to kill his children if they did not adhere to his commands.

"I had to kill somebody," he said. "Anyhow, but somebody had to be killed. I could not forsake my god."

Figure 43
Robert Harris, so-called 'Voodoo Slayer'

288

resist the officers," we are told, "smiling enigmatically when told he was under arrest."[591] *The Detroit Free Press* continues:

> At police headquarters he evaded questions cleverly. With the complacent smile of an oriental fakir, Farad (sic) calmly told detectives that he was the 'supreme being on Earth'."[592]

Fard stated that, while he did not know Harris, he had *"apparently misunderstood my teachings."*

> Although the precepts of the worship command the death penalty for persons who 'disturb the peace in our temples'...human sacrifices were not tolerated.[593]

Berry and Snyder took a picture with Fard as he explained to them from scripture his teaching (Figure 44).[594] When the police searched Fard's room on Saturday, November 26 they found "1, 000 letters from all sections of the country," that is to say 1, 000 letters from Blacks throughout the country requesting from Fard their righteous names.[595]

Described in the press as an "Arabian," Fard was held at the Detroit station for immigration authorities.[596] He and Ali were transferred to the psychopathic ward of Detroit Receiving Hospital where they were examined by psychiatrist Dr. David Clark. Dr. Clark's preliminary observations were that Ali's "mental processes (were) radically deviated" and that Fard, the "Arabian leader," was "suffering from delusions that he is a

[591] "Negro Leaders Open Fight," *The Detroit Free Press* November 24, 1932 A02,09.

[592] Ibid.

[593] Ibid. 09.

[594] Ibid., 20; "Member Lists Are Checked By Police," *Detroit Evening Times* November 24, 1932 A01.

[595] "Voodoo Killer Tied Up After Starting Fire," *Detroit Sunday Times* November 27, 1932 A03.

[596] "Harris, Cult Slayer, Faces Court Friday," *Detroit News* November 24, 1932 A01.

# Figure 44

Page 20 of *The Detroit Free Press* (Nov. 24, 1932) Fard is shown discussing Islam to dets. Berry and Synder after confessing to them that he is "the Supreme Being on earth." The caption reads: "Here's My Authority." Wallace Farad, head of the Order of Islam, explains from his 'bible' to detectives the workings of his cult. It was an offshoot of the Order of Islam which led Robert Harris, Negro, to slay James Smith in a cult rite, police charge. Farad is held."

"HERE'S MY AUTHORITY." Wallace Farad, head of the Order of Islam, explains from his 'bible' to detectives the workings of his cult. It was an offshoot of the Order of Islam which led Robert Harris, Negro, to slay James Smith in a cult rite, police charge. Farad is held.

divinity."[597] Fard thus confessed to the detectives and the psychiatrist that he was "the supreme being on earth."[598]

On Thursday, November 24th 500 Temple members, led by Ugan Ali's wife Lillie Ali, marched to the First Precinct demanding Fard's and Ali's release. When told they had already been moved to the psychopathic ward of the Receiving Hospital for questioning and observation, Lillie declared: "we will march down here every day until they are let out."[599]

It was discovered that some 8, 000 Blacks in the Greater Detroit area were members of Fard's 'Nation of Islam.' The Black clergy in the city were appalled at the obvious success Fard had in attracting so many Blacks to his allegedly 'anti-Christian' message. On November 28 it was announced that an interracial commission of clergy was formed for the purpose of "digging out and strangling" the deeply planted roots of "Islamism." Rev. J.D. Howell, speaking from his pulpit in the St. Stephen's African Methodist Episcopal Church, declared that "the Arabian leader is solely to blame...The Islamic 'Bible' and the Nation of Islam must go!"[600]

On Tuesday, November 29 Dr. Clark released his report on his five-day diagnosis of Fard and Ali. The latter was found 'unsound.' Fard, however, was "apparently *not* driven into his sinister teachings through insanity (emphasis added)."[601] Thus, while Fard repeatedly claimed to be 'the supreme being on earth,' the diagnosis was that he was sane. They were both released on December 6. Though declared 'unsound' Ugan Ali was released in order to "use his influence in disbanding" the Allah Temple of Islam. Detectives Berry and Snyder were called in to "persuade" Fard to leave the city by Tuesday.[602] This is odd because these

---

[597] "New Human Sacrifice With a Boy as Victim is Averted by Inquiry," *The Detroit Free Press* November 26, 1932 A01.

[598] See below also.

[599] "500 join March to Ask Voodoo Kings' Freedom," *The Detroit Free Press* November 25, 1932 A01; "Cult Slayer Pleads Guilty," *Detroit News* November 25, 1932 A01.

[600] "Pastors Decry Growth of Cult Practices Here," *The Detroit Free Press* November 28, 1932 A01.

[601] "Voodoo Chief Held Unsound," *The Detroit Free Press* November 30, 1932 A03; "Voodoo Chief Abnormal," *Detroit Evening Times* November 30, 1932 A02.

[602] "Voodoo's Reign Here is Broken: Slayer Held Insane; Farad Quits City," *The Detroit Free Press* December 7, 1932 A03; "Voodoo Ranks Disbanding," *Detroit Evening Times* December 7, 1932 A02.

detectives were no longer assigned to the case. On Friday, November 25 they were removed as homicide detectives because the crime was solved.[603] The case was turned over to a Special Investigation Squad handled by detectives Srgt. Barney Seleski and Harry Mikuliak and headed by Lieut. John Hoffman. Why not just force Fard to leave the city? Why bring in Berry and Snyder to "persuade" him to leave? Recall that it was these detectives who had their picture taken with Fard after he confessed to them that he was "the supreme being on earth." Fard agreed to leave and was escorted by the detectives to a train heading for Chicago. *The Detroit Free Press* announced happily: "Farad Quits City".

Fard went to Chicago and there "organized 20, 000 worshipers." He returned to Detroit on several occasions, but on May 25, 1933 he was picked up again at the Traymore Hotel by Det. Berry and the Special Investigation Squad on the charge of investigation of disorderly person. Fard was held pending an investigation into his activities since his reappearance in the city. He boasted to Berry: "Already I have 10, 000 followers in Detroit." On May 26 Fard was discharged by the superintended of police at the request of Lieut. Hoffman who lead the Special Investigation Squad assigned to the Allah Temple of Islam. Det. Berry reiterated his ultimatum that Fard leave the city and not return. This time Fard was booked and photographed and given twenty-four hours to 'quit the city' again.[604] Before leaving Fard gathered at Elijah's home with thousands of "sad and weeping" followers. He announced to them: "Don't worry. I am with you; I will be back to you in the near future to lead you out of this hell."[605]

Fard went again to Chicago, getting arrested and locked up almost immediately. He telegrammed Elijah to come see him in the Chicago jail. Upon his release Fard traveled "all over America." His activities and whereabouts become increasingly difficult to pinpoint now. He was apparently back in Chicago by

---

[603] "Intended Voodoo Victims Number Still Mounting," *The Detroit Free Press* November 27, 1932 A01, 04; "Suburbs Also in Voodoo Net," *The Detroit Free Press* November 29, 1932 A03.

[604] "Voodoo Chief Back in Cell," *Detroit Evening Times*, May 26, 1933 A08; "Banished Leader of Cult Arrested; Farad Found in City Despite Promise to Leave," *The Detroit Free Press* May 26, 1933; FBI File on Wallace D. Farad, August 29, 1963.

[605] Elijah Muhammad to Hatim A. Shahib in 1951 interview. Sahib, "The Nation of Islam," 71.

February 1934,[606] whence he left to (probably) return to Detroit. In March 1934 Fard was in Mexico; from there he sent a letter to the Hon. Elijah Muhammad.[607] That same month truant officers investigating the 'alarmingly' increasing number of Black children dropping out of city schools to attend the University of Islam discovered that Fard had "made several...visits to Detroit" since being ordered out of the city.[608] On April 16 the University of Islam was raided: 13 administrators were arrested and the Flag of Islam was pulled down(Figure 45).[609] During the trial that month Recorder's Judge Arthur E. Gordon inquired about the whereabouts of Fard but leaned only that he had been in the city "about two months ago," i.e. February-March. He was last heard from in Gary Indiana.[610]

According to Jesus Muhammad Ali, the Hon. Elijah Muhammad's grandson, Master Fard Muhammad received 'Official Notification' in the spring of 1934 from U.S. Immigration.[611] He was given 14 days to leave Chicago or face deportation "due to unrest stemming from his activities in the Negro community." June 30, 1934 is given as the date he was last in Detroit,[612] but this is probably an error. It is likely the last day Fard was in Chicago, for the Hon. Elijah Muhammad told the FBI in 1942: "The last time I saw Allah was in Chicago in 1934."[613] According to the Hon. Elijah Muhammad he was with Master Fard Muhammad at the airport when he was deported.[614] Fard told Elijah that he (Fard) was "going up in the mountains where the cavies would not find him."[615] On the other hand we are also told by Benjamin and Clara Muhammad that in 1935 the Hon.

[606] Sahib, "The Nation of Islam," 71.

[607] Elijah Muhammad to Hatim A. Shahib in 1951 interview. Sahib, "The Nation of Islam," 71.

[608] "Voodoo Cult Revived in the City," *The Detroit Free Press* March 27, 1934 A01, 02.

[609] "Voodoo University Raided by Police; 13 Cultists Seized," *The Detroit Free Press* April 17, 1934 A01.

[610] "Girl Recounts Lore of Islam," *The Detroit Free Press* April 26, 1934 A01, 02.

[611] *The Evolution of the Nation of Islam: The Story of the Honorable Elijah Muhammad* (n.p.: JMA Publishing, 2002) 35.

[612] Beynon, "The Voodoo Cult," 896.

[613] FBI File on Wallace D. Fard September 30, 1942 #100-9129.

[614] Quoted by Arna Bontemps and Jack Conroy, *Anyplace But Here* (Columbia: University of Missouri Press, 1966), 222.

[615] According to Ayman Muhammad, eldest child of the Hon. Elijah Muhammad. See Barboza's *American Jihad*, 268.

Figure 45
Detectives 'haul down' Flag of Islam after raiding Temple on April 16, 1934

Elijah Muhammad told them that he last "saw Allah" in Milwaukee, Wisconsin prior to arriving in Washington D.C.[616] In any case, as Lincoln notes: *"Fard vanished as mysteriously as he had arrived. Even the police seem to have been baffled."*[617]

14.4. *The FBI, W.D. Fard and Wallace Dodd Ford*

The July 28, 1963 issue of the Los Angeles *Herald-Examiner* contained an article by Ed Montgomery entitled, "Black Muslim Founder Exposed as a White." It read in part:

Black Muslims by the thousands pay homage to Wallace Farad, their "Prophet From Mecca," in the mistaken belief

---

[616] Barboza's *American Jihad*, 80.
[617] Lincoln, *Black Muslims in America*, 17.

that as founder of the black supremacy cult he is one of their own...Yet Wallace Fard is, admittedly, an enterprising, racketeering fake.

He is not a Negro. He is a white man masquerading as a Negro.

His true name is Wallace Dodd. He was born in New Zealand, on February 26, 1891. His father was British – arriving in New Zealand via Australia on a sailing schooner. His mother was a Polynesian native.

Dodd's police 'rap sheet' includes conviction for bootlegging and a San Quentin Prison term for the sale of narcotics.

Displaying a mug shot of Wallace Dodd Ford and listing various convictions in California, Montgomery goes on to mention that Dodd had a son by a common-law wife in California who, upon learning of Dodd's activities in the Black communities of Detroit and Chicago, changed the boy's name from Wallace Dodd Ford (Jr.) to Wallace Max Ford in order to conceal any relation. Montgomery concludes:

According to his former common-law wife, Dodd went from (Detroit) to Chicago and became a traveling salesman for a mail order tailor. Working his way through the Midwest, Dodd arrived in Los Angels in the spring of 1934...Finally he sold his car and boarded a ship for New Zealand with the announcement he was going back to visit his relatives, including an uncle who had paid the fare for his trip to America in 1913.

Thus the revered holy man to whom Black Muslims pray and whose February 26 birthday marks the opening of each annual convention of the black supremacy cult, returned to the land of his birth – as close to Mecca as he has ever been.

295

"Wallace Do•

Figure 46
Ed Montgomery's infamous 1963 *LA Herald-Examiner* article alleging W.D. Fard is really Wallace Dodd Ford, ex-felon and drug dealer. Photo on right that of "Wallace Dodd."

Needless to say this article, which was syndicated, was not well received by the Hon. Elijah Muhammad and the Muslims. It was a complete fabrication, it was argued. The Wallace Ford shown in the photo, supposed to be Fard in Detroit police custody in 1933, is not Fard but is a 'phony'. On July 29 Muhammad sent John Shabazz (Abdul Allah Muhammad), Bernard Cushmeer (Jabril Muhammad and (?) John Ali to the Hearst newspaper with a $100, 000.00 check. He offered to pay all expenses to bring Wallace Dodd to the US and air nationally a debate with him and the Honorable Elijah Muhammad over his claim to be the 'Fard' the Hon. Elijah Muhammad was representing to the people. On August 16, 1963 the Hon. Elijah Muhammad responded to this 'exposé' in the *Muhammad Speaks* newspaper, which read in part:

I, Elijah Muhammad, Messenger of Allah, told the Los Angeles "Herald-Examiner" -- on Monday, July 29, 1963, that my followers and I will pay the Los Angeles "Herald-Examiner" Newspaper $100,000.00 (one hundred, thousand dollars) to prove the headline charge ("BLACK MUSLIM FOUNDER EXPOSED AS A WHITE") made against us; that we are following one Wallace Dodd with many aliases including the name Fard; that he is the man that I am representing to my people as being Master Fard Muhammad (Allah in Person) who appeared among us in Detroit, Michigan in 1931 and is the same person (Wallace Dodd).

The Los Angeles "Herald-Examiner" also printed his prison history is San Quentin Federal Penitentiary on a charge of peddling dope, and that he admitted he was teaching us...

I would like the Los Angeles "Herald-Examiner" to prove that this man (Dodd) was my teacher by bringing him to this country at our expense.

Mr. Wallace Fard Muhammad, Whom Praises are due forever, The Finder and Life-Giver to we, the LOST FOUND MEMBERS OF THAT GREAT ASIATIC BLACK

297

NATION from the TRIBE OF SHABAZZ, speaks 16 different languages. Can Mr. Wallace Dodd speak 16 different languages?

MR. WALLACE Fard Muhammad also writes 10 of the languages He speaks fluently. His native language is Arabic (does Mr. Dodd speak Arabic?) of which we have in His handwriting and it is the best writing or penmanship in the Arab World.

Let Mr. Dodd prove that he was among us; prove that he gave us our names. Let Mr. Dodd prove who was his secretary and where were the identification cards printed, of which we have with us today and did he write the Arabic on them himself?

If Mr. Dodd was the Mr. Wallace Fard Muhammad, why did not the F.B.I. arrest him for this teaching of truth? Let this paper prove these things before it headlines us as liars and worshippers of white devils.

I would like to ask the Herald Examiner to give us a minute closeup of this fake (Mr. Dodd) who they would like to make the public believe is our Saviour. Even the description of this man's height and weight does not correspond to Master Fard Muhammad's (to Whom Praises are due forever) measurements. I know His height, His weight, the size of clothes, and shoes.

WHEN MASTER Fard Muhammad left us, it was 1934. Again, let Mr. Dodd prove that he and I were together and that the Lessons that I am teaching to my followers are from him and where were they given to me and did he ever examine me on what he gave me, and where?

There are many questions that I could ask this Mr. Dodd about, that would prove to the world that this man is a fake that the Los Angeles Herald-Examiner has published. We believe this by the reasoning of such unfounded truth.

Let the Herald-Examiner Newspaper put us in contact with this Mr. Wallace Dodd. We will show the world that the entire statement is false: that this Mr. Wallace Dodd is not Master Fard Muhammad; To Whom Praises are due forever.

Figure 47
The. Hon. Elijah Muhammad's reply to Ed Montgomery's charge that Master Fard Muhammad is one Wallace Dodd Ford

This Fard=Ford claim has become pretty much accepted in mainstream media today, due in no small measure to the writings of Karl Evanzz of *The Washington Post*.[618] Muslims vehemently deny it, charging the government with manipulating the evidence as part of a smear campaign. What is the truth? Are Muslims simply in denial or is the Fard=Ford claim more in a long list of 'misinformation' spread by the government, through its 'friends in the media' to arrest the spread of Islam in Black America?

A close and careful reading of the 816 pages of the FBI Files on Master Fard Muhammad made available through the Freedom of Information Act (Wallace D. Fard) leave no room to doubt: Fard is not Ford, and the 'Detroit Mug Shot' displayed in Montgomery's article, which the Hon. Elijah Muhammad said was a 'phony,' is indeed just that: it is a 1926 San Quentin mug shot of Wallie D. Ford, not a 1933 Detroit mug shot of W.D. Fard.

*14.4.1. FBI Launches Search For Fard*

In 1939, the NOI became the subject of FBI counterintelligence. J. Edgar Hoover, FBI Director, linked the Muslims with the Japanese Black Dragon Society led by seventy-year-old Satahota Takahashi. The group was thought to be a fifth column of Japan who was to eventually engage America in World War II. In 1940, after word got back that the Honorable Elijah Muhammad urged his followers to oppose the war, Hoover initiated a covert operation against the movement. He placed in charge of the operation Assistant FBI Director Percy J. Foxworth. In March of 1942, the Alien Enemy Hearing Board recommended the custodial detention of Takahashi. Shortly thereafter, President Roosevelt issued an Executive Order to have the Honorable Elijah Muhammad locked up and taken off the streets. On May 8th, the FBI arrested the Honorable Elijah Muhammad in Washington, DC. In his oral statement to special agents Muhammad mentioned that W.D. Fard, the founder of his movement, instructed his followers not to register for Selective Service. The Washington Field Office then contacted Detroit and suggested checking the Detroit Police Department records for a criminal

---

[618] *The Judas Factor: The Plot to Kill Malcolm X; The Messenger: The Rise and Fall of Elijah Muhammad.*

record, photographs, or any information they might have on Fard and his whereabouts. The Detroit Field Office checked the records of the Identification Division of the DPD and discovered that a Wallace Fard was arrested in Detroit for "conversion." His number there was 45138. He was described as "White Male, 33, 127 lbs, 5'6", Slim build, black hair, maroon eyes, Arabian." W.D. Fard was thus recognized by the DPD as a white skinned Arab (see below).

On May 16, the Detroit office raided Temple #1 located at 623 Medbury Street; agents confiscated a picture of the Flag of Islam and of Fard.[619] These would help, the Bureau hoped, to "positively identify Fard." On September 20, 1942 the FBI raided the Hon. Elijah Muhammad's Chicago home and confiscated two more images of Fard. One was a steel cut photo. At that time, newspapers were printed by using heavy steel squares. Photos were processed on metal, pasted onto a piece of wood the size of the intended photo, and inserted into the metal frame for printing. When the FBI printed the confiscated steel cut image it was a photo of "Prophet Fard addressing a congregation."[620] The other was a

Pen and ink sketch entitled "Calling the Four Winds" which was a picture of a US map containing a figure in the center identified as Fard. Guns, bearing the name Asia on the barrels, pointed to the US from each side. The drawing bore the signature R. Sharreiff.[621]

These photos along with the authentic Detroit mug shot made available to the FBI on August 8, 1942 were displayed to individuals in hopes of making identifications and locating Fard. On February 9, 1943, the Chicago Field Office forwarded the following memo to Hoover:

Director
Federal Bureau of Investigation
Washington D.C.

[619] FBI File on Wallace D. Fard, June 13, 1942, #100-6989.
[620] FBI File of Wallace D. Fard, Correlation Summary February 15, 1958, #105-63642, page 32.
[621] Ibid.

Re: Allah Temple of Islam, wa,
etal Sedition, Internal Security J
Selective Service

Dear Sir:

It is requested that a warning notice be placed in the files of the Identification Division against the record of the following individual:

| | |
|---|---|
| Name: | Wallace Don Fard |
| Aliases | W.D. Fard, Allah |

FBI number    56062(or) Local Registry number
F.P.C.

The above individual is wanted for questioning.
In the event of apprehension of this individual notify the Chicago Field Office.

The FBI thus initiated, in the words of Karl Evanzz, "one of the most exhaustive and expensive searches on a noncriminal matter in its history."[622] On November 9, 1943 the Washington Office reported that: "Allah has proved to be very much a human being since he has an arrest record in the Identification Division of the FBI."[623] His FBI number was 56062, and the record goes back to the 1933 Detroit arrest.

This 1942-43 search turned up very little. In the files for this period no mention is made of Wallie D. Ford. The latter wasn't discovered until 1957. After receiving reports of the continuous "explosion in the Nation of Islam membership,"[624] the FBI's Chicago field office requested that Hoover renew the investigation on Fard. Based on a review of files on Fard conducted April/May 1957 the Chicago Office inspector noted:

---

[622] *Messenger*, 264.
[623] FBI File on Wallace D. Fard, Washington Office, Nov. 9, 1943: I.C. 100-6582.
[624] Evanzz, *Judas Factor*, 141.

From a review of instant file it does not appear that there has been a concerted effort to locate and fully identify W.D. Fard. In as much as Elijah Muhammad recognizes W.D. Fard as being Allah (God) and claims that Fard is the source of all his teachings, it is suggested that an exhaustive effort be made to fully identify and locate W.D. Fard and or/members of his family. *It appears that Fard may have been of Arabian descent,* rather than an American Negro, and may have spent some time in Arabia or the Middle East.[625]

Again, investigation of Fard initiated in 1942 suggested Fard was an Arabian, not a New Zealander. An October 3, 1957 memo stated,

For the information of the Honolulu, Portland, and Washington Field Offices [and] as a result of a recent inspection of the Chicago office, it was suggested that a concerted effort be made to determine the whereabouts of W.D. Fard, reportedly the founder of the Nation of Islam [NOI].

When the Bureau conducted a search on Fard's various aliases, they submitted "Ford" based on the Erdmann D. Beynon article ("the Voodoo Cult") that lists "Professor Ford" as an alias of Fard. Two "Wallace Fords" were discovered. After searching INS records in November of 1957, the FBI found a Wallace Ford born 2/12/98 at Bolton, England. He entered the US at San Pedro California 7/25/37 having resided in London. This was not their man, however, as a November 29 memo confirms: "It would appear the above individual is the former prominent movie actor."[626]

Another Wallace Ford of California came up. He is Wallie D. Ford, arrested by Los Angeles PD, #16448, as Wallie Ford on November 17, 1918 on a charge of ADW (assault with a deadly weapon); by the LAPD January 20, 1926 for violation of the

---

[625] FBI File on Wallace D. Fard, May 16, 1957, CG 25-20607.
[626] FBI File on Wallace D. Fard, November 29, 1957

California Wolverine Possession Act; LAPD, February 15, 1926 for violation of the State Poison Act. Wallie Ford was sentenced to six months to six years at San Quentin Penitentiary on June 12, 1926. The FBI concentrated its efforts for the next year on finding Wallie Ford.

Wallie Ford told the California State Parole Authorities that he was born in Portland Oregon on February 15, 1891 to Hawaiian parents. He had a common-law wife, Hazel Barton, with whom he had a son, Wallace Dodd Ford, born September 1, 1920. In the Los Angeles County Birth Index 1920 listing for the boy, however, his father is listed as having been born in New Zealand rather than Oregon. This Hawaiian/New Zealand ancestry is clearly the background of his description, given frequently, as "dark complected" (see below) .[627]

On October 14, 1957 three photos of Walli D. Ford SQ #42314 taken in June of 1926 were forwarded to the FBI. At this time the Bureau would only say that "W. D. Fard *may* be identical with one Wallie Ford, FBI #56062, who was arrested on February 15, 1926, by the Los Angeles Police Department, their number 16448, for violation of the State Poison Act and subsequently received a sentence of one-half year to six years at San Quentin Prison, San Quentin, California, their number 42314."[628] After suggesting a search in Hawaii for Ford's family or Ford, the FBI says again, "If any relatives or if Wallie D. Ford are located, consideration should be given to interviewing them to determine *if Wallie D. Ford is identical with W.D. Fard.*"

On October 17, 1957 the FBI located and interviewed Hazel Barton-Ford, Wallie Ford's common-law wife, who described Wallie Ford as a New Zealander, 5'8", 140 lbs., slender build, black curly hair, black eyes, Caucasian features but "extremely swarthy complexion, (he) had the appearance of a very dark skinned Mexican."[629] Wallie Ford's "dark-skinned Mexican" look and curly hair, his 5'8", 140 lbs build contrasts markedly with that of Master Fard, of whom Mother Clara Muhammad said: "He looked to me like a poor white man."[630] [631]Warith Deen

[627] FBI File on Wallace D. Fard, March 8, 1965.
[628] FBI File on Wallace D. Fard, October 3, 1957 n.n.
[629] FBI File on Wallace D. Fard, October 18, 1957, LA 105-4805.
[630] Muhammad-Ali (Grandson), *Evolution of the Nation of Islam*, 31.

# Figure 48
## Wallace Dodd Ford Mug Shots

---

[631] *As Light Shineth*, 27.

Muhammad also described Fard as having "straight hair and very light features." Nor do the builds of the two men agree, as the Hon. Elijah Muhammad pointed out in the *Muhammad Speaks* article. While Ford was 5'8" 140 lbs, Fard was around 5'6", 127 pounds. According to Jesus Muhammad-Ali, Elijah's grandson, Master Fard Muhammad and the Hon. Elijah Muhammad had the same height and build and were therefore able to wear the same suits.[632]

In February 1958 Hoover forwarded to the Chicago SAC (Special Agent in Charge) a 52 page "Correlation Summary on Wallace Don Ford (Wallie D. Ford), summarizing the investigation and all of the evidence up to that point. The FBI admitted: "It was not definitely determined whether the individual referred to as W.D. Fard...was identical with the subject of this summary (i.e. Wallie Ford)."[633] In April Hoover terminated the investigation. On April 15, 1958, he sent a memo to Special Agent in Charge in Chicago stating:

The Bureau feels that continued expenditure of investigative time in this matter is not warranted. Therefore, this matter is being closed by the Bureau. You should take similar action in your office.

In a note added to this memo after the fact the FBI admits, after listing possible records of Fard:

Actually, since birth has not been verified, SUBJECT'S TRUE IDENTITY UNKNOWN (emphasis added – True Islam).[634]

Thus, at the conclusion of the FBI's year long investigation of Wallie Ford and its broader search for Fard the Bureau concedes that FARD'S TRUE IDENTITY REMAINED UNKNOWN! They were not able to identify Ford with Fard.

---

[632] *Evolution of the Nation of Islam*, 34.
[633] FBI File of Wallace D. Fard, Correlation Summary February 15, 1958, #105-63642, page 37.
[634] FBI File on Wallace Dodd Ford, April 15, 1958.

## 14.4.2. COINTELPRO Against W.D. Fard and the NOI

After the infamous documentary called *The Hate That Hate Produced* aired in 1959 the ranks of the NOI swelled with new recruits. Three weeks after the June 13th broadcast, the Los Angeles mosque gained 500 new members. As a result, the FBI initiated its *"second major counterintelligence offensive aimed at destroying the Nation of Islam."*[635] Since "Fard's true identity (is) unknown" the Bureau decided to discredit the movement by publishing a fabricated biography of its founder. The FBI fabricated a fallacious biography according to which Fard was a Turkish born nazi agent for Hitler during World War II. They reported that Fard and Elijah Muhammad had concocted the idea of the Nation of Islam while they both were in prison together in Milan, Michigan in 1943. The FBI sent this slander to its *"friends in the media."* One of those friends was the *New Crusader* newspaper of Chicago. On August 15, 1959, Mohd Yakub Khan published the slander under the title "White Man Is God For Cult of Islam." Karl Evanzz, in his *Judas Factor,* says Khan

> had gotten his information from a selection of the FBI's file on Wallace Fard, which it released in response to the surge in the NOI membership that had followed the television broadcast 'The Hate That Hate Produced.'[636]

This first attempt at disinformation was very sloppy and backfired. The article was "riddled with demonstrable errors and obvious contradictions." For example, this Nazi from Turkey supposedly met Elijah Muhammad while they were allegedly in prison together in 1943. However, in another paragraph, the two are said to have met in 1934. Such sloppiness allowed the Honorable Elijah Muhammad and Malcolm X to successfully discredit the "white Nazi from Turkey" story with articles of their own in *Muhammad Speaks* and *The Los Angeles Herald Dispatch.* Notice that the FBI's first attempt at discrediting the NOI through an 'exposé' on Fard did not use the Wallie D. Ford file. If the Bureau identified the two men, they would have used the file

---

[635] Evanzz, *Judas Factor,* 131.
[636] Ibid.,145

instead of spinning a biography from whole cloth. The FBI would, however, learn from this mistake and the failure of their couterintelligence offensive.

On August 14, 1962 South Carolina Congressman L. Mendel Rivers held a press conference on the steps of the Capital Building and promised to "open up the unsavory history of the Black Muslims for all America to see."[637]  On his urging the congressional House Rules Committee recommended a congressional investigation of the NOI. After gaining support for the probe by the House Un-American Activities Committee, hearings on the NOI were scheduled to begin in September. Subpoenas were issued to the Hon. Elijah Muhammad, Malcolm X, and other top officials. Congressman Rivers' crusade was apparently inspired by a meeting he had weeks prior with top FBI officials, including Hoover. Congressman Rivers, having been supplied the Wallie Dodd Ford file by the Bureau, "contemplated building the hearing around Wallace Farad, aka Willie D. Ford".[638] During the short (a couple hours) hearing, Rivers revealed what he received from the FBI.[639]

What was the FBI's intention in sharing the Ford file with the Congressman for presentation at the hearings? The Bureau closed the Ford file admitting being unable to identify him with W.D. Fard. We do not have to speculate on the Bureau's motives, as they are laid out explicitly in a Chicago memo:

> In connection with efforts to disrupt and curb growth of the NOI, extensive research has been conducted into various files maintained by this office (Chicago). Among the files reviewed was that of Wallace Dodd Ford...It is felt that if the whereabouts of Allah could be inconclusively determined, the impact on Elijah Muhammad and his followers would be tremendous and could well serve to make Muhammad appear ridiculous.[640]

---

[637] "Black Muslim Inquiry Tentatively Approved," *The Washington Post*, August 15, 1963 A03.
[638] FBI File on Wallace D. Fard, August 3, 1962; Evanzz, *Messenger*, 251.
[639] Evanzz, *Messenger*, 251.
[640] FBI File on Nation of Islam, February 19, 1963 CG 25-330971.

The release of the Ford file to Congressman Rivers was a part of the FBI's counterintelligence offensive against the Nation of Islam designed to "make Muhammad look ridiculous" and thus curb the growth of the NOI. But feeding the file to the House Un-American Activities Committee was just the beginning of what will end up being, in the words of Karl Evanzz, "among the most successful COINTELPRO actions against the NOI."[641]

In an effort to "inconclusively determine the whereabouts of Allah," the FBI followed the leads suggesting that Ford was born in New Zealand and that, according to his common-law wife, he was returning to New Zealand. The Bureau traveled to New Zealand with photos of Fard. They had hoped to be able to finally identify Fard and Ford by tracking down the latter's family. On December 7, 1962 the Bureau received the answers to their queries in a letter from the Willington, New Zealand Chief Commissioner of State Police. The letter read in part:

> In the course of these inquiries I spoke to a number of men in Willington [unintelligible] with Maori affairs and welfare. One such person –a Mr. Steve [unintelligible] informed me of the fact that it is most unusual to discover a Maori family named Ford, but he was able to recall that such a family lived in the Thomas District some years ago. He was also able to recall that a relative of this family had, many years ago, traveled to California in the United States of America. Further inquiries by the Thomas Police established that this person was Walter [D. Ford]. His brother – [unintelligible] is now residing at 843 Weeton Road...and when interviewed recently he gave the following particulars concerning his brother: Full name – Watana (?) [unintelligible] (usually known as Walter [Ford]) – born at Thomas in October, 1881 and went to America about 1912; that he joined the American Forces during the 1914-18 World War; that in 1957 he returned to New Zealand for about six months; that he returned to New Zealand for a further six months in 1959; that he married and is at present residing at 1103

[641] Evanzz, *Messenger*, 264.

Pacific Avenue, [unintelligible], California. From the photograph supplied, however, those persons who knew 'Walter [Ford]', say that he is not identical with Ford, alias Farad.[642]

This is vitally important: The FBI tracked down Wallie Ford's family in New Zealand, showed them the photo of Fard, AND THEY DENIED THAT HE IS WALLIE FORD!

Nonetheless, the FBI would move forward with its counterintelligence offensive against the NOI, hoping still to 'make Elijah Muhammad look ridiculous.' In February 1963 the Chicago field office learned that the Hon. Elijah Muhammad would not be speaking at the upcoming Saviour's Day due to health complications. On February 19 Hoover sent a memo to the Chicago field officer stating *"now [is] the time to use the dossier on Fard to neutralize the NOI."*[643] The FBI sent the Ford file to several large newspapers on July 4, 1963. On July 28, 1963 Ed Montgomery of the *Los Angeles Evening Herald-Examiner* printed the story under the title "Black Muslim Founder Exposed As White," as quoted above. Through wiretaps and a system of informants the FBI closely monitored the reaction to these stories from Muslims. It was noted that during a conversation with John Ali about the article "Elijah was quite riled up about the story."[644] Informants were asked to update the Bureau on "discussions at the NOI Temple or by individual members."[645]

14.4.3. *FBI Docs Prove Hoax*

The story was a hoax. In Bureau documents at the time the FBI confessed the spuriousness of the history written in Montgomery's article. According to Ed Montgomery, Master Fard Muhammad's "true name is Wallace Dodd. He was born in New Zealand, on February 26, 1891. His father was British – arriving in New Zealand via Australia on a sailing schooner. His mother was a Polynesian native." But in a July 30, 1963 memo concerning the

---

[642] FBI File on Wallace D. Fard, LA 105-2604, August 29, 1963, page 13.
[643] Evanzz, *Judas Factor*, 145
[644] FBI File on Wallace D. Fard, July 31, 1963.
[645] FBI File on Wallace D. Fard, July 30, 1963 CG 100-33683, page 6.

Montgomery article the Bureau admits: "We have not been able to verify his birth date or birth place nor identify his parents. W.D. Fard has not been seen or heard from since 1934."[646] In an internal note appended to an August 6 letter Hoover sent to an inquirer regarding the article it was affirmed:

Farad has been reported to be both Negro and white; however, fingerprint cards and Identification Division records at time of arrests show his color was white and of Arabian descent.[647]

The FBI knew Fard was a white skinned Arab, not a "dark, Mexican looking" New Zealander. These FBI confessions completely contradict not only Ed Montgomery but also Karl Evanzz who claimed in his book, *The Messenger,*

During the investigation, the FBI discovered that Master Fard Muhammad was actually Wallace Dodd Ford, a Californian with an extensive criminal record...Ford, as the FBI later learned, was born in 1891 in Hawaii on February 25.[648]

Remember, in the 1958 "Correlation Summary" on Wallie Dodd Ford the FBI admitted: "It was *not definitely determined* whether the individual referred to as W.D. Fard...was identical with the subject of this summary (i.e. Wallie Ford)."[649] And in another memo that year the Bureau admits:

Actually, since birth has not been verified, SUBJECT'S TRUE IDENTITY UNKNOWN.[650]

The Bureau thus admits that W.D. Fard's "true identity" remained unknown. Later in 1974 in an August 12 memo from the

---

[646] FBI File on Wallace D. Fard, July 30, 1963.
[647] FBI File on Wallace D. Fard, letter to G. W. Jackson of Hollywood, California, August 2, 1963.
[648] Evanzz, *Messenger,* 142.
[649] FBI File of Wallace D. Fard, Correlation Summary February 15, 1958, #105-63642, page 37.
[650] FBI File on Wallace Dodd Ford, April 15, 1958.

Chicago SAC to the Director regarding Montgomery's *LA Herald-Examiner* article, it is confessed:

> As the Bureau (i.e. Director) is aware, efforts were made in 1963 to verify the birth and identity of Wallace Farad or Wallace Dodd, THESE ATTEMPTS MET WITH NEGATIVE RESULTS.[651]

The Chicago SAC says also regarding the Montgomery article: "this document contains neither recommendations nor conclusions of the FBI." The FBI is here admitting failure in their attempt to identify W.D. Fard. This too contradicts Evanzz's claim that:

> Though most Muslims have refused to look at the evidence, the Bureau *correctly concluded* that Wallace D. Fard and Wallace D. Ford were one in the same.[652]

The Bureau in 1974, in fact, specifically noted that these were *not* its conclusions and in 1958 admitted that "It was *not definitely determined*" whether W.D. Fard and Wallace Ford were identical. In 1963, after tracking down Ford's relatives in New Zealand and showing them a photo of Fard, the Bureau actually discovered that *they were not identical*. On December 5, 1963 the Bureau closed its file on Ford.

14.4.3.1. *The Photo Hoax*

Karl Evanzz, in his book, *The Messenger: The Rise and Fall of Elijah Muhammad*, displays what he claims is the 1933 Detroit mug-shot of W.D. Fard (Figure 49). In a 1965 follow-up to his original article Ed Montgomery also presents this mug-shot as the 1933 Detroit photo.[653] Indeed, scribbled on the left-hand corner of the photo are the numbers "45138, 5-26-33." This is the date Fard was arrested and booked in Detroit (May 26, 1933) and his

---

[651] FBI File on Wallace D. Fard, August 12, 1974.
[652] *Messenger*, 399.
[653] "Violence, Dissension Hit the Black Muslims," *San Francisco Examiner*, February 28, 1965 A13.

identification number there (45138). But why is it scribbled on the photo as if an afterthought? Because it was an afterthought. It was scribbled on the photo decades later. Why?

Figure 49

Mug shot of Wallie Dodd Ford. Notice the dark complexion and the 'scribble' on the left-hand corner of the photo.

In Montgomery's 1963 article the photo was not identified as Fard's 1933 Detroit mug-shot. In fact, in Montgomery's **Boston Record American** article "Muslim Founder, White Masquerader" (July 28, 1963), he displays the photo without the scribble (Figure 50) and correctly identifies it:

> Profile features of British father and dark eyes and complexion of Polynesian mother was evident in THESE LOS ANGELES POLICE SHOTS OF WALLACE DODD, ALIAS FARAD. PICTURES WERE TAKEN JUST PRIOR TO HIS CONFINEMENT IN SAN QUENTIN FOR THE SALE OF NARCOTICS.

PROFILE FEATURES of British father and dark eyes and complexion of Polynesian mother are evident in these Los Angeles police shots of Wallace Dodd, alias Farad. Pictures were taken just prior to his confinement in San Quentin for sale of narcotics.

Figure 50
Ed Montgomery's *Boston Record American* edition of his "Fard-is-Ford" exposé correctly identifying the so-called 'Detroit mug shot' of Fard as actually a San Quentin mug shot of Ford.

These are thus not 1933 Detroit photos of W.D. Fard; they are 1926 LA photos of Wallie Ford. We have a good idea what inspired the hoax evident in the "scribble." On July 30, 1963, 2 days after the Montgomery article appeared in the papers, the Hon. Elijah Muhammad was interviewed concerning the story and the photo in particular by a Mrs. R. Simmons from the *California Eagle.* The following exchange took place:

E (Elijah Muhammad): It is not the picture of Mr. Farard Mohammed.
R (Mrs. Simmons): It is not?
E: It is not, I know the other person well, and it is not his age.
R: Not his age. How old is he?
E. It is not Farard Mohammed. He is 86 years old and he

314

was born in the city of Mecca and he is an Arab. This is not an Arab and he speaks 16 different languages.

R: Then the whole story is false?

E: It is completely false...

R: Do you have a picture of (W.D. Fard)?

E. I certainly do. I have lots of them...

E: I know him perfectly well and we have pictures of him and *if they want to prove this why don't they write and get his picture from the Detroit police Court* there or send for it from Washington.[654]

A photo was taken of W.D. Fard in Detroit during booking before his release from police custody on May 26, 1933. Elijah Muhammad's challenge here to prove their "Fard is Ford" claim by obtaining the Detroit mug shot clearly inspired the "scribble" on the 1926 LA mug shot of Ford identifying it with the Detroit arrest of Fard. What happened to the authentic Detroit mug shot? When I requested the W.D. Fard file from the Detroit Police Department in the summer of 2002 I received the same doctored 1926 LA mug shot. The answer to this mystery is likely provided in a June 2, 1971 memo to the Chicago SAC concerning a "Destruction Project" during which pre-1961 files and photos associated with the Wallace Fard investigation were destroyed. The memo notes: *"In re 1-A file, only one photo and/or negative was retained of photos prior to 1961."* Thus photos from the Fard file were destroyed. According to an Indices Search Slip dated May 5, 1957 file 65-411-706 on Wallace D. Ford was destroyed on April 5, 1957. File 100-11506-531 on Wallace Fard was destroyed on the same day. Indices Search Slip October 20, 1957 notes that File 100-7006-979-24 on Wallace Ford destroyed. Thus files and photos of Fard and Ford were destroyed by the Bureau. The Destruction Project and the scribble on the LA mug shot are evidence of an FBI hoax and cover-up.

[654] FBI File on Wallace D. Fard, July 30, 1963 CG 100-33683, pages 2, 4.

## 14.5. *Prophet or God?*

The Apostle Paul makes an important claim about the Son of Man (Christ Jesus) in Phil. 2:6-8:

> Who, being in the Form of God,
> Did not regard equality with God as something to be exploited
> He emptied himself (or: He made himself nothing)
> Taking on the form of a servant
> Becoming as (ordinary) human beings are;
> And being in every way like a human being,
> He was humbler yet,
> Even to accepting death, death on a cross.

In this passage we learn of the coming Son of Man's *kenosis* (self-humbling). The verb *kenoo* means metaphorically to "deprive" or "make of no effect." Christ being in the "form of God," *morphe theos* means both that he was born with a glorious divine body and that he was born with the very nature of God himself.[655] Yet, he deprived himself of these, or, better, he "made them of no effect." That is to say he did not exploit this divine form and nature. He instead assumed the appearance and condition of a normal human being, allowing himself to serve and suffer. Habakkuk 3:4 therefore prophesizes that God, when he comes from Arabia at his advent, will "veil" or "conceal" his power. He will appear to all as a simple human; a lowly human because he will serve and he will suffer, though having the very nature of God he did not have to do either.

It is in this context that we must understand Master Fard Muhammad's statement, recalled by one who heard his very first addresses in Detroit: "My name is W.D. Fard and I came from the Holy City of Mecca. More about myself I will not tell you yet, for the time has not yet come. I am your brother. You have not yet

---

[655] See Markus Bockmuehl, *The Epistle to the Philippians* (London: A & C Black, 1997) 126-29; Gordon D. Fee, *Paul's Letter to the Philippians* (Grand Rapids, MI.: William B. Eerdmans Publishing Company, 1995) 204.

seen me in my royal robes."[656] The "royal robes" are clearly metaphor for his glorious divine form and status.

Thus in the Lessons as well as in the editions of the Allah Temple of Islam's early newspaper, *The Final Call to Islam*, Fard is referred to by the Hon. Elijah Muhammad as a Prophet, not God. He came among the Black community in Detroit humbly, not as God; as a servant (posing as a silk-peddler). Some have understood these early descriptions of Fard as 'Prophet' to indicate that he was not therefore God. The claim is that he never called himself God. He called himself prophet, but Elijah unilaterally exalted him to "God-status" after Fard left. This is incorrect.

Firstly, Master Fard Muhammad never called himself "prophet"; he called Himself God. The Hon. Elijah Muhammad told Hatim Sahib in 1951:

> He did not teach us that he (Master Fard Muhammad) was a prophet. We used to call him a prophet. I made the followers call him prophet because I (did) not know exactly what name to give him. No one called him prophet before me. First, I thought we should call him Master; later I thought we should call him prophet, and later I told them that he (is) neither of either one; I said that we should call him the 'Almighty God"...He (Fard) came to Chicago and delivered a speech in which he said, "I am God himself," and I looked at him and he looked at me when he said so...He did not say that "I am a prophet," but he said that "'I am the one who comes in the last day."[657]

It is thus inappropriate to seize these early characterizations of Fard as 'prophet' as the final word. The author of this characterization, the Hon. Elijah Muhammad, admits to only 'trying it out' as he was searching for the right terminology. When Master Fard Muhammad and his secretary Ugan Ali first visited Elijah at his home in the fall of 1931, according to the Hon. Elijah Muhammad, "(Fard) said that he was Mahadiah and that he was

---

[656] Quoted from Beynon, "The Voodoo Cult," 896.
[657] Elijah Muhammad to Hatim A. Shahib in 1951 interview. Sahib, "The Nation of Islam," 93-94.

Allah who everyone expected to come two thousand years after Christ who was crucified at Jerusalem."[658] It is thus Master Fard Muhammad himself who is the source of his characterization as "God."

Fard's divinity as a Black man was apparently part of the teaching at that first Temple on Hastings Street. Robert Harris, after sacrificing his roommate Josef Smith on a make-shift altar in his home on November 21, 1932, claimed that he was ordered to do so by the "Gods of Islam," by which he is believed to have meant Master Fard Muhammad (who wrote about "sacrificing four devils" in his book, *Secret Rituals of the Lost-Found Nation of Islam*) and Ugan Ali. Thus, when the detectives (Oscar) Berry and (Charles) Snyder entered the Temple on November 22, 1932 to arrest the two of them, Ali, Fard's right-hand man at the time, was at the podium proclaiming himself "God of the Asiatics."[659]

It was not just to 'gullible Negroes' that Master Fard Muhammad revealed his divine identity to. At the First Precinct police station Fard told detectives Berry and Snyder that "he was the supreme being on Earth."[660] He told Dr. David Clark, psychiatrist at the Detroit Receiving Hospital who observed and diagnosed him for five days, that he was the Supreme Being on Earth.[661] Fard's claim to divinity was published not only in the Detroit papers, but in the Chicago papers as well. Thus *The Chicago Defender* December 3, 1932 states: "Farad, one of the leaders, told detectives that he was the 'supreme being on earth'."[662] These reports are likely the basis of the claim made by Brother Yussuf Muhammad, one of the early followers of Fard, that

> When the police asked him who he was, he said: 'I am the Supreme Ruler of the Universe.' He told those police more about himself than he would ever tell us.[663]

---

[658] Elijah Muhammad, statement to the FBI September 20, 1942. FBI File on Wallace Fard, September 30, 1942, #100-9129.

[659] "Raided Temple Bares Grip of Voodoo in City," *The Detroit Free Press* November 23, 1932 A01.

[660] "Negro Leaders Open Fight," *The Detroit Free Press* November 24, 1932 A02,09.

[661] "New Human Sacrifice With a Boy as Victim is Averted by Inquiry," *The Detroit Free Press* November 26, 1932 A01.

[662] "Probe Weird Rites of Detroit Voodoo Cult," *Chicago Defender* December 3, 1932 A01, 04.

[663] See Beynon, "The Voodoo Cult," 897.

It was thus Master Fard Muhammad who was the source of the claim that he is God, and Elijah Muhammad who first claimed he was prophet, not the other way around. But the Hon. Elijah Muhammad clearly did not mean to deny Fard's divinity by calling him by names such as 'prophet' or 'master.' These were the terms of honor that the would-be preacher was most familiar with. He tried them out in his presentation of Master Fard Muhammad to the people, then abandoned the one ('prophet'), knowing all along they did not adequately define Who He Was. We know for a fact that calling Fard 'prophet' did not mean for Elijah that Fard was not God. The Hon. Elijah Muhammad tells us that during that time "I used to go to my clothscloset (sic) and pray to Fard who brought us the truth that I was longing to hear."[664] The Hon. Elijah Muhammad is here admitting to *praying to Master Fard Muhammad as God, even while calling him 'prophet.'*

Not only did the Hon. Elijah Muhammad originate the early practice of calling the God a 'prophet,' it was he, not the Hon. Louis Farrakhan, who first thanked Allah for *sending* Master Fard Muhammad to us. He said to Hatim Sahib in 1951:

> Mr. W.D. Fard taught us what to eat, when to eat, and how to eat. That was a great lesson to us. *We all today pray and are thankful to Allah for sending him.*[665]

He thanked Allah in 1951 for sending Mr. W.D. Fard even though Mr. W.D. Fard was "Allah himself incarnated."[666] These are no contradictions. The Hon. Elijah Muhammad was displaying profound theological insight. In the Hebrew Torah, God Himself appears at time *incognito.* Instead of coming in his glorious, divine body[667] he comes in a normal human form called *mal'ak Yahweh,* often translated "the Angel of the Lord." But we now know that this *mal'ak Yahweh* is no 'angel' but is God himself in an unrecognized human form. The term *mal'ak* means literally

---

[664] Elijah Muhammad to Hatim A. Shahib in 1951 interview. Sahib, "The Nation of Islam," 93.

[665] Elijah Muhammad to Hatim A. Shahib in 1951 interview. Sahib, "The Nation of Islam," 95.

[666] Elijah Muhammad to Hatim A. Shahib in 1951 interview. Sahib, "The Nation of Islam," 98.

[667] See True Islam, *Truth of God,* 57-60 § 2.5. "The Transcendent Body of God."

'ambassador' or 'sent one/messenger.' Thus in these biblical narratives (e.g. Gen. 16; Judges 6) God himself appears to people as a "sent one" looking like a normal human.[668] Who "sends" God in these biblical contexts? The Council of the Gods (Elohim). Who do we thank for sending Master Fard Muhammad? Allah, i.e. the Council of the Gods. This biblical tradition of the God coming among humans as an unrecognized, ordinary human described as a 'sent one' sent by the Divine Council exactly parallels Master Fard Muhammad's (God's) coming among us as an unrecognized ordinary human being and referred to as a 'sent one' or prophet sent by the Divine Council.

As the apostle Paul in the Philippians passage noted with regard to the coming Son of Man or Christ Jesus: he will humble himself and suffer, not because he has to, but because he *doesn't have to.* That he would suffer on our behalf when he did not have to demonstrates his Godhood. The Honorable Elijah Muhammad noted as well:

> Mr. Fard Muhammad (God in Person) chose to suffer three and one-half years to show his love for his people who have suffered over three hundred years at the hands of a people who by nature are evil, wicked, and have no good in them.
>
> He was persecuted, sent to jail in 1932...He submitted himself with all humbleness to his persecutors. Each time he was arrested, he sent for me that I may see and learn the price of Truth for us (the so-called Negroes).[669]

### 14.5.1. *The Messianic Secret*

The evidence indicates that Fard told some persons he was God, the Supreme Being on earth. He certainly did not tell all of his 35, 000 followers, which is why Brother Yussuf Muhammad could be surprised to read Fard's confession in the Detroit papers. How does this self-identification as "Supreme Being on earth" to law enforcement and hospital personnel relate to the Hon. Elijah

---

[668] See especially James Kugle, *The God of Old.*
[669] Elijah Muhammad, *The Supreme Wisdom*, 2 vols. (New Port News, Virginia: The National News and Commentator, 1957) 1:15.

Muhammad's statement below, recalling his first encounter with Fard:

And finally I happened to get to him. And when I saw Him, I said to Him, myself, after looking at Him, it came to me that this is The Man that the Scripture prophesied of that would come in the Last Day, called the second-coming of Jesus or The Son of Man or God in Person.

So I mound my way to Him, and I'd taken Him by the hand. He shook hands with me. And I told him, I said, "You are the one that the Bible prophesied of that would come in The Last Days, The second-coming of Jesus. And some is sent to be the Son of Man. And as I spoke to Him, He says to me in my ear, "Yes, I am He that they have been looking to see for the last 2,000 years, but who else knows that. You are the only one that knows it. So keep quiet." He ordered me to keep quiet. For the next two or three years He refused to allow me to preach to the people He was The One. He told me to wait until He was no more among us. And then I could tell the people what I wanted to of Him. So this went on for a time. And today, after about 32 years, the Truth of this Mighty One, the Long-looked-for-to-come All Mighty God, IN PERSON!

Muhammad is here commanded secrecy regarding Master Fard Muhammad's identity as "the one that the Bible prophesied of that would come in The Last Days" and "the Long-looked-for-to-come All Mighty God, IN PERSON." These are very specific designations and have a different connotation from Fard's self-identifying title "God" or "Supreme Being on earth." "God" does not mean the same thing as "God in Person" or "The One who Comes in the Last Days." Let me explain.

The ancient traditions that we have been examining, including Biblical and Islamic tradition, draw a distinction between The Gods, God, and the God who Comes in Person in the Last Days. The term "The Gods" has two meanings: (1) it is used of the general population of original people, the direct descendants of the Creator who was the first Black man in existence. These are the *neteru* of Kemet; the *Annunaki* of Sumer; the *ha'elohim* or *bene eleohim* of the Bible, etc. (2) "The Gods" also refers to the Council of the Gods that serve as the ruling body governing the Black Nation (see above).

"God" also has two significances. "God," used in the singular and as a concept, alludes to either the Creator-god or the God that heads the Council of the Gods. In Kemet the Council was called *paut neteru aa'* and *paut neteru netchest* ("The Great Company of the Gods" and "the Little Company of Gods"), each consisting of Twelve gods with one God sitting as King; in Sumer it was the twelve Annunaki who constituted the *puhur ilani* or the "Council of Gods," with one God serving as *Lugaldimmerankia* or 'King of the Gods of the heavens and the earth." And so on. The head of this Council is he who wears the title "God." This "God" however is not actually an individual god but a position, as we saw above, like President. The individual incumbent will change, but whoever sits in that seat is called "God."

"The God" or "God in Person" is a figure distinct from simply "God." According to the Original Man's ancient traditions, including the Biblical and Islamic traditions, "God in Person" is the God who comes at the Eschaton or at the End of Days. This 'Coming God' is described as having some ambiguous relationship to the Creator: he is clearly distinct from the original creator-god, but is in some way identified with him. As the ancient Egyptians (Kemetians) prophesied the end-time coming of the great *Iu-em-hept*, the Apostle Paul spoke of the Son of Man/Christ and Prophet Muhammad spoke of the divine *shabb*.[670] This figure's coming is described as the coming of "God in Person" because prior to his coming the people did not encounter "God", the king of the Council of Gods, directly or "in person." Even the Prophets only encountered him during theophanic visitations in dreams and visions or, as in the case of ancient Kemet and Sumer, also through the mediation of the cult-statue. But "God" was not directly encountered by the general population (the high priests, under special conditions, did). "The God," however, he who comes at the Eschaton or End Time, does

---

[670] See True Islam, *Truth of God*, 96-100, 244-50.

not mediate his presence through dreams, visions or cult-statues: he comes "in the person."

When this One comes, according to these traditions, his identity as 'God in Person' would be concealed. This is what scholars of religion call the "Messianic Secret." We find the motif, for example, in the Gospel of Mark 8:27-30:

Jesus went on with his disciples to the villages of Caesarea Philippi; and on the way he asked his disciples, 'Who do people say that I am?' And they answered him, 'john the Baptist; and others, Elijah; and still others, one of the prophets.' He asked them, 'But who do you say that I am?' Peter answered him, 'You are the Messiah.' And he (Jesus) sternly ordered them not to tell anyone about him.

Thus, it was Master Fard Muhammad's identity as "God in Person," "the Coming God," that was kept strictly secret. Listen to the words of the late John Muhammad, the physical bother of the Hon. Elijah Muhammad:

in 1933, I and all of the Teachers were taken on a picnic by Master Fard Muhammad into Ferndale, Michigan. After he had finished with the Teachers, we danced a while. But that dancing was not for us to continue and then go back to that which he brought us out from. Do you understand me?! It was that we enjoy ourselves in a good manner and not do the "boogie-woogie!" Do you understand me, now? We are not to do what you and I see them doing on T.V. In doing so, he asked the question, "How many of you will be here and keep up my Teaching until I come back?" That is the question that Master Fard Muhammad asked. The Messenger was there. We all held up our hands and said we would do so. He said to us, "Will you continue this Islam?" We all said, "YES!" So that is why I am continuing, today, because I made that promise. At that time, I did not know that Master Fard Muhammad was God in Person. Remember this. I didn't know it then, that He was God in Person! But I made that promise and later on Messenger Elijah Muhammad, my brother, told me, "Brother

John...that man that we called 'Brother Fard' was none other than The Beneficent God. (All Praise Is Due Allah)." I looked around. I said, "Sir?" He said. "That man is none other than Allah in Person. He is The Allah that is to come in this day!"[671]

The claim is not just that Master Fard Muhammad is Allah, but that he is "The Allah that is to come in this day". When Fard first visited the Hon. Elijah Muhammad's home with Ugan Ali in the fall of 1931 he pulled Elijah into the living room away from Mother Clara and the children and said that "he was Mahadiah and that he was Allah who everyone expected to come two thousand years after Christ who was crucified at Jerusalem."[672] The stress is always on him being the One who was "to come" at the end.

Master Fard Muhammad identified himself as Supreme Being on earth to some, but to others he did not, thus Yussuf Muhammad's lament that "He told the police more about himself than he would ever tell us." This is the nature of the Messianic Secret.

> Throughout the gospels...we have regular examples of Jesus' admonishing both people and demons (i.e. whites) not to reveal to others who he truly was. This has puzzled many scholars...Today...the problem of why Jesus would be depicted as counseling silence and secrecy remains. It's a complex issue because there are also plenty of examples where Jesus DOESN'T command silence and where it is clear that a message about who he is and what he is doing is spreading among the people, well in advance of his crucifixion and resurrection.

---

[671] John Muhammad, "Black Man Unite!" *The Muhammad Speaks Continues* (March-April 1991).

[672] Elijah Muhammad statement to the FBI, 1942).

## 14.8. *White Arab, Black God?*

An important hadith (report from Prophet Muhammad) is found in the hadith collections of Al-Bukhari, Muslim, and Ibn Hanbal in several versions narrated by the Companion Abu Said Al-Khudri:

> We said, "O Allah's Apostle! Shall we see our Lord on the Day of Resurrection?" He said, "Do you have any difficulty in seeing the sun and the moon when the sky is clear?" We said, "No." He said, "So you will have no difficulty in seeing your Lord on that Day as you have no difficulty in seeing the sun and the moon (in a clear sky)." The Prophet then said, "Somebody will then announce, 'Let every nation follow what they used to worship.' So the companions of the cross will go with their cross, and the idolators (will go) with their idols, and the companions of every god (false deities) (will go) with their god, till there remain those who used to worship Allah, both the obedient ones and the mischievous ones, and some of the people of the Scripture. Then Hell will be presented to them as if it were a mirage.

> Then it will be said to the Jews, 'What did you use to worship?' They will reply, 'We used to worship Ezra, the son of Allah.' It will be said to them, 'You are liars, for Allah has neither a wife nor a son. What do you want (now)?' They will reply, 'We want You to provide us with water.' Then it will be said to them 'Drink,' and they will fall down in Hell (instead). Then it will be said to the Christians, 'What did you use to worship?' They will reply, 'We used to worship Messiah, the son of Allah.' It will be said, 'You are liars, for Allah has neither a wife nor a son. What (do you want now)?' They will say, 'We want You to provide us with water.' It will be said to them, 'Drink,' and they will fall down in Hell (instead).

> When there remain only those who used to worship Allah (Alone), both the obedient ones and the mischievous ones,

it will be said to them, 'What keeps you here when all the people have gone?' They will say, 'We parted with them (in the world) when we were in greater need of them than we are today, we heard the call of one proclaiming, 'Let every nation follow what they used to worship,' and now we are waiting for our Lord.' Then the Almighty will come to them in a form (*sura*) other than the one which they saw the first time, and He will say, 'I am your Lord,' [They will say: "(God protects us from you!) We associate nothing with God!" (We will stay here until our Lord comes to us. When our Lord comes, we will recognize Him!")[673] And none will speak to Him then but the Prophets, and then it will be said to them, 'Do you know any sign by which you can recognize Him?' ["Yes!" they will say. "*So, a leg will be uncovered* (68:42)."] and so Allah will then uncover His Leg whereupon every believer will prostrate before Him..."

God will thus appear on the Day of Judgment in a visible form (*sura*), but one that the believers don't recognize. It differs, we are told, from the form God had the 'first time' the people saw him. The commentators tell us that 'the first time' is a reference to the Primordial Covenant (*mithaq*) alluded to in *surat al 'Araf* 172. The pre-incarnate souls of humanity, prior to the creation of Adam's physical body, entered into a primordial covenant with their creator to serve him alone once they are sent to earth. The first time the people saw God, then, was prior to creation; they saw then God's true form. It is this divine form the people expected to see on the Day of Judgment. Instead, however, God shows up in a new, unrecognized form. Orthodox exegesis understood the point of this test (*imtihan*) as a means of distinguishing the true believers from the hypocrites and others.[674] The faithful are expected to recognize their Lord, the strange form notwithstanding.

The important question is, of course, what is the nature of these two forms? In a variant of this hadith, it reads, "Then the Lord of the worlds will come to them under a more lowly form (*fi anda suratin*) than that under which they had seen Him

---

[673] Ibn Hanbal, *Musnad*[1], 2:275; idem, *Kitab al-Sunna*, 42.
[674] See Gimaret, *Dieu à l'image*, 139.

[before]."[675] It is not clear what makes this form "lowly" or how exactly it differs from the form God had the 'first time' the people saw him prior to creation. That this first form is God's true form is indicated in two versions of this hadith reported by Ibn Hanbal, where we find the words, *ya'tihim Allahu 'azza wa jalla fi suratihi*, "God will (again) come to them in 'His form'," i.e. His true form.[676] This true form, the form that the people saw "the first time" or "before," is anthropomorphic; its sign is somehow marked on God's "Leg," his disclosure of which convinces the incredulous Muslims that this is God, however unrecognized his new form.

In other reports the form God will don in the Last Days is specifically identified with that of a white skinned, black haired Young Man (*shabb*).[677] God will, according to certain narrations, descend on the Day of Judgment in this form ridding a red camel, dressed in a *jubba* (long outer garment, open in front, with wide sleeves).[678] The *jubba* will probably be green. God, at creation and at the sending of the prophets, was Black.[679] On the Day of Judgment, we are told, he will look white. Warith Deen Mohammed, son of Elijah Muhammad, recalled looking at the famous picture of Master Fard Muhammad, white-skinned and black-haired, and wondering "why this man looking so white was supposed to be black and a black god."[680] We can answer that question. It was prophesied that the Black God will appear on the Day of Judgment in an unexpected and unrecognized form - a white form. He will not be white, he will only be white-complected. The Apostle Paul said that when the Lord comes He will come "in the likeness (*homoiōma*) of sinful flesh (Rom .8:3)," the flesh of the man of sin. The Lord's is only a 'likeness' of this white flesh, not the actual white flesh. The Hon. Elijah Muhammad said regarding Master Fard Muhammad:

---

[675] Al-Bukhari, *tawhid* 24/5.

[676] Ibn Hanbal, *Musnad*[2], 13:304, #7927 and 16:527, #10906.

[677] See True Islam, *Truth of God*, 96-100 .

[678] Al-Fadl b. Shadh§n, *Al-Idah* (Tihran, 1972), 15f. See also Ibn al-Jawzi, *Kitab al-mawdu'at*, 1:180; al-Suyuti, *Al-La'ali*, 28.

[679] See True Islam, *Truth of God*.

[680] Quoted from the Imam in Steven Barboza, *American Jihad: Islam after Malcolm X* (New York: Doubleday, 1993)100.

We are going to get over to you the history of this Man who is the Almighty God in Person as he gave it to me...His father was a Black Man, very much so. His mother was a white woman. He said that His father knew that his son could not be successful in coming into a solid white country being a solid black man. So He taught that His father said, "I will go and make me a Son and I will send my Son among them looking like them...And my Son, Whom they will think is one of them, will find our lost people." So Almighty God, in the Person of Master Fard Muhammad, said to me that His father said, "I will have to make One look like them."[681]

---

[681] *Theology of Time,* 166.

# CHAPTER XV:

# *The Wheel and the War of God*

## 15.1. *A Close Encounter in Detroit Michigan*

W.D. Fard shared with Elijah Muhammad a strange and very unorthodox theology which he called Islam. This theology consisted of the histories of the various races of man, measurements of the earth, universe, and all of the major heavenly bodies in our solar system (which were extremely accurate, even though most were made years before science was able to verify), as well as a description of an apocalyptic race war which he said will take place in America. At the center of Fard's teachings was a description and history of a huge, circular warplane called the Wheel or the Mothership.

This was 1931-1934. Kenneth Arnold had not yet made his infamous flight over Mount Rainer, the flight that slung "flying saucers" into national attention and national consciousness (July 1947). The words "flying saucer" wwere not even a part of the vernacular yet. What Fard told Elijah concerning these soon to be dubbed "unidentified flying objects" flies in the face of nearly all of the ufological theories being propagated today. What is most important about Fard's discussion of the "Mother Ship" is that his information apparently didn't originate from second hand sources. Fard had reportedly come to America from Arabia on this craft. In fact, he was reportedly the "captain of the ship." Fard thus was able to give a very detailed account of the design, construction, abilities, and purpose of these craft, as well as a profile of the builders and its pilots.

What Mr. Fard told Elijah concerning these craft has never made it into ufological discussions. Even though this is the first and most detailed "Close encounter," complete with a newspaper photo of the "Occupant" and thousands of witnesses to him, this case never made it into the writings of Leonard Stringfeild.

## 15.2. *Chariot of the Black Gods*

According to Fard, the Mother Ship is a huge circular craft a half mile by half mile in size. It serves as, among other things, a carrier for 1,500 smaller crafts called Baby Planes which are the disked shaped crafts labeled "UFO's" by the press. The Mother Ship or Wheel is said to travel at 9,000 mile/hour, in any direction, without making a complete turn. The Baby Planes have the same maneuverability. They are also called Bomber Plans because each on caries three highly explosive bombs (said to be 30% more powerful than those used by America).

According to Fard, the Mother Ship and her fleet of Baby Planes were built on a Niponese Island situated off the cost of Japan. They were built by a fraternity of Black Scientists that has been operating clandestinely for thousands of years-the Twenty Four Scientists. Construction of the craft began in 1909 and was completed in 1929, the year it took flight. One million dollars in gold were reportedly covertly drawn from the treasury of Mecca every year to finance this operation, at a total cost of $20 million ($100 million is reported to have been drawn from the treasury, but the rest went into other operations.)[632] The Blue Prints were reportedly made in the Holy city Mecca thousands of years ago and turned over to the Japanese at the time of the operation.[633] The motor, we are told, was built in China over the course of nine years.

This fraternal order of Black Scientists spent a year recruiting the best minds from the Aboriginal Nation to work on this project, many of them said to originate from the Hidden Civilization discussed in above. 25, 000 workmen are said to have been assembled from various non-white countries. Each Scientist and workman worked on a specific part of the craft which they had no knowledge of. Security on this project was of paramount importance as to not alert the western governments who would have attempted to arrest this development. The Niponese Islands were best suited for this purpose. The entire population of 500 islands looks exactly alike and is spaced so tightly that they

[632] Except where otherwise noted, information in this section comes from an internal Nation of Islam document called "Science and Teachings of the Mother Craft." Unpublished.
[633] Elijah Muhammad's Statement to FBI upon his arrest in Chicago September 20, 1942.

provide heavy camouflage. Once one departs from an island, it is almost impossible to return to that same island. Maintaining compass direction is difficult because of the high magnetic interference.

The construction of the Wheel was reportedly undertaken in an underground shelter that was excavated for this operation. This shelter was said to be 1,000 feet deep and 5,280 feet in width. The walls and ceilings, we are told, were crystallized to protect against magnetic radiation bombardment and to provide light which maintained a constant temperature on 75.04 degrees in the shelter. The temperature was never under or over the ten-thousandth of 75 degrees. This was for the special metal that was used to build the craft. This was the only temperature at which the metal would fuse together (there was no welding or seams used). The metal was mined in Outer Mongolia and around the Gobi Desert, we are told.

The Mother Ship or Wheel displays the supremely advanced level of scientific and mathematical understanding possessed by this hidden civilization. The motor is actually six motors enclosed in one big motor measuring 1, 320 feet in diameter. It is designed to take in oxygen from the atmosphere and convert it into electro-magnetic energy that is distributed throughout the craft. This energy causes the metal of the craft to pulsate or breathe. The craft is able to produce its own gravity and travel on the lines of magnetic force, allowing it to reach astonishing speeds.

There is reportedly a radar television system within the Mother Ship so advanced it allows its pilots to read the names of street signs from 300 miles above the earth. The craft also employs an infer-red system that enables the pilots to see five miles within the earth's crust.

15.3. *Fire This Time*

The most shocking aspect of Fard's teachings on the Mother Ship is the reason for which it was created. According to Elijah Muhammad, the Wheel has one primary purpose: to usher in the Destruction of the Western World, the enemy of God and of righteousness. The white race is said to have been given 6,000 years to rule the earth, which they did with bloodshed, tyranny, licentiousness and deceit. Accordingly, the Apocalypse is the time when God (the fraternal order and their Judge) breaks western hegemony and punishes the people for their six thousand-year abuse of the aboriginal peoples of the earth.

> The Wheel, the Mother Ship, is one of the greatest wonders of man, in making military weapons...The Mother Plane was made to destroy this world of evil and to show the wisdom and mighty power of the God who came to destroy an old world and set up a new world.[634]

Muhammad says further,

> The Scientists of the Black Man will plan and execute the destruction of the devil (whites). They will do to the devil what the Muslims did to those people who live over there next to Turkey. Turkey almost annihilated them when they fought the last war but some of them are still around. They are a little group of Christians who live next to Turkey. They are called Armenians.... They (Turks) went out and slaughtered Armenians until they were told that it was not time to kill all white people. Although the Turkish people are white, they have gained the mercy of Allah because they are Muslims by belief and practice.[635]

The Baby Planes each carry three bombs. The bombs are attached to drills that, when they hit the surface of the earth, will drill one to six miles before it explodes.

> These bombs, when they strike the earth, will start right into the earth. These bombs have timers and motors which, when they strike the earth, automatically turn on and take the bombs one mile into the earth before the explosion. When they explode it sends up a mountain one mile high. That is a powerful bomb...These mountains

---

[634] Muhammad, *Message to the Black Man*, 290-294.
[635] Muhammad, *Theology of Time*, 475.

pulling up out of the earth from that blasting by the bomb, will kill people for fifty miles around the crater.[636]

These planes will take one trip across America, who is regarded as that Mystery Babylon (which is why America has most of the UFO sightings), dropping bombs. America will be engulfed in flames that will burn for 300 years. When the fires finally subside, America will be uninhabitable for six centuries. Three bombs will be dropped on England and she will be destroyed, Muhammad says.

The defense apparatus of these craft precludes any harm coming to them or their crew.

The well-trained crew of the Mother Ship, the Wheel, can dodge the enemy and make the enemy to look for the Wheel where the Wheel is not...

When America thinks that she is going after this Plane...then those scientists on the Plane go to work and create a barrier (force field-author) so that she can't come forward towards the Plane. She can not shot at it...They are going to get rid of (America's) jets on the ground first...(The Scientists) will destroy all of America's airplane bases which will also destroy her planes that you now see running up in the air at the speed of sound or faster...There are Scientists on it (the Plane) who know every spot where America has her dreadful planes, searching around with deadly weapons, seeking to destroy the Mother Plane.[637]

The well-trained crew, ranging from the ages 12 to 25, were raised since six years old to bring about the "Destruction of the Devil." They are said to participate in a ritual in which they get into a circle and do a particular dance, chanting "Death to America." These Scientists are so advanced they can manipulate the forces of nature, sending storms and earthquakes. There are

---

[636] Ibid., 510-11.
[637] Ibid., 512, 517-18.

333

seven Scientist who will be the vanguard in this war with the western world.

> The seven Angels are capable of cutting a corridor in the air between this country and the other countries and confining all of his destruction in this hemisphere...They (Black People) have been wise enough to make a chemical which, if the devil releases poison gas on us, will separate the non-poison gas in the air from the poison gas, and it will be powerless to do harm...
>
> They have orders from Allah to do a certain job. Each one is to do a certain job, just as you read in the Bible...There are seven of them...They are not spooks, they are men...The devil is bound to attack us one day. But we have what they call, in the Bible seven Angels with us and Allah said, 'The devil is not enough for one.' All seven would like to get a hold of him (devil)...(These) are seven Scientists that Allah sends to His Messenger in the Destruction. Last of all is that dreadful Angel who places one foot on land and one on sea. That's the dreadful one, the Seventh one. The Book says, and Allah confirms it, that he lifted up his right hand and his left hand to heaven. This is the way Muslims pray...He said these words, 'Time, time, shall soon know no more.' Then he cut a shortage into gravity and set the nation on fire. Cutting a shortage means to cut a shortage into the atoms of the gravity of the earth and make the atoms over the earth explode.[638]

Muhammad says further of this dreadful Seventh Angel,

> The Angel is a very beautiful sight here. He put one foot on water and one foot on land...Since this is true out of both books, here is the secret of it: the man was raised off of the food and water out of the Earth, and out of the water he also obtained food to survive. So the Angel is cutting

---

[638].Ibid., 527, 532.

them off from both. He puts His foot on land and water because without either one of these two you can't exist.[639]

When the fighting starts, the righteous will be given instructions to avert destruction.

> On every corner of the streets, the Messengers of God will be separating the people for the Fire and Destruction. They will ask you 'What side are you on?' 'I am on America's side.' One will (then) tell you where to stand so that they (bombs) want miss you. They'll ask another, ' What side are you on?' 'I'm on Allah's side, the Muslims.' 'O.K., come with me. This is the way it will be done and it won't be long before it happens...
> But I say to you Brothers and Sisters, on the Day when that thing is seen in the sky over America, make haste and run for safety. There will be two Scientists every two blocks and they will be guiding you, telling you where to go. Everything has been prepared while we were sleeping, to save us."[640]

While America and Europe burns, the People of God will be airlifted to safety in a secret location on the earth.

> They angels will come from Heaven, all right enough, but they are men and not spooks like you think. They will come in planes to take you up out of the troubled area and fly you to another peaceful area out in the far Pacific.

## 15.4. *The Prophecy of the World King*

The most important feature of the Agharti-Shamballah tradition is the Prophecy of the World king. This is the prophecy of the Apocalyptic Battle between the King of the World and the evil king who ruled the surface of the earth. According to the prophecy, 32 kings will rule Shamballah. With each successive reign, the conditions on the surface will get progressively worse.

---

[639].Ibid., 531.
[640] Ibid., 494-495, 512

Dishonesty, selfishness and materialism become the way of life. The rulers of the outside world are a "race of barbarians" who, though small in number, consumed and slaughtered the whole earth. One tribe of the "barbarians" soon exercises dominion over the earth. Its evil king, called Chipa or Lalu Desum, "Childish Mind," whose power is now unrivalled, will be enjoying his hegemony when the 32nd King of Shamballah, called *Rudra Cakrin*, comes to the Throne. The most powerful of the Agharti Kings, Rudra Calkrin is he who will vanquish the Barbarians in a bloody End-Time-Battle.

Feeling himself "the King of the World" because he subdued every nation and ruler on the earth, the Evil King will be informed that there is yet one kingdom he had not brought under his control, the Kingdom of Agharti. The Barbarian King, stung by the revelation, will conduct an aerial surveillance of the earth in search of Agharti and he will find it. Enraged by the sight of this sovereign nation, Chipa will launch his attack with an army of terrible weapons against Rudra Cakrin and his Army of Panditas. Armageddon has begun. The King of Agharti, after a bloody fight, will destroy the evil king and his race of barbarians and establish the Kingdom of Heaven on Earth.

The Hindus of India have a similar prophecy. The Redeemer of the World here is the Black God *Kalki*. According to tradition, as the conditions on the earth grow worse and worse, Vishnu, the Supreme God, will be born on the earth in a series of ten divine incarnations who fight the growing forces of evil, temporarily checking them. When the conditions on earth reach the all time low, Vishnu will come to earth as the Divine Warrior, the tenth incarnation called Kalki. Kalki is depicted as a Black god riding a winged horse and holding a sword in his hand. Kalki destroys the same Barbarians that Rudra Cakrin destroys. In fact, in one Sanskrit tradition, Kalki and Rudra are identified as one and the same. [641]

What is important about these prophecies is the means by which Rudra Cakrin-Kalki defeats the Barbarians. In a popular Tibetan prayer to the World King, it reads:

---

[641] E. Bernbaum, *The Way to Shamballa* (Garden City: Anchor Press/Double Day, 1980) 83.

You, the best of holy teachers, shall ride a stone horse with
the power of wind;
Your hand shall thrust a spear into the heart of Chipa,
King of the barbarians.[642]

Rudra Cakrin is depicted in a famous picture riding his stead and
trusting a spear through the heart of Chipa.    This horse is
significant in the Hindu tradition as well.

Like Gesar and the future King of Shambhala, Kalki rides a
horse of supernatural power of flight.  In the Hindu myth
it has a special significance as the attribute or symbol that
identifies    and    distinguishes    Kalki    from    the    other
incarnations of Vishnu; Indian art invariably depicts him
with either a winged steed (Figure 51) or the head of a
horse...In the Buddhist myth, the King of Shambhala
defeats the barbarians by entering into "the meditation of
the best of horses."...the role of the supernatural horse in
both myths shows that it symbolizes the power that
enables Kalki and the King of Shambhala to overcome the
forces of evil.[643]

Figure 51
10th Avatar Kalki with Winged Steed

---

[642] Ibid., 22.
[643] Ibid., 84.

This "stone horse with the power of wind" is, according to E. Bernbaum in his study of these traditions, airplanes:

> As for the stone horses with the power of flight, lamas tend to interpret them as airplanes. According to Chopgye Trichen Rimpoche, the stone refers to petroleum fuel that comes out of rocks in the ground. Others think that the texts are talking about metal used in the construction of the aircraft.[644]

These airplanes symbolized by the winged steed are not ordinary planes, however. It is a wheel-shaped craft. In fact, Rudra Calkrin means "The Wrathful One With the Wheel." This craft is referred to as "the Wheel." According to Tibetan tradition, *"a wheel of iron will fall from the sky to mark the beginning of his reign."* Thus, like Kalki, the rule of the Last King of Shamballah is identified by the "Iron Wheel." Rudra Calkrin, the Wrathful One with The Wheel, uses this Wheel *"like a spinning discus to cut down his enemies."*[645]

This "Wrathful One with the Wheel" has been identified with W.D. Fard Muhammad, the current World King and Judge of the Council of Twelve whose rule is identified with the Mothership or the Wheel. This Wrathful One has come to destroy the barbarians and their unrivalled King, America.

As you see, Fard's explanation of these mysterious UFO's is quite at odds with the speculations of current ufology. But as you will see in the following chapters, the most reliable reports of UFO sightings and encounters confirm many of the details provided by Fard and the apocalyptic scenario he painted.

---

[644] Ibid., 242.
[645] Ibid., 239.

Figure 52
Famous 1952 Passiac, New Jersey Photo

## 15.5. 'Most Highly Classified Subject in the United States Government'

Though public statements issued by governmental agencies give the impression that UFO's are purely fictitious entities, behind the scenes practically every government on earth has been scrambling to cope with a true menace flying around in our skies which these governments acknowledge as a grave concern. In a July 1947 FBI/Army intelligence report, the FBI and Army concluded:

> This flying saucer situation is not all imaginary or seeing too much in some natural phenomenon. Something is really flying around.[646]

On September 23, 1947, Lieutenant General Nathan Twining, Commanding General of Air Material Command, sent a secret memo to Brigadier General George Scgulgen, Chief of the Air Intelligence Requirements Division at the Pentagon. The memo was in response to request from Air Intelligence concerning "flying disks" and reflected the conclusions of a recent conference attended by personnel from the Air Institute of Technology, Intelligence T-2; the Office, Chief Engineering Division; and the Aircraft, Power Plant, and Propeller Laboratories of Engineering Division T-3. The memo read in part:

> The phenomenon reported is something real and not visionary or fictitious...There are objects probably approximating the shape of a disk, of such appreciable size as to appear to be as large as man-made aircraft...The reported operating characteristics such as extreme rates of climb, maneuverability (particularly in roll), and action which must be considered evasive when sighted or contacted by friendly aircraft and radar, lend belief to the possibility that some of the objects are controlled either manually, automatically, or remotely.[647]

---

[646] Jenny Randles, *The UFO Conspiracy* (New York: Barnes & Nobles, 1987) 15.
[647] Timothy Good, *Above Top Secret* (New York: Quill, William, Morrow, 1988) 476.

On December 30, 1947 General Twinning received a security coding for his "Project Saucer," the first governmental study of the UFO phenomenon. Project Saucer was changed to "Project Sign" and responsibility was given to Wright Patterson Air Force Base in Dayton, Ohio.

On September 15, 1950, Wilbert Smith, Senior Radio Engineer of the Canadian Department of Transportation, interviewed Lt. Col. Bremner of the Canadian Defense Attaché at the Canadian Embassy in Washington, D.C. and Dr. Robert Sarbacher, Director of Research for WEDD Laboratories and consultant to the U.S. Government's Research and Development Board (R&DB). The interview concerned the "flying saucer" phenomenon. On November 21, 1950, Smith forwarded a memo containing the substance of this interview to C.P. Edwards, Director of the Canadian Department of Transportation. It stated:

We believe that we are on the track of something which may well prove to be the introduction of a new technology. The existence of a different technology is born out by the investigations which are being carried on at the present time in relation to flying saucers...

I made discreet enquiry's through the Canadian Embassy staff in Washington who were able to obtain the following information:

a. The matter is the most highly classified subject in the United
   States Government, rating higher even than the H-bomb.

b. Flying saucers exist.

c. Their modus operandi is unknown but a concerted effort is
   being made by a small group headed by Doctor Vandovar
   Bush.

d. The entire matter is considered by the United States authorities to be of tremendous significance."[648]

---

[648] Ibid., 464-465.

The CIA even expressed great concern over the mysterious and unidentified craft flying around its skies. On December 2, 1952, H. Marshall Chadwell, Assistant Director of Scientific Intelligence, sent a secret memo to the CIA Director stating:

> Recent reports reaching CIA indicated that further action was desirable...At this time, the reports of incidents convince us that there is something going on that must have immediate attention...Sightings of unexplained objects at great altitudes and traveling at high speeds in the vicinity of major U.S. defense installations are of such nature that they are not attributable to natural phenomena or known types of aerial vehicles.[649]

The UFO phenomenon is indeed a real phenomena and not the wild visions of crackpots or eccentric and diluted citizens. There is actually something unexplained and perplexing to authorities flying around the skies. Ufologists have suggested various origins for these anomalous craft, from a secret WWII aerial program of Germany to a friendly contingent of "Space Brothers"-EBE's-from Venus, Clarion, or Zeta Reticulti. By the 1990's, UFO's had become a real concern among common citizens, but ufology had abandoned a critical, scientific study of the phenomena in favor of "leaks" and revelations from anonymous individuals purportedly connected with the intelligence community. These "leaks" have been so outlandish, sober-mined researchers have been turned off by the study.

What is the answer to the UFO Question? With all the theorizing about what planet these craft originated from and what the true purpose of their Earthly Mission is, there is yet one close encounter case that took place long before reports of Abductions or even the Kenneth Arnold sightings. The "contactee" was given details that have not been reported in any UFO publication. The information this contactee was given by the UFO "occupant" goes against the grain of all current ufological theorizing but is supported by the weight of the actually evidence to a surprising degree. With photos of the occupant, thousands of witnesses, and

---

[649] Ibid., 335.

a duration of 3 ½ years, the 1934 Close encounter of Elijah Pool is by far the most complete case not on record.

## 15.6. *The Mother Ship Observed*

Figure 52
The Mother Ship. Joe Ferriere took this photo when the object appeared over Woonsocket, Rhode Island. He reported seeing a flying disk emerge from the huge object, which he also photographed.

On June 29, 1954, a British Overseas Airways Corporation Boeing Stratocruiser, G-ALSC, Flight 510-196, commanded by Captain James Howard, left New York for London via Goose Bay. Thirty minutes after takeoff, Captain Howard was rerouted to Cape Cod without explanation. As he crossed the St. Lawrence estuary near Seven Islands, Quebec, he saw some strange objects moving parallel to the plane and at the same speed. He said in his report that the "shy was clear, visibility unlimited." The objects fly parallel with the plane for twenty minutes, giving Captain Howard and several passengers the opportunity at a good look. In his report Howard stated:

There was one large object and six smaller globular things. The small ones were strung out in a line, sometimes 3 ahead and 3 behind the large one, sometimes 2 ahead and 4 behind, and so on, but always at the same level. The large object was continually, slowly, changing shape, in a way that a swarm of bees might alter its appearance. They appeared to be opaque and hard-edged, gray in color, no lights or flames visible.

After ten minutes, Howard asked his co-pilot, Lee Boyde, to radio ground control for information. They told Boyd they had an F-94 on patrol which they would vector toward the Boering. As Boyd was talking to the fighter, something strange occurred:

I gave him a bearing of the objects from us, and as I did so I noticed that the small objects had disappeared. My navigator who was watching them closely at this time said they appeared to converge on, and enter, the large one.[650]

Another interesting encounter with the mother ship and Her Baby Planes was reported by an Australian pilot in 1968. On August 22, Captains Gordon W. Smith and Walter Gardin of Murchison Air Services/Southern Airlines of Western Australia, were flying an empty Piper Navajo, registration VH-RTO, returning from Adelaide. Gordon Smith, in his report, stated that he was awakened from his sleep by Gardin who excitedly pointed out an object in the vicinity.

Some distance ahead at the same level, and about 50 (degrees) to my right...I saw a formation of aircraft. In the middle was a large aircraft, and formatted to the right and left and above were four or five smaller aircraft. We were on a track of 270 (degrees) and these aircraft appeared to be maintaining station with us...

After radioing to Kalgoorlie Department of Civil Aviation, something even more errie occurred:

---

[650] Ibid., 191.

At about this time we lost communications with Kalgoorlie on all frequencies...In the next ten minutes I transmitted about seven times and I believe Walter did about five times with no results.

Also at this time we noticed that the main ship split into two sections still maintaining the same level, and the smaller aircraft then flew out left and right but staying on the same level and coming back to the two main halves of the bigger ship. At this time there appeared to be about six smaller aircraft taking turns of going out and coming back and formatting on the two halves.
Sometimes the two halves joined and split, and the whole cycle continued for ten minutes. The shape of the main ship seemed to have the ability to change, not drastically, but from, say spheroid to a slightly elongated form with the color maintaining a constant dark gray to black.

However, the smaller craft had a constant cigar shape and were of a very dark color. Their travel out and back had a peculiarity not associated with normal aircraft in that they appeared to travel out and come back without actually turning like a normal airplane would have to do.

At 0950 GMT the whole formation joined together as if at a single command, then departed at a tremendous speed. It did not disappear as, say, gas would, but it departed in about three or four seconds diminishing in size till out of sight.

Captain Smith reported that immediately following the departure of the Mother Ship and Baby Planes, radio communications were restored. Air Chief Marshal Lord Downing, Commander-in-Chief of RAF Fighter Command during the Battle of Britain in 1940, stated that this craft had *"been tracked on radar screens...and the observed speeds have been as great as 9,000 miles an hour."*[651]

---

[651] Ibid., 47.

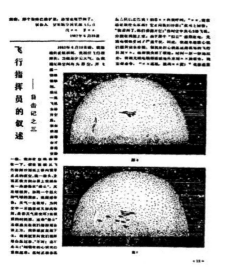

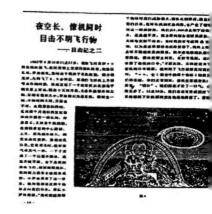

Figure 53

On June 18, 1982, five Chinese Air Force pilots on patrol over North China observed a huge craft *"as big as a mountain of mist."* Smaller craft looking like black dots behind the luminous glow of the huge craft appeared to exit it. The huge craft flew toward the pilots at a high rate of speed. It caused the electrical power systems, as well as the communication and navigation systems to malfunction. The pilots returned to base and prepared reports. The report above shows the "huge craft" which looks a lot like pictures of the Mother Plane which circulated in the temples of the Nation of Islam.

346

## 15.7. *Aliens or Asiatics?*

The most reliable Close Encounter reports confirm that the pilots of these craft are not "aliens" or emissaries from other planets. They are human beings, Scientists, who were supremely advanced in aviation and warfare. But these reports are always suppressed, in favor of the "Little Green or Gray Man" contact experience that, as we will show shortly, is completely fabricated. One of the most important of these authentic accounts comes from Papua, New Guinea in June, July, and August 1959. The observers were William B. Gill, an Anglican priest in charge of the mission to Boianai, Papua, and thirty others: six teachers and the remainder children. After the sighting, twenty-four signatures appeared on a statement testifying that they observed the phenomenon.

The first sighting took place on June 26. The report issued by Gill, and signed by the witnesses, read in part.

A large UFO was first sighted by Annie Laurie at 6:00 P.M.I called Ananias and several others and we stood in the open to watch. Although the sun had set, it was quite light for the following 15 minutes.

We watched as figures appear on the top-four of them. I HAD NO DOUBT THAT THEY WERE HUMAN. It was possible the same object that I took to be the "Mother Ship" last night. Two smaller UFO's were seen at the same time, stationary...

On the large one, two of the figures seemed to be doing something near the center of the deck. They were occasionally bending over and raising their arms as though adjusting or 'setting up' something that was not visible. One figure seemed to be standing, looking down on us (a group of about a dozen).

Several days later, Father Gill added an addendum to his report:

Have been having further experiences lately with the UFO. On Saturday night I counted one large and seven small

UFO's; on Sunday one large and two small; on Monday one large and four small.

Believe it or not, Ananias, Mission boys and I exchanged hand signals...with the occupants of the 'Mother Ship' a little after 6:00 P.M. There is no doubt that she is occupied by at least four men...

Figure 54
Sketch based on witnesses to the New Guinea sightings

This is one of the few impeachable cases in ufology. Multiple witnesses, the duration of the sighting, and the integrity of the observers, make this the darling of UFOlogists. [652]

Another close encounter experienced by a group occurred on the night of July 4, 1978 in Mount Etna, Sicily. Two Italian Air Force sergeants, Franco Padellero and Attilio di Salvatore, with Maurizio Esposito, an Italian Navy officer, were off duty that night when they noticed a triangle of three red lights pulsating in the sky above them at a distance. One of the lights suddenly separated from the others and approached the group. It disappeared, however, behind a nearby slope.

[652] Carl Sagan and Thorton Page, *UFO's-A Scientific Debate* (New York: Barnes & Noble, 1972)146-148.

The group drove where the light had landed to investigate. As they looked over the edge, they saw a *"saucer-shaped object about forty feet across, with a brilliant yellow (illuminated) dome."*

The rest of the object was of a reddish hue with blue and red lights of top. By the side of the craft were five or six very tall beings...with black overall-type tight-fitting suits...Their features were...HUMAN AND BEAUTIFUL.[653]

As two of the men from the craft started to climb up the slope toward the witnesses, they (witnesses) found themselves immobilized by an unknown force. This is reminiscent of the effects that the appearance of the Scientists had on the Prophets.[654] The men from the craft stop short of reaching the top of the slope and returned back to the saucer which by this time was glowing with yellow, red, and blue lights. When a car passed, the lights went out, only to resume again when the car was gone. After the witnesses recovered their mobility, they left the scene in a hurry, not waiting for the craft to depart. They all reported to have felt drained of all energy for some time after the event.

One of the most impressive cases occurred in October of 1973 in Falkville, Alabama. The Police Chief and only policeman of that small town was Jeff Greenhaw, a man well respected in his town prior to the October 17th encounter. Around 10:00 p.m., Greenhaw was telephoned at his home by a woman reporting that an object with flashing lights was landing in a field west of Falkville. Because there were many reports of UFO sightings previously, Greenhaw grabbed his Polaroid camera and started out to the scene.

About two miles outside of town, a man with a metallic suit (Figure 55), about six-feet in height, was standing in the middle of the road. Greenhaw got out of his car and said, "Howdy, stranger, " but the man refused to respond. The Police Chief then proceeded to take four pictures of the man. After getting back into his car and turning on his police lights, the man started running.

---

[653] Good, *Above Top Secret*, 146
[654] See above.

I jumped into my car and took off after him, but couldn't catch up with him in a patrol car. He was running faster than any human I ever saw.[655]

Figure 55
Polaroid taken by Officer Greenhaw

His car reached speeds of 30-40 mph before it spun out on the gravel road. One is reminded of a statement of the Hon. Elijah Muhammad: "One of our brothers from Asia came to Detroit and outran a car by twenty miles." In one of the pictures Greenhaw snapped, reproduced below, the out line of the man in his metallic suited is easily discerned. Unfortunately, Greenhaw suffered much for reporting the incident to NBC-TV. He received threatening phone calls, had his mobile home burned down, his car engine blew, his wife left him, and he was asked to resign from his job, all within two weeks of the incident.

---

[655] Ibid., 302.

## 15.8. *Battle in the Sky*

Figure 56
UFO's seen in formation over Italy, September 26, 1960

Though the fullness of the War of Armageddon has not yet begun, there have been skirmishes in the sky; some of them very ghastly in their implications. On September 24, 1952, a four-page memorandum was sent to General Walter Bedell Smith, Director of the CIA (DCI) from H. Marshall Chadwell, Assistant Director of Scientific Intelligence, concerning "unidentified flying objects."

1. Recently an inquiry was conducted by the Office of Scientific Intelligence to determine whether there are

national security implications in the problem of "unidentified flying objects," i.e. flying saucers...

2. It was found that the only unit of government currently studying the problem is the Directorate of Intelligence, ESAF, which has charged the Air Technical Intelligence Center (ATIC) with the responsibility for investigating the reports of sightings...A worldwide reporting system has been instituted and major Air Force bases HAVE BEEN ORDERED TO MAKE INTERCEPTIONS OF UNIDENTIFIED FLYING OBJECTS...

The Air Force was ordered to INTERCEPT these craft! This policy had disastrous consequences. The following year, General Benjamin Chidlaw, former Commanding General of Air Defense Command, told researcher Robert Gardner,

We have stacks of reports of flying saucers. We take them seriously when you consider WE HAVE LOST MANY MEN AND PLANES TRYING TO INTERCEPT THEM.[656]

One disastrous attempt at interception occurred over Michigan. On November 23, 1953 after the Air Defense Command Ground Control Intercept controller was alerted by an unidentified and unscheduled target on his radar over Soo Locks, Michigan, he scrambled an F-89C Scorpion jet from Kinross AFB. The jet was flown by Lieutenant Felix Moncla, Jr and Lieutenant R. R. Wilson. As the GCI controller vectored the F-89 to the unidentified target, he noted that the UFO changed course, heading in the direction of the jet. The jet closed the gap between itself and the UFO. As the controller advised the men that the target should be in their sight, the two blips on the GCI radarscope merged into one, as if they collided. A single blip remained on the scope and then suddenly vanished.

The controller flashed an emergency message to Search and Rescue. After an air/sea rescue search that lasted all night, no trace of the plane or the men were found. The Air Force press release read:

---

[656] Ibid,, 272.

352

The plane was followed by radar until it merged with an object seventy miles off Keweenaw Point in upper Michigan.

Incidents such as this reportedly prompted the US Navy in 1956 to issue orders to its pilots to engage UFO's in combat if they appeared hostile.[657]    According to Navy physicist Dr. Bruce Maccabee, in the spring of 1959 an USAF jet was ordered to intercept an object off the coast of Japan (Nippon?) that was stationary on radar. The pilot was authorized to fire on the object, but the rockets had no effect on the UFO.  Radar followed as the craft began chasing the jet. Then, suddenly, the two blips on radar merged, just as in the Michigan case.    The object remained stationary for a while, then disappeared.    Search and Rescue missions conducted over several days failed to find any trace of the jet or the pilot.[658]

The US had to change its policy again.  Major General Ramey of the Air Defense Command is reported to have instructed his pilots, *"Intercept but don't shoot except in the case of an obvious maneuver on the part of the UFO."*[659]    According to UFOlogists Robert Carr, there have been over 1,000 failed attempts by the Air Force to shoot these craft down.[660]

There have been many "battles in sky" reported from America, Russia, Cuba, Japan, and Africa. I will describe some of the most disturbing.

## 15.8.1. *America*

On February 25, 1942, a million California residents were awakened by the scream of air raid sirens.  At 2:15 a.m., radar picked up an unidentified target 120 miles out to sea. At 2:25, the cities of Los Angeles County had blacked out.  At 3:18, the 37th Coast Artillery Brigade's anti-aircraft artillery (AAA) began firing batteries of 12.8 pound shells at "unidentified aircraft" coming in over the ocean.  Searchlights pursued the craft through the sky.

---

[657] Ibid, 268.
[658] Jacques Vallee, *Confrontations* (New York: Ballantine Books, 1990) 113.
[659] R. Vesco and D. Childress, *Man-Made UFO's, 1944-1994* (Stelle, Illinois: AUP Publishers Network, 1994) 21.
[660] "What On Earth?" *Clearwater Sun*, October 27, 1974. P. 1-A.

There was one "enormous UFO" and several smaller ones. Thousands of Los Angelinos witness the huge craft remain stationary as anti-aircraft shells bounced off of it. The Los Angeles *Herald Express*, published a picture of the event clearly showing the disked shaped UFO in the search lights (Figure 56), reported that many shells burst directly in the middle of the object and was not moved.[661]  The smaller UFO's "*arrived in formation and then appeared to dodge their way through AAA salvos at speeds of up to 5 miles per second.*" [662] According to witness Paul T. Collins, the smaller UFO were consistently "*appearing from nowhere and then zigzagging from side to side.*" Others would "*mix and play tag with about 30 to 40 others moving so fast they couldn't be counted accurately.*" The huge "mother ship" proceeded at a "leisurely pace" over the coastal cities between Long Beach and Santa Monica.

Figure 56
February 26, 1942 Los Angeles *Herald Express* photo of disc-shaped aircraft and
US military munitions bouncing off its structure.

---

[661] Good, *Above Top Secret*, 15.
[662] Peter Brookesmith, **UFO: The Government Files** (New York: Barnes & Noble, 1996) 15.

On February 26, 1942, Chief of Staff General George Marshall sent President Franklin D. Roosevelt a memorandum on the event which read in part:

The following is the information we have from GHQ at this moment regarding the air alarm over Los Angeles of yesterday morning:

...1. Unidentified airplanes, other than American Army and Navy planes, were probably over Los Angeles, and were fired on by elements of the 37th CA Brigade (AA) between 3:12 and 4:15 a.m. These units expended 1430 ROUNDS OF AMMUNITION (emphasis mine)
2. As many as fifteen airplanes may have been involved, flying at various speeds...
3. No bombs were dropped
4. No casualties among our troops (three residents did die however-author)
5. No planes were shot down.
6. No American Army or Navy planes were in action...

Another disturbing American incident reportedly occurred in 1964. Dr. Robert Jacobs, who later became Assistant Professor of Radio-Film-TV at the University of Wisconsin, was at the time of the incident first lieutenant in the Air Force. On September 15, 1964, he was responsible for the filming of missile tests at Vandenberg AFB in California. In order to have clear films of all missile test firings over the Pacific, according to Roberts, a TV camera affixed to a high-powered telescope was placed on a mountain. What was caught on film on that day was nothing short of incredible. Roberts told researcher Timothy Good:

We kept the telescope locked on to the moving missile by radar, and it was while we were tracking one of the Atlas F missiles in this way that we registered the UFO on our film.
We had a crew of 120 men, and I was in charge. As we watched the Atlas F in flight we were delighted with our camera, which was doing fine, in fact we were jumping

355

around with excitement, with the result that…we actually missed seeing the most important bit of all – our missile's close encounter, at an altitude of 60 miles, with a UFO!

I only heard about it, in fact, a couple of days later, when I was ordered to go and see my superior, Major Florenz J. Mansmann, Chief Science Officer of the Unit. With him there in his office were a couple of men in plain clothes. He introduced them to me only by their first names and said they had come from Washington, DC.

Then Major Mansmann had the film of the test run through. And, just at the point where my men and I had been busy congratulating ourselves and each other, Major Mansmann pointed to the screen and said: "Watch this bit closely." Suddenly we saw a UFO swim into the picture. It was very distinct and clear, a round object. It flew right up to our missile and emitted a vivid flash of light. Then it altered course, and hovered briefly over our missile…and then there came a second vivid flash of light. Then the UFO flew around the missile twice and set off two more flashes from different angles, and then it vanished. A few seconds later, our missile was malfunctioning and tumbling out of control into the Pacific Ocean, hundreds of miles short of its scheduled target.

They switched on the office lights again, and I found myself confronted by these very intense faces. Speaking very quietly, Major Mansmann then said: "Lieutenant, just what the hell was that?" I replied that I had no idea. Then we ran the film through several more times, and I was permitted to examine it with a magnifying glass. Then Mansmann again asked me what I thought, and I answered that in my opinion it was a UFO. Major Mansmann smiled and said: "You are to say nothing about this footage. As far as you are concerned, it never happened!…

It's been 17 years since the incident, and I've told nobody about it until now. I have been afraid of what might happen to me. But the truth is too important for it to be concealed any longer. The UFO's are real. I know they're real. The Air Force knows they're real. And the U.S. government knows they're real. I reckon it's high time that the American public knows it too.

As Timothy Good pointed out, this was an incredible case of true Star Wars. And America lost.

### 15.8.2. *The Soviet Union*

Some of the most interesting cases were reported from the Soviet Union. According to science writer Alberto Fenoglio from Italy, who got the information from Soviet sources in the West, an incident occurred in the summer of 1961 near Rybinsk, 150 kilometers from Moscow. New missile batteries were being set up when a huge disk-shaped object surrounded by an assortment of smaller objects appeared 20,000 meters up. The battery commander panicked and gave an unauthorized order to fire a salvo at the giant object.

> The missiles were fired. All exploded when at an estimated distance of some two kilometers from the target, creating a fantastic spectacle in the sky. The third salvo was never fired, for at this point the smaller 'saucers' went into action and stalled the electrical apparatus of the whole missile base. When the smaller discoidal UFO's had withdrawn and joined the larger craft, the electrical apparatus was again found to be in working order.[663]

The larger craft apparently had some sort of "force field" around it which caused the shells to explode two km before reaching it. This is reminiscent of what Elijah Muhammad has stated about the Mother Ship.

> When America thinks that she is going after this Plane...then those Scientists on the Plan go to work and create a barrier so that she can't come forward towards the Plane. She can't shoot at it.

---

[663] Good, *Above Top Secret*, 227.

An even more sinister incident occurred in 1990 in Turkmenistan, one of the Turkic republics. At the time, the airspace in the region was under strict control because of the war in Afghanistan. The Soviet Air Defense Forces were divided up into regional Air Defense armies. The town of Mary fell under the control of the 12th Air defense Army whose Air Defense division was commanded by Colonel Anatoli Kurcky.

On May 25, 1990, during the day light hours, a huge disk-shaped object hovered over the town of Mary at an altitude of 1,000 meters. Military personnel observed the craft from less than 3,000 meters away. When informed about the craft, Kurchy gave the order to fire three ground-to-air guided missiles at it. The UFO made a slight horizontal maneuver and disintegrated the missiles with beams of light emanating from its port side. The Colonel then ordered two interceptor jets scrambled. At approximately 1,000 meters from the UFO, the jets were thrown to the ground, killing the pilots and destroying the aircraft.

The Air Command immediately removed Colonel Kurchy from his post and, according to Paragraph 1, Item 5 of the Turkmenistan Criminal Procedures Code, military prosecutors of the 12th Air Defense Army instituted procedures against him.[664]

## 15.8.3. *Cuba*

In March of 1967, a security specialist from a unit of the Air Force Security Service reported an alarming incident. His unit was based with the 6947th Security Squadron whose mission it was to monitor all Cuban military communications. He reported in his statement.

In March of 1967…Cuban radar installations reported a bogey (UFO) approaching the Cuban landmass from northeast. 2 MiG-21 interceptors were scrambled when the bogey crossed Cuban air space at an altitude of approximately 10,000 meters and at a speed approaching Mach [1]. The interceptors were directed to the bogey by

[664] Timothy Good, *Alien Contact, Alien Contact.* (New York: Quill, William, Morrow, 1991)184-185.

Cuban Ground Control Intercept and were guided within 5 kilometers of the object.

The wing leader reported the object was a bright metallic sphere with no visible markings or appendages. After a futile attempt to contact the object for identification, Cuban Air Defense headquarters ordered the wing leader to arm his weapons and destroy the object. The wing leader reported his missiles armed and his radar locked-on.

Seconds later the wingman began screaming to the ground controller that the wing leader's aircraft had exploded. After regaining his composure he further reported that there was no smoke or flame; the aircraft had disintegrated. Cuban radar reported the object quickly accelerated and climbed beyond 30,000 meters and at last report was heading south-southeast toward South America.

A spot report was sent to National Security Agency headquarters, which is standard procedure in any case involving aircraft loss by an enemy country…Within hours we received orders to ship all tapes and pertinent intelligence to the Agency and were told to list the incident in the squadron files as aircraft loss due to equipment malfunction.[665]

### 15.8.4. Japan

On June 9, 1974, Major Shiro Kubota and Lieutenant Colonel Nakamura of Japan's Air Self-Defense Force (JASDF) were flying an F-4EJ when a fatal encounter with an UFO occurred. According to Kubota's report:

We thought at first we were going up to intercept a Soviet bomber, of the type which sometimes tests our northern air defenses. After Toshio got us airborne, our Ground Control Intercept (GCI) explained to us that we were going upstairs to check out a bright-colored light reported by dozens of observers and showing on radar. Several

---

[665] Good, *Above Top Secret*, 421.

minutes later, we broke out of the clouds and leveled off at 30, 000 feet on a clear, moonless night. That was when we spotted the light a few miles ahead.

Even at first, I felt that this disk-shaped, red-orange object was a flying craft, made and flown by intelligent beings. It appeared to be about 10 meters in diameter, with square-shaped marks around its side which may have been windows or propulsion outlets. Toshio aimed us straight toward it and, as it grew larger in our gun sight, it dipped into a shallow turn, as if sensing our presence...

Toshio armed our 20mm cannon and closed in on the UFO. Suddenly, the object reversed direction and shot straight at us...Toshio threw the stick to the left and forced us into a sudden, violent dive. The glowing red UFO shot past-missing us by inches. Then it made a sharp turn and came at us again...The UFO began making rapid, high-speed passes at us, drawing closer and closer. Several times, the strange object narrowly missed us.[666]

According to Kubota, the UFO then struck the Phantom jet, causing the pilots to eject. While Kubota landed safely, Nakamura's parachute caught fire and he fell to his death. After a lengthy investigation by the Japanese Air Defense, they released only that Phantom number 17-8307 crashed following a collision with "an aircraft or object unknown," killing Nakamura.

15.9. *A Base On The Moon?*

Dr. von Braun acknowledged the uncertainty with regard to the base of operations of these craft and their Mother Ship. Elijah Muhammad said the Wheel stays 40 miles above the earth's surface for six to twelve months, then reenters to take in air from the atmosphere with huge suction devices for the crew. Muhammad says the primary base of operations is here on Earth where it was created, but there are reports of a possible auxiliary base on the Moon.

---

[666] Ibid., 430-1.

Reports of lunar UFO activity goes back to 1956. The University of Ohio reported receiving "*code like radio chatter from the Moon.*" In October 1958,

America, Soviet, and British Astronomers detected something speeding toward the Moon at better than 25,000 miles per hour. They not only saw the strange object; they heard it emitting radio signals that no one could interpret![667]

The most astonishing evidence of a lunar UFO base came from the Apollo 11 landing on July 21, 1969. Neil Armstrong and Buzz Aldrin reportedly observed disc shaped craft on the Moon when they landed. This historic landing was of course televised for the whole world to see. Viewers heard Armstrong report to Mission Control that he observed a "light" in or on one of the craters. After mission Control requested more information, all sound was terminated. We watched the remainder of the landing in silence.

According to Otto Binder, former NASA employee, unnamed radio hams with their own VHF receiving facilities were able to bypass NASA's broadcasting outlets. They captured the following exchange, according to Binder:

Mission Control: What's there? Mission Control calling
                 Apollo 11.

Apollo 11:    These babies are huge, sir...enormous...Oh,
              God, you wouldn't believe it! I'm telling
              you there are other spacecraft out
              there...lined up on the far
              side of the crater edge...they're on the
              moon watching us...

In 1979, Maurice Chatelain, former chief of NASA communications specialists and one of the conceivers and designers of the Apollo spacecraft, confirmed that Armstrong indeed reported seeing on the rim of a crater two enormous

---

[667] David Barclay, *Aliens, The Final Answer?* (London: Blandford Books, 1995) 59.

UFO's.[668] Soviet scientist Dr. Vladimir Azhazha, a physicist and Professor of Mathematics at Moscow University, confirmed the same.

> According to our information, the encounter was reported immediately after the landing of the module...Neil Armstrong relayed the message to Mission Control that two large, mysterious objects were watching them after having landed near the moon module. But his message was never heard by the public-because NASA censored it.

### 15.10. America Prepares for War

During the Los Angeles air raid of 1942, the Mother Ship and her Baby Planes formally introduced themselves to the U.S. government. Even though Chief of Staff Marshal's memo concluded that the *"unidentified airplanes...may have been from commercial sources, operated by enemy agents for the purpose of spreading alarm,"* President Roosevelt apparently knew better. In September, by Executive Order, he had the FBI arrest Elijah Muhammad in Chicago. They confiscated all of Muhammad's material concerning the Wheel, including a blackboard which contained pictures of the Wheel drawn by Muhammad and explanatory notes. In his statement to the FBI, Muhammad responded to their inquiries concerning the Mother Ship. When finally released, the FBI kept the blackboard.[669]

Based on this information, Roosevelt then initiated plans for surviving an attack from the Wheel and its deadly fleet. He ordered the construction of a series of "hidden cities," communities built one mile underground. They were built on large platforms supported by giant springs to withstand the shockwaves caused by the bombs from the Baby Planes. Three of these hidden cities were built: one in the Blue Ridge Mountains in Northern Virginia; one in the Appalachian system along the west back of the Hudson, in the Catskill Mountains of south east New York; the other in Mount Diablo in central California east of

---

[668] Good, 1988, p. 384.
[669] Muhammad, *Theology of Time*, 512.

Oakland. The Virginia hidden city is called Mount Weather and the New York City is called Iron Mountain.[670]

These subterranean communities are complete with private apartments, streets, hospitals, water-purification systems, mass transit system, and power plants. An independent government consisting of a president, Cabinet, and federal departments is in place. Ted Gup, in his report in *Time Magazine* called "Doomsday Hideaway," notes:

> Mount Weather is a city unto itself, with a resident compliment of scientists, computer programmers, engineers, fire fighters, craftsmen and security guards. The government bureaucracy is well represented by branch chiefs, financial managers, supply officers, secretaries and stenographers. Mount Weather's communication facilities are an integral part of the National Emergency Management system, with a direct line to the White House Situation Room.[671]

The caves are said to be protected by steel doors that are 13 by 13 by 10 feet and take ten minutes to open. Only the President holds the three keys, and they are passed down from President to President. It is commonly believed that this program, called Continuity of Government (COG) Program was initiated by President Eisenhower. According to other sources, however, Eisenhower only inherited the Survival Plan that had been started by his predecessor.

When the bombing starts, selected government officials, prominent newsmen, and other pre-approved persons, will be airlifted to these cities by an elite unit of helicopter crews. The unit, the 2857th Test Squadron, was initially stationed at Olmsted Air Force Base in Pennsylvania but later relocated to Dover Air Force Base in Delaware. That squadron was made in-operational in 1970, being replaced by another unit.

The justification given for these underground cities has been that they are designed to survive a nuclear attack by an enemy

---

[670] Bill Cooper, *Behold A Pale Horse*, 117; Ralph Epperson, *Unseen Hand* (Tucson: Publius Press, 1985) 252.
[671] Ted Gup, "Doomsday Hideaway," *Time Magazine*, December 9, 1991, 28.

state such as Russia or a terrorist country. But according to a CNN Special Assignment Report on this "Doomsday Government" as they called it, other considerations were involved in its construction. CNN Special Assignment Investigator David Lewis said in the November 17, 1991 broadcast,

> It is overseen directly by the White House because of its fundamental mission, to make sure that the constitutional government SURVIVES ARMAGEDDON (Emphasis mine).[672]

"Armageddon," the ultimate war between Good and Evil, God and Devil. The President (Roosevelt) saw this war as the fulfillment of the Prophesy of the World King. The evidence suggests that Roosevelt saw his nation as the Lalu Desum or Evil King of the Barbarians. In 1934, Roosevelt authorized Secretary of Agriculture Henry Wallace to send Nicolas Roerich on a government-sponsored expedition to Central Asia. The Press was told the purpose of the trip was the search for drought-resistant grasses. *Newsweek* (March 22. 1948) however, noted

> Around the Department of Agriculture the Secretary's assistants freely admitted that he also wanted ROERICH TO LOOK FOR SIGNS OF THE SECOND COMING.[673]

"The Second Coming" was understood by Wallace as the coming of Rudra Calkin, the World King whom Roerch taught Wallace and Roosevelt of. The President's fascination with the Shamballah Prophecy would display itself again before he left office. He built a hide-away in the hills of Maryland and called it "Shangri-La," the novel name for Shamballah. The hide away would later be renamed Camp David.[674] During WWII, Roosevelt announced that General James Doolittle's bombing raid of Tokyo originated at "Shangri-La."

---

[672] "The Doomsday Government, " **CNN Special Assignment** Transcript # 104, Air Date: November 17, 1991.
[673] "The 'Guru Letters'..." *Newsweek*, March 22, 1948, 28.
[674] Bernbaum, *Way to Shamballa*, 3-4.

Offensive preparations are said to have begun in the 60's by the Air Force's Directorate of Operational Intelligence. These programs were logged under USAF code number 7795 which was listed as anti-satellite weapons systems. Two of the earliest proposed programs were Project Saint and Project Blue Gemini.

Project Saint, short for Satellite Intercept, was an orbital UFO inspector according to researcher Howard Bloom.[675] A television camera and a radar system were to be affixed to an Agena B satellite used by the CIA. After being launched by an Atlas rocket, Saint would get within fifty feet of the UFO and photograph it. These reconnaissance photos would then be relayed to NORAD.

Project Blue Gemini called for a militarily converted manual Gemini capsule from NASA to be launched so that it could *"approach, capture and disable an uncooperative satellite or unidentified flying object."*[676]

Projects Saint and Blue Gemini never made it off of paper. What developed instead was Strategic Defense Initiative (SDI) or "Star Wars." Many writers, such as William Cooper, former member of the Office of Naval Intelligence Briefing Team, believe that Star Wars is an operation specifically designed to do battle with the Wheel. Major Colman S. VonKeviczky of Russia told the *Final Call Newspaper* in 1989 that *"the super powers, America and Russia, were actually planning to do battle with the UFO's, and that the Star Wars Defense System was not aimed at Russia, but at UFO's."*[677]

There is reason to believe such claims. The brains behind SDI are said to be the RAND Corporation (Research and Development Corporation). RAND is a civilian organization of elite scientists that does research and consulting work for the USAF. RAND has also been involved in UFO investigations. In the General Nathan Twinning memo which we cited earlier, he recommended that all UFO data be sent to various governmental agencies, including RAND. In fact, RAND joined the Scientific Advisory Board, the Weather Bureau, and the FBI, in the first attempt in 1948 at working out a preliminary plan for a standardized approach to

---

[675] Howard Bloom, *Out There: The Government's Secret Quest For Extraterrestrials*, (New York: Pocket Books, 1990) 67.

[676] Ibid., 68.

[677] *Final Call*, November 30, 1989.

studying the UFO problem.[678] Phillip J. Corso, retired Army-intelligence officer, says in his *The Day After Roswell*,

> [The U.S. and U.S.S.R.] both knew who the real targets of SDI were…When we deployed our advanced particle-beam weapon and tested it in orbit for all to see, the (UFO's) knew and we knew that they knew that we had our defense of the planet in space.

### 15.11. *The Duplication Program*

Since World War II, the governments of the world have been trying to duplicate the technology of the Mother Ship and Her Baby Planes. The Germans were the first to get anywhere in this regard. Walter Schauberger, Ruldolf Schriever, Habermohl, Miethe, and Dr. Bellonzo from Italy, were the chief architects of Germany's "duplication program." They are reported to have succeeded in test-flying a "flying-disk" of their own on February 14, 1945, achieving a vertical lift at an altitude of 12,400 meters in three minutes and a speed of 2,200 km/h in horizontal flight.[679]

After the war, the U.S. took the baton and carried the duplication program to another level. In General Twinning's 1947 memo quoted above, he acknowledged:

> It is possible, with the present U.S. knowledge - provided extensive detailed development is undertaken - to construct a piloted aircraft which has the general description of the object in subparagraph (e) (UFO) above which would be capable of an approximate range of 7000 miles at subsonic speed.[680]

This capability in 1947 was due to the fact that Meithe, Dr. Wernher von Braun, and Dr. Henry Wang, the German scientist who worked on the German Duplication Program, were brought to the U.S. and Canada after the war.[681] The two nations thus

---

[678] Vesco and Childress, *Man-Made UFOS*, 337.

[679] Ibid., 242.

[680] Good, *Above Top Secret*, 477.

[681] William Steinman and Wendelle Stevens, *UFO Crash at Aztec*, (Wendelle Stevens, 1986) 368-71.

collaborated in their efforts to reproduce the technology reported to be involved in the "UFO" phenomenon. The Air Force worked through Avro Aircraft Ltd., Canada, with the aid of Wilbert Smith in the |Canadian Department of Transport. On December 2, 1950, Commander C.P. Edwards, Deputy Minister of Transport for Air Services, established Project Magnet, with Smith appointed as Engineer-in-Charge. The purpose of Project Magnet was clearly stated in the June 25, 1952 and August 1953 interim reports by Smith:

> If, as appears evident, the Flying Saucers are emissaries from some other civilization, and actually do operate on magnetic principles, we have before us the fact that we have missed something in magnetic theory but have a good indication of the direction in which to look for the missing quantities. It is therefore recommended that the work of Project Magnet be continued and expanded...
>
> It appears then, that we are faced with the substantial probability of the real existence of extraterrestrial vehicles, regardless of whether they fit into our scheme of things. Such vehicles of necessity must use a technology considerably in advance of what we have. It is therefore submitted that the next step in this investigation should be a substantial effort toward the acquisition of as much as possible of this technology, which would without doubt be of great value to us.

Smith is under the impression, because of the advanced technology, that these craft are from another planet. He could not conceive that a civilization on this earth, a Black Civilization, could produce such. But he/they were wrong.

The U.S.-Canadian efforts to duplicate the technology of God failed. Smith concluded in a 1958 article:

> But it soon became apparent that there was a very real and quite large gap between this alien science and the science in which I had been trained. Certain crucial experiments were suggested and carried out, and in each case the

367

results confirmed the validity of the alien science. Beyond this point the alien science just seemed incomprehensible.

Another scientist which acknowledged this fact was Dr. Herman Oberth. In 1955 Oberth was invited by Dr. Von Braun to come to the U.S. and aid in the work done at the Army Ballistic Missile Agency and NASA to study the 'alien technology.' Oberth said concerning the work:

> today we cannot produce machines that fly as UFOs do. They are flying by means of artificial fields of gravity. This would explain the sudden change in directions...This hypothesis would also explain the piling up of these disks into a cylindrical or cigar-shaped Mothership upon leaving the earth, because in this fashion only field of gravity would be required for all disks.

Russia, Japan, France, Britain, America, Germany, Canada, all attempted to produce similar craft which exhibit the same technology as that of the Mother Ship and Baby Planes. They failed dismally, littering the terrain with residue of "crashed-saucers." Flying Saucers did crash at Roswell and Aztec. But it is as likely that this were not "alien" or Asiatic craft. It is possible they were the crafts of these various nations trying to imitate God's Wisdom.

# Project Saucer

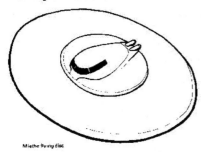

Miethe flying disc

Serious German interest in disc-shaped aircraft seems to have originated from about the spring of 1941, when Rudolf Schriever, a Luftwaffe aeronautical engineer, designed his first "Flying Top", the prototype of which was being test-flown in June 1942. Schriever followed these experiments – carried out in collaboration with three colleagues, Habermohl, Miethe and Bellonzo – by constructing an even larger flying disc in the summer of 1944. It is not clear how these early designs were to be powered, but a bigger version with advanced jet engines was reportedly designed at the BMW factory near Prague.

Information on this aspect of German jet aircraft development is very sketchy. The project was always highly secret, and documents that may have existed were probably either destroyed, lost or taken by the Russians when the war ended. A last possibility is that the Allies discovered Schriever's work and considered it too important to reveal. However, in the late 1950s Rudolf Schriever himself described his work on a wartime research programme named "Project Saucer"

The Schriever and Habermohl design comprised a large-area disc rotating around a central cupola-like cockpit. The disc was made up of adjustable wing surfaces which could be positioned for take-off or level flight. Dr Miethe also developed a 138ft (42m) diameter flying disc powered by vectorable jets. This machine is said in many references actually to have flown, and one source even pinpoints the date of the first flight as February 4, 1945, and the place as Prague. On that

flight the machine, designated V-7, is supposed to have climbed to a height of 37,600ft (11,450m) in just three minutes, reaching a level speed of 1,218mph (1,960km/hr). But Schriever claimed after the war that while his flying disc was made ready for testing early in 1945, the preparations were cancelled in the face of the Allied advance, and the machine was destroyed and all information lost or stolen. The factory at Breslau at which Schriever's saucer is said to have been built fell into Russian hands, and the prototype and the technicians working on it are believed to have been captured and taken to Siberia to continue the project under Soviet control. Also rumoured was another near-complete flying disc which was expected to be capable of reaching 3,000mph (4,830km/hr).

Although the evidence for the existence of a German flying-disc programme is very tenuous, the senior official of a 1945 British technical mission revealed that he had discovered German plans for "entirely new and deadly developments in air warfare". These plans must obviously have gone beyond normal jet aircraft designs, as both sides already had jet-powered aircraft in production and operational service by the end of the war. Moreover, before Rudolf Schriever died some 15 years after the war he had become convinced that the large numbers of post-war UFO sightings were evidence

Schriever flying disc

Schriever and Habermohl flying disc

From Vesco, and Childress, *Man-Made UFO's*, 241.

## Model I

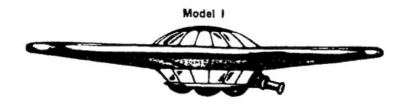

**Model I**

                                This prototvpe was first test-flown in 1941-42; it is also the world's first vertical take-off flying vehicle. It has similar flight characteristics as the Schauberger models but it was less stable. The wings which issued from the centre of the craft like spokes towards the outer rim, were tiltable. The Germans called that "Flugelrad" or Wingwheel. This caused the designers immense problems because the smallest imbalance caused the wingwheel to vibrate and this vibration increased at high speeds and was the cause on many occasions of wrecked machines. Perhaps the best comparison is to the tire of a car that is not properly balanced or is unevenly worn. Since the r.p.m.'s were so utterly fantastic, the problems faced by the designers can be easily appreciated even by the layman. Whilst car wheel balancing can be corrected by adding lead slugs to the rims of the wheels, German UFO scientists could employ no such crude remedy and so it was repeatedly "back to the drawing board" and it was absolute perfect workmanship which finally eradicated the problem. This model was test-flown with the standard German Rocketmotor then in use and called the Walterrohr. Because of its tremendous speeds, fuel consumption was very high and there was not sufficient tank space on board. At first, the pilot sat in a reclining contour seat as in an airplane. Later the position was changed to lying flat. Provision was made for one flight mechanic whose compartment can be seen below the "Flugelrad". The jet engines on all conventionally propelled flying saucers were manouverable or tiltable in order to achieve what is called the "Coandaeffeckt" which results in the vertical take-off of the craft. Many improvements were naturally made in the course of the experiments and flight trials.

From Vesco, and Childress, *Man-Made UFO's*, 241.

From Vesco, and Childress, *Man-Made UFO's*, 241.

# CHAPTER XVI

# The Black God, The Mars Enigma, And The Moon

## 16.1. Black Life on Mars?

Some on the early UFO reports suggested that the base of operations of the anomalous craft was some other planet. One of the first candidates was Mars. Consequently, wild stories of "little green men from Mars" proliferated and became the textbook image of the forces behind the UFO's.

The base of operations, according to Mr. Muhammad, is here on earth. However, he did make reference to an advanced civilization on Mars peopled by, not little green men, but by tall Black Men. He says in *Theology of Time*

> God has taught me about the Martian people. He said that they (whites) have pictures of them (Martian people). The devil (whites) believes it because they have come near to looking at the surface of Mars for creatures on it. But they (the Martians) are very wise and very skillful so Allah taught me. When they hear the devil's space vehicles coming they can hide away. They live up to one thousand Earth years...

He says further,

> Now he (devil whites) is making instruments to look at the civilization on Mars. When he sees what is on Mars he won't see any mark of his. It's our Mars and our people, so God taught me. He didn't know that they were there until just a few days ago. He used to look at Mars and just call it a star. Our Fathers made it with some type of intelligent beings like ourselves. They are not animals. They are intelligent people. The marks that we see on Mars are not from an ignorant, silly, uncivilized people. They show signs of civilization and they look something

similar to us. Not exactly, but they look similar. They walk on two feet and they are not white folks...

The Martian people have civilization but it is not equal with ours, so God has taught me. We are their superior.

What are these "marks" or "signs of civilization" to which Muhammad referred? It has commonly been held by the scientific community that Mars was inhospitable to life forms. That view has now been demonstrated false. In June of 2000, the Mars Global Surveyor (MGS) and Mars Orbiter Camera (MOC) relayed images which NASA is interpreting as signs that liquid water has seeped onto the surface in the geologically recent past. Fox News reported:

What Malin's (Michael Malin, the chief scientist for Mars Global Surveyor's camera) team has presented is dozens of images of features on Mars which appear to have been formed by water in recent times, possibly continuing to the present.

Scientists generally agree that liquid water existed on Mars in the distant past. There are massive channels with teardrop shaped islands which were almost certainly formed by flooding. But there's also no doubt that there isn't any liquid water on Mars' surface now — the atmosphere is too thin for it to exist.

Water does however still exist on Mars as ice in the polar caps and may exist beneath the surface. But the surprising conclusion of Malin's paper, *Evidence for Recent Groundwater Seepage and Surface Runoff on Mars*, is relatively young features on Mars formed by water.

In their survey of Mars, Malin's team found gully-like features in many areas on the planet. ...

Ken Edgett, a member of Malin's team and the co-author of the paper said, "I was dragged, kicking and screaming to this conclusion. I've always had a hard time whenever anybody invokes water on Mars because it's not there now in liquid form. The thing that really sold me is some of these things cluster in specific regions, particularly in Gorgonum Chaos we see a single layer and many troughs and craters puncturing through that layer and in every one of those troughs and craters. We see these features coming down the slopes from that same layer. That's hard to do unless there's liquid seeping through that layer."

So what's the big deal about liquid water on Mars?

Most important is the potential for life. On Earth wherever there's liquid water there's some form of life. So if life ever existed on Mars in its distant past then it's a logical conclusion that if liquid water still exists then life probably still exists in some form.

Evidence that indeed life existed on Mars came as early as August of 1996. CNN reported:

WASHINGTON (CNN) -- NASA announced Wednesday that a primitive form of microscopic life may have existed on Mars about 4 billion years ago.

The announcement was made in Washington at a news conference to discuss the findings, made by researchers from NASA and various universities.

Before the news conference, a source close to the agency told CNN, "I think it's arguably the biggest discovery in the history of science."

NASA Administrator Daniel Goldin had said Tuesday the research is based on a sophisticated examination of an ancient Martian meteorite, labeled Allan Hills or ALH 84001, that landed on Earth about 13,000 years ago. The meteorite was found in Antarctica in 1984...

"It means a lot," astronomer Richard Berendzen of American University told CNN. "It means a long-lost discovery, a thing that astronomers have been looking for for decades." Astronomer and author Carl Sagan, who has studied the possibility of extraterrestrial life and investigated the origins of life on Earth, called the discovery "glorious." "The chance of independently arriving at the same kind of life on two independent planets is very small. That is one of the great excitements -- to see what two different planets, how their evolutionary history proceeds," he said.

## 16.2. *The Discovery of Marks of Civilization on Mars*

There is thus evidence that life could and indeed did exist on Mars. But it is a huge leap to go from there to "The Black Man has a civilization on Mars." The first hints of evidence that Muhammad was in fact correct came in 1971 when NASA's *Mariner 9* satellite photographed the entire surface of Mars and revealed, contrary to previous scientific notions, a living planet with a history of geologic and volcanic activity as well as the marks of flowing water. In the southern hemisphere, *Mariner* photographed surface structures that suggested the presence of intelligent life. A series of steppe walls made up of square segments brought to mind similar Walls from the pre-Inca civilization of Peru (Figures 60, 61). Astronomers have thus dubbed the area "Inca City." NASA geologist John McCauley said the "ridges" were "*continuos, show no breaching, and stand out among the surrounding plains and small hills like walls of an ancient ruin.*"

As the steppe walls can arguably be attributed to some natural erosive process, they are inconclusive as evidence of a Martian civilization. However, photos of pyramids strengthened the suggestion of life on Mars. Images sent back from *Mariner 9* (Frames 4205-78) show a three-sided pyramid in the region called Trivium Charontis. Astronomer David Chandler, in *Life on Mars*, noted

Given the lack of any easily acceptable explanation, there seems to be no reason to exclude from consideration the most obvious conclusion of all: perhaps they were built by intelligent beings.

Figure 60

The "Inca City Walls" found in the southern hemisphere of Mars.

Figure 61

Ruins found in Peruvian Sacred Valley.

In 1975, *Viking Orbiter* launched from Cape Canaveral. *Viking 1* and *Viking 2* landed July/August on Mars and began snapping thousands of photos. On Orbit 35, 1,000 miles above an area dubbed "Cydonia" 41 degrees above the Martian equator in the north, *Viking* snapped Frame 35A72. The image was conveyed through Deep Space Network to the NASA imaging area. Toby Owen of the imaging team saw the image and exclaimed: "*Oh my God!*" It was the now infamous photo of "The Face" – a huge human head that appears to be carved into a plateau in the Cydonia area. The photo was subsequently dismissed as a "trick of light" and laid away for two years as an Archive Photo at the National Space Science Data Center in Greenbelt, Maryland.

Figure 62
Frame 35A72 from Viking photo of the anomalous "Face" structure on Mars

Composite of frames 70A13 and
35A72 flipped to create image of
the missing half of the "Face."

The photo was rediscovered by Vincent DiPietro, engineer who designed, built, and ran the digital image records for Landsat and Nimbus programs for the NASA Goddard Spaceflight Center. Together with colleague Gregory Molenaar, a computer scientist, they digitally examined the photo to see if it was truly a "trick of lighting." They discovered another photo of the Face taken 35 days after the original photo was taken (70A13) which showed the Face was no mirage. In the same frame they found a huge five-sided pyramid, a mile by 1.6 miles. Called the "D & M Pyramid" after its founders (DiPietro and Molenaar), it appears to be badly eroded and mashed on one side due to impact from space debris. After four months of image processing and computer enhancement, DiPietro and Molenaar reported "*the non-uniformity*

377

*of alignment between adjacent pyramids and the bisymmetry of the face leave doubt that nature was totally responsible.*"[682]

In 1983, Richard Hoagland, science writer and one-time consultant at the Goddard Space Flight Center, organized a computer conference to have all pertinent data studied by a representative body of scientists and specialists. Called the Independent Mars Investigation Team, it consisted of astronomers, architects, artists, anthropologists, physicists, and computer programmers. Their results were very convincing.

Physicist John Brandenberge from national defense contractor Sandia Laboratories in Albuquerque, New Mexico, after scientifically examining the "Face" or "Head" photo, observed:

> It appears completely bisymetric. It has two eyes, a nose, and a mouth. It appears to have an eye in one socket and also, by careful study, to have cheek ornaments below the eyes
> It is pleasing aesthetically, it looks (like) a King...
> All objects resembling this object, found on earth are man-made...[683]

Artist Jim Channon reached similar conclusions:

> For an artist, there is yet a more precise way to judge the authenticity of this form. The expression expected from one powerful enough to be so memorialized by a monument of this scale would not be random. The artistic, cultural, mythic and spiritual considerations behind such a work of art would demand a predictable expression. The expression of The Face on Mars reflects permanence, presence, strength, and similar characteristics in this range of reverence and respect.
> The image appears to be a powerful male about the right age to be a ruler...
> It is the face of a powerful male character with the strength and age known to have created similar artifacts on Earth.

---

[682] V. DiPietro and G. Molenaar, *Unusual Martian Surface Features* (Maryland: Mars Research, 1982).

[683] Randolfo Pozos, *The Face on Mars* (1982), 91.

As an artist with anthropological training...the evaluation just presented is overwhelming evidence that the structure...is a consciously created monument typical of the archeology left to us by our predecessors. [684]

In 1988, Dr. Mark Carlotto, an expert in digital image processing and satellite remote sensing from the Analytical Sciences Corporation, reconstructed the 3-D image using a single image shape-form-shading technique. In his report published in *Applied Optics* ("Digital Imagery Analysis of Unusual Martian Surface Features", Vol. 27, No. 10 May 15, 1988), Dr. Carlotto concluded:

> The image enhancement results indicate that a second eye socket may be present on the right, shadowed side of the Face. Fine structure in the mouth suggesting teeth are apparent in the enhanced imagery as well as crossed symmetrical lines on the forehead. The results of the 3-D analysis show that the impression of facial features is not a transient phenomenon. Facial features are evident in the underlying topography and are shown to induce the visual impression of a face over a wide range of illumination conditions and perspectives.
> It is the author's belief that although the Viking data are not of sufficient resolution to permit the identification of possible mechanisms of origin for these objects, the results to date suggest that they may not be natural.

Better imaging techniques showed that there was an eyeball with a pupil within the socket, teeth within the mouth, a helmet with a chin strap (a warrior-king) and, interesting, a tear drop falling down the cheek. In a follow-up report ("Evidence in Support of the Hypothesis that Certain Objects on Mars are Artificial in Origin, *Journal of Scientific Exploration* - Vol. 11, No. 2, Summer, 1997), Dr. Carlotto observed:

---

[684] Ibid., 51.

The formation known as the Face possesses all of the salient features of a humanoid face: head, eyes, ridge-like nose, and mouth. This fact has been verified by two images taken at slightly different sun angles (35A72 and 70A13)...Instead of an ordinary rock formation, this second image not only confirms the facial features first seen in 35A72, but also reveals the overall symmetry of the head, the extension of the mouth, and a matching eye on the right side - features not visible in 35A72 because they were in shadow...

Measurements between the eyes, nose, mouth, chin, and crown of the head fall within conventional humanoid proportions...

In addition to its gross humanoid features, the Face contains a number of subtle details or embellishments. They include a dark cavity within the eye socket that looks like an eyeball, broad stripes across the face, thin lines that intersect above the eyes, and fine structure in the mouth that appear as teeth. These features are visible in both images and so it is very unlikely that they are due to noise in the imagery or artifacts of image processing. It is also noted that if erosional processes are responsible for the Face they would also have to explain these subtle details - details that one would expect to have been obliterated by erosion over time...

The visual impression of a face persists over a wide range of sun angles and viewing geometries. Such is not the case for naturally occurring rock formations that look like faces when viewed in profile...

By using fractals to model images, areas that are least natural can be identified according to how well they fit a fractal model. The Face was found to be the least fractal object in Viking frame 35A72 and was also highly anomalous in frame 70A13. Results of fractal analysis indicate that the Face is the least natural object over an area of about 15,000 square kilometers...

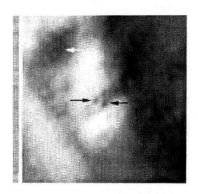

Figure 63

Magnified image showing "eyeball" (white arrow) and "teeth" (black arrow)

Vincient DiPietro, one of the two original re-discovers of the Viking images, developed a new digital image enhancing process called SPIT (Starburst Pixel Interleaving Technique). After applying this technique in conjunction with bit-slicing to the images, DiPierto published a report in 1996. This process indicated "three concentric circles in the eye cavity area," which would suggest pupils.[685]

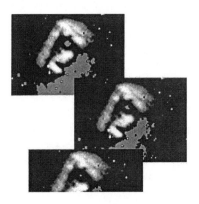

Figure 64
Three concentric circles ("pupils") discovered by DiPietro.

---

[685] Vincent DiPietro, "Report of Findings of the Face on Mars in the Cydonia Region," July 1, 1996. Now available at http://planetarymysteries.com/mars/dipietroface.html.

The D&M Pryramid was subjected to equal scientific scrutiny. In 1988 a cartographer from the U.S. Defense Mapping Agency, Erol Torun, challenged Hoagland's claim that the objects of Cydonia – the Face, the Pyramid, a "City Square," a cliff and a fortress - displayed complex geometries that are unlikely to occur naturally. But after conducting his own measurements, Torun found Hoagland to be accurate. He went on to note:

One of the most important aspects of the Martian geology is that Mars is geologically similar to the Earth...Partly because of this similarity it is difficult to dismiss the unusual objects of Cydonia as simply the product of an utterly alien environment. Any natural explanation would need to provide a specific geomorphological model for the formation of a five-sided structure that appears to include six mathematical constants and whose apparent axis of symmetry points directly at an object bearing the likeness of a humanoid face.

Considering the Face, the City, the City Square, the Cliff and the Tholus, we now have a complex of objects that exhibit architectural, anthropomorphic and other visually-anomalous qualities. In addition to their appearance, we must also consider whatever geometry is present, and the information that this geometry may represent. In Cydonia, specific angles and mathematical values are represented, not once but abundantly. Furthermore, this pattern seems to relate to the physics of stellar and planetary bodies.

Thus we have here key elements of solid science...It is this recovery of useful information that speaks most eloquently for the PROBABILITY OF INTELLIGENCE ON MARS.

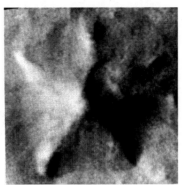

Figure 65
D&M Pyramid


Torun released a report on his concentrated study of the D&M Pyramid ("The D&M Pyramid of Mars", 1996).[686] His study was based on a geometric reconstruction of the object as it appears in the Viking images. Torun's research demonstrated:

> The reconstructed geometry of the D&M Pyramid shows a five-sided object having facets with differing angles. The object has bilateral symmetry, with a pair of congruent angles forming the front, and another pair of congruent angles forming the sides...
> The D&M Pyramid appears to be positioned with architectural alignment to other enigmatic objects nearby that have also been studied as possibly artificial.

Torun concludes:

> This investigation of the D&M Pyramid reveals a morphology that is inconsistent with the surrounding geology. The geomorphological processes observed to exist on Mars not only fail to provide a potential mechanism for the D&M Pyramid's formation, but seem to preclude its very existence. Analysis of the object's geometry, and its alignment with other anomalous landforms, reveal intricate relationships that are numerous

[686]Erol Torun, "The D&M Pyramid of Mars" at http://well.com/user/etorun/pyramid.html.

383

and logical, and are suggestive of highly sophisticated design...

The same techniques used for most of this century in air photo interpretation show that the D&M Pyramid may be artificial, or may be a natural landform modified by intelligence.

In his early working out of what he called "the Cydonia mathematics," Hoagland discovered 12 small formations dubbed "mounds" which appeared to be angularly placed on the surface. When Dr. Horace Crater of the University of Tennessee Space Institute analyzed the structures, he reported persuasive findings.[687] He noticed that the mounds formed two specific types of triangles, isosceles and right triangles. It was then discovered that 19 triangles can be discerned with their vertices within the 12 mounds so that only a single point within each mound is used as a vertex. In Crater's report, co-authored with Prof. Stanley McDaniel, he observes:

In this paper we established the existence of an anomaly on Mars in the form of angular placements of 12 relatively small surface features we call mounds. The anomaly has four aspects: geometry, number, precision, and location. The geometrical aspect is most compelling, in that the relative locations of all 12 mounds show striking redundant appearances of right and isosceles triangles.

Compounding this anomaly is the finding that as we go from mound to mound the right and isosceles triangles uncovered at the highest frequencies by far (19 occurrences) are not independent but are geometrically related to one another. The right triangles we see have proportions that are the same as what you would obtain if you split the isosceles triangle down the middle.

---

[687] See Stanley V. McDaniel and Horace W. Crater, "Dr. Horace Crarer's Latest Results to be Published by JSE" and Stanley V. McDaniel, "SPSR Issues Report to NASA; Analyses of MGS images by Carlotto, DiPietro, Brandenburg, Moore, and Erjavec provided to NASA officials" found at http://mcdanielreport.com.

Furthermore this anomaly of number and geometry is accompanied by one of precision. The vertices of the triangles are for the most part nearer the centers of the mounds than those for fictitious mounds from a computer simulation. And finally, the actual locations of the mounds in this region of Cydonia are such as to take advantage of a unique feature of the geometry that defines the proportions of the triangles. That feature is that the defining angle for the triangles (the center angle of the isosceles), increases the number of appearances of these triangles drastically to19 when it is equal to [pi/2-arcsin (1/3)], well over what would occur if the angle was even slightly different from this value.

Our systematic Investigation of the geometric relationships between these mounds takes the form of a test of what we call the random geology hypothesis. This hypothesis presupposes that the distribution of the mounds in the specified vicinity (i.e. the area of other recognized anomalous formations such as the Face), however orderly it may seem, is consistent with the action of random geological forces. Our question is: Does the random geology hypothesis succeed or fail in the case of the small mound configuration at Cydonia?

After testing the hypothesis with computer simulations of the positions of the mounds in an area similar in size to that in which the actual mounds appear, Crater concluded:

Our conclusion is that the random geology hypothesis fails by a very large margin, and therefore that a radical statistical anomaly exists in the distribution of mound formations in this area of Mars.

Figure 66
Mounds


Even the skeptic Dr. Ralph Greenberg, professor of mathematics from the University of Washington, who had previously challenged the mathematical relationships posited by Hoagland and Torun for the D&M Pyramid, was unable to impugn the geometries attributed to these mounds. He noted:

The repetitive appearance of these special triangles is intriguing and puzzling to me. I am not able to dismiss this kind of evidence... The repetitive appearance of the interesting special triangles that Crater and McDaniel discuss does seem rather striking... Hoagland and others had been thoroughly scrutinizing the locations and shapes of various objects in the Cydonia region. Hoagland pointed out that certain triangles formed by the mounds appeared to be right triangles or isosceles triangles. Crater then noticed that if one chose points within four or five of the mounds as vertices, then one could find several of the special triangles shown above in illustration 3. This by itself does not seem very remarkable, especially given the leeway allowed by the size of the mounds (which amounts to a few degrees of leeway for the angles). But Crater then discovered that these very same triangles continue to appear. In the end, he found that 12 of the 220 possible triangles formed by the twelve mounds would be in the shape of the special right triangle and that 5 would be in the shape of the special isosceles triangles. It is the appearance of the additional triangles beyond the several which Crater originally noticed that seems rather remarkable. It is for that reason that I cannot dismiss the pattern discovered by Crater. [688]

The perplexing Cydonia mathematics is therefore maintained and is strong evidence for the artificiality of the Mars structures, and thus intelligent life on Mars. But full confirmation would not come until 1998, and when it did it came disguised as proof to the contrary.

On April 5, 1998, after twenty years of debate, the Mars Global Surveyor (MGS) re-imaged the Face. The raw image released by the Jet Propulsion Laboratory (JPL) gave the impression that the "Face" was a natural mountain after all. On closer examination, however, it was learned that this released image was seriously defective and thus untrustworthy. Before the Public Information Office released the image to the world-wide media the JPL manipulated it, suppressing the details so as to make it look like a natural mesa.

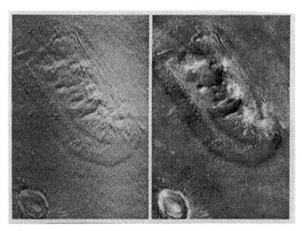

Figure 67
JPL manipulated image (left) and restored image (right)

---

[688] Ralph Greenberg, "The D&M Pyramid on Mars and Richard Hoagland's Theories About Cydonia" at http://www.washington.edu/~greenber/DMPyramid.html.

Dr. Tom Van Flandern, who spent 20 years at the U.S. Naval Observatory where he became the Chief of the Celestial Mechanics Branch, after analyzing the photos, noted:

The MGS spacecraft took a high-resolution photo of the "Face on Mars" in April 1998. That image suffered from four handicaps: a low viewing angle; a low Sun angle from the direction under the "chin"; an almost complete lack of contrast; and enough cloudiness to scatter most of the light and eliminate shadows... The appearance is much less face-like in the high-resolution MGS image in Figure 2 than in the original Viking image...for the following reasons:

(1) The MGS spacecraft took its image from a low-perspective angle well to the west, rather than from nearly overhead as in the Viking spacecraft view. Mainly the western half of the "Face" is seen...with the eastern half largely hidden behind the nose ridge.
(2) Sunlight shines on the Face mesa from the low west in the Viking image, but from the low southeast in the MGS image. The latter tends to distort facial features, much like a flashlight held under the chin.
(3) The Viking image had a normal variation of grayscale levels to provide contrast between adjacent features. The range of grayscale levels in the MGS image was inadequate to provide the amount of contrast normally utilized by the human eye.
(4) Following analysis, it became apparent that the major face-like features on the mesa have the characteristic that they cast shadows that enhance the face-like appearance at almost any Sun-angle. For example, the eye socket is a depression that contains the shadow of its walls while the Sun is anywhere but overhead. It is similar for the mouth feature, which casts a shadow into the ravine between the lips at most times of day. The facial appearance is enhanced by such shadows, but is difficult to separate from the background when the shadows are absent. By bad luck, the sunlight was so scattered by thin cloud cover that light on the Face was mainly ambient (omni-

directional, shadow-free) light. This partially ameliorates difficulty (2), but creates a greater problem by removing one element important to the perceived appearance of the mesa. Photographs of actual human faces and of face sculptures taken under similar viewing perspective and lighting conditions... are commonly no longer recognizable as faces...

Compounding these natural deficiencies in the image was the JPL's inexcusable tampering. Van Flandern continues:

When the first picture arrived at JPL, its Mission Image Processing Laboratory (MIPL) passed the image through two filters, a low-pass filter and a high-pass filter. It is difficult to see how usage of these filters on this image before release to the media could be scientifically justified. Indeed, usage of the high-pass filter gave an especially damaging impression. From Adobe's Photoshop software, we find the following description of the function and purpose of this filter:

"High Pass Filter: Retains edge details ... and suppresses the rest of the image. ... The filter removes low-frequency detail in an image ... The filter is useful for extracting line art and large black-and-white areas from scanned images."

The usage of these filters on the "Face" image is documented on the JPL web site <http://mpfwww.jpl.nasa.gov/mgs/target/CYD1/index. html> The same day that the raw spacecraft image data was received at MSSS and posted to the Internet, the JPL Public Information Office (PIO) released the MIPL-created, filtered image to the world media.

With all of these deficiencies in the image, both natural and man-made, it still provides powerful confirmation of artificiality. After correcting the handicaps through computer enhancement, Dr. Carlotto reviewed the new images and published his results in a paper, "Analysis of Global Surveyor Imagery of the Face on Mars."[689] According to him, the corrected images provide:

*Confirmation of facial features first seen in Viking imagery.* Although the Face looks different in the MGS image we show that its appearance can be predicted from, and is consistent with the Viking data. Even though on cursory inspection the two images look different, most of the features seen in Viking are present in the new MSG image of the Face.

*High degree of lateral symmetry.* It is shown that certain processed images released by JPL do not accurately depict the Face. In one, the Face looks flat and featureless; in another its true shape has been distorted by up to 100 pixels making it appear less face-like. Using an elevation model derived from Viking, feature locations in the MGS image are mapped into an orthorectified coordinate system. Measurements of lateral features in this coordinate system reveal that the Face is highly symmetrical...

*Nostrils* - Corresponding to a flattened area near the tip of the nose ridge in the Viking images is a pair of circular depressions that look like nostrils. These features are on either side of lateral axis of symmetry of the Face as discussed in a later section.

*Lip structures* - Rather than being a sharp cut through the central ridge, the top and bottom of the mouth slope gradually down to the level of the platform. The shape of these sloped areas are not unlike lips. Adding to this impression is what could be referred to as a "harelip" which comes together between the base of the nose and the mouth.

---

[689] http://www.psrw.com/~markc/Articles/MGSreport/paper.html

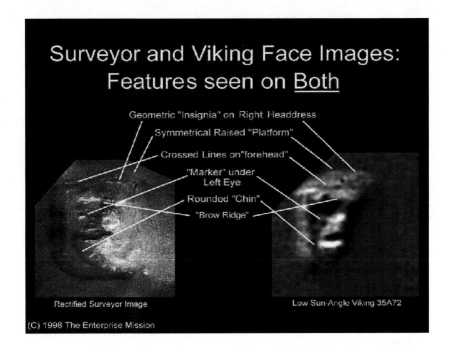

Surveyor and Viking Face Images:
Features seen on Both

Geometric "Insignia" on Right Headdress
Symmetrical Raised "Platform"
Crossed Lines on "forehead"
"Marker" under Left Eye
Rounded "Chin"
"Brow Ridge"

Rectified Surveyor Image

Low Sun-Angle Viking 35A72

(C) 1998 The Enterprise Mission

On July 5, 1998, Dr. Horace W. Carter, as president of the Society for Planetary SETI Research, sent a summary report to NASA on analysis of the new MGS images. The report reads in part[690]:

During the month of April, 1998, the Mars Global Surveyor (MGS) obtained three new images of objects in the Cydonia region of Mars. These three images included one of the "Face" and two of the area that has been referred to as the "City." Premature announcements by a few scientists, accompanied by a very early, poorly processed picture of the Face, were widely disseminated by the news media as final "proof" that nothing on Mars can be considered possibly artificial. SPSR regrets these early

---

[690] See Stanley V. McDaniel and Horace W. Crater, "Dr. Horace Crarer's Latest Results to be Published by JSE" and Stanley V. McDaniel, "SPSR Issues Report to NASA; Analyses of MGS images by Carlotto, DiPietro, Brandenburg, Moore, and Erjavec provided to NASA officials" found at http://mcdanielreport.com.

391

announcements, which were made prior to any significant study of the images.

In fact, the new images provide strong evidence of artificiality:

An unexpected finding in the new image is the presence of a more pronounced feature corresponding to a "nose" which is in the appropriate location, has the appropriate shape, and most surprisingly appears to have symmetrical circular indentations suggestive of nostrils. Both of the independently derived orthorectifications display this symmetry.

The report concludes:

The question of possible artificiality remains open. While at a cursory glance, using poorly processed and unrectified images, the Face may give the impression of an entirely natural feature, close analysis shows that there are a number of consistencies with the morphology predicted from the Viking images. There remains overall symmetry, possible decorative ornamentation, and other features placed in a manner consistent with a highly eroded artificially constructed object. This, in combination with the lack of data for the east side due to the camera perspective, means that we do not yet have sufficient information to invalidate the hypothesis of possible artificiality or to establish the validity of that hypothesis with regard to the Face.

The astronomer Tom van Flandern noted as well in his "Preliminary Analysis of April 5 Cydonia Image from the Mars Global Surveyor Spacecraft (1998)":

An asymmetrical or highly fractal appearance of the Face mesa would have been compelling evidence for a natural origin of at least this one feature, and with it the significance of six of the eight tests of artificiality for Cydonia. But the reality is that the object has a high degree of symmetry and very low fractal content, consistent with artificial origin...

The features of a near-perfect face are all present, and almost every feature seen on the mesa has a size, shape, and orientation that enhances the appearance of a decorated face in headdress...The humanoid facial features that first drew attention to this area are confirmed by this photo despite poor lighting and poor viewing angle. One feature, the headdress, is so much a symmetrical combination of right-angle linear and rounded features as to suggest artificiality strongly.

In a follow-up report, Van Flandern elaborates:

In science, an improbable event that has already happened is called "a posteriori" (after the fact), and generally is taken to have no significance no matter how unlikely it might appear. By contrast, if we specified a certain specific highly improbable event in all its detail "a priori" (before the fact), and it happened anyway, that would be significant, and we would be obliged to pay attention.

As all this pertains to the "Face" on Mars at Cydonia, the discovery of the face-like object was an a posteriori event. No one predicted it, nor could they have done so based on known facts. But once our attention was called to a particular object in a particular place on a particular planet as possibly being of artificial (constructed) origin, anything else found out about it that is highly improbable but related to the artificiality question becomes a priori. We can safely ignore a posteriori claims, but not a priori ones.

At Cydonia, almost everything we see in the new, high-resolution "Face" image fulfills highly unlikely a priori predictions. So when we found a "nostrils" feature, that was impressive. The fact that the relative size, positioning, and orientation is also correct for nostrils makes it a significant a priori prediction. The additional fact that no other nostril-like features can be found nearby means that our minds are not free to pick and choose such face-like features we may want to see. Because it is a priori, that single feature would be strong evidence for the artificiality hypothesis by itself.

But when we consider the perspective, lighting, and contrast Limitations of the new image and use old Viking images to fill in missing items, we now see that a priori predictions for a "pupil" and an "eyebrow" are also fulfilled. These are a priori even if no one had verbalized them because the face hypothesis implicitly predicts such facial details before the fact. And each feature is unique on the mesa and its surroundings, and properly shaped and positioned relative to the face with the right relative size and orientation. All this makes the a priori probability of chance operating vanishingly low.

But there is much more. The eye socket is a well-formed 3-D cavity and not in any way shaped by shadows. The mouth is smooth and regular with inner and outer portions, curled just below the nose, and continues to the opposite side.

He concludes:

The reason I have concluded that the case for artificiality of the "Face" is well-established is the fulfillment of so many a priori expectations, combined with the lack of extraneous features that might allow us to see patterns that might arise by chance. We have almost no degrees of freedom, yet everything in the image appears to work. Each of the new a priori points such as the nostrils, mouth curl, pupil, and eyebrow has individually only very small chance to occur at all, let alone with the correct relative size, shape, location, and orientation. Each such feature by itself indicates artificiality at perhaps 1000-to-1 odds (some much more) just because of their a priori nature.

Collectively, they say "artificial" beyond a reasonable doubt.

It is not the odds of occurrence of these features that is convincing, because even a long list of 1,000,000-to-1 a posteriori coincidences has no persuasive ability. It is the low probability of these features combined with their a priori nature that makes them persuasive. Real faces do have just such features, and all major facial features are present in the Martian "Face". In truth, the thought never crossed my mind before the fact that the Face should have eyebrows, nostrils, pupils, and a lip curl. But of course, if it is a real face depiction, it should have those features. Anyone could have predicted those things, but most of us dare not hope for so much. Now we have them!

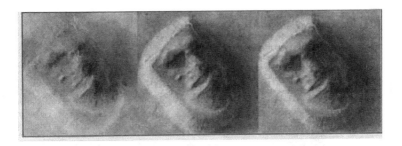

Figure 69
Left: Negative of the Face as seen by MGS spacecraft in April, 1998. Center: Lighting source switched from SE to NW. Right: Viewing angle switched from 45° west to overhead.

Final confirmation of the artificiality of the Face came in April of 2001. NASA/JPL/MSSS finally took a high-resolution image of the full Cydonia Face under good lighting conditions. Mirror-symmetry for the two sides, especially the mesa enclosure, is confirmed, as well as the existence of the eastside eye, nostril, and mouth with parted lips.[691] The new image also reveled that the east side of the Face suffered some sort of crater-forming event

---

[691] Tom Van Flander, "Preliminary Analysis of 2001 April 8 Cydonia Face Image."

which also caused some melting, which indicates that some artificial materials were used in the construction of the Face.

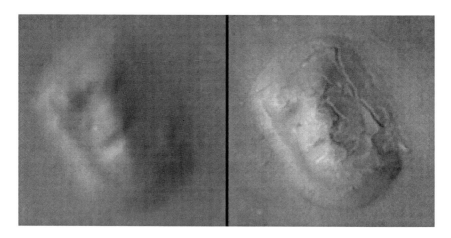

Figure 70
Original 1976 *Viking* image (left) and 2001 MGS image (right)

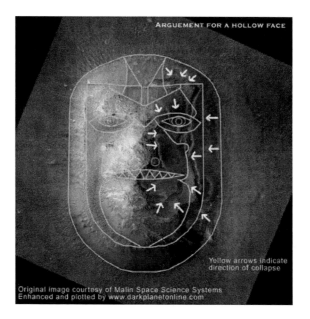

Figure 71
2001 MGS image enhanced and plotted, showing the facial features and symmetry maintained, even after suffering an obvious collapse on the structure's east side.

Thus, the evidence is strong that the anomalous surface structures on Mars, particularly the "Face," are artificial. What does it tell us about its builders? The new MGS images allow us to get a better look at any cultural or racial markings (in as much as either term has relevance outside of earth). When the left side of the new image is copied and mirrored onto the right, as has been done with the Viking images, a stunning picture emerges. Investigator Fiontar McEghan observes:

> I was stunned by what I saw, what to me was a face, with an Egyptian style head dress, complete with the cobra emblem, which the Pharaohs wore, at the center of the forehead. Two eyes, topped with a thick brow, broad nose, perfectly formed mouth and chiseled chin.

Richard Hoagland discovered a feline look by mirror imaging the new MOS images. He sees in the Face a "Martian Sphinx." He has argued for a connection between the Ancient Egyptian Civilization and the Civilization of Cydonia in his *The Monuments of Mars*. This not only supports Hogland's suggestion (though one should not go too far with this), it more importantly confirms the Honorable Elijah Muhammad's claim that the "Martian civilization" is a BLACK CIVILIZATION!

*16.3. A Russian-Mars Confrontation in 1988?*

In July 1988, the Russians launched two unmanned satellite probes - Phobos 1 and Phobos II - in the direction of Mars with the primary intention of investigating the moon, Phobos. Phobos 1 was lost en route in September, reportedly because of a radio command error. Phobos II arrived safely at Mars in January 1989 and entered into orbit around the planet as the first step at its destination towards its ultimate goal: to transfer to an orbit that would make it fly almost in tandem with Phobos and explore the moonlet with highly sophisticated equipment. On March 28, Phobos II aligned itself with the moonlet. Suddenly, and inexplicably, communication was lost between Phobos II and the Soviet mission control center. According to Tass, the official Soviet news agency, Phobos failed to communicate with Earth as scheduled after completing an operation yesterday around the Martian moon Phobos. Scientists at mission control have been unable to establish stable radio contact.

Soviet authorities subsequently released a taped television transmission Phobos II sent in its last moments. Missing from this released transmission were the last frames, taken just seconds before the spacecraft fell silent. The television clip was shown by TV stations in Europe and Canada. One of the pictures, released on Canadian TV, presents an infrared scan radiometer image of the Martian surface that showed clearly defined rectangular areas. These are interconnected with a latticework of perfectly straight channels, much resembling a city block. There were no corresponding surface features taken by regular cameras. This suggests the heat signature of what may be a set of underground cavern or channels that are just too geometrically regular to be formed naturally. According to Dr. John Becklake of the London Science Museum, "The city-like pattern is 60 kilometers wide and could easily be mistaken for an aerial view of Los Angeles." This brings to mind a statement by Muhammad quoted earlier.:

The devil (Caucasian) believes it because they have come near to looking at the surface of Mars for creatures on it. But they (the Martians) are very wise and very skillful so Allah taught me. When they hear the devil's space vehicles coming they can hide away.

Is it possible that the Black "Martians" hide away in underground cities? The evidence would suggest so.

One of the most important pictures from the clip shows a shadow on the Martian surface shaped like a "thin ellipse." The following news item appeared on AP (Associated Press) at 4:41 PM EST March 30, 1989:

SOVIET RESEARCH CENTERS ARE NOW TRYING TO INTERPRET SO FAR 'UNEXPLAINED OPTICAL PHONOMENA' ON THE PICTURES OF THE MARTIAN

SURFACE. THE PICTURES SHOW AN ENIGMATIC STRIP 23-25 MILES WIDE AND A LARGE SPINDLE-SHAPED FORMATION.

It is certain that the shadow is not that of the moonlet Phobos whose shadow was photographed on the surface by *Mariner 9* and is shown as a rounded ellipse with fuzzy edges. The shadow in this photo is thin with sharp edges.

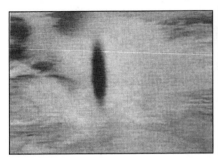 

Mystery Shadow on Mars surface

1971 Mariner 9 photo of Phobos shadow on Mars surface.

Dr. John Becklake of the London Science Museum noted that the shadow was created by "something that is between the spacecraft and Mars, because we can see the Martian surface below it." Alexander Dunayev, chairman of Glavkosmos, the Soviet equivalent to NASA, told *Aviation Week & Space Technology*:

One image appears to include an odd-shaped object between the space craft and Mars. It may be debris in the orbit of Phobos or could be Phobos II's autonomous propulsion sub-system that was jettisoned after the space craft was ejected into Mars orbit-we just don't know.

It was demonstrated that neither debris nor any part of the spacecraft could account for the shadow cast on the Martian surface. On March 30, *Vremya*, the main evening Soviet news program, reported some astonishing information. The Spanish daily, **La Epoca** (March 31, 1989) reported the dispatch by the Moscow correspondent from the European news agency EFE under the headline, "Phobos-2 captured Strange Photos of Mars Before Losing Contact with its Base." The text read:

> The TV newscast Vremya revealed yesterday that the space probe Phobos 2, which was orbiting above Mars when Soviet scientists lost contact on Monday, had photographed an unidentified object on the Martian surface seconds before losing contact.

> The TV broadcast devoted a long segment to the strange pictures taken by the spaceship before loosing contact, and showed the two most important pictures, in which a large shadow is visible in one of the pictures...Scientists characterize the final picture taken by the spacecraft, in which the thin ellipse can be clearly seen, as 'inexplicable.'

> The phenomenon, it was stated, could not be an optical illusion because it was captured with the same clarity both by color camera as well as by cameras taking infrared images...

> According to calculations by researchers from the Soviet Union the "shadow"...is some twenty kilometers [about 12.5 miles] long. A few days earlier, the spaceship had already recorded an identical phenomenon, except that in that instance the 'shadow' was between twenty-six to thirty kilometers [16-19 miles] long.

This is indeed amazing. Some "unidentified object" that was "between Mars and the spacecraft," i.e. in the sky, was responsible for casting a 12-19 mile long shadow on the surface of Mars. It was observed seconds before the spacecraft communicated with ground control for the last time. What was this "unidentified object." It could not be any piece of the craft, which is only a few feet in length. Nor could it be debris. The object would have to be much bigger, say a half mile, in order to cast a shadow that big. Dr. Becklake said while commenting on this picture:

> As the last picture was halfway through they (Soviets) *saw something which should not be there.* (The Soviets) have not yet released the last picture, and we won't speculate on what it shows.

The Soviets later advanced two contradictory explanations for the mysterious shadow. In 1993, A.S. Selivanov and U. M. Gektin of the Institute of Space Device Engineering, Moscow, reported in the Jan/Feb issue of the Planetary Society's *The Planetary Report* that the shadow was that of moonlet Phobos. We have seen, however, that a photo of Phobos' shadow was taken in 1971 by

*Mariner 9* and it looks nothing like the "thin elliptical" shadow here discussed. The Russian scientists here attribute the awkwardness of the shadow to: Phobos' orientation; distortion from Mars surface curvature; dispersion of radiation; and deviation of the spacecraft's axis. All of this, they said, conspired to produce the strangely unusual shadow of the moonlet on the Martian surface. Australian science writer Brian Crowley disagrees. According to him, the convex cats-eye shadow which, because of the overhead solar inclination, prevented shadow-casting by Martian surface features, implies a shadow thrown on the surface from something in orbit - beyond the orbit of Phobos II itself. The shadow is inconsistent with any possible shadow cast by the moon Phobos, which is an irregular potato shape.

Alexey Kuzmin of the Department of High Energy Astrophysics of the Russian Space Research Institute (IKI), the man responsible for handling of information during the mission, had a different explanation. He told Jorgen Westman of WUFOC in 1997 that the shadow was that of the probe itself. He said, "*it has such shape and size because of the scanning mode of the instrument it was produced by.*" Nevertheless, Kuzmin admitted that some from within IKI attributed the lost of the spacecraft to a UFO.

> Most of the people consider the Phobos-2 was lost because of the mistake in the control and because of imperfect intelligence of the on-board computer. I think the same. But there are the persons who consider the probe was lost because of UFO influence. There is no complete conclusion. (JW) Who believed that a UFO was the reason to the loss of the Phobus-2 probe? I don't know the believers in UFO around Mars in IKI, they were the guys, but they are not in IKI now.

So what was it? Was the strange shadow produced by the spacecraft or was it produced by the moonlet? The two contradictory stories emanating from the Russian space science community appears awfully like damage control or a cover-up. But where there is a cover-up, there are usually whistle-blowers. And indeed there were.

As noted above, the final photo taken right before Phobos II lost communication was not released to the public. This "highly secret" photo was later given to the Western press by Russian astronaut and pilot Colonel Dr. Marina Popovich. Colonel Marina Popovich, Ph.D., the Soviet test pilot and engineer who set 13 world records, is a graduate of the University of Leningrad where she graduated from the Military Flight School. Dr. Popovich's former husband is General Paval Popovich, the first man to rendezvous with another space craft in orbit during the Vostok 4 flight in August, 1962.

According to Colonel Popovich, the last transmission from Phobos II was a photograph of a gigantic cylindrical spaceship - a huge, cigar-shaped 'mothership', that was photographed on 25 March 1989 hanging or parked next to the Martian moon Phobos by the Soviet probe Phobos II. After the last frame was radio-transmitted back to Earth, the probe mysteriously disappeared; according to the Russians it was destroyed. It was apparently this cigar shaped craft in the final frame taken by Phobos II which is the object responsible for casting the oblong shadow on the surface of Mars in the earlier photo.

The photo in question shows a long cylinder shape approaching the moonlet Phobos. It is believed that the cylinder shape is the huge "mothership." Alexey Kuzmin, who claims to have been the man who produced the photo, says the image is explained by a defect in the CCD matrix. But then he goes on to make an astonishing admission:

> I have no explanations for the other strange effects, it could be an artificial UFO, but they can be the other kinds of things. The situation in IKI (our institute) is difficult enough (as well as for the whole space research in Russia) to work on the problems without the concrete results. Some Russian probes were lost in the Earth orbit without detailed explanation, but it's normal for the incidents with the complex devices.

This scientist is willing to countenance the idea that a "UFO" was indeed involved. AND HE IS FROM AMONG THE SKEPTICS AT IKI!

It will probably never be known what really happened to Phobos II in 1988. Whether this last photograph contributes anything will also probably never be known. What is certain, however, is that there is strong scientific evidence, some scientists now say proof, pointing to the presence of intelligent life and civilization on the planet Mars. There is strong scientific evidence that the architects of this civilization belong to a "race" (for lack of a better word) not unlike Black people on Earth in physical appearance. This thus goes a long way in validating Mr. Muhammad's claim that there exists on the Red Planet a Black Civilization.

16.4. *Mars, the Moon, and an Angry Black God.*

The evidence is convincing that Mars was not originally a planet, but a moon of a larger planet that no longer exists as such.[692] In 1772 astronomer Daniel Titus discovered that each of the six known planets at the time was roughly twice the distance of the previous one from the sun, with one exception: between Mars and Jupiter there is a gap just the right size to hold another planet. Within that space there are now asteroids. In 1972 Canadian astronomer Michael Ovenden argued convincingly that these asteroids or 'minor planets' were the remnants of a Saturn-sized planet that had once existed there but exploded, blasting debris out into the solar system.[693] Mars was likely the satellite of this planet.[694] The tilts and orbital ellipticity of the tens of thousands of asteroids filling the space show 'explosion signatures' and "evidence from…comets, planets and their moons, and meteroroids (leave) little doubt that such an explosion did happen."[695] This explosion sent a blast wave of dark carbonaceous matter – completely vaporized material mixed with ash and soot - throughout the solar system coating all atmosphere-less bodies such Iapetus, Saturn's moon, which is completely covered on one side with this dark material.

Figure 75
Iapetus, showing coating by black "blast debris" from the exploding planet.

---

[692] See especially Tom Van Flandern, *Dark Matter, Missing Planets & New Comets: Paradoxes Resolved, Origins Illuminated* (Berkeley, CA: North Atlantic Books, 1993) Chapter Seven.
[693] See M.W. Ovenden, "Bode's Law and the Missing Planet," *Nature* 239 (1972): 508-509.
[694] Van Flandern, *Dark Matter*, 277.
[695] Ibid., 215.

Because of its close proximity as a satellite to the exploding planet Mars got severely affected. The southern hemisphere, which clearly was the face turned toward the planet, is heavily cratered, while the northern hemisphere is only sparsely so. This southern cratering is likely due to the blast debris.[696] The planetary explosion also shifted Mars's original pole by 90°. Evidence of water erosion on achondrite meteorites thought to have originated in the explosion indicate that the exploding planet contained abundant water.[697] Comets and asteroids, which are 20% water by bulk, suggest that the explosion was "the source of a sudden, short lived massive influx of water".[698] Mars apparently got inundated.[699] *Viking*-orbiter photos show that vast quantities of water flowed on Mars, but not peacefully; a variety of troughlike features are likely "catastrophic flood channels," evidencing "scour on a massive scale," "water...released in phenomenal quantities...followed by collapse of overlying rock to form chaotic terrain."[700] In other words, when this planet exploded it dumped massive amounts of water on its satellite, Mars.

The so-called Cydonia complex with its central 'Face' was built after the explosion, otherwise it would have been buried under the 21 km of debris now littering the southern hemisphere. The post-Explosion origin of this artificial complex on Mars is confirmed by the fact that the complex is aligned with the post-Explosion equator.[701] Why would this complex be built on the damaged side of the new planet, rather than the non-impacted northern hemisphere? Maybe as a 'ground-zero' memorial. This may explain the 'teardrop' feature observed falling from the western eye of the Face.

What caused this planet to explode? Planets are unlikely to generate enough energy to explode through known chemical or collisional processes. The meteorite evidence indicates nuclear processes were involved, but planets are not hot enough in their

---

[696] Ibid., 427.
[697] Ibid.
[698] Ibid., 226.
[699] Ibid., 161.
[700] Victor R. Baker, "The Spokane Flood Controversy and the Martian Outflow Channels," *Science* 202 (1978): 1249.
[701] Van Flandern, *Dark Matter*, 438.

cores for nuclear reaction.[702]   It had to have been an unnatural explosion.   But what was the source? Van Flandern laments: "Unfortunately, we have almost no evidence yet as to what the cause may have been...What we do know is that enormous energy was involved".[703] The Hon. Elijah Muhammad in fact told us the source of this planetary explosion.

### 16.4.1. *Jatu and the Deportation of the Moon*

The earth is currently approximately 25, 000 square miles in circumference, but according to the Hon. Elijah Muhammad it was originally approximately 35, 000 square miles in circumference. History was written by the Gods then to last 35, 000 years. This proto-earth was a different planet then. It existed in a different pocket than where it is currently. At that time, this bigger planet was also without its companion, the Moon. But we know it had to have a satellite because this bigger planet had an enormous area of water which, if unchecked by tides, would have overrun the land.

This all changed some 66 trillion years ago when one of the Gods, tradition has called him Jatu, failed in imposing his will on the world. Jatu was the God with "power over the Earth and the heavens above the Earth."[704] However, what he wanted was a natural impossibility: he wanted everyone to speak the same dialect, though climate and atmospheric pressure preclude this. In angry frustration the God, Muhammad says, sought to punish the 'rebellious' world with a fiery destruction. He drilled a shaft some 3, 000 miles into the planet and filled it with a powerful dynamite much more explosive than that used in this world. The explosion was catastrophic for the planet and civilization. It split the planet in two: one part shot up 35, 000 miles becoming the Moon. The other part dropped 66, 000 miles from the original pocket becoming the current 'Earth.' This catastrophe caused both a goliath fire and a global deluge. The water that had been on the 'Moon' part of the planet fell onto the newly formed Earth, causing great devastation and death.

---

[702] Ibid., 163.
[703] Ibid.
[704] Muhammad, *Theology of Time*, 276; idem, *Message to the Black Man*, 31.

Ancient tradition remembers this catastrophe of global fire and deluge and the God who caused it. The Tupenambra Indians of Brazil called this God who "destroyed the [old] world with flood and fire" Monan, meaning "ancient, old."[705] In Norse mythology he is the 'giant Surt' who

> set the entire earth on fire...Flames spurted from fissures in the rocks, everywhere there was the hissing of steam. All living things, all plant life, were blotted out...the rivers, all the seas, rose and overflowed. From every side waves lashed against waves. They swelled and boiled slowly over all things. The earth sank beneath the sea. Yet not all men perished in the great catastrophe...[706]

This was not the deluge of Noah that occurred approximately 6, 000 years ago. These are memories of a primordial deluge and fire that goes back to a much earlier period in the planets history. José de Acosta recounts a legend from the Cuzco area (Cuzco was the capital of the Inca Empire):

> For some crime unstated by the people (of Cuzco) the people who lived in the most ancient times were destroyed by the creator...in a deluge. After the deluge the creator appeared in human form from Lake Titicaca. He then created the sun and moon and stars. After that he renewed the human population of the earth...[707]

This anthropomorphic creator god destroyed the people with a flood before even creating the sun, moon and stars. In a Yamana legend from Tierra del Fuego the Moon is specifically cited as the origin of the flood-waters, just as the Hon. Elijah Muhammad taught.

> The moon woman caused the flood. This was at the time of the great upheaval...Moon was filled with hatred towards

---

[705] *New Larousse Encyclopaedia of Mythology*, 426; Graham Hancock, *Fingerprints of the Gods: The Evidence of Earth's Lost Civilization* (New York: Three Rivers Press, 1995) 192.
[706] *New Larousse Encyclopaedia of Mythology*, 275-7; Hancock, *Fingerprints of the Gods*, 205.
[707] José de Acosta, *The Natural and Moral History of the Indies*, book 1, Chapter 4.

human beings...at the time everybody drowned with the exception of those few who were able to escape to the five mountain peaks that the water did not cover.[708]

The most remarkable description in the ancient literature of this earth-and-moon producing event is found in the ancient Babylonian myth, *Enuma Elish*, which describes the origin of the gods, the cosmos and man in seven tablets, not unlike the biblical seven days.[709] According to this poem, in the beginning there was only the undifferentiated primordial waters called Apsu/Tiamat, from which emerged the gods. The Black king of the gods Anu emerged from these black waters, as did his son Ea (Enki). Ea/Enki, the Black creator-god, goes to war with the Apsu and slays it, as the Hon. Elijah Muhammad says the Black God went to war with the darkness after he emerged therefrom. While Apsu, the masculine side of the primordial waters, was slain, Tiamat, the feminine aspect of the waters, was not. Tiamat represented the more material aspect of the primordial waters. Indeed, she represented the primordial, proto-earth covered in water (like the biblical waters that, when gathered together, reveal dry land, Gen. 1:9).

According to this ancient Babylonian poem the population growth of the primordial gods exceeded what the watery proto-earth (Tiamat) could handle.[710] "They were too overbearing," we are told.[711] The proto-earth seems to have become stressed and unstable, which in turn caused dissatisfaction among the gods ("Tiamat did not like being upset and so disturbed. She moved and moved, day and night. The gods could not rest").[712] Some of these dissatisfied gods organized and mounted a rebellion against Anshar, King of the Gods, and his Divine Council of Twelve. The divine rebels organized an "anti-Council" themselves and somehow succeeded in stealing from the Divine Council the

---

[708] John Bierhorst, *The Mythology of South America* (New York: William Morrow & Co., 1988) 165; Hancock, *Fingerprints of the Gods*, 192.

[709] On this text see Richard J. Clifford, *Creation Accounts in the Ancient Near East an in the Bible* (Washington, DC: The Catholic Biblical Association of America, 1994) 82-93.

[710] On the 'noise' of the gods as overpopulation see Clifford, *Creation Accounts*, 82.

[711] Translation by Virginia Hamilton, *In the Beginning: Creation Stories from Around the World* (San Diego: Harcourt Brace Jovanovich, 1988) 80

[712] Ibid., 81.

*Tablets of Destinies* (i.e. the Holy Qur'an containing the 25, 000 year prophetic history). These rebels formed some sort of alliance with Tiamat, the proto-earth, an alliance which gave birth to "monstrous gods." The king of this monstrous "anti-Council" was a valiant god named Kingu, called "Tiamat's consort."[713]

The Divine Council of Anshar convened in order to formulate a response to the rebels' threat. The young god Marduk, Anshar's grandson, was appointed to subdue and 'calm Tiamat' and her host.[714] As a reward, Marduk is elevated to King of the Gods, replacing Anshar. Marduk subdued Tiamat by producing a deep and wide cleavage in the proto-earth, in which he drove his Evil Wind and shot his electric arrow, recalling the shaft Jatu drilled in the proto-earth and filled with high explosives. The Evil Wind and electric arrow of Marduk "charged" and "tore (Tiamat's) belly." Her body was distended as the arrow "cut through her inside, splitting her heart." Then

> The Lord (Marduk) paused to view her lifeless body. To divide the monster he then artfully planed. Then, as a mussel, he split her into two parts.

One half of the subdued proto-earth became the sky, including the asteroid belt and the moon, which Marduk "bade...to allow not her (Tiamat's) waters to escape," an obvious reference to the moon's 'checking' of the Earth's waters via tides.[715] The other half of the proto-earth became the Earth.[716]

> He (Marduk) opened the Euphrates and the Tigris from her eyes...He piled up clear-cut mountains from her udder; bored waterholes to drain off the catchwater.

The *Enuma Elish* thus shows remarkable agreement with the Hon. Elijah Muhammad's teaching on the Deportation of the Moon: A god, king of the Divine Council of Twelve, creates an

---

[713] James P. Pritchard, *The Ancient Near East.* **Volume I:** *An Anthology of Texts and Pictures* (Princeton: Princeton University Press, 1958) 33.

[714] Translation in Mircea Eliade, *Essential Sacred Writings From Around the World* (New York: HarperCollins Publishers, 1967) 102.

[715] Translation in Eliade, *Essential Sacred Writings*, 106.

[716] Clifford, *Creation Accounts*, 91.

opening in the proto-earth ("shaft"/"cleavage"), in which he inserts an explosive device (dynamite/electric arrow) which splits the proto-earth in two, producing the Earth and the Moon.

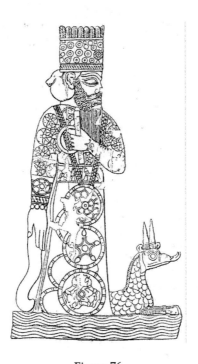

Figure 76
Marduk, King of the Gods who was responsible for Exploding the planet, creating Earth and Moon, according to the ancient Babylonians.

Astrophysics and ancient tradition thus converge to provide strong support to the claims of the Hon. Elijah Muhammad. Geological evidence supports these claims as well.

Certain regions of the Earth's surface retain evidence for a unique, massive flood several million years ago. For example, the Spokane Flood evidence indicates that a short-lived event involving not less than 2000 cubic kilometers of water discharged per day. This singular event might have been caused by a major impact event in the Pacific Ocean; or it might be the direct result of a massive influx of water from the planetary breakup, as suggested by evidence on other planetary surfaces.[717]

If the Spokane Flood is evidence of a catastrophic deluge several million years ago that was somehow centered in the Pacific Ocean (see below), the Cretaceous-Tertiary (K/T) Boundary is evidence of a global, catastrophic fire several million years ago. The K/T Boundary is a global layer of carbon deposits, usually dated around 65 million years ago, but could be much older. This boundary indicates that the earth experienced a global fire.[718] The presence in the boundary layer of shock deformation features (such as shock-altered quartz stones) suggests that a goliath explosion was involved. Mass extinctions are evidenced in the record; maybe as much as half of the living genera (plural of *genus*) at the time perished.[719] What caused such a catastrophic explosion? It has been suggested that a large meteor hit the earth, producing the recorded effects.[720] But the mineralogy and physical evidence of the boundary is inconsistent with a meteor-impact event.[721] According to geologist Anthony Hallam the cause is likely "one intrinsic to the earth, involving significant disturbance in the mantle."[722] This is a critical key because, as we will explain below, the moon was likely formed out of the earth's mantel that was "significantly disturbed" by an explosion event.

## 16.4.2. *The Origin of the Moon*

There are three main scientific models of how the earth's moon originated. The first, the 'Capture Hypothesis' according to

---

[717] Van Flandern, *Dark Matter*, 224.

[718] Wendy S. Wolbach et al, "Global fire at the Cretaceous-Tertiary boundary," *Nature* 334 (1988): 665-69; Wendy S. Wolbach et al, "Cretaceous Extinctions: Evidence for Wildfires and Search for Meteoritic Material," *Science* 230 (1985): 167-170.

[719] Luis W. Alvarez et al, "Extraterrestrial Cause for the Cretaceous-Tertiary Extinction," *Science* 208 (1980): 1095.

[720] Ibid.

[721] Anthony Hallam, "End-Cretaceous Mass Extinction Event: Argument for Terrestrial Causation," *Science* November 27, 1987: 1237-42; C. Jéhanno et al, "The Cretaceous-Tertiary boundary at Beloc, Haiti: No evidence for an impact in the Caribbean Area," *Earth and Planetary Science Letters* 109 (1992): 229-241; Charles B. Officer et al, "Late Cretaceous and paroxysmal Cretaceous/Tertiary extinctions," *Nature* 326 (1987): 143-49.

[722] Hallam, "End-Cretaceous Mass Extinction Event," 1237. See also Officer et al, "Late Cretaceous and paroxysmal Cretaceous/Tertiary extinctions."

which the earth seized a fully formed moon that came too close, suffers from fundamental problems, not the least of which is the fact that "the gravitational capture of one body by another is a virtual impossibility under ordinary circumstances."[723] Also, lunar samples show that the Moon and the Earth have similar quantities of oxygen isotopes, suggesting a close kinship between the two. Indeed, University of Michigan geochemists Der Chuen Lee et al analyzed isotopes of tungsten in rock samples from the Moon's surface and announced in 1997 that the tungsten isotopic composition is "consistent with the hypothesis that the moon was derived from Earth".[724]  Likewise, A.E. Ringwood et al studied terrestrial and lunar depletions of Cr, V, and Mn and noted a remarkable similarity suggesting that "the protolunar material was derived mainly from the earth's mantel."[725]  Thus Van Flandern asks: "So did the Moon originate from the Earth?" He summarizes the "preponderance of evidence":

We know that the moon shares certain properties with the Earth's crust...which are unlikely to have arisen unless the Moon was indeed once a part of that crust.[726]

The question now becomes, By what manner did the protolunar material separate from the Earth's mantle? The most popular theory at one time was the "Giant Impact Hypothesis," according to which a Mars-sized meteor impacted ('hit') the Earth, ejecting the material into orbit, which eventually accreted into the Moon. But this hypothesis too suffers from too many fundamental shortcomings to be plausible. Fragments from a collision site cannot get into orbit under normal circumstances.[727] Also, as Robin Canup and Larry Esposito pointed out, the accretion of an impact-generated protolunar disk into a single large moon is implausible. The natural expectation based on satellite systems of other planets would be for multiple small moons to arise and thus

---

[723] Van Flandern, *Dark Matter*, 262.
[724] Der Chuen Lee et al, "Age and Origin of the Moon," *Science* 278 (November 1997): 1103.
[725] A.E. Ringwood et al, "Partitioning of Cr, V, and Mn between Mantels and Cores of Differentiated Planetsimals: Implications for Giant Impact Hypothesis of Lunar Origin," *Icaraus* 89 (1994): 122.
[726] Van Flandern, *Dark Matter*, 264.
[727] Ibid., 265.

"explaining the formation of a single Moon from an impact generated disk becomes...difficult."[728] Ringwood et al thus concluded their study of terrestrial and lunar depletions of Cr, V, and Mn:

> ...the observed depletions of Cr, V, and Mn in the Moon are inconsistent with the hypothesis that protolunar material was derived primarily from the mantle of a differentiated Mars-sized planetismal which impacted the Earth...Indeed, the depletions of Cr, V, and Mn in the Moon constitutes a serious and perhaps fatal obstacle to the giant impact hypothesis of lunar origin.[729]

How, then did the protolunar materials get ejected from the Earth's mantle? In the later part of the 19th century British astronomer and mathematician George Darwin took note of the fact that the Earth's continents would nearly fit together like a jigsaw puzzle if the Atlantic Ocean were removed. Darwin proposed the 'Fission Hypothesis,' according to which early in the Earth's development it was spinning so fast, a critical overspin was reached, eventuating in a sizable chunk of the mantle being thrown off, forming the Moon. The protolunar material would have derived from the crustal area where the Pacific Ocean now is. The crust then split into continents and produced, on the opposite side, the Atlantic Ocean basin.

Recently Van Flandern has supported this theory.[730] However, it too has some fatal weaknesses. Calculations have shown that for the Earth to have the necessary centrifugal force to throw its mantel into orbit it would have to have been rotating once every 2.5 hours. The slow accumulation of dust grains in the early stages of the Earth's origin tell against this overspin. Most fatal to this theory, however, is the evidence that an explosion event of some kind is at the origin of the moon. As Space.com reported in August, 1999:

---

[728] Robin M. Canup and Larry W. Esposito, "Accretion of the Moon from an Impact-Generated Disk," *Icarus* 119 (1996): 445.

[729] Ringwood et al, "Partitioning of Cr, V, and Mn between Mantels and Cores of Differentiated Planetsimals," 127.

[730] Van Flandern, *Dark Matter*, 265.

Magnetic readings taken by the Lunar Prospector probe support the increasingly popular theory that the moon had a unique -- *and violent* -- origin.[731]

Lunar crustal evidence indicates that a large portion of the moon was once molten. A high degree of energy is necessary to melt the rock and form such a magma ocean. Some Moon rocks called *breccias*, which are rocks that result from the shattering of solid rock and its re-welding by extreme and sudden heat, evidence an explosion event. According to Apollo 16 and Apollo 17 astronauts the moondust they handled smelled like burnt gunpowder. The moon "smells like someone just fired a carbine in here," said Apollo 17 astronaut Gene Cernan. According to Apollo 16 astronaut Jack Schmitt "All of Apollo astronauts were used to handling guns," so they knew of what they spoke. The question is, what explosion event melted the protolunar material, produced these breccias stones, and left its residue in the burnt gunpowder aroma of the moondust? The University of Michigan's *The University Record* even used the language "Earth's 'Big Bang'."[732] What explosion event produced the K/T boundary? A 'giant impactor' is unlikely in both cases (moon, K/T boundary), as we saw above. The astrophysical evidence indicates that a planet did indeed explode in our solar system. That exploding planet likely produced the Earth as we know it, the Moon, the asteroid belt between Mars and Jupiter, and Mars itself as a planet. Ancient tradition attributes this explosion event to one of the Gods. The Hon. Elijah Muhammad said that God was the angry Black God, Jatu.

### 16.4.3. *Concluding Remarks*

There is thus an enormous amount of astronomical, astrophysical, geological, and ancient literary evidence supporting the Hon. Elijah Muhammad's seemingly most fantastic claims.

---

[731] Kenneth Silber, "Magnetic Data Hint at Moon's Unique Origin," August 10, 1999 at http://www.space.com/scienceastronomy/solarsystem/moon_core.html.
[732] "U-M Scientists Date Origin of Moon In Earth's 'Big Bang'," *The University Record* November 19, 1997.

This is truly a case of Truth being stranger than fiction, but apparently truth nonetheless. The planet Earth was a much bigger planet in the past, and Mars served then as its satellite. On that satellite was a Black civilization, akin to that on the proto-earth, whose architectural remains have been photographed by *Viking*-orbiter and Mars Global Surveyor. Mars became a planet only after the explosion of the proto-earth, an explosion confirmed by the gap and asteroid belt between Mars and Jupiter; by the dark carbonaceous blast debris coating atmosphere-less bodies throughout the solar system; by the evidence of pole shift and catastrophic flooding on Mars; by the geological evidence, such as the K/T boundary and the Spokane Flood indicators, which point to the fact that the Earth has suffered a catastrophic explosion and flooding; and by the lunar evidence confirming that the moon was once a part of the earth but was blasted off as a result of some supernova-like explosion.

What caused this goliath explosion? Science does not know. However, a number of ancient literary traditions describe an event remarkably similar to that described by the Hon. Elijah Muhammad: God, the Lord among the Council of Gods, caused the explosion and subsequent flooding. The ancient Babylonian creation poem, *Enuma Elish*, specifically describes the god making a cleavage in the proto-earth and inserting some explosive devise, causing the explosion and splitting the proto-earth into Earth and Moon. The Yamana of Tierra del Fuego even remember that the flood was caused by the moon-water, just as the Hon. Elijah Muhammad suggested.

When evidence from such widely disparate fields converge to lend support to seemingly incredible claims, the one making those claims must be looked at a little more seriously.

# Conclusion

The Honorable Elijah Muhammad answered three very important questions concerning the make-up of the human family:

*Who is the 85%?*

The uncivilized people; poison animal eaters; slaves from mental death and power; people who do not know the Living God, or their origin in this world, and they worship what they know not what-who are easily lead in the wrong direction, but hard to lead in the right direction.

*Who is the 10%?*

The rich; the slave makers of the poor, who teach the poor lies - to believe that the Almighty True and Living God is a spook and cannot be seen by the physical eye.

Otherwise known as the Blood-Sucker of the Poor.

*Who is the 5% in this Poor Part of the Earth?*

They are the poor, righteous Teachers, who do not believe in the teachings of the 10%; who are all-wise; and know who the Living God is; and teach that the Living God is the Son of Man, the Supreme Being, the (black man) of Asia; and teach Freedom, Justice, and Equality to all the human families of the planet Earth.

Otherwise known as Civilized People.
Also is Muslim and Muslim Sons.

The masses (85%) don't know God. They worship a philosophical construct given to them by a small but powerful click (10%) who publicly share their faith but secretly acknowledge the True and Living God. The 5% have the perilous task of imparting this Divine Knowledge to the masses, the 85%. This task is perilous because what they are doing threatens to topple an entire world which has been built on a lie: the Lie of the Mystery God.

God Most High does indeed possesses a spiritual essence (*pnuema, ruach*), but this essence resides in and is manifest through a material reality. While all of creation has some portion of this essence in their very atoms and DNA, this essence manifests itself most fully in the Divine Body of the Original Black man and woman, the direct descendants of the Originator, who was Himself the first Black Man under the sun.

> There is One God and Father of All, who is above all, and through all, and *in you all*. (Ephs. 4:6)

The Spirit of God is the true Self of the Black man - his 'higher self.'

> As men, we are never without this pure essence, and upon it we as men rely for our continuance, and for it is our essential being. As men we know that this essential being is in all, passing through different stages of our daily life and taking our bodies through birth, old age, and death, but itself remaining unchanged by anything and calls itself (I). In us all, it is therefore the one (I) in the whole Universe, and it is the One source of all that is in the Universe. You and myself are but different expressions of the (I). Because you say (I), and I say (I). Who then is (I)? If we are not (I), is it not evident that...man is only an expression of his Creator, and that he and his Creator are one?...The suffering we try to excuse ourselves of, and blame it on the Creator, Who is within ourselves, and (is) our very selves. If we were aware of the creator within

ourselves we would be at a loss to blame anyone but ourselves.[733]

According to ancient Indic tradition the incorporeal God Most High, called *Parabrahm*, is the very self of man, his *atman*. When man unites with this divine self within, he becomes God. The *Upanishads* declare:

That which is the finest essence – the whole world has that as its soul. That is Reality. That is Atman. That art Thou.

The individual who successfully unites with Atman or his God-self is said to be an *avatar* of Vishnu or Parabrahm , which "incarnates" within him. In esoteric Islam, this process of incarnation, *hulul* in Arabic, or uniting with one's God-self is called *fana*, "annihilation." Man's personal ego is gradually dissolved or annihilated until the core of his being is reached which is Allah Ta'ala, God Most High. At this point of complete annihilation it is no longer the individual – Karreim, or Elijah or Muhammad – who walks, talks, and acts. It is Allah himself walking, talking, and acting through the physical body of the individual who became submerged in the Mind of Allah. As Allah says in a Hadith Qudsi:

My servant does not come closer to Me with anything more dear to Me than that which I made obligatory upon him. My servant keeps coming closer to Me with more volunteer deeds, until I love him. When I love him, I become his ear by which he hears, his eyes by which he sees, his hand by which he holds and his foot by which he walks.[734]

The Knowledge of God is the most precious Jewel. When given to a people who have walked in darkness for so long, it can be (with some) tantamount to throwing pearls before swine. Some of us simply lack the ability to appreciate it. The Honorable

---

[733] "The Science of Islam," Lesson, Department of Supreme Wisdom, Nation of Islam.
[734] Al-Bukhari 6021.

Elijah Muhammad once said, *"there are some people so stupid, God can't even help them."*

With others, this Jewel in their hands becomes very dangerous. Some of our people have taken this knowledge that the Black Man is God and have become devils. Others receive this Wisdom, but because it came to them without the Understanding, which is the best part, it (this Wisdom) actually precludes their growth into Godhood. They become arrogant and thus unwilling to grow into their true Godhood. The Black Man is God, but he is *Kiakkiak*, God of the Gods who sleeps for 6, 000 years. With the exception of a small population of "true Gods" scattered across the planet, the masses of Black men have fallen far from the Glory of God. The difference between God and Man is this: God is an Immortal Man and man is a mortal god. Man is a god whose Third Eye (Pineal Gland) is closed. God is a man whose Third Eye is open. What we see in Atlanta, Detroit, New York, Philadelphia, and through out the inner cities and suburbs of America are Black men, i.e. mortal gods. The brother strung out on drugs, or the graduate from college doped out on a false sense of belonging, are gods whose Eye is closed. This happened as a result of our fall.

> I have said, Ye are gods; and all of you are children of the Most High.
> But you shall die like men, and fall like one of the princes.
> Arise, O' God, judge the earth: for thou shalt inherit all nations.

We are gods. But we have fallen. We are admonished to "Arise, O' God." That process of "arising," called in scripture "Resurrection," is the process of awakening the Spirit of God in us (our Higher Selves) and becoming One with It. This process of Resurrection was the purpose for which Master Fard Muhammad, the World King, came out of hiding and chose to dwell among His people. He deposited in the head of the Honorable Elijah Muhammad the Wisdom necessary to facilitate our Resurrection. The Hon. Elijah Muhammad said:

> The Father (Master Fard Muhammad) is our own kind. He wants to make you and ME, not just believers, but Gods.

Everyone of you, according to what He has taught me, will be Gods...There is no doubt that we are really Gods, but we lost our power and knowledge as shown in the parable of the Jesus. "Salt is good as long as it has saving power. When it no longer has saving power it is not good for anything, but to be thrown out and trampled under people's feet." This is referring to us. We had knowledge and we will be powerful when we are restored to what we originally were. But, we have been robbed of power through depriving us of the Knowledge of Self....

Allah has taught me that He would like to restore you. You have lost everything of self. Now He wants to restore you back to Self...He didn't come here just to show us who He was. He came here to show us who He was, who we are, and then to make us rulers.[735]

The process by which one goes from a mortal god to an Immortal Man (Living God) is much more involved that just memorizing Lessons or excelling at Final Call sales. It requires years of discipline, self-denial, and spiritual development, all predicated upon humility. In Egypt, it took 42 years to achieve Summum Bonum or Godhood. Master Fard Muhammad, the God of Gods, Himself studied 42 years. He came to America, by Himself, and brought the blueprint where by the mortal gods living in the slums and lost in the white communities of America can be raised to Immortal Men.

Some time ago a brother e-mailed me asking an important question regarding my work to vindicate the teachings of the Hon. Elijah Muhammad and show and prove that the Black Man is God. The brother asked: "Where is this taking us as a people? Will the knowledge of understanding 'The Black Man is God' evolve us into God again?" Because this question is so important I will close with my response:

Peace

---

[735] Muhammad, *Theology of Time*, 118-19.

Thank you for the time you have given to my work. You have asked the right question: What is the real relevance of this material for our people? Is the science of the Black man being God merely academic?

The current state and condition of our people speaks for itself. I am a father: I have a seven year old daughter and a four year son. I lament the fact that they must grow up in this cipher. The Black man and woman, especially 35 and younger, are in a horrid state when judged by the criterion of righteousness as defined by the Bible, the Qur'an, the teachings of the Honorable Elijah Muhammad, the 42 Negative Confessions of Ancient Kemet (Egypt), the ancient Code of Hammarabi of Babylon, etc. What is the answer?

First and foremost: knowledge of self. If black folk would just *be self*, our true self, then the quality of life in our community would drastically improve. A god, in whom the principles of righteousness are incarnate, could never prey on the community in the way we, black men, are (wittingly or unwittingly) preying on our community: the violence, the abuse of our wives and daughters and our women in general, the destruction of our mental faculties and bodies through harmful foods and substances, all while the devil (the Caucasian) manipulates the whole thing in order to secure his permanent position as world-ruler. This teaching, the Black man is God, must inspire the desire to 'be' God. To 'be' God requires a change in life style. This was the reason Allah, in the person of Master Fard Muhammad, came: to make us gods. The life-style he requires of us - the diet, the rules of conduct, etc - all have the purpose of putting us on the path to 'being' God again. The Hon. Elijah Muhammad said once he has made us gods, we can leave him: we don't need him anymore.

That is the point brother. The knowledge of God, which is the knowledge of self, is prerequisite to a better lifestyle for our people, individually and collectively. What is more important to an individual on a day-to-day basis than the quality of his/her life? It is a true knowledge of self/God that allows us to begin the process of truely improving our lives and the lives of our babies.

I hope this helps dear brother. I truely appreciate the question.

True Islam

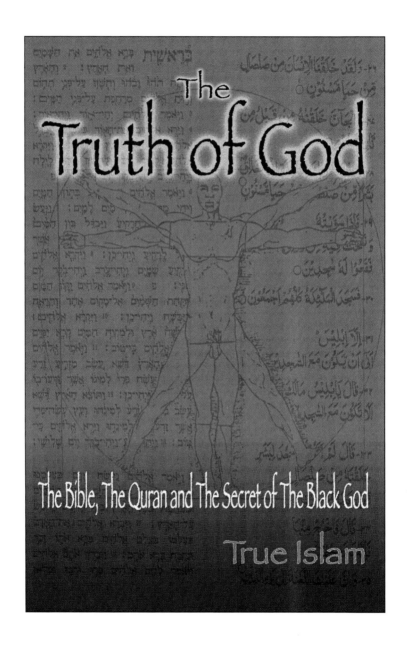

*The Truth of God* is a History-of-Religions study based on a critical examination of the primary texts of scripture (Bible, Qur'an, Sunnah) in Hebrew, Greek and Arabic, as well as the critical scholarship in the secondary literature: English, German and French. This multi-lingual literacy has enabled True Islam to answer the question, 'Who is God?' from the scriptural perspective with a depth not heretofore seen in writing. True Islam has also drawn extensively from the religious texts, in translation, of the ancient Near East and India. With these primary and secondary sources True Islam has been able to demonstrate that:

(1) According to a widespread ancient Near and Far Eastern tradition, as evidenced in Egyptian, Sumerian/Babylonian, and Indic sources, God the creator was a black god, with a black body. The answers to such questions as: how did this body develop, of what substance was this body made, and why was this body black, were the focus of the mysteries in these nations.

(2) The Creator God of Ancient Israel was this same Black God, and those responsible for forming the Hebrew Bible (Old Testament) were devotees of this Black God.

(3) The Black God of ancient Near Eastern and Semitic monotheistic traditions was a self-created black man-god, whose *physical* (though not spiritual) beginnings were from an atom hidden in a primordial darkness. The Hebrew of Genesis I specifies that this was a triple-darkness in which this atom was hidden and from which Elohim (God) emerged.

(4) According to the Hebrew Bible and Arabic Qur'an the original black man, in his original state, was God on earth.

(5) The Bible and the Qur'an/Sunnah, when allowed to speak their own languages (Hebrew, Greek and Arabic) affirm that God is a transcendent *man*, not a transcendent, formless spirit.

(6) The God of Prophet Muhammad (PBUH) and the Qur'an is this same Black God of the ancient Near East and ancient Israel. The claim of modern Muslim theologians that God has no form and could never be a man is based on later theological developments away from the Qur'an and Sunnah, developments inspired by the introduction of Greek philosophic ideas into Islam.

(7) Biblical and Islamic tradition expects God to appear on earth as a man in the last days.

To order your copies or to read more from True Islam and view lectures
visit

# www.theblackgod.com

www.allahteam.info
www.myspace.com/truislam
www.myspace.com/theblackgodd
www.myspace.com/thetruthofgod
www.myspace.com/thebookofgod

Send all correspondence to:

True Islam
P.O. Box 4102
Ann Arbor MI, 48106

Or email True Islam: truislam@yahoo.com

426